"A compelling, no frills account of this legal and human horror show."
—*Washington Post Book World*

"*IN A CHILD'S NAME* is well written and crammed with facts. They range from the gruesome . . . to the poignant. . . . All these elements combine to elevate *IN A CHILD'S NAME* to a level of humanity not often seen in crime tales."
—*People*

"A gripping exposé of domestic violence . . . Mr. Maas masterfully conveys the horror of Ken's act and the grief and anger that Teresa's guilt-ridden family and friends feel, and sustains a sense of stunned outrage through a fascinating description of the police and legal investigation."
—*Baltimore Sun*

"Not merely an account of the atrocities of a sociopath . . . but an allegory for American society, where clashing cultures, religions and ethnicities produce the nation's diversity and, sometimes, its evil."
—*Boston Globe*

"A chilling and often disturbing book—painstakingly researched and dispassionately written by the bestselling author of *Serpico*."
—*San Francisco Chronicle*

"Maas is a superb storyteller as well as a highly skilled investigative reporter. This is a taut, fascinating journey into the mind of a sociopath. Don't miss the trip."

—*Buffalo News*

"Maas . . . recounts every bloody detail of the 1984 murder of Teresa Benigno by her husband, dentist Kenneth Z. Taylor. . . . The story takes an unusual and significant turn when it begins to focus on the struggle between two families over custody of the infant, Philip. The truly disconcerting aspect of this case lies not in anomalous issues related to the murder but in general questions about the ways in which courts resolve child custody disputes."

—*Newsday*

"Maas has written a dramatic account, the story behind the story, one that readers won't soon forget."

—*Staten Island Advance*

"Maas provides a dark, compelling portrait of a sociopathic middle-class professional who ruined many lives. A wrenching story . . ."

—*Library Journal*

(more . . .)

**Books by Peter Maas**

NONFICTION

In a Child's Name: The Legacy of a Mother's Murder*
Manhunt
Marie: A True Story*
King of the Gypsies
Serpico
The Valachi Papers*
The Rescuers

FICTION

Father and Son
Made in America

*Published by POCKET BOOKS

# IN A CHILD'S NAME

# PETER MAAS

**POCKET BOOKS**

New York   London   Toronto   Sydney   Tokyo   Singapore

Grateful acknowledgment is made for permission to quote from the song "Deacon Blues." Words and music by Walter Becker and Donald Fagen. Copyright © 1977 by Duchess Music Corporation. Rights administered by MCA Music Publishing, a division of MCA Inc., New York, NY 10019. Used by permission. All rights reserved.

POCKET BOOKS, a division of Simon & Schuster Inc.
1230 Avenue of the Americas, New York, NY 10020

ISBN: 0-671-74619-7

First Pocket Books printing October 1991

10  9  8  7  6  5  4  3

POCKET and colophon are registered trademarks of Simon & Schuster Inc.

Cover photo courtesy of the Benigno-White family

Printed in the U.S.A.

*For Suzanne*

"I'd always looked forward to being a jolly grandfather with a house or yard full of rowdy grandsons and cute little tomboyish or dainty granddaughters."

—DR. KENNETH Z. TAYLOR

# CONTENTS

# IN A
# CHILD'S
# NAME

# PROLOGUE

When the first state trooper arrived at the scene and un-wrapped the padding around the young woman's body, he recoiled in horror. Who, he thought, was capable of such savagery?

As hideous as the murder was, no one involved in the case could imagine the religious, regional and ethnic passions that it would unleash, revealing not only the fragility of American society, but, paradoxically, its extraordinary resiliency.

In an age inured to excuses, it got down finally to an issue quite absolute: Good versus Evil.

At stake was the future of an infant, then five months old.

# Part 1

## THE MURDER

# Chapter

## ONE

Marion, Indiana (pop. 35,874), is sixty miles north of Indianapolis. On both sides of Route 37 as you enter Grant County, of which Marion is the seat, fields of corn and soybeans fall away as far as the eye can see. Silos rise against a cloud-fleeced sky. You know at once that you are in the nation's fabled heartland—industrious, independent, God-fearing.

Indeed, according to marketing researchers, Marion is an archetypal American community, ranking twelfth in the country, for instance, as an ideal place to test new products and advertising campaigns.

These days, though, there's a down-at-the-heels look to the city, as if time is passing it by, which triggers a certain defensive "Well, it's good enough for me" posture among local boosters. The population, with a median household income of $17,031, is of overwhelmingly English and German stock. Over the years there has been a lot of white migration from the South—"rednecks," according to old-guard Hoosiers—especially from Kentucky and Tennessee.

About 12 percent of the citizenry is black, none of whom are either lawyers or doctors. The two biggest employers in town are General Motors and a French electronics conglomerate which, in a transaction that has caused considerable unease, recently took over an RCA color TV picture-tube factory. The most famous native son is the late actor James Dean, who started his career at the age of four at Zina Glad's Marion College of Dance and Theatrical Arts. His grave is the major tourist attraction, along with displays of plates, mugs, jigsaw puzzles, and bubble-gum cards bearing his likeness.

In basketball-mad Indiana, what gives Marion a special identity is its high school team, which won an unprecedented three consecutive state championships from 1985 through 1987. The high school is the largest in Indiana, with a gymnasium seating eight thousand fans. A few years ago, it became clear that academic needs would be best served by having two high schools, one for the city's north side, the other for the south, but this plan was scotched for fear of diluting the basketball program.

Marion is also Bible Belt territory. The marquee in front of a big supermarket doesn't announce a sale, say, on pork chops; it says, "Love Jesus." A used car dealer knows his potential buyers. *His* sign says, "Christ is Free."

For years Marion was the world headquarters for the Wesleyan church and remains today the site of the World Gospel Mission, a nondenominational, fundamentalist organization that runs militant ministries in Africa, Latin America and Asia. Besides such traditional Protestant faiths as Presbyterian, Lutheran and Methodist, there are dozens of other congregations, among them the Assembly of God, Church of Christ, Disciples of Christ, Nazarenes, Mennonites, Pentecostals and any number of Baptist variations.

Nevertheless, an unchristian blot lurks in Marion's past. On page 311 of *Alistair Cooke's America* a photograph shows two black teenagers dangling from a huge elm tree while a crowd of men and women look on, some of them laughing. The caption suggests that the lynching took place in the Deep South, circa 1919. Actually it occurred a little later—and in Marion—on August 7, 1930. A mob of five thousand had seized the two teenagers, accused of raping a white girl and murdering her boyfriend, and hung them from the elm, one of many that shaded the Grant County Courthouse.

• • •

Jean and Everett Z. (Zach) Taylor moved to Marion from Oak Hills, a middle-class suburb west of Cincinnati, in 1967. Zach had been a production-line supervisor at Andrew Jergens, the lotion company. Both Taylors had grown up in the Cincinnati area, but Zach, then forty, figured he had reached a dead end at Jergens. A similar job at the RCA plant in Marion appeared to offer opportunities for advancement.

After methodically sampling Marion's array of religious possibilities, Jean Taylor chose the First Baptist Church, a large, modern structure a couple of blocks from the courthouse. Its theology was upbeat, reflected in messages on a display out front like, "The worse air pollution is not smog, but a sour disposition."

The Taylors came to Marion with their second child, Nancy, and their youngest son, Tom. Their oldest boy, Ken, who was in the middle of his senior year at Oak Hills High, remained behind till graduation.

Ken Taylor would describe his adolescence in the most halcyon terms, but with a curious, unsolicited protestation. His mother and father "were not tyrants at all," he insisted. "They were teachers, guidance directors, genuinely loving parents." He'd never forget when he and his mother and father were featured on the cover of the annual Church of Christ calendar back in Oak Hills. "Apparently we were the 'picture' of the American Protestant family," he said. He couldn't remember why his sister and brother had not been included. Maybe Nancy was busy changing from her choir robe, and Tom, nearly six years younger, was probably in Sunday school.

The trouble was that there was no church calendar with Ken and his parents on it. Once, Jean Taylor remembered,

7

a photographer came by trying to get members of the flock to pose outside the church for individual family portraits, but she refused, cottoning neither to the photographer's hustling manner nor the price he was asking.

Their old neighbors agreed that Jean "ruled the roost" and that she was, well, "odd." It was little things, nothing really dramatic. Jean didn't like parties, found them frivolous, and the Taylors never engaged in any of the usual suburban socializing, did not give or accept dinner invitations. Life at home was highly regimented, run like a "quasi-military camp," one neighbor said. After the dishes were done, the table was immediately set for the next meal. Friends of Ken and his siblings were limited to the basement recreation room, and the days when each age group could drop by was strictly regulated, as was the use of the backyard pool the Taylors had installed. The mother of a chum of Ken's remembered the one time she was inside the Taylor home on a church-related mission. Jean had offered her a glass of lemonade and before she was out the door, Jean had taken the glass and was wiping the ring it had left even though it was on a presumably impervious plastic TV dinner tray.

The most memorable incident for all of Ken's teenage friends was when, enraged by his sister's constant tattling to Jean, he tied her to a chair "in front of everyone" and painted her hair green. After Jean and Zach Taylor discovered what had happened, one of his friends recalled, "You could hear the screams up and down the street. I mean it was weird, what he did, and how he thought he'd get away with it. It was like, suddenly, he didn't care."

When Ken joined the Cub Scouts, Jean Taylor became the den mother and Zach the scout master. But it was in the sports activities of their children that the Taylors were especially zealous. Ken was encouraged to participate in knothole baseball, grade school basketball, and tackle football. His father was always on hand to help manage and coach, while Jean was ever present cheering and keeping score. One of Ken's high school coaches, Stephen Moore, said, "Ken was very serious and dedicated. He didn't have

8

great ability, but made up for it in effort. Ken's father was very involved. He was a fiery guy and very, very competitive."

During his senior year, Ken finally became the starting end on the high school football team. His sister Nancy, a year behind, played the glockenspiel in the marching band. By then, though, the family focus had shifted to Tom, who was an extraordinarily gifted athlete. Jim Lockwood, a classmate of Ken's, recalled, "You could tell Ken was hurt by the attention Tommy was getting, but he never talked about it."

When the Taylors moved to Marion, coach Moore remembered Ken's father telling him that he'd "had enough" of Oak Hills. "I sensed that he was dissatisfied with the program here and the way things had gone for Ken. He was hoping for better things for Tom."

Ken's peers in high school found him generally affable and easygoing, popular enough to be elected vice president of the student council his senior year. Although Ken could have resided with his maternal grandparents when the Taylors moved to Marion, he arranged instead to stay at the home of his best friend, Tom Chatham. Jean was secretly relieved. Relations between her and her mother had always been tense. Her mother, by all accounts a remarkably pretty woman, smoked cigarettes and drank liquor and was, according to Jean, an outrageous flirt who "sat on men's laps at parties, smiling at them and patting their cheeks." She was eighteen when Jean was born, and when Jean herself reached her teens, her mother would introduce her as her "younger sister." Jean, who had inherited much of her mother's fine-boned good looks, decided that her mother resented the attention her father gave his only child, and early on, Jean determined "never to be like her."

Jean herself married Zach when she was twenty, right after Zach was discharged from the army following the end of World War II. Two years later, when she was pregnant with Ken, her mother snapped at her, "I'm too young to be a grandmother." One of Zach's great attractions had been that he alone of the boys who came calling did not play along with her mother. After Jean announced that she was marrying him and her mother said, "I don't like him," Jean relished the memory of telling her, "That's too bad, Mother. He's coming to see *me*."

For Ken, life at the Chathams' was more like being at a boardinghouse than a foster home. Liberated from rigidly enforced curfews and dress codes, about the only stricture he had was a kidding "be back before sunrise." And driving around in the eight-year-old white Rambler station wagon his grandfather provided, he was able at last to indulge in such forbidden delights as the burlesque house on downtown Cincinnati's Vine Street and some of the clubs in wide-open Newport, Kentucky, across the Ohio River.

The Rambler also gave Ken, till then shy around girls, a chance to consummate his first hot romance with an aggressive sports-loving classmate with shoulder-length brown hair named Patsy Duncan. Rick Hillman, another teenage pal, said, "That Rambler was the talk of the school. Everyone called it the Sex Mobile. It was like Ken needed a daily injection. He'd pick her up at seven A.M. every day, and he'd always be off somewhere parking with her."

Ken even gave up the baseball team. He got a job after school in a shoe store to earn money to date Patsy, and Tom Chatham remembered how he began skipping lunch to save up enough to buy her an engagement ring. After graduation, she enrolled in college at Eastern Kentucky and so did he. Then during their freshman year, she dropped him for another boy. "He was crazy about her and you just knew he was crushed," Chatham said, "but he held most of it in. The thing about Ken was that he never really laid all his cards on the table."

He promised himself, however, that no female was ever going to get the better of him again. This vow was made easier when he transferred to Ball State University in Muncie, Indiana, where the ratio of girls to boys at the onetime teachers college was close to four to one.

By now Ken was six feet one, one hundred eighty pounds, with beachboy blond hair and in great shape after a summer working in a small steel mill in Marion. At Ball State, he meticulously followed a weight-lifting regime and carefully cultivated an "aw-shucks" manner when he discovered how that could bring out the maternal instinct in a certain type of woman. He enjoyed such success dating that it actually became a drag. Then, as he would tell it, during his junior year Emily Latrelle, an Indiana farm girl, an English major a year ahead of him, with whom he'd been sleeping for three months, suddenly said, "Do you want to get married?" and he said, "Okay, let's do it now." They eloped to North Carolina. He was twenty.

When he brought Emily back to Marion to meet his parents, he told his mother, "I wanted to marry someone just like you, Mom."

His sister soon married a career enlisted man in the army who would be stationed in Germany, which gave Jean Taylor a vicarious thrill since she was of German descent. Visiting Germany herself was an experience Jean would never have, since she hated to travel and would not eat in restaurants or stay in hotels and motels. Tom, meanwhile, was fulfilling every sports dream his parents had for him. He became an eight-letter man at Marion High in football, basketball and baseball, with a collegiate athletic scholarship if not a contract in organized baseball seemingly a sure bet.

Then Ken had another startling surprise for his mother and father. He'd been an indifferent student, but he always did quite well in biology and he announced that he was switching to a pre-med major. He was going to be a doctor. The news truly made Jean and Zach take notice of their oldest offspring. No one on either side of the family had graduated from college, much less dared such professional heights.

Emily, after graduating, was unable to find a teaching position in the Muncie area and settled for a secretarial job. Ken also worked as an orderly at Ball Memorial Hospital. In the end, although his grades improved considerably, they were not good enough to qualify him for medical school. But, as Zach Taylor proudly told coworkers at the RCA plant, Ken had a "fall back" position. He would still be a doctor—a dentist. He applied to and was accepted by the dental school at Indiana University's medical center in Indianapolis.

Ken, however, had another version of why he shifted from medicine to dentistry, one that he especially liked to share with various women later on. One night while on duty as an orderly at the hospital, a nurse in the operating area summoned him, handed him a bundle wrapped in linen and a plastic bag, and instructed him to take it down to the autopsy room. He vaguely thought that the bundle contained an amputated arm or leg, but when the nurse said to make sure to use the service elevator, that the mother and father might be outside, he suddenly realized that he was holding a dead baby, and the picture flashed in his mind of being a physician someday and having to face distraught parents with the news of a child's death. It was something, he'd confide with an appropriate shudder, that he would never be able to bring himself to do.

• • •

In Indianapolis Emily had to take another secretarial job to help support them. Then Jean Taylor spotted a U.S. Navy ad offering full dental scholarships in return for four years of active service. Ken applied and was accepted. While other applicants had better academic credentials, the Navy judged him to be an "outstanding officer candidate."

Emily finally landed a teaching post during Ken's second year in dental school. But it was in Ohio, which meant that they'd be together only on weekends. And Ken, free not only from his parents but also from being a husband most of the time, began doing drugs with three other dentistry students who, like him, sported jeans and dingo boots and sneered at the "white shoe nerds" making up the rest of the class. At Ball State he had smoked a joint now and then. But this was heavy stuff—acid and pounds of pot and bricks of hash from a connection at the Indianapolis airport. There was an occasional cocaine score, which they really didn't need with all the available uncut amphetamines—"speed"—from a chemist at the Eli Lilly pharmaceutical plant who was researching their effect on animals. Barbiturates—"reds" and "bluepoints," dopers called them—were also available from another contact. And there was an extra added attraction. "You had the drugs, you got the girls," hordes of them, according to Ken.

During the fall term of his junior year, Emily told him she was pregnant. At first, she recalled, he appeared pleased and excited. Then he grew increasingly sullen and remote. One weekend when she came home, she found three garbage bags in a closet filled with hashish or marijuana, "I don't know what." She flew into a rage and ordered him to remove the bags. A couple of months later she arrived a day ahead of schedule because she wasn't feeling well. Ken walked in carrying some plastic bags full of pills. He claimed that they weren't his, that he was holding them for a friend. "Then get new friends, or leave," she said. She wasn't going to put up with it, the way he was messing up his life with drugs.

About a month after that, Ken abruptly said, "Look, you can stay here until it's born and then I'm leaving or you're leaving, one or the other."

"But what about our baby? Don't you care?"

As she listened in speechless horror, he said, "It's not my kid. You've been fucking around."

Somehow she forced herself to believe that this was a nightmare that would work itself out.

• • •

Emily was in her seventh month when Ken was working nights as a desk clerk at the airport's Ramada Inn. He had gotten the job through one of his buddies in a softball league. Meeting plane crews was a regular chore, and one evening he drove out to pick up the crew of an Allegheny flight into Indianapolis. When he spied her, a flight attendant, there was instant—"electric," he said—eye contact. She was a slim, long-legged redhead. Her name was Marilyn Hope. She sat in front next to him in the hotel station wagon. After she changed, she came down to the lobby and invited him to have a drink.

He arranged to get off early and they went into the lounge. Marilyn was a revelation to him. She was from

Brooklyn and lived in midtown Manhattan. She had vacationed in Hawaii, skied in Aspen, been to London, Rome and Paris. He'd never met anyone so sophisticated, and she was a knockout. She was twenty-nine, four years older than Ken. He told her he was a dental student and then launched into the story of his switch from medicine. He knew he was in business when she said she hadn't realized Indiana men could be so "sensitive."

She gave him her phone number in New York, and when he called, she said she'd trade flights with one of the other attendants and be back in Indianapolis the next week.

While Emily had always been a willing, if docile, sex partner, he'd never experienced the edgy tension Marilyn exhibited in bed, or her knowledgeable moves. At first, she didn't know he was married. When she found out, finally, during one of the trips she was now regularly making to Indianapolis, she threatened to end the relationship. He said his marriage was one in name only. He was getting a divorce. She'd heard that one before. Forget it. She was going to get married by the time she was thirty, she said, and time was running out. She wanted children.

He pulled out all the stops. He'd love nothing more than to have a child with her. Look, he said, he'd been crazy in love with a girl in high school and she had thrown him over. He never thought he'd be in love again like that until he met her. He had just been marking time. He'd been with a lot of girls, but none of them meant anything. He didn't know why he married Emily. He had realized right away it wasn't going anywhere, and then she tricked him by getting pregnant.

Give him a chance, he told Marilyn. She'd see.

In June 1974, in her ninth month, Emily came home to find that Ken had cleared out, no note, nothing. She never saw him again. About a week later, she learned that he had moved into a trailer with one of his dental school pals.

When Marilyn flew in, Ken met her at the airport and drove her to the trailer to prove what he'd done. She was impressed. "See," he said, "it's just you and me now." He lit up a joint and she shared it with him to celebrate.

Then his trailer mate walked in lugging a huge bag of pot, dumped it on the table, and started dividing it. Marilyn freaked out. "My God," she said, "what if the police come?" Don't worry, he said. He was quitting. All he needed was someone like her. And in fact, he was cutting down, especially with downers. He'd been so spaced out that he hadn't been able to complete a lot of required clinical work, and it was clear that he would need an extra year to graduate. He had already written to the Navy's Bureau of Medicine in Washington about this, explaining that he'd had personal, family problems. To his relief, the Navy granted his request.

That same month Tom Chatham, now an insurance agent, happened to be in Indianapolis on business and decided to drop in on Ken and Emily. He had visited them at Ball State and was fond of her, a big step up from Patsy Duncan at Oak Hills High, he thought.

Chatham couldn't believe what he saw. Emily, about to give birth, huddled alone in this tiny sweatbox of an apartment without air conditioning, the temperature outside over a hundred degrees—Emily, devastated, weeping.

It was inconceivable that Ken, his old, decent, loyal friend, was capable of this. He called him and said, "Good God, man, what are you doing?" He remembered the familiar soft, lazy voice coming over the line, not at all defensive or argumentative, saying, "I'm happy. I've met someone I'm in love with." Ken didn't even ask how Emily was.

Jean and Zach Taylor were beside themselves. They discovered what had happened when they phoned Emily to see how the pregnancy was progressing. She told them that Ken had left her. They phoned him at once at the number Emily gave them and told him that he had to "try harder, life was a two-way street," and that "you're supposed to work these things out together." Divorce was "unacceptable."

"What are we, suddenly Catholic or something?" he said.

He was not being "responsible," they said. That struck a raw nerve. During his adolescence, responsibility had been drummed into him endlessly, and for the first time he became openly defiant. "It's none of your business," he said.

Zach happened to be in town for an RCA engineering conference and called Emily, who said she was expecting any moment. He got in touch with Ken and said that he should at least "fulfill the responsibility" of taking his wife to the hospital, but Ken would not do it. So Zach himself was on hand, along with Emily's mother, when she gave birth to a daughter around one A.M. on July 3, 1974.

Privately, Jean Taylor thought that Emily had brought it on herself. She recalled how much pleasure "Kenny" got out of playing softball, but that Emily would never go watch him. And she particularly harked back to the time he had come with Emily to cheer on Tom in a basketball game at Marion High, and how right in the middle of it, "kind of sullen and bored," she got up and left. Still, Jean concluded, that was no excuse for this.

"God will not forgive you," she warned Ken.

"It's not my baby," he said.

Ken never saw the child. Eventually Emily remarried and her new husband offered to adopt her daughter. She would need Ken's permission and wrote to him for it.

He refused.

• • •

Within five years, on the night of April 16, 1979, Ken would try to murder Marilyn.

After he had left Emily, he spent the summer in New York at Marilyn's place. He pretended to enjoy visits to the Museum of Modern Art and the theater, and loved watching major-league ball at Shea Stadium. In the fall Marilyn went back to Indiana with him. Although the airline based her in Boston, she had enough seniority to commute to Boston from Indianapolis. They rented a garden apartment in a complex near the small town of Noblesville, off Route 37 on the way to Marion. Marilyn wasn't too happy "living in the middle of nowhere," but Ken had to finish his schooling. He was sure he'd get an East

Coast billet from the Navy. He wanted to be away from all the dopers he'd been running with, and she'd say yes, okay, she was sorry, and then they'd jump into bed for what he called "fantastic sex" and everything would be smoothed over.

That fall the divorce from Emily, handled entirely by lawyers, became final. Ken was required to pay twenty-five dollars a week in child support. Over the years she had to take constant legal action to collect whatever she could. In December Ken and Marilyn were married by a local justice of the peace.

Although Jean and Zach Taylor were not more than a half hour away, they were not present. Nor would they ever meet Marilyn during the marriage. Earlier Jean had phoned her son at the apartment. When Marilyn answered, Jean said, "You could have at least waited until the divorce before you moved in." Marilyn said, "Who the hell do you think you are?" and Jean said, "I'm Kenny's mother." Marilyn hung up on her.

Ken was impressed. Marilyn was as hard-nosed as his mother. Every girl he'd previously taken home had gone through the motions of catering to her. And later, when Jean even tried to make amends, Ken told her she had been out of line. It was going to take time to patch things up.

A peculiar event occurred the following June. Except for occasional joints, Ken was off drugs, although he was boozing more. He'd always drunk beer, but now he was tossing down a new favorite, Jack Daniel's sour mash. One Sunday morning he dropped Marilyn off at the airport in her blue Buick Skylark convertible and went on to a softball game. After the game he had some beers and a couple of drinks, and on the way home he ran off the road and hit a utility pole. He made it back to the apartment, but the driver's side was caved in. He parked out front and later abandoned the Skylark on a country lane where the police found it. His story was that it must have been stolen since he returned to the complex with the car in perfect condition and spent the rest of the day by the pool without noticing that it was missing. But witnesses in three nearby apartments said that they had noticed the parked Skylark, all smashed up, throughout the afternoon. An attorney for Ken then advised authorities that there had been no theft and plea-bargained a fifty-dollar fine for falsely reporting a crime. Ken told Marilyn that he had panicked at the thought of her fury and begged her to forgive him. What made the whole thing so peculiar to the investigating cop, Robert A. Smith, was how Ken expected to get away with such an obvious cock-and-bull tale.

His last act of rebellion in Indiana was to skip his graduation ceremonies, disappointing especially Jean Taylor. However, a confrontation between his mother and Marilyn was avoided. He was assigned to the Navy submarine base in Groton, Connecticut, across the Thames River from New London. They rented an apartment in a complex filled with singles and young marrieds in Cromwell, a town south of Hartford, equidistant from Groton and the airport at Windsor Locks from which Marilyn could fly to Boston.

Some of the ardor in the marriage had cooled. Ken felt a new confidence. He was no longer a student, but a full-fledged dentist, and an "officer and gentleman" to boot. Little things began to rankle. Like Emily, Marilyn was disparaging of his passion for sports.

His very first week on duty, when Marilyn was off on a flight, an enlisted female dental assistant—he remembered her well, "twenty-one years old, a pretty blonde with blue eyes, a muscular body and coarse manner"—said, "You're some hunk, lieutenant." If he wasn't doing anything that evening, she and her roommate could make dinner for him and "welcome him to the base." After a number of drinks, they started playing strip poker and he had them both.

They were the first of many. He realized more than ever how playing a slightly country bumpkin role was such an effective come-on. They were all the same, he decided—dental assistants, female hospital corpsmen, female officers, the wives of officers, secretaries at the complex where he lived, even business executives, married or not—they all wanted him. He loved the oohs and aahs he heard when they saw how big his penis was and how they'd say, "Please, please don't hurt me."

The trouble with Marilyn was that she believed she could turn him into her creature. He had married a harridan. She'd hooked him like a big, dumb catfish, and he had only himself to blame.

They had a serious fight when she wanted to go to Hartford to see Angela Lansbury in a play the same evening he was supposed to play in a softball game at the submarine base. She began to suspect that he was screwing around. When she was away on a flight trip, she would call late and he wouldn't be home. Once they returned from a weekend in New York, and she found a note under the door that said, "Missed you while you were gone. Where were you?" He said that it had to be a mistake, that there was another guy down the hall named Ken.

A neighbor had told her about the partying in their apartment when she was off on flights—"every size, shape, color and creed," she was told. She was mortified when she contracted crabs. He accused her of getting them on one of her trips. She knew this couldn't be so; she wasn't fooling around. She screamed at him not to touch her, and grew increasingly cold and distant.

It always annoyed him that she had retained her maiden name—"If it's such a big deal," she said, "why don't you change yours to mine?" The breaking point came at a gala given by the commandant of the base. A gift for each officer's wife was the high point. When "Marilyn Taylor" was called out, she remained seated.

"What's wrong with you?" he whispered. "Go up and get it."

"That's not my name. My name's Marilyn Hope."

"Relax, will you, and just get it."

"No."

In the end he had to step forward and accept the gift

himself, suffering the humiliation of having to say, "Thank you on behalf of my wife, Marilyn Hope."

He moved out. He rented a house on the Connecticut coast in Waterford, a few miles west of Groton. He resumed doing drugs, lots of pot and "black beauties," a powerful amphetamine in capsule form that many users snapped open and snorted like cocaine. He had always been a rock music addict, listening for hours, especially when he was stoned. The lyrics of Steely Dan's "Deacon Blues" became his battle cry: "I crawl like a viper through the suburban streets/Made love to these women, languid and bittersweet/I rise when the sun goes down, cover every game in town/A world of my own, I'll make it my home sweet home."

A couple of months later, Marilyn called him, sobbing hysterically. Her father, to whom she was devoted, had throat cancer. Ken rather liked the old man and did his best to console her. There were more talks and finally she joined him in the Waterford house. He traveled with her to visit her father at the Memorial Sloan–Kettering Cancer Center in Manhattan. For a while she thought it would all work out.

In December 1978, she became pregnant.

At first, as with Emily, it seemed as if he couldn't be happier at the news, but then he started withdrawing into himself. Marilyn didn't know about the drugs at the time, but it was clear he was seeing other women again, stumbling in at all hours of the morning.

Angry and miserable, desperately worried about her father, she told Ken in her fourth month that she was through with sex until after the baby was born.

Maybe they should seek counseling, she said, but Ken refused.

• • •

In early April Marilyn discovered that three hundred dollars was missing from a cash hoard she was keeping in the kitchen to buy baby clothes. When she questioned Ken, he denied knowing anything about it. They shouted at each other. Suddenly he raised a clenched fist and she was already starting to duck. At the last moment he hit the refrigerator door instead and stormed out. The next time she saw him, his hand was in a cast. He had broken it.

A week later, the night of April 16, she returned from New York after visiting her father. Ken was in the study, poring over a Florida state dental board exam. He'd been thinking about practicing there after he got out of the Navy. Exhausted after a harrowing day—her father was back in Sloan–Kettering for more treatment—she asked Ken if he would make her a cup of hot chocolate. He'd be glad to, he said, but when he brought her the chocolate, it smelled funny to her. Ken sniffed it, as though surprised, and said it must be a residue of dishwasher detergent. He'd make her another cup. She was touched by his solicitousness, but she said no, the hell with it, she was beat, she'd just go to bed, and left him bent over his papers. "Sleep well," he said.

Actually, the chocolate had been laced with chemical chloroform. If ingested, it can be fatal to the liver. If inhaled, it can cause death in two to five minutes. In all likelihood, its presence would not be detectable in an autopsy.

In bed, Marilyn tossed fitfully. Around midnight, she wasn't sure of the exact time, she sensed a presence in the room. She opened her eyes and vaguely saw a figure standing in the doorway. It was Ken. She watched him walk over to her side of the bed and sit down. In the old days, when everything had been so splendid between them, he'd often break off studying and come to kiss her good night and wish her sweet dreams. She thought contentedly that he was doing that now, trying to make up for what had happened, attempting to comfort her.

She remembered him putting his arm across her chest, so hard that she said, "Please, you're hurting me." But the pressure continued. Ken didn't speak. Then "this thing" came over her mouth and nose, and she smelled the same fumes that had been in the chocolate, only stronger.

21

Pressed against her face was a kitchen towel, and wrapped inside the towel was a sponge soaked in chloroform.

She tried to break free, clawing at Ken, trying not to breathe. Once, for a second, she managed to say, "Please don't kill me! I'll do whatever you want." Still, he said nothing. The towel slipped off, and now the sponge was held directly against her. She could feel its roughness.

Her mind raced crazily. Why was he doing this? Did he hate her that much? Was it the baby? She was going to die, she thought, at the hands of her own husband in her own bedroom, "like some stupid soap opera." She couldn't struggle anymore.

All at once she had the image of her father, battling for his own life. What would happen to him if she died? Who would look after him?

She thrashed violently in a last-ditch effort. His hold loosened momentarily, and she was able to roll off the bed onto the floor. He was right on top of her, trying to get the sponge back on her face. She twisted over on her stomach. Now she felt his cast on the back of her neck, and she thought, He's going to start hitting me with the cast. She cried out, "Oh God, help me, please help me!"

The pressure suddenly stopped. The light went on. Dazed, she looked up and saw Ken standing a few feet away, staring at her. She didn't know if she was hallucinating or what, but she believed God *was* in the room, had saved her life, and she got to her knees and began praying out loud, giving thanks. Then Ken was on his knees beside her, also praying, also thanking God.

He mumbled, "What have I done? I've got to call the police. They have to take me away."

Marilyn was so confused. She tried to think clearly. Ken was sick. He needed help, for sure. But were the police the right answer? She wondered if Ken would snap again. She decided she had to stay very calm.

She'd call the Navy chaplain, she said. He'd know what to do. He lived right down the street. She told him over the phone that something terrible had occurred, that he had to get right over. Her face hurt. She looked in a mirror.

She could barely recognize herself. Her face had blown up and was covered by what seemed to be burns. Later, she was told that they were caused by the chloroform and the coarse sponge.

When the chaplain arrived, Ken sat there immobile, his head bowed, while she tried to explain what happened, to make some sense of it.

The chaplain drove them both to the base hospital so that Marilyn could be treated for her facial injuries and Ken admitted to the psychiatric ward.

The senior psychiatrist on the base, Commander W. F. Pettit, was on leave, so Ken was placed in the care of Lieutenant Commander Ronald C. Smith. Ken confessed to Dr. Smith that he had attempted to do away with his wife, but his conscience had gotten the better of him. He said that he was a heavy user of marijuana and amphetamines, obtaining them from enlisted sources on the base that he wouldn't name. He had taken three black beauties the Monday night he attacked Marilyn and at least seven more over the weekend. He had heard voices telling him to kill her. His first marriage had failed, which angered his parents. He said his mother was "very judgmental" and that it had been a "constant struggle" to gain his father's approval. His current marriage was about to break up. He feared the reaction of his parents and was, as Ken phrased it, "in a bind."

When Marilyn came to the hospital two days later to check on Ken, Dr. Smith advised her that her husband was a "homicidal maniac" and that it was only a matter of time before he "would finish off the job" if she remained with him. For her own good, he told her to report the matter forthwith to the police. Only she could do it.

It was more than she could bear. First her father wasting away, and now this. *Homicidal maniac?* She didn't know what to do. Memories of wonderful moments she'd had with Ken flooded through her. Of course he needed help, but was prosecution the solution, possibly ruining his life, his career?

She discussed it with the chaplain, who sympathized with

her dilemma. "But what it boils down to," he said, "is that you can't take the chance. I understand you don't want to destroy his life, but he did do this, whether it's drugs or psychosis or whatever. You have to worry about you and your baby."

She contacted the police. She said that while she wasn't prepared at this stage to sign a formal complaint, she wanted it made a matter of record that the incident had taken place. She also said she thought her husband had gone over the edge because he was afraid that the baby would take attention away from him. And after an investigation, in which additional evidence was gathered, Ken was charged with attempted murder.

Then Dr. Smith was superseded on "the Taylor case" by his superior, W. F. Pettit. The switch was unusual, but the Navy didn't welcome the sort of publicity a trial would bring. Ken was a popular figure on the base, most valuable player on the champion intramural softball team, who also performed the dental work on the top brass. The only complaints about him were that his "military bearing" needed improvement and that he fraternized a bit too much with enlisted personnel.

Pettit told Marilyn precisely what she wanted to hear. According to his findings, Ken was "neither psychologically nor physically dependent on drugs." There was no evidence of "psychosis." Ken was the kind of man who "has difficulty in dealing directly with his emotions and tends to allow things to build up to where he experiences chronic tensions and anxiety." That, plus excessive alcohol intake and his plunge into drugs, led to the "alleged incident." He cited other contributing factors that filled Marilyn with guilt, among them a "growing lack of respect and appreciation from his wife" and "more recent feelings of abandonment related to his wife's absence due to her father's sickness."

There was no reference to Ken's philandering.

Pettit also said that Ken had entered group therapy and was undergoing counseling for alcohol abuse. He had agreed to marriage counseling as well. Meanwhile, Ken, once released from the hospital, would remain on the base in quarters for bachelor officers. Pettit urged her to cooperate.

• • •

In a phone call to Marion, Ken gave Jean and Zach Taylor his version of what had happened. He had a problem, he'd lashed out physically at Marilyn. He had stressed out, he said. Too much coffee and too many pills, pills to wake up and pills to sleep because of marital tensions. A senior Navy psychiatrist had said that most of it was caused by the way Marilyn had been treating him. Now he was in therapy, straightening himself out, building his "self-esteem" which had suffered greatly. Everything was going to be fine. The problem, though, was that he needed ten thousand dollars to post bond and to retain a lawyer. The Taylors were hardly admirers of Marilyn. Zach withdrew the money from his savings account and wired it to Ken. It was supposed to be a loan, one Ken never paid back. Considering her view of Marilyn, Jean wasn't at all surprised that the marriage had gone sour.

Marilyn was completely reassured when Ken's attorney showed her a letter from the superintendent of a state psychiatric center, Fairfield Hills Hospital, who had personally examined Ken. The possibility that Ken would repeat his "assaultive behavior is virtually nonexistent," he wrote. Moreover, "further psychiatric treatment on an ambulatory basis would restore this young doctor to his intended role as someone beneficial to society."

Marilyn agonized over her decision for a time and finally declined to sign a formal complaint. That ended the matter and under Connecticut law all the records in the case were sealed.

There hadn't been any media coverage. There would never be public knowledge of what had occurred. Inside the base, of course, it was different. According to Ken, even more women flocked to him, intrigued by what they'd heard. He particularly remembered the good-looking wife of a marine officer who had come in complaining of a toothache. He couldn't find anything wrong. He happened to remark on her excellent tan, and she asked him how he liked the rest of it, raising her sweater to expose her breasts. Her husband was away, she said. How about dinner? Marital counseling or not, he couldn't pass this up. He'd just have to be more discreet.

Still, as far as Marilyn could tell, she had made the right choice. When their daughter Astrid was born, Ken was a doting father. In her own father's last days, he was supportive in every way. And he appeared steadfast in his therapy. When he was discharged from the Navy in July 1979, he acceded to her desire to move back to New York and got a job running a newly established dental center in Brooklyn. She compromised, too. He didn't like the city, so she agreed to live in New York's most remote borough, Staten Island, with its large stretches of green, and single-family houses. In a way it was reminiscent of a midwestern town, and the Verrazano Bridge over New York Harbor provided easy access to work—to Brooklyn for him and to LaGuardia and Kennedy airports in Queens for her security blanket, the flight attendant's job she had never relinquished.

Very soon, however, Ken reverted to his old ways. He started drinking again. He had to relax, he said, after the long hours he devoted to building the dental center's business. She found the remnants of a joint in the house they had bought. While she had never actually seen him doing other drugs, she noted that he was walking into walls and falling over things. Oh, brother, she thought, here we go again.

And obviously he had resumed seeing other women. She blamed herself partially for that. Try as she might, she was never sexually comfortable with him after Connecticut. But it was intolerable, the way he would stroll into the house at five A.M. She imagined her daughter waking in the morning and saying, "Oh, here comes my daddy."

There was a new crisis. After one of their rare instances of intercourse, she became pregnant again. Fearful of the future, of a repeat of Connecticut, of being alone now with two children to care for, she had an abortion.

"What is it you want, an open marriage?" she asked him.

She never got a straight answer. "Whatever," he said.

She zeroed in on one particular rival, a young woman he had hired for the Brooklyn office. She had seen her two or three times and had gotten a whiff of her perfume. Then, after returning home from one of her flights, she sniffed the same fragrance in the house.

Marilyn was right. Her name was Teresa Benigno, then twenty-one, a newly graduated dental hygienist who had dark brown flowing hair and deep-set electric blue eyes.

She would become Ken Taylor's third wife.

# Chapter

## TWO

When Teresa Benigno graduated from Moore Catholic High School in Staten Island in 1977, her father, Albert, wrote in her yearbook, *The man you marry will make the ultimate difference in the outcome of your life. He must be your equal in intelligence and maturity. No man must ever be your master. No man must ever dictate the terms of your security through force or fear. A marriage can only endure through mutual love and respect for one another.*

It's not customary for parents to write in their children's yearbooks, but the Benignos were an emotional clan. And it would seem even more unusual for words like these to have been written by Al, as everyone called him, who was not only Italian, but also Sicilian, a tradition not especially noted for fostering equal rights for women.

His father had come to New York from Sicily in 1910. Al was born and raised in Brooklyn. A poor student and an eventual high school dropout—"The only class I passed was lunch," he liked to joke—he enlisted in the Navy in 1948, and served as a radioman during the Korean War.

After his discharge, though, he got his high school diploma and with the aid of the GI Bill of Rights trained to be a draftsman. He then began work as an assistant architect in the New York City public school system in the department responsible for the design and rehabilitation of school buildings. After ten years there, he taught drafting for another twenty years at a vocational high school in Brooklyn.

In 1955, he had married Louise Arico, also Sicilian, a shy, pretty girl, then working as a secretary for a ship line, whom he had known since childhood. Three years later, Louise became pregnant. Their rented apartment inadequate for a growing family, Al started thinking about buying a house. Financially, Brooklyn was out of reach, so he began looking in Staten Island. And in 1960, a year after their first daughter, Teresa, was born, he purchased a three-bedroom ranch-style home in the New Dorp section on Staten Island's south shore.

With a mortgage, he could just make the $17,000 price tag. Until the Verrazano Bridge to Brooklyn was built four years later, he had to commute by ferry. At first, the Benigno house was surrounded by dairy and vegetable farms. Now, because of the bridge, the area is middle-class suburban, with blocks of similar homes and well-kept lawns, predominantly owned by Italians. Indeed, a third of Staten Island's population of four hundred thousand is Italian. The borough, one of five in New York, is really a series of villages, isolated both spiritually and geographically from the rest of the city. Most other New Yorkers, except perhaps for taking a spectacular round-trip ferry ride from the skyscrapers of lower Manhattan past the Statue of Liberty—still the world's best travel bargain at only fifty cents—have never set foot on it.

After Teresa was born in 1959, a second daughter, Celeste, came in 1961, and finally a son, Philip, named after Al's father, in 1964. There were problems with Phil—a handsome, husky kid, rebellious, an indifferent student—but a kid who reminded Al very much of himself at that age, a kid who in the long run would straighten out.

And there was Celeste, the family beauty, outshining

even Teresa. Her pale luminous gray eyes contrasted with Teresa's vivid blue ones. She was outwardly scatter-brained, unfocused in school, apparently marching to her own drummer, oblivious to curfews and chores. Yet Al never doubted her rock-solid substance. At twelve she'd fallen for a neighborhood boy named Jeff White and never looked left or right after that. It brought back memories of his own courtship of Louise.

If he ever questioned Celeste's resiliency, her ability to rise to the occasion, it was resolved when at the age of eighteen she drove into Brooklyn to try on a wedding gown for her marriage to Jeff. On a street under elevated subway tracks she saw a couple of police cars on the corner with cops crouched behind them, guns drawn. Wow, they're filming a movie, she thought, and pulled into a parking space to watch. All at once this fellow with a sawed-off shotgun was yanking open the passenger door and pointing the gun at her and saying, "Drive, bitch." And she did.

At the first red light, she said, "Oh no, what'll I do?" and he said, "Drive through it." There was another red light, and another. Here she was speeding through red lights, and where were the cops? she thought.

"Listen," she said, "I'm only eighteen years old. I just tried on my wedding gown today. Don't kill me. You notice I'm not looking at you because I can't identify you. I don't know who the hell you are," she kept babbling on, "so don't kill me, you hear me!"

She could hear sirens behind her and up ahead more sirens and saw flashing red lights coming toward her. "Pull over," the fellow said, and she remembered saying, "Why?" If she had to, she was ready to take him to California. "Just get out," he said, and she did, and then she remembered the leather jacket Jeff had bought her that meant so much to her and she yelled, "Wait, my jacket!" and the fellow threw it at her, and then it was her pocketbook, and she cried, "My pocketbook! My pocketbook!" and, cursing, he tossed it at her as well.

She scrambled away and ducked behind a parked car. There was a guy sitting on a stoop taking this all in, and she called to him, "Is he gone?" and then she peeked and saw the fellow with the shotgun running across the street into an alley and then the cops arrived and went in after him.

The guy on the stoop, who had not stirred throughout the entire episode, stared at her bemused and said, "Hey, I thought you were having a fight with your boyfriend."

Well, she thought, that's New York for you.

Later on, Ken Taylor would know none of this, would not comprehend at all the spunk and determination of his third wife's sister, and would dismiss her as a ditzy bubblehead.

• • •

*Please know that you can always come to me with your problems,* Al had also written in Teresa's yearbook. *Above all, always remember this: no matter how old a lady you get to be, you will always be daddy's little girl.*

Al was concerned about Teresa because she had so much promise. Unlike her siblings, she was a whiz at St. Charles Parochial School in New Dorp and was immediately accepted at Moore, Staten Island's elite diocesan high school, where she continued to get A's with little apparent effort. He was afraid that she would jettison all of this over someone unworthy of her. It wasn't that she slept around. It was just the opposite. Teresa was incurably romantic, always one boy at a time who was going to be *the* one whom she would marry and have children with and be forever happy. And she wore her heart on her sleeve. On her page of the yearbook of her current boyfriend, it said, "I love Pat 4ever," along with a photograph she had picked of the two of them gazing into each other's eyes. Her favorite verse was from Goethe, about the true measure of love: "When we believe that we alone can love/That no one has ever loved so before us."

It drove Al crazy that her boyfriends weren't up to snuff, weren't nearly as smart as she. He worried that she could be as submissive with her boyfriends as she was willful and stubborn at home. It wasn't only his imagination. One of her girlfriends in high school remembered, "Teresa seemed to be drawn to, I don't know, like to the underdog. Like she was going to help them realize their potential. And they, some of them anyway, could be mean to her and slap her around."

Something else also was deeply troubling to Al. It surfaced one night during Teresa's senior year when they sat alone talking about college. Al said that he wanted her to apply wherever she wanted to go, even if it meant moving away. With the scholarship aid her grades would bring, he'd be able to scrape together any additional funds that might be needed. "I've made so many mistakes," he said, "and as I grow old, I see my life going downhill, and I want it to be different for you. It's not that I'm not happy, it's just that I don't think I've fulfilled myself."

He said, "I want to give you everything, but I can't." At the time she was constantly with a group of girls that neighborhood boys started calling the "Glitter Chicks"— determinedly sporting the latest in makeup, nail polish, and hairstyles, spending every spare dollar on fashionable outfits. The other "Glitter Chicks" came from well-off families and to keep up with them, Teresa, who was an expert seamstress, had to make all her own clothes. Al told her how much it saddened him that her friends had beautiful cars and beautiful things to wear which she couldn't afford.

When he had been hospitalized with back problems for a lengthy period that temporarily reduced his income, she had lied about her age and got a job at Burger King and turned over every paycheck to her mother. "It breaks my heart that I can never be the father I want to be," he told her that night. "This is how I pay for my mistakes, the reminder always of them. So whatever college you want to go to, please fill out the applications."

Then Teresa, eyes tremulous, displaying an unexpected vulnerability, said that she didn't want to go away right now. "You may think I'm smart and everything," she said, "but I make mistakes, too, and I cry. I want to stay at home for a while."

Weeping, she had started out of the room when Al said,

"Teresa," and she turned back to her father and they silently hugged and kissed.

"The thing you remembered most about Teresa in school," Karen Oliveira, her closest friend at Moore Catholic, said, "was how vivacious and full of life she was, how she could take the littlest story and make it so dramatic with her voice and eyes and hands. She just made you feel good. And she was so caring. When we were freshmen, my grandmother died, and my mother and father had to go make the funeral arrangements, and I told her I had to stay home and fix dinner for my little brothers and I didn't know what I was going to do, I could hardly boil water then, and around six o'clock she showed up with two pizzas, not store-bought pizzas, but ones she'd made herself from scratch, dough and all. Not many fourteen- or fifteen-year-olds would be that thoughtful."

In high school, according to Karen, Teresa tried pot. "Almost all the kids did, me included. But Teresa didn't like it." She also tried THC, a distilled form of marijuana that could cause hallucinations. "It just arrived at the school," Karen said. "That's what all those references in the yearbook to 'T-day' mean. I didn't try it. Teresa did, but only once. She said it made her feel sick and dizzy. She did take diet pills because she was so worried about her hips and thighs—it made her mad that Celeste didn't have anywhere near the problem—and she hardly drank, a little wine and maybe a gin or vodka at a party. The first time she brought Ken Taylor over, I couldn't believe it when she asked me for Jack Daniel's. That's what Ken and she drank, she said, and I had to send out for it. I remember thinking, God, if she's suddenly drinking something that tastes that strong, she'll do anything for this guy."

After graduating with honors from Moore, Teresa decided she'd do the practical thing. She enrolled in Brooklyn College for an associate degree in dental hygiene, which offered the prospect of an immediate, well-paying job. It also gave her some time to decide what else she might want to do. Besides, she had a new love, a local boy named Sal Aurelio.

While Al thought Aurelio—an accountant with a Wall

Street firm—was a cut above her other swains, he was not enamored of the young man's arrogant ways. He'd heard that his adoring mother referred to him as "Saint Salvatore." How did his daughter find them? he thought. When Al wanted to include Teresa in a family summer vacation trip to California, Aurelio actually complained to him, "What am I going to do while she's gone?"

"Baloney," Al said. "Do whatever you want. You're a grown man. She's still my daughter, she's living at home. If you two get married, she'll be yours forever. I'm tickled pink to have her on the trip and she wants to go."

So when suddenly Aurelio was out of the picture, replaced by this dentist from Indiana, Al wasn't exactly unhappy. Okay, he was different, but so what? He was from another part of the country with a different background. It was unfair to expect him to fit hand-in-glove with an often volatile Italian-American family which had practically no familiarity with anyone outside its own parochial community. And it didn't bother Al one whit that Ken was, according to Teresa, divorced. It troubled Louise Benigno a great deal, however, and almost at once she and Teresa fought about Ken. Louise was a devout Catholic, even though Al had long since fallen away from the church. And Teresa herself, once she finished high school, had ceased being a communicant of consequence except for the big feast days like Christmas and Easter.

At that time, none of the Benignos, except for Teresa, knew that Ken Taylor was in fact still married to Marilyn Hope, who lived only a few miles away. They did not know, nor did even Teresa, about the sealed court documents in Connecticut which recorded that he had attempted to murder her. They had no idea that Ken had a former wife he had left to languish alone in the pitiless heat of a room in Indianapolis days before giving birth to a daughter he never saw.

And Ken, in turn, did not comprehend, nor would he ever really understand, that all the tumult of the Benignos, their combativeness, their emotional highs and lows, meant little. He listened to Teresa grumble endlessly that her mother always looked over her shoulder, always finding fault; he never knew that when Louise, who suffered heart trouble, had a particularly bad siege, Teresa dropped everything without a second's hesitation to be by her side, to nurse her and to run the household. He didn't know that however much Teresa complained to him about Celeste, she had burst into nearly hysterical sobs the day Celeste was to marry Jeff White, crying inconsolably, "I'm losing my sister," while Jeff kept saying, "Hey, come on, Teresa, we're only going to be living three blocks away." He had no conception of how this family could instantly and fiercely unite when it perceived itself threatened.

In truth, Al rather liked Ken. He found him personable and respectful to him and Louise. And Ken was a professional man—a dentist. "You can't take that away from him," he told Louise.

• • •

Teresa first met Ken in September 1980, at the Fulton Family Dental Center in central Brooklyn. The center, founded by two Brooklyn dentists with thriving private practices, had been under his direction since his discharge from the Navy. Now there was an opening for another hygienist.

He was immediately taken by her big blue eyes and her "classic Italian hourglass figure." Ken's deal with the center provided a base salary against commissions. In a highly visible location, the center attracted many of its patients off the street. It was vital, though, to keep tabs on followup treatments, which produced the major income. After talking to Teresa, he realized that she was extremely intelligent. He told her that while he needed a hygienist, his most pressing problem was supervising the appointment books, keeping the reception room filled and the three dentists he had hired busy. She would have some hygienic duties, but her main job would be organizing the office, manning the front desk.

He liked how she made eye contact and said, "I'm sure I can handle everything to your satisfaction."

He had come to pride himself on being able to enter a woman's mind. He was sure that she was intrigued by him, but they had talked enough for him to sense that she was not the kind to hop right into bed, like one of the assistants in the office who was always available, no questions asked. This was going to require some time.

And in another way, *time* was a problem. He was putting in at least sixty hours a week at the center, Monday through Saturday. Besides the office assistant, he had scored with a couple of patients. Cocaine kept him going. Much of the center's clientele was black. He despised blacks and made no secret of it. When the psychiatrist who treated Ken at the submarine base learned that one of the enlisted women he was seeing was black, he advised Marilyn that it was a perfect example of how low her husband's self-esteem had sunk. But Ken figured that streetwise blacks might be good connections, trading off, say, some dental care for a gram or two. And if he had to pay, so be it. He'd also discovered a joint on the west side of Staten Island that featured go-go strippers, a hangout for bikers, where if you knew the right people, you could get just about anything you wanted. He didn't have to be concerned with anyone he knew spotting him there, and he would sit with a drink at the bar watching the girls perform. It wasn't the anticipation of seeing one of them naked, guys all around yelling, "Take it off," it was imagining the girl dancing just for him.

Teresa was still driving a used Skylark she had bought her senior year in high school. One day a month or so after she had been hired by Ken, she phoned the dental center to say she'd be delayed. She had to take the car in for repairs. She would be coming in by bus. Look, Ken told her, the Skylark was on its last legs. He worried about her driving across the bridge during rush hours in that rattle-trap. You didn't know what could happen. Why didn't she drive to his house? It would be an easy ten minutes. Then she could ride in with him.

He rather enjoyed the image of Marilyn, now almost thirty-six, peering into the mirror for signs of wrinkles, having to meet this lush twenty-one-year-old. And it worked out as he suspected. Marilyn was in her robe in the kitchen having coffee when Teresa rang the bell and asked for "Doctor Taylor." She turned glacial and headed instantly for the bedroom. Ken told Teresa to wait for him in his Buick. He went to the bedroom to get his briefcase.

"So that's your latest tramp?" Marilyn said.

"Don't be ridiculous. She works for me."

"Yeah, sure. Well, at least do me a favor. Don't bring your punchboards around here."

In the car, Teresa said, "What was that all about?"

"It's what I have to live with."

Afterward, Teresa would park by the Staten Island side of the bridge where Ken picked her up every morning.

During these rides, they began to exchange confidences. Teresa told Ken about her boyfriend, Sal Aurelio, how they'd been going together for nearly two years and that he was pressuring her about marriage. She had thought she was madly in love with him, but now she was uncertain. He was so demanding and once, during an argument, he had hit her. Her father didn't like him much, but then her father hadn't really liked most of her boyfriends. This time, though, maybe he was right. She didn't know what to do.

His life with Marilyn, he said, was miserable. She was an unbearable know-it-all. If he said it was noon, she would say no, it's twelve o'clock. On top of everything else, she was frigid. Once when he was in the Navy and they were living in Connecticut, she had even brought rape charges against him. "How can you rape your own wife?" he said. She eventually dropped the charges, but it showed what she was capable of. She'd seduced him into marrying her. She'd been around and knew all the tricks, and he'd been just an innocent kid in dental school. She took him like Grant took Richmond. He would have been long gone, if it weren't for little Astrid. He adored their daughter, he said. Considering Marilyn's lack of interest in sex, it was a miracle she'd been born in the first place.

Teresa told him that when she was studying to be a hygienist and had to learn all about anatomy, she had thought of becoming a doctor. That was funny, he said. He also had contemplated doing the same thing, and he related how he'd been a hospital orderly at Ball State and was handed the body of the dead infant, and when he finished the story, Teresa uttered a gasp and impulsively squeezed his arm.

They talked about music and traded record albums. She was a fan of David Bowie, and he gave her two of his old favorites, a Neil Young and a Steely Dan.

Eventually the Skylark broke down completely, and Ken said he would stop by for her at home. Blushing, she said that she had told her parents that he was divorced. She didn't know exactly why, it just seemed easier.

Well, it was the whitest of lies, he said. He would be, sooner or later. Meeting her had caused him to think about many things.

Sometimes when Teresa was late getting her makeup on, he'd come in for a cup of coffee. Louise Benigno questioned him closely about his divorce. While he wasn't Catholic, he said, his own parents were extremely religious people who did not believe in divorce, nor for that matter did he. What could he say? he said. He'd married too young. He and his wife were totally incompatible. It had been a terrible mistake, but you had to be man enough to admit it, pull yourself together, and go on to lead a productive life.

Louise painted for pleasure, and he complimented her on her work and her dressmaking talent. Obviously, Teresa had inherited her sewing skills. He commiserated with Al about the task of trying to teach inner-city ghetto kids, who with few exceptions didn't seem to care. Should the Benignos ever need dental work, feel free to call on him, he said. With their wonderful daughter on hand to help him, it would be his pleasure.

They had not dated. Occasionally they'd have a drink after work or a bite at a fast-food restaurant. She made an awful face the first time she tasted Jack Daniel's, but he noticed that the next time she asked for it on her own. Then Ken made his move. When Marilyn was flying, she had arranged to leave Astrid in the care of a woman whom she found through the classifieds. The following March, while his wife was off on a three-day trip, he asked Teresa if she was free that night. He wanted her to think about it, he said. After all, she was practically engaged, wasn't she?

It was precisely what Teresa had been waiting for. She told Louise she was staying overnight with one of her girl-friends. They had dinner in a Manhattan steak house. Then he drove her to his place. According to Ken, it was the best sex he ever had. He used all the same raves he'd once reserved for Marilyn. Awesome. Unbelievable heights of passion. Skyrockets going off. It was as if in his head Teresa had become Marilyn, and Marilyn was now Emily.

Early in the fall, Teresa told him she was pregnant.

"Is it mine?" he said.

She slapped him. It was the first time he had been hit by a woman since his mother had done it when he was a child. To his surprise, he felt chastened. He apologized and leaned over and kissed her. "That's some right you pack," he said.

She had no choice, she said. He was still married and she couldn't face her parents. She'd have to have an abortion. He didn't argue. When it was over, he held her hand and said, "Our time will come."

On Thanksgiving Day, after dining with Marilyn, Astrid, and Marilyn's brother and his wife, Ken left for good, without a word. Marilyn found a note in the kitchen that said he'd be in touch.

A few days later he phoned to set up a visit with Astrid.

"It's that Italian girl, isn't it?" Marilyn said.

"It's a lot of things," he said. After all the fights they'd had, he thought, she was actually jealous. She was blaming everything on Teresa. He still had her number, and he tucked that in the back of his mind.

He rented an apartment on Staten Island and now he could have Teresa almost every evening. But never for the whole night. Sometimes they'd fall asleep, and the phone would ring, at three or four A.M., and Louise would be on the line saying, "Get home." It led to bitter confrontations between mother and daughter. Once Teresa shouted, "You don't think I'm a virgin, do you?" Al was livid. "Never speak to your mother like that again. There are rules in this house, and as long as you live here, you will abide by them."

The Benignos customarily had a big Sunday dinner. And every so often there'd be an extended family get-together of assorted aunts and uncles, nieces and nephews and cousins. On one of these occasions, an incident occurred that nobody present, including Ken, would ever forget.

Ken was standing with Teresa on the top step at the front door as her grandfather Philip, Al's father, made his way slowly along the walk with the aid of a cane. He was then ninety-three years old, retired from a lifetime of counseling hundreds of Italian immigrants applying for citizenship papers.

It was the first time he had seen Ken, and as Ken bent forward to help him up the steps, he suddenly lashed out, catching Ken by surprise, causing him to stumble off the steps. "Away," he cried. "Get away from me!"

Ken turned toward Teresa and said, "What did I do?"

"Nothing," Teresa said, tears of embarrassment streaming down her cheeks. "He's an old man. He's not right in the head. Let's get out of here."

Afterward, inside, Louise said, "Papa, what's the matter?"

"He's no good," Philip Benigno snapped. "I can tell. He's a man with a past."

"What should we do?"

"Throw him out."

Louise threw up her hands, tears rolling down her face as well. "This is nineteen eighty-two. It's not like the old days. I throw him out, I throw her out, too."

That spring Teresa lost her job at the Fulton Dental Center. The two dentists who owned it were constantly second-guessing Ken. One of them, Dr. Irwin Azar, would arrive weekly to examine the books. Azar was being particularly harsh in his review of procedures during an evening visit. Teresa leapt to Ken's defense. Words were exchanged, and the next morning, Ken told Teresa that Azar wanted her fired for insubordination.

She didn't care, she said, she hated working there anyway, she would get another job and, indeed, that same day she was hired as a hygienist in the office of a Staten Island dentist. Besides, she said, she needed time for herself. She'd been so preoccupied with Ken that she had neglected her friends. Maybe she should go back to school for more study.

"Study what?"

She didn't know, but she was tired of being "the other woman." Ken had used Astrid as an excuse for dragging his heels about a divorce for too long. "People get divorced every day," she said.

"And children get hurt every day," he said.

Teresa still did not know about Emily and his daughter back in Indiana. Nor would she.

She calmed down when he told her that Marilyn had finally retained a lawyer. Then a couple of months later he said he had some bad news. Marilyn had informed him that her lawyer had died. "But she'll find another one," he said. "The divorce is still on."

"Yes, on hold," Teresa said.

To jolly her out of her anger, he took her on a weekend trip to Connecticut. It was the first time they had gone anywhere together. Louise and Al couldn't do anything about it. They stayed overnight in New London, at a motel Ken had regularly used for his liaisons when he was stationed at the submarine base. It was kind of spooky, he remembered, lying next to Teresa, thinking about all those others.

On February 7, 1983, the eve of Ken's birthday, Teresa sat waiting for him in the kitchen of his apartment. She had bought him an expensive stereo set and champagne. First, he'd said, he had to stop by to see Astrid. But he never came home. Teresa left him a letter: *It's now 9:31 P.M. You probably don't realize you are torturing me right now, hon. I just don't know whether you are dead or alive—maybe in the emergency room of some hospital, maybe at your house on Travis Avenue (excuse me—"Astrid's house"), whoever's house I don't really care . . . I don't have the guts to call Travis Ave. 'cause maybe you left a long time ago and then I would really flip out 'cause that would mean something really happened to you . . . You are the only one I live for. I only live for you and I only want to be with you and spend my life with you . . . I need you to hug and kiss me and tell me you love me . . . Hon, please, I don't care if you're divorced or not. I need you, only you, and I will wait—I mean eventually you will be divorced. I don't care if I'm too old to have kids. I don't care as long as I have you.*

Actually, Ken was at his house on Travis Avenue that night—in bed with Marilyn.

She had recently undergone plastic surgery to enlarge her breasts. When he stopped by to be with Astrid, Marilyn said that everything had gone well and they ought to celebrate. She wanted him to be the first to see the results. Boy, he thought, weren't women really something? He was sure she'd had the implants just to entice him, regretting, because of Teresa, all the times she had rebuffed him. Well, he'd be big about it, show her what she'd been missing.

He apologized profusely to Teresa on the phone. He swore it would never happen again. He wouldn't do anything to hurt her. Time had simply slipped away while he visited with Astrid and he hadn't noticed. And he had good news, which was why he had been concentrating so on his daughter. The divorce was now imminent. At most a matter of weeks. It was going to be his surprise for her.

He wrote a note for Teresa to find when she arrived at the apartment later: *Understand my feelings of loss, and perhaps you can forgive me. I could never leave you. I hope you can forgive me . . . I love you with all my heart and will soon make you my wife if you will still have me. I have gained strength and pledge my everlasting love to you. On my birthday, I love you.*

*All my love forever. Ken.*

There were many things Teresa would never know about Ken Taylor. One of them was that right after professing his undying love for Teresa, he asked Marilyn to drop the divorce proceedings. It had been exciting with her the other night, he thought, just like the old days, so exciting to see her practically beg to have him. Besides, there were other considerations. A divorce was going to cost him five hundred dollars a week in alimony and child support. And Marilyn was going to get the house, which was appreciating rapidly. Okay, so she had put up most of the down payment—after all, he was fresh out of the Navy, working his ass off to get a career started—and half of the mortgage payments, but it still wasn't fair.

"I've been thinking about you and Astrid," he told her. "Teresa's so immature. Maybe we can work things out and put it back together."

Marilyn hesitated. The truth was she couldn't stand the image of "that receptionist." Teresa wasn't like the others whom she had never actually seen. Since her separation from Ken, much of the tension between them had evaporated. He'd been really good to Astrid and good around the house, mowing the lawn and everything, she thought. She had talked about her problems with Ken to a couple of other flight attendants and they both said, "You know, if a guy's not getting sex at home, he's not just going to live without it." She recalled what the psychiatrist had said about Ken's low self-esteem, how he needed bucking up, but in the end, she decided that it would be better to let the divorce go through. Then they would see what happened.

A month later, the divorce was finalized. And on March 27, Teresa's twenty-fourth birthday, Ken sent a bouquet of flowers to Louise, thanking her for having brought such a beautiful daughter into the world.

Teresa was floored. Karen Oliveira remembered that Teresa called her, exclaiming how wonderful and romantic a gesture it was, how wonderful Ken was. Neither Karen nor other old high school friends had seen much of Teresa since this Indiana dentist had entered her life. It seemed so unlike Teresa, and yet so purposeful. Karen, a 4.0 graduate of Wagner College on Staten Island, who had gone into commercial banking, was unimpressed by Ken when she finally met him. He seemed remote, disinterested, smug, taking little part in the conversation. She concluded he had to be responsible for keeping Teresa away from everyone. Karen hadn't taken the romance that seriously. After all, Teresa was always in love. Marriage was usually just around the corner. Now, though, after hearing about the bouquet that Ken sent to Louise, she wasn't so sure.

They agreed to meet for Saturday brunch the next week. When Karen arrived, Teresa appeared terribly upset. She told Karen a bizarre tale. According to Ken, his ex-wife was threatening to blackmail him for more money. She had photographs of Teresa naked on some beach that she intended to send to Teresa's parents.

Teresa had not seen them. Ken said he just couldn't bring himself to show them to her.

"I've never been nude on a beach in my life!" Teresa said. How could this be? But then, after a moment, she brightened considerably. Ken, she said, had told her he had studied the pictures and concluded that it couldn't have been Teresa, that her head was superimposed on someone else's body, and he wasn't going to cave in.

What kind of mind games is this guy playing? Karen thought. She wanted to say this to Teresa, but she didn't. She was certain it would be futile.

• • •

Their marriage was set for July 10, 1983.

Ken had planned on just going down to City Hall or finding a justice of the peace somewhere. But Teresa wanted a big wedding. "Don't worry," she said. "My father will pay for it."

In deference to Louise, she tried to have the ceremony at the parish church, St. Charles, but once the crusty old monsignor learned that Ken was divorced, he would have none of it. They finally settled on the Reform Huguenot Church near Ken's apartment. Her matron of honor Celeste and her bridesmaids would wear pink and mauve. Ken said he wanted his brother Tom to be best man, and Teresa said that she would need his measurements; all the men participating in the ceremony were wearing light gray tuxedos.

Teresa spoke to Jean and Zach Taylor over the phone. She told them how deliriously happy she was, how good their son was to her, and how obvious it was to her that it was the result of his upbringing. She couldn't wait to meet them. She was the luckiest girl in the world, she said.

In Marion, Jean, occupied by her Sunday school classes at the First Baptist Church, active in the Women's Baptist Circle, and a regular at Thursday night Bible studies, felt waves of satisfaction. Teresa Benigno, Catholic or not, was a far cry from that stewardess who had gotten her hooks into "Kenny."

Odd incidents occurred that were largely ignored at the time by everyone caught up in the preparations.

A week before the wedding, Ken approached Al Benigno and said that his brother Tom wouldn't be able to come after all. Did Al think that Teresa's brother Phil would fill in as his best man? Al said that he was asking the wrong person, but Phil then agreed.

Ken was vague about the reasons why Tom could not come. Tom in fact had another agenda. The brilliant sports career envisioned for him by his parents was over. Just out of high school, he wrecked his knee in a freak accident during a weight-lifting session. No more athletic scholarships or professional contracts were in the offing. Living at home, bouncing from one job to the next, he had tuned out first with marijuana and hashish, and then with cocaine, which he found easily available on Marion's south side.

Jean and Zach did nothing to address his problem. It was as if it were an unacceptable intrusion in their ordered life.

On Wednesday night before the Sunday wedding, Karen Oliveira told Teresa that the bright blue eyeliner she used might not be appropriate. Why not go down to Garber's, a local department store, the next day and have the ladies in the beauty salon make her up? If she liked it, they could do her for the wedding. They went together. Afterward, Teresa panicked. She was late. She had to pick up Ken. Ken was waiting for her. Ken's parents would be arriving. "So what?" Karen had said. "You're doing things for the wedding. How could he be mad at you?" Karen had seen

Teresa upset, but never out of control like this. There was something in her eyes that was different, close to fear.

When Ken was asked for his list of friends, the only two names he produced were fellow dentists from the Fulton Center. In all, one hundred fifty guests attended the ceremony.

At a cookout Al and Louise gave on the eve of the wedding, Jean Taylor was withdrawn. She wasn't used to, as she said, "that Italian custom of hugging and kissing."

The hit of the festivities was Jean's mother, who had flown up from Florida. In a limousine on the way to the church, she said to the bridesmaids, "Do you ladies mind if I smoke?" When they said no, she sighed and said, "With *them* I can't smoke or drink, can't do anything. I can't wait to get back to Florida, get all my clothes off, and lie in the sun nude with a gin and tonic."

The reception was held at Dellwood Manor, a popular Staten Island catering hall. The theme song, from the Boz Scaggs group, was "Love, Look What You've Done to Me."

• • •

Jean and Zach left for Marion the next morning. On her return, Jean told a neighbor, "It was just like a Hollywood wedding."

Marilyn Hope learned about Ken's marriage when a friend called after reading a notice in the local paper, the *Staten Island Advance*.

Ken and Teresa spent their first night as husband and wife in a hotel at Kennedy Airport. Then they flew to Mexico, to Las Brisas, the famous Acapulco resort, the culmination of all of Teresa's romantic dreams. John F. Kennedy had taken Jacqueline there on their honeymoon.

They were to be there a week.

The following Sunday night Al and Louise drove to Kennedy to meet their flight. Teresa and Ken were not on it. Al made inquiries at the counter. No, an agent told him, there was no Dr. Kenneth and Mrs. Taylor on the passenger manifest. They had not boarded the flight.

By now it was almost one A.M. On the way back to

Staten Island, Al said, "They're probably having a good time and decided to stay over. Maybe they went somewhere else."

"Why didn't they call?"

"Look, they're busy. They're on their honeymoon."

Near dawn, Al awoke. Louise was not in bed. He went into the kitchen and found her at the table. She was saying her rosary.

"Don't worry," he said. "I'll call if we don't hear from them."

# Chapter

## THREE

The response to Al Benigno's first call on Monday morning—to the Las Brisas Hotel—left him reeling. After a pause, a voice said that there was no Dr. or Mrs. Taylor registered.

Al demanded to speak to someone in authority. Then a second man, identifying himself as an assistant receptions manager, told Al that the Taylors had checked out the previous Thursday. When Al tried to question him further, the man said that he was sorry, but he was unable to provide any more information. While the man had been quite polite, Al could sense there was something he wasn't telling him, a hesitancy in the way he spoke. "I regret, sir, I can't tell you any more than this," he insisted.

Al next telephoned the Mexican Consulate in Manhattan, which referred him to the Mexican Tourist Office. A woman there suggested that he contact the American government representative in Acapulco. While the United States did not maintain a consulate in the resort city, there was a consular agent. If anything untoward had occurred,

48

he would certainly know about it. She gave Al his name, L. J. Bon Urbanek, and his number.

Al got right through. He explained that his daughter was on her honeymoon and that she and her husband, Dr. Kenneth Taylor, had, according to the hotel, checked out well ahead of schedule. That's all he knew, Al said. It didn't add up.

Urbanek, it then turned out, was quite aware of what had happened. Teresa was in a hospital, recovering from a "terrible beating." The Mexican police had charged her husband with the beating.

Al's knees sagged. He gripped the door frame by the wall phone in the kitchen.

Hospital, what hospital? he said.

The Centro Medico in Acapulco, Urbanek said.

Had Urbanek seen Teresa?

No, he had not.

Had he seen her husband?

Yes, Urbanek said. In jail, where he was being held.

What was the number of the hospital?

After Urbanek gave it to him, he said that if he could be of any more service to please call. Al could tell from his distant, bureaucratic tone that he was hoping that it would be the last conversation they'd have.

He turned to Louise and related what he'd just heard. Tears sprang to her eyes. There was something else in them, too. Hate. "He did it to her?" she said.

"That's what they say."

Al dialed the hospital. A Spanish voice answered. He didn't speak Spanish, Al said. Was there somebody who spoke English? *"Espera un momento,"* the voice said. After what seemed an eternity, another voice said, "Yes?" Al said he wanted to speak to his daughter, Teresa Taylor, who was a patient. It was urgent. There was a second long hiatus before the same person said that Señora Taylor was being wheeled out to a phone.

Al closed his eyes. *Wheeled out!*

Then a voice so pathetically weak and slurred that he could barely hear it said, "Hello."

Al struggled to keep his own voice calm. "Teresa, it's Daddy. Teresa, what happened?"

"I don't know."

"How are you?"

"I don't know."

"Well, what's wrong with you?"

"I don't know."

"Where's Ken?"

"I don't know."

Al couldn't restrain himself. "Teresa, how can you be in a hospital and not know why?"

"Daddy," she whispered, "all I know is that I went to sleep in my hotel room and I woke up in the hospital. Daddy, I have to go back to my bed now."

"Teresa, I'll get down there as soon as I possibly can."

He didn't know if she had heard him. There was no answer, and then the connection was lost.

Al called Celeste and Jeff. They said they'd be right over. Just before they arrived, the phone rang. To Al's amazement, it was Ken.

"Ken, where are you?" Al said.

"In the hospital with Teresa."

"But they said you were in jail."

"I was. I had to pay my way out. Five hundred bucks. I got here just after you called Teresa."

"Ken, what's going on?"

He and Teresa, he said, had been in their casita, their villa, asleep. Sometime in the middle of Thursday night burglars had broken in and stolen jewelry and cash. He had been hit on the head and knocked unconscious, and Teresa had been brutally beaten. When he came to, he saw her lying in a pool of blood. He called for help. Then he passed out again. The next thing he knew, the hotel doctor and the police were standing over him. Teresa was taken to the hospital. He was carted off to jail. He'd been held there in horrible conditions ever since, except when the police had escorted him back to the hotel to retrieve five hundred dollars he had hidden in a suitcase. It was only after he had given them the cash that he was finally released. He had been the victim of a sadistic shakedown. "Al," he said, "get down here as soon as you can. And bring plenty of money."

Al looked at Louise, Celeste and Jeff. "He says that he didn't do it. He said burglars broke in and robbed and attacked them."

"What else would he say?" Celeste snapped. There was no way, she said, that her father would leave for Acapulco without her. Al thought that was a good idea. If Teresa was as badly hurt as it seemed, having her sister on hand might reassure her. Besides, he dreaded going alone.

He called a friend, a travel agent who had booked the honeymoon trip for Ken and Teresa. The agent said he'd get them priority ticket status and reminded Al to bring birth certificates as proof of U.S. citizenship. Celeste suddenly let out a wail. When she had been abducted briefly in Brooklyn, the gunman had filched the wallet with her birth certificate. She had never replaced it. Then she remembered that Teresa had an extra one. She'd use it. Who would know the difference?

They landed in Acapulco on Tuesday afternoon, July 19, just nine days after Teresa and Ken were married. On the flight down, Celeste remembered how, like everyone else, she hadn't taken Ken seriously at first. Teresa loved all her boyfriends and planned to marry them all. When it seemed that this time it was going to be different, she took another look at Ken. She personally didn't think he was all that great. She didn't like the way he always put down New York, his talk of nigger this and spic that, and how everything was so filthy and the schools so lousy, and so forth. Of all the guys Teresa had gone out with, the one Celeste liked the best ended up being a plumber, but Teresa, of course, wasn't going to settle for that. Before Ken, none of Teresa's boyfriends had been college graduates. That was his big attraction, Celeste decided. Intellectually, he was on her level, and he was a doctor. And even if Celeste found him uncomfortably "different," she chalked it up to his being from Indiana. He wasn't a New Yorker. He wasn't like "us."

"If that son of a bitch touched her, I'll kill him myself," she said.

"Celeste, please," Al Benigno said.

They took a cab to the hospital and were directed to Teresa's room.

Nothing they had imagined prepared them for the sickening sight. Celeste struggled to suppress the scream rising inside her. She recognized her sister only by her hair. The entire right side of her face was swathed in bandages covering multiple wounds from broken glass. The other side was a grotesquely swollen, purplish mass. Her one exposed eye was no more than a slit. Her puffy lips were black and cracked. Her mouth was slightly open so that they could see the broken, jagged fragments of her front teeth. There was a big bandage on her neck, by her jugular, where her throat had been deeply slashed.

Ken was seated next to her on the bed. He started to get up when they entered. They ignored him.

Celeste rushed to Teresa's side, took her hand and squeezed it gently. "I'm here," she said.

The slit that was Teresa's one good eye widened a little. She tried to smile. "Hi, sister," she mumbled.

Aghast, Al stared at her. Ken stood there, but it was as though he weren't present.

"Teresa, how do you feel?" Al said.

"I don't know."

"Who did this to you?"

"I don't know."

"The police say that Ken did this to you. Did Ken do it?"

"No."

"How do you know he didn't do it?"

"Because Ken loves me."

"See," Ken said, speaking for the first time. "I told you."

Al took him into the hall. Ken repeated the same story he had told on the phone. Al believed him. How could he not believe his own daughter?

• • •

The physician attending Teresa arrived. He told Al that the lid of her bandaged right eye had a deep cut which had been stitched. Bits of glass had been removed from the eye itself. The surgery had gone well, and he was confident the eye would not suffer permanent impairment. At the worst, she would have blurred vision for a while. There were stitches on her face and neck. There'd be scars, he said, but nothing disfiguring. Best of all, there was no evidence of neurological damage. Meanwhile, she was on antibiotics to guard against infection.

When would she be able to travel? Al asked. The doctor said he'd have to see.

Ken said he was hungry. He hadn't eaten during his four days of incarceration. Celeste went with him to find a restaurant.

As they walked down a dark street, she suddenly felt waves of panic. If he and Teresa had been attacked as he had described, why was this big, strong guy able to stride alongside her while her sister lay immobile in a hospital bed? It didn't make sense. He could kill her on the spot, and who would know?

While they were gone, four men appeared at the door of Teresa's room and motioned to Al. After Al explained to them who he was, they said they were police. They asked where Ken was, and after Al said that he was out for some supper, they said they would return in the morning. Al started to get uneasy.

Right after that, a second physician appeared, Dr. Esteban Ortiz Pavon, who handled medical problems at Las Brisas and who had first treated Teresa. It was a miracle she had lived, he said. Lying as she was in a pool of blood, he initially believed that she was dead until he discovered a faint pulse.

Al had not noticed any visible injuries to Ken, and it bothered him. He asked Dr. Ortiz what Ken's condition was at the time. Other than some scratches on his hand and knees, undoubtedly from the broken glass that littered the room, Ortiz said that he only had a small lump on his head, certainly nothing that might require attention before he was led away by the police.

Then Dr. Ortiz dropped a bombshell. On his way to Teresa's room, a nurse said to him that she had overheard police talking about getting some more money from the Americans. He advised Al to speed Teresa out of the country as soon as possible.

After Al relayed this to Ken and Celeste, Ken said that it simply confirmed everything he'd been saying. It was all an outrageous shakedown.

Al tracked down Urbanek, the U.S. consular agent, who said that since it was a criminal affair, it was out of his hands. He advised Al to retain a lawyer.

Before Al had left for Acapulco, a neighbor of his in New Dorp had provided him with the name and number of a lawyer in Mexico City in case he needed any legal help.

In the morning, Al went to the central telephone office in Acapulco to make the call. To his relief, his neighbor had already alerted the lawyer. After listening to Al, the lawyer said he would get right on it and told Al to return to the hospital.

A man and a woman came to the room. The woman was a very attractive redhead; the man with her, well-dressed, was obviously Mexican. The woman did all the talking. Whatever her citizenship, she sounded very American to Al. She questioned Ken about the supposed break-in at Las Brisas. Ken gave his version again. When he had finished, the woman said, "Okay, I guess that's it." Then the man handed Ken a release absolving the hotel of any responsibility for the assault. Ken and Teresa signed it.

A few minutes later Teresa's physician reappeared. Now he said that he was very pleased with her progress and that she was able to leave the hospital.

Bewildered by these curious and contradictory events, consumed with getting Teresa safely home, Al booked seats on an afternoon flight out. He advised the airline that his daughter had been severely injured and would be traveling as an invalid.

Then Dr. Ortiz reappeared. He offered to drive them to the airport. On the way, Al and Celeste were on edge worrying that she did not have her own birth certificate. If the cops wanted to stop them—to shake them down for more money, as Ken kept insisting—all they'd need was the excuse that Celeste had entered Mexico under an assumed name.

But at the airport they were whisked through, bypassing the normal formalities. Teresa was wheeled to the plane and carried on board. She and Ken were put in first class. Al and Celeste would be in coach. Nothing doing, Celeste said. She was staying with her sister. The crew was the same one as on the flight down, and finally she was allowed to crouch by Teresa's feet.

Once seated, with a chance to reflect, it occurred to Al that whatever else had been going on, everyone in Mexico wanted to wash their hands of the whole business.

Throughout the flight to New York, Celeste remained close to Teresa, reaching up continually to wipe the drool from her mouth. Ken kept giving Teresa pills and taking some himself. Celeste demanded to know what they were. He said Valium. It had been prescribed by the hospital, and she should take a couple herself. They all needed to relax, he said. Celeste said to him, "You did it to her, didn't you?" and he said, "No, I didn't," and she remembered how Teresa pushed angrily at her.

They landed around midnight. Louise broke down when she saw her daughter and had to be supported by Teresa's brother Phil. Teresa whispered, "Hi, Ma," which produced more tears, but this time in relief. At least Teresa knew who Louise was.

Teresa was taken directly to Staten Island Hospital. Louise and Phil stayed by her bedside through the night. Exhausted, Al went home to sleep, as did Celeste. Ken, after being examined in the emergency room, returned to his own apartment.

Hospital records show that Ken was admitted at 12:40 A.M., July 21: "Pt. states he was hit in head and passed out. Was in Mexico when assaulted. No bumps on his head noted." They also recorded that while at first Ken appeared to be "in a dazed state," he was "alert and orientated" when he left.

Teresa remained in the hospital for a week. The records note that along with everything else she was suffering from "retrograde amnesia," that she was "very frightened and needed much assurance," and that she "states her husband told her a group of people entered the room and beat them up."

• • •

After Ken's efforts to persuade Marilyn Hope to drop the divorce, after all the hints of his getting back together with her, she was livid when a friend phoned to say that there was a notice in the paper that he had gotten married.

He had told Marilyn that he wouldn't be around to see Astrid for a week or so because he was going on a short vacation, possibly to see his parents in Indiana, and he set the date for his next visit for Monday, July 19. When he didn't show up, she called the dental center in Brooklyn. At first, she was simply told that he wasn't in. Then she was told that he might not ever be in, that Ken wasn't working there anymore.

Alarms went off in her head. She wouldn't put anything past him. Maybe he had sneaked off with Teresa to avoid alimony and child support payments. Maybe she should start planning to sell the house.

She felt funny calling the Benignos, so her sister-in-law spoke to Louise and reported that Ken and Teresa apparently had been attacked on their honeymoon in Acapulco, that she was in the hospital, and that he was being detained.

Marilyn decided she better get this firsthand and finally telephoned Louise herself. Louise was crying so hard that it was difficult to get a coherent story. One thing was clear, however. The police suspected Ken. Then Louise blurted out, "Is Ken a wife-beater?"

Marilyn hesitated. It was all so confusing. She didn't know what really had taken place in Acapulco. She remembered the psychiatrist advising that what had happened in Connecticut was an "isolated incident." How could she say, Well, he did this, this, and this, and wind up wrecking his life? What did she owe these people, anyway?

"You're not answering me," Louise said.

And Marilyn Hope said, "Ken never beat me."

Then, perhaps three days after that, Ken was at her front

door, smiling and saying the lawn needed mowing. He would get right to it. She really needed a man around the house.

He said that they had been "mugged" and robbed in Acapulco. He had been knocked out, he said, and Teresa was beaten. He said that he had been told by various people down there, among them even a lawyer, that the muggers often acted in cahoots with the cops so that it would look as though the husband were the assailant, thus absolving Acapulco itself of any blame, not hurting, you know, the tourist trade.

He said it was Marilyn's fault that he'd gotten married. If she had only agreed to postpone the divorce. But she had rejected him, and Teresa had been so relentless in her pursuit. It was important for him to believe that someone cared for him, loved and respected him. He saw, though, that it wasn't going to last with Teresa, and he would soon be in the throes of another divorce. Yeah, well, she said acidly, in that case he had better get to it before he knocked up Teresa and discovered what it was like to contend with two weekly alimony and support checks.

Ken visited Teresa at the hospital everyday. Louise had warned the floor nurses never to leave him alone with her daughter. Of course, as a practical matter, this was not possible. One nurse recalled that she heard a cry from the room, and when she went in, she observed Teresa stumbling backward against a wall. Ken was standing nearby. He said that she had tried to get up and lost her balance. While the nurse thought it strange, there was no evidence of an assault, certainly Teresa did not say anything, and she reported nothing about it at the time.

Ken told the Benignos that because he wanted to be with Teresa throughout her recovery, he was quitting his position at the Fulton Family Dental Center. He would launch his own practice on Staten Island. He was even thinking of hiring young Phil as a sort of office manager.

Celeste remembered being present when Ken was on the phone—presumably to the center—explaining to someone that he would not be returning because he had to stay with his wife, she needed his support. His voice choked as he described Teresa's condition.

In fact, although none of the Benignos was aware of it, he had no choice. During his absence, the two dentists who owned the center, Irwin Azar and his partner Edward Sutton, discovered that Ken had stolen at least five thousand dollars—actually, closer to ten thousand—in cash and checks. They elected not to press charges; they just wanted him out of their hair. To hide this, Ken subsequently submitted a letter of resignation which he showed to Al and Louise. He did not mention that the Internal Revenue Service had also begun an action to garnishee his wages.

At dinner at the Benignos, Ken went into more details about what had occurred that Thursday in Acapulco. They both had awakened a little hung over. The night before they'd been in town to pick up a dress Teresa had wanted. They'd bought the dress two days before, but a substitute had been boxed. According to Ken, the girl wrapping the dress had accidentally spilled Coke on it. Teresa spotted this and there'd been a dispute, but the guy who owned the store had been very accommodating and said he would have another dress, in the style Teresa wanted, ready on Wednesday. Teresa tried it on and looked gorgeous. Afterward, they found a pleasant open-air restaurant and had a "real nice time," except that they drank too much.

On Thursday, they lounged around the small private pool that went with their casita, clearing their heads. In the evening they drove into Acapulco to a restaurant that a couple of Teresa's girlfriends had told her about. When they finally located it, it was closed, and they wound up in another restaurant. They had drinks and ordered dinner, but were never served, even though other customers, who had come in after them, were already eating. Teresa got angry, he said, and cussed out the maitre d'. After they left, he calmed her and they decided to go to a restaurant at Las Brisas called El Arsenal. Teresa had just taken a bite into a mango in her salad when she spied a worm. Now, according to Ken, she was really in a state, thinking that she had swallowed part of the worm. She ran to the rest room, sure that she was going to throw up, but didn't.

As soon as they returned to the casita, though, she headed straight to the bathroom and this time she vomited. After taking off her rings and a bracelet and putting them on a night table, she washed and went to bed. He was starving by now, he said, and ordered room service for himself. Around ten o'clock that evening he thought he might either have a swim or go to bed himself. He opted for bed. He still wasn't feeling all that well from the previous night.

He got into bed next to the sleeping Teresa. He was dozing off, he said, when he thought he heard a noise by the glass door leading to the balcony. He got up and flipped the switch that illuminated the balcony and the pool below. He didn't see anything, so he turned off the lights and returned to bed.

He was asleep—it couldn't have been more than a few minutes—when he received a terrific blow to his head. He felt hands grabbing his feet and pulling him off the bed. His forehead hit the stone floor. Ken said that he staggered up, only to receive a karate-like kick in the back of his neck. After that everything went black.

When he recovered consciousness, he was lying on the floor. He saw Teresa nearby, also on the floor. She was splattered with blood. There was blood on the wall. Shards of broken glass were everywhere on the floor between the bed and wall. He saw the telephone on the floor. He crawled over the glass to it. His first call reached the kitchen. He tried again and this time, the front desk answered. He couldn't recall what he said exactly, but he had cried out for help. He went to Teresa and checked her pulse. She was unconscious and bleeding profusely, but she was alive. He was afraid to move her. He didn't know what might have happened to her neck. He said that there were pieces of glass in his cheek and in his hands and knees. He made it into the bathroom to cleanse himself. He tottered to the balcony to see if anybody was in sight, stumbled on a step, and fainted. The next thing he knew, he was surrounded by hotel personnel and then cops.

He wouldn't wish the jail he was taken to on his worst enemy. He was confined in a compound where the sun beat down mercilessly. Flies and roaches were everywhere. There was no place to bathe. The only toilet was an open hole in the ground. The stench was unbelievable. The food was revolting just to look at. He had managed to bring a few dollars with him and on his second day purchased some doughnuts and coffee. They wouldn't let him write to Teresa nor would they tell him how she was. By Sunday night, he realized that he would have to buy his way out. He told them that he had money at the hotel, and on Monday morning he was brought to Las Brisas to get it. He was sure they'd want more, which was why he had asked Al to bring as much as he could.

Listening to this, eyes boring into Ken, her normally soft voice up a notch, Louise Benigno said, "Ken, what I don't understand is how nothing happened to you, and my daughter is lying in a hospital."

At that, Ken bent his head, hunched his shoulder, and slowly swiveled his neck, his hand reaching to the back of his neck, rubbing it lightly, as if in mute testament to the marvel of his survival from the karate kick. He acted as if they were incapable of understanding the implications of the miracle that he was not permanently paralyzed instead of sitting there at the table dining with them. "I was lucky," he said.

The real marvel, Celeste remembered, was how bland and cool he was about it. Never being at all defensive, not once raising his voice, never showing the slightest irritation or temper, as though he understood completely their misgivings, doubts and suspicions.

"The psychiatrist at the hospital thinks you did it," Louise said.

"What does the psychiatrist know?" he said, waving his hand derisively. "I know. He's like everybody else. You want to believe I did it, then believe it. Why doesn't anybody believe Teresa?"

That was the failure of the psychiatrist at Staten Island Hospital, Karen Oliveira always believed. After talking to Ken, he had concluded that Ken was guilty of the assault. However, he was incapable of drawing Teresa out, and became, in her eyes, simply another one of Ken's silent accusers. Teresa managed to recall seeing "bare feet" during the attack, but that was before she retreated into a shell. "Ken would never do that to me," she insisted, and abruptly halted her sessions with the psychiatrist.

Like almost everyone else, Karen was convinced that Ken had done it. "What happened?" she asked her dearest friend, and got the same story from Teresa. But it wasn't what Teresa said, it was how she said it that so disturbed Karen. Usually Teresa was so animated, so full of life. Now, though, when the subject of Acapulco came up, she got a faraway look in her eyes, as if her mind were a blank, and then she'd begin in this monotone to speak of people breaking into the room. It was not genuine but something rehearsed, something she was parroting. Finally Karen gave up. Teresa wouldn't—or couldn't—recall the events of that night.

It was the same thing for Celeste. She kept hammering at the theme of Ken's guilt until Teresa turned on her and said, "Stop it! How would you like it if you were me and I told you that it was Jeff who beat you up?"

Celeste told Louise, "Ma, you better cool it, because Teresa is getting mad and she'll want to take off and that'll be that. He's her husband and you just have to let it go."

That was the overriding fear of the Benignos when they discussed the situation privately. "We have to consider Teresa's attitude," Al said. "He's a dentist. If we treat him badly, he could just pick up and go anywhere, and we'll never see her again. The best thing is to try to keep them as close to us as possible."

And for Al, as he hashed Acapulco over and over again in his mind, nothing made sense. It'd been their honeymoon! He could imagine they'd had a fight. Even that a husband might slap his wife around. But it was too much for him to accept that Ken could have committed this terrible crime.

After she was released from the hospital, Teresa and Ken stayed with Al and Louise for nearly a month in the room that she and Celeste used to share. The slightest sound in the night would bring Louise upright in bed, straining her ears for anything untoward. She secretly wrote a letter to Las Brisas asking for information about what had occurred. The executive administrative assistant replied that in his opinion, as well as that of his security director, Ken was the culprit. Louise did not confront Teresa with this. She could hear Ken telling her, What do you expect them to say? Ken even talked to Al about suing the hotel for its lax security, but since this would require his returning to Mexico, it was a rather empty gesture.

• • •

For Karen Oliveira, there would be another jarring note. To launch his new practice, Ken had entered into an arrangement with two Staten Island dentists to lease two of their offices and equipment. The two dentists would also share in the profits. The advantage for him was that the offices were already functioning. But he needed some seed capital.

Karen's father was a bank officer, who coincidentally had been instrumental in providing financing for the Fulton Family Dental Center. Teresa asked her to speak to him about helping Ken get started.

Karen's father was not sympathetic. He'd heard from Karen, of course, about her views on Acapulco, but besides that, he had met Ken two or three times and didn't trust him. "It wasn't anything in particular," he later said. "This fellow just didn't come across clear." But because of Teresa, he told Karen, he wouldn't do anything to prevent a loan; he'd stay out of it and let the application go through the normal process.

The result was startling. Ken was about as bad a risk as you could find. He had no credit at all. In a time when every credit card company in the country was beginning a massive, competitive campaign to enroll new customers, every card Ken possessed had been canceled. Sears was after him for arrears of nearly $6,000. Ken had to use Teresa's American Express card to pay her hospital bill.

Once again Ken escaped a confrontation. Karen decided simply to tell Teresa, after the bank had turned down Ken's application, that her father's hands were tied, that there wasn't anything more he could do. Finally, Ken got $7,500 from a bank in Marion after Zach Taylor co-signed the loan.

Neither Jean nor Zach rushed east to see their new daughter-in-law in the hospital; in fact, they never came at all. "Well, there was the cost, the expense, taking off from work, that kind of thing," Zach said, and Jean said, "I felt that the Benignos and Teresa had a lot of friends and relatives, and we'd be too much. And the way Ken talked, *he* was all right."

Gradually Teresa recovered, the scars on her face and neck fading. Ken did root-canal work and the crowns for her fractured teeth. He wanted to remove one root entirely. It was sure to abscess eventually, he told her. But she was adamantly against that. She didn't want another hole in her head, she said. She was, though, in constant pain. Ken prescribed extraordinarily large amounts of codeine.

She returned to her job as a hygienist in the office of Dr. Roland Avis on Staten Island. He was delighted to have her back.

And like her scars, the trepidation everyone felt also began to fade. "It just faded in time," Celeste remembered. "We talked about it still, but as she healed, you know, life just went on and it just kind of got pushed aside. She'd get so mad if you said anything about it."

One of the few people who accepted Acapulco according to Teresa was Angela Arone, a cousin on Al's side. Angela admired Teresa intensely, had always looked up to her, and she'd said from the beginning, "Look, Teresa wouldn't lie. If she says that's what happened, that's the way it did." Inevitably, except for Louise, who had dark forebodings that she kept to herself, friends began to adopt this attitude.

And then even Louise came to have a new focus. That autumn, Teresa announced that she was pregnant. It was the catharsis everybody desperately needed. Acapulco, for any practical purpose, was forgotten.

•  •  •

Ken appeared to be a new man, exultant and proud, hovering protectively over his wife. To the annoyance of Dr. Avis, he would often visit Teresa at work, using office forms there to write out prescriptions in her name for Tylenol 3, which contained codeine.

Ken's three-room apartment would be too cramped with a baby. Teresa wanted a house. She had always been jealous of the house Marilyn had on Staten Island. Ken said that he wanted to be in the country. They began looking in New Jersey. She found her dream house in rural Manalapan Township in Monmouth County. A two-story wood shingle structure on a corner lot in a relatively new development, it had a backyard swimming pool and was less than an hour's drive to work for them both.

Although the township was on the verge of a population explosion, real estate values had temporarily flattened out and they were able to negotiate an $89,000 purchase price. On December 3, 1983, Teresa provided the down payment from her savings.

That December, during one of his visits with his daughter, Astrid, Ken first told Marilyn that he was going to be a father again. She remained his true love, he said, and he yearned with all his heart to be back with her, but now that Teresa was pregnant, what could he do? He had to stay with her, for a while anyway.

At the end of the year, Teresa resigned from her job with Dr. Avis. She said that her husband needed her to help him in his own practice. Before departing, she confided her worry about finances to Ann Toppino, another hygienist in the office with whom she had become quite friendly.

Teresa also said that Ken had tried to get her to terminate her pregnancy.

# Chapter

# FOUR

In March, in her sixth month, right after her twenty-fifth birthday, Teresa went into premature labor. She was rushed to St. Peter's Medical Center in New Brunswick, New Jersey.

She remained hospitalized for four days. Tests showed that the fetus was unharmed and that she was carrying a boy. No physical reasons were found for her early contractions. After talking to her, her gynecologist concluded that her concern over her husband's practice had been a contributing factor.

Further work in Ken's office was out of the question. Teresa was to have absolute bed rest for three weeks. After that, she was restricted to minimal activity around the house. Louise and Celeste were constantly in attendance.

It was a particularly bittersweet time for Teresa. Her sister had just discovered that she also was pregnant. Soon after the move to Manalapan, the house next door to the one she and Ken had bought came on the market, and Teresa—thrilled with the thought of having Celeste and Jeff as neighbors—did everything she could to get them to buy it, even calling Karen Oliveira to ask her father if he would be able to help on the mortgage. But Jeff, who worked as an oiler on the Staten Island ferry service, decided that they simply couldn't swing it on his salary, and he and Celeste settled for a condominium apartment in New Dorp not far from Louise and Al.

The one echo that reverberated from Acapulco was Teresa's paranoia about being left alone. Once, while confined to bed, she asked Al to please install a lock on the door between the house and the attached garage. She'd been after Ken to do it, but he never seemed to have time. He was so preoccupied with building his practice, she said.

When Louise or Celeste weren't available, especially after she could get out of bed for brief periods, Teresa's cousin Angela filled in. Geography especially had drawn them close together. Angela, who now had a baby girl of her own, was married to Peter Rozek, a husky Polish steelworker, and lived in East Brunswick, about twenty minutes away by car.

Angela had been one of Teresa's bridesmaids, and of all those around Teresa, she was the least critical of Ken. He appeared to her to be a "nice enough guy, quiet, reserved and smart." She noticed that Teresa was the one who displayed all the external signs of affection, hugging and kissing Ken and holding his hand. Clearly, Teresa was the "lover." But wasn't that what love did to some people? she thought. She herself had been a lot like that with Peter.

And of all the people who knew Teresa and Ken, the Rozeks, after the move to Manalapan, socialized the most with them. Both women had bubbly, outgoing personalities, and their husbands, athletic and reserved, shared a common interest in golf and tennis.

Every so often, though, the specter of Acapulco would return. Once, in February, the Taylors, the Rozeks, and Peter's brother and his wife went to a "couples only" weekend at a resort in the Pennsylvania Poconos. They had adjoining rooms. But suddenly, as they were checking in,

Teresa insisted on the middle room. "If something happens," she said, "I want everyone to hear it."

Then two incidents occurred which, except for their curious nature, didn't mean that much to Angela at the time. She was the least judgmental of people; everyone, she believed, had his or her hangups, and whatever went on behind closed doors really was nobody's business. But in late March, she and her mother—Teresa's aunt—and her nine-month-old daughter met Teresa for lunch at a shopping mall. Midway through lunch, Angela's mother took the child off for a diaper change, and out of the blue, Teresa said, "Tell me something. Does Peter ever like to eat you right at your period?"

Angela stared at her and said, "Ugh, no."

"Well, Ken does."

"God, that's gross."

Angela remembered thinking that with Teresa pregnant this couldn't be a major issue right now. Before anything more was said, Angela's mother and daughter returned to the table. Then, three days later, Teresa went into premature labor and Angela forgot all about it.

In the weeks afterward, whenever Angela couldn't get over to visit Teresa, who was still fearful of being alone, the two of them would talk on the phone for hours at a clip, "just girl talk," Angela would recall, "you know, junk stuff, what was going on in the soap operas, stuff going on with movie stars, what the current stories were, that kind of thing."

Around the beginning of May, a major drug bust was in the news and during one of their conversations, Teresa said, "Ken smokes pot to relax. And he does coke. He does it to get through the day."

"He treats people stoned?"

"Yes."

A majority of his patients, Teresa said, were on Medicaid. It was dreary, tedious work, and he'd go into his office and do a couple of lines. And besides, Ken was killing himself trying to keep his practice afloat. What with the overhead, the phone bills, and the payroll, and her not able to be there, the business was losing money. The pressure on him was endless.

At home occasionally, she said, she did coke with him. He had told her how it enhanced sex, and she had to admit that he was right. But she had stopped when she became pregnant.

So Ken was doing coke, Angela thought. So stop the presses! She and Peter didn't do it, but she knew plenty of others who did.

Angela was deeply touched when Teresa, in spite of instructions to remain home, came to her daughter's first birthday party on May 20. And she noticed how Ken helped Teresa to a chaise lounge and made sure she was comfortable, getting her food and pampering her. Angela observed, too, that at the Manalapan house he had thrown himself into a frenzy of activity, planting rose bushes, petunias, azaleas, putting in a stand of pine trees in the backyard, and turning over and fertilizing a large vegetable garden. As a matter of fact, she used Ken as an example to her husband.

On June 3, there was a surprise baby shower for Teresa at her house. Angela remembered how impressed she was with all the cute little outfits decorated with rocking horse buttons that Teresa had fashioned for her son. That day Peter and Ken had arranged to play golf and later, while the shower was still going on, Angela glanced out of a window and saw the two of them drinking beer in the backyard.

Afterward, while driving Angela home, Peter Rozek revealed that it had been quite a day for him. On the course, Ken had hooked a shot. Peter had never seen a temper tantrum like it. You hooked shots all the time, that was part of the game, but this time Ken had flown into an unbelievable, uncontrollable rage, flinging his iron maybe thirty or forty yards, stomping around kicking and screaming and cursing.

And then, when they returned and were in the backyard, Ken picked up Teresa's calico cat—what was her name, Cleo? Cleo apparently had bitten him, at least that was what he said. Anyway, Ken had taken the cat and slammed it twice against the garage wall. Peter was sure that was it for Cleo, but to his relief she'd raced off with eight lives to go. "Goddamn fucking cat," Ken had said.

A week later, on the night of Sunday, June 10, Teresa was on the phone with Angela when she suddenly exclaimed, "I'm getting wet. Oh, I think I broke my water!"

Teresa was admitted to Middlesex General–University Hospital in New Brunswick just after midnight. With stomach muscles weakened by so much time in bed, her labor was painful and exhausting, lasting more than fifteen hours. At one point, it appeared that a cesarean section would have to be performed. But then Philip—named after her brother and grandfather—was born.

That day Ken wrote a note to Teresa that said, *Today you shared with me the greatest gift of all—the gift of life. Your pain, your hurt, your joy and exaltation have motivated me and inspired me more than you can ever realize. I would rather die than see you hurt, ever at any time. Your love for me is endless and totally giving. My feelings for you run so deep inside me they will forever be a part of me. I must do my best for you and I always will. I love you so much, Thank you for allowing this miracle to transpire. Your husband, with love as always, Ken.*

• • •

Angela Rozek remembered Ken as a "proud father," who decorated the front of the Manalapan house with streamers of blue crepe paper and strung three dozen blue balloons from the trees and shrubbery to greet the return of Teresa and baby Philip the following Thursday.

The next day Jean and Zach Taylor flew in from Marion. According to Ken, Teresa could not abide the thought of having her "haranguing, cantankerous mother" underfoot and her "dingbat sister" making a nuisance of herself. So Jean and Zach were "pleased to accept Teresa's humble plea for their guidance with her newborn baby."

Jean was working as a hostess at a Marion restaurant to supplement Zach's income, but she was, she said, happy to step into the breach. She recalled asking Teresa about Louise and Celeste and quoted Teresa as saying, "My mom bosses me around all the time," and as far as Celeste was concerned, she wouldn't let her sister look after her cats, much less a baby. In his recollection of that time, Zach said, "Teresa and Celeste definitely did not get along. As soon as Teresa was eighteen, she left home and the room she shared with Celeste and got her own apartment." When it was pointed out to him that this was not at all the case, his face reddened, and he said, "Well, that's what Ken told me."

For Jean, Teresa was then a "nice, sweet girl." Jean was particularly gratified when she raised the question of Teresa's religious intentions regarding the baby. Teresa, still angry over her parish priest's refusal to marry them and acutely aware of Ken's feelings, told Jean that she was more than open to suggestions. It didn't necessarily have to be the Baptist church, Jean said. She would make sure to send Teresa literature on various options. There were many fine Protestant denominations. Just so long as he wasn't baptized Catholic.

Those attending the surprise baby shower for Teresa had a different memory of Jean and Zach's imminent arrival. Teresa said that Ken was insistent that his mother be on hand, and she, of course, acceded. But it was no big deal. In-laws were part of married life. Both Angela Rozek and Karen Oliveira remembered how Teresa laughed, a little ruefully, about it. Skip all the mother-in-law jokes was all she asked.

Suddenly, though, it wasn't so funny. Jean Taylor was a strict vegetarian, and although she did not force her strictures on the men in her family, she did with Teresa. Meanwhile, Teresa was breast-feeding the baby, and the baby wasn't gaining any weight. "I'm starving. What I need is some beer and red meat," Teresa complained to Angela, "and all I'm getting is raw carrots and grapes. I can't wait for them to leave."

Teresa and the baby underwent extensive testing but there were no specific findings. Finally the infant was put on formula feeding and the weight problem vanished.

On July 6, Ken took out a $100,000 Equitable Life Insurance policy on Teresa, paying the first premium of $247 in cash. Teresa knew about it. She'd had a rough time giving birth, and if something happened to her, the insurance would cover nursing and housekeeping expenses for the baby.

Then Ken got stunning news. Marilyn told him that she was selling the Staten Island house and moving with their daughter to Pittsburgh, her flight base.

Ken tried to convince her to reconsider. He had even more stunning news for her. Teresa, he said, was freaking out on cocaine. Ever since Acapulco, after he prescribed codeine for the pain she was suffering, she had begun forging his name on prescriptions and also signing his name to checks to support her habit. In case Marilyn wasn't aware of it, codeine was more than a pain killer; codeine kept you flying longer after doing coke and it gave you a soft landing.

Although there was no history of Ken ever previously mentioning anything about Teresa's plight to anyone else—not even to her gynecologist—he said now that this was the real reason for Teresa's premature labor as well as her inability to breast-feed the baby.

He was at a crossroads. He wanted to leave Teresa, get custody of the baby, and rejoin his "family," namely Marilyn and Astrid. He feared for the baby's safety, he said.

He was crazy to think a mother was going to give up custody of her child, Marilyn said.

No, Ken said, the way things were, he didn't think that Teresa would want custody. Besides, to ensure that he would win if it came down to it, he was keeping precise records to prove her drug abuse and thievery. He was just waiting until his son was "well established." Then he would begin life anew.

He himself had stayed off drugs, he said. He told Marilyn that he had learned his lesson in Connecticut, had learned about "life, responsibility, caring." The tables had been turned. He was now in the same situation that he had put her in.

Later, Ken would embellish this story. Teresa had been

into cocaine well before he had met her. The first night she went to work at the Fulton Family Dental Center in Brooklyn, she offered coke to him. She was wired on coke all the time. It was the reason why she'd been fired from the center. Her supplier was her brother Phil, who had Mafia connections in Manhattan. As promised before his wedding, he had hired Phil to manage his two new offices on Staten Island, to oversee the appointment books, keep the flow of patients going, and handle the billings. He said that he had caught Phil in a small apartment above one of the offices with scales and glassine envelopes, the whole bit, measuring out cocaine for distribution.

He had pleaded with Teresa, cajoled her, threatened her, but it was futile. Nothing worked. She wouldn't stop.

When Karen Oliveira eventually heard about this, she said, "I've known Teresa all my life. We exchanged secrets nobody else ever heard. If Teresa was doing cocaine at all, it was because of Ken. She'd do anything for him."

Other than Marilyn, no one was cognizant of Ken's claims. On weekends, Louise and Al and Jeff and Celeste would drop by to see the baby and lounge around the pool. Teresa often wore a halter and shorts. Al, mindful of Acapulco, would furtively observe her body for any telltale marks or bruises. He never saw any.

Once in late August, Celeste, by now more than five months pregnant, went shopping with Teresa in Staten Island. They were selecting material for maternity dresses for Celeste that Teresa wanted to make. Afterward, driving away, with baby Philip in his chair in the back seat of her Cutlass Supreme, Teresa glanced at her watch and said, "My God, it's late. I've got to get home."

"Oh, we're having such fun. Let's go somewhere for coffee. Call Ken and tell him you'll be late."

No, Teresa said, white-faced. She had to go. Celeste thought her reaction was a little extreme, but mostly, right then, she felt guilty about being so cavalier about Jeff, and she vowed to be a better wife, like her sister.

Over Labor Day weekend, Ken and Teresa drove with the baby to Marion. Jean was to undergo colon surgery, and Ken wanted to be with his mother.

Both Jean and Zach remembered that Teresa fell in love with Marion. If anything ever happened to her, they said she said, she wanted her son to be raised there.

She attended Sunday service with Ken and his parents at the First Baptist Church where Philip was "dedicated."

The pastor, Darrel Parris, would recall that Teresa told him how wonderful it was to be in a church filled with people who wanted to be there—unlike her own church where attendance was mandatory.

Back home, when Angela asked what life in Marion was like, Teresa said that it was okay, a little dull, you know, Smalltown, USA. Jean Taylor was a "nut case," so was Ken's brother, Tom. The only normal ones seemed to be Ken and his father. When Teresa told her about the dedication, Angela said, "You mean he was baptized a Baptist?"

No, Teresa said. It had been explained to her by the pastor. It meant that Philip had been introduced to the congregation. It wasn't official. You could not be baptized a Baptist until you reached the age of reason. The dedication was a first step. Teresa said she didn't know what she would do, except that she'd never forgive the Catholic church. Ken's mother was bombarding her with brochures, and Ken's attitude had to be considered. She was thinking maybe Presbyterian; the local minister was very nice.

But that wasn't her principal concern. Uppermost in her mind was Ken's desire for her to return to the office. With her on the job, they could inch past the break-even point. She wasn't too happy about it. She wanted to spend her days with the baby, but she had no choice.

So she went back to being a hygienist for Ken. She would drop Philip off with Louise in the morning and pick him up at day's end.

On September 29 an unsettling incident caused Angela Rozek to wonder again about Acapulco. For the first time, her acceptance of Teresa's story was shaken. The week before had been Angela's birthday, but she told Teresa she was just going to celebrate quietly with Peter and her parents. They arranged for a post-birthday get-together on the twenty-ninth. Angela was pregnant with her second child, and Teresa wanted to measure her for some clothes.

To make the occasion more festive, Teresa invited Al and Louise. She baked a birthday cake and gave Angela a pair of gloves and a silk blouse. During the evening Teresa started looking for something—Angela couldn't remember what—and opened Ken's attaché case.

All at once, Teresa said, "Oh," and lifted a pair of earrings out of the case. "Ken, aren't these my earrings from Acapulco? I thought they got ripped off. How did they get in here?"

Angela recalled the way Ken stared at Teresa. "You're making a mistake," he said. "It was a different pair."

Teresa seemed so bewildered as she looked down at the earrings in her hand. Finally, after a moment, she said, her voice barely audible, "Okay."

What so disturbed Angela was how quickly Teresa had acquiesced to Ken, although clearly there was turmoil inside her. "Wasn't that strange?" she said to her husband as they left. "It's like she knows something, but doesn't know."

Other unexpected tensions surfaced. In mid-October, after dropping the baby off at her mother's, Teresa arrived alone at Ken's main office where she had a full schedule of patients.

"Where's Ken?" her brother asked.

"Right after breakfast," she said, "he said he had to get something at the store. He'd be right back." When he didn't return, Teresa said, she went outside and found a note under her windshield wiper. She showed Phil the note. It said, "I'm leaving for a couple of days to get my head together." It also said, "My business is a failure."

"I think he must have gone to Pittsburgh," Teresa said. "That's where his ex-wife is." He'd been complaining about not being able to see his daughter, she said. Teresa told him to invite her to visit them, she was more than welcome. He'd said that his ex-wife wouldn't agree. Well,

Teresa had said, was there something in the visitation decree that gave her that right? Ken hadn't really answered.

There was more to it than his daughter, Teresa said. It was hard to fathom what was going on inside his head. He'd even talked about suicide. She was at wit's end and she was scared. Despite the humiliation, she was seriously thinking about a divorce. She told this to Celeste and Angela and also to Karen. And she told them something else. She said that she had been having nightmares recently, nightmares in which she heard Mexican voices.

During Ken's disappearance, Karen called Teresa. Her banker father had a number of gift certificates—for stores like Gucci and Tiffany—from some of his clients. She was going to Manhattan with her mother the next day, a Saturday, to use them. Teresa should come along. At first, Teresa said no, she had too much on her mind, and Karen said that was exactly why she should come. It would be like old times.

But it wasn't. When Teresa finally agreed, leaving the baby in Louise's care, she was subdued, as if she were in another world. Gradually, though, as the day wore on, Teresa began to recover some of the spirit Karen always associated with her, giggling over the outrageous prices being charged at the various Fifth Avenue stores they went to. They topped off the day with afternoon tea at the Trump Tower. Karen remembered the startled Yuppies around them, looking at them as if they were counterfeiters, when Teresa exclaimed, "Well, we got rid of the money."

That was when Teresa spoke about the nightmares and the Mexican voices. Karen thought, Good, maybe it's all coming back to her, and she'll get rid of this guy.

* * *

Ken in fact had gone to Pittsburgh. And it had not been that sudden a decision. He called Marilyn the night before he left and told her what flight he'd be on.

She had met him at the airport with their daughter. He had a toilet kit and a camera. He immediately began taking pictures of Astrid. Then they went to a store where he bought her some dresses.

He said he wanted to stay overnight, which became two nights. On the second night, they made love. He could tell how pleased Marilyn was to be elevated over his new, sexy young wife. He made certain to compliment her on her breast implants. It had been really unnecessary, he said. He'd loved them the way they were.

She asked him if Teresa knew where he was.

It didn't matter, he said, she had gone off to her sister's.

She said, "You leave with no clothes, and you're just going to show up three days later, and she isn't going to say anything?"

She realizes the marriage is ending, he said.

Marilyn laughed, and he asked why. She was looking at his camera, she said, remembering how he would tell *her* that he was going out to photograph the fall foliage and show up three days later.

That was different, he said. She'd been a real bitch then.

•  ✓  •

Teresa told both Angela and Celeste that Ken had returned begging forgiveness. He'd been desperate to see Astrid, and Marilyn had made it so difficult. And then he'd gone off by himself, trying to rethink his practice, trying to get his act together. He needed a break, he said, he was trying his best for her and the baby.

She said that it had better be so, she wasn't going to submit to this treatment. Otherwise, although she hated to say it, she wouldn't hesitate to split up.

On November 9, a Friday, Phil and his girlfriend Kathy came by the Manalapan house about ten P.M. Phil brought wine. Ken was very upbeat. He said that the practice had finally turned the corner. He could see nothing but light ahead. Phil wasn't so sure. He had found a pile of follow-ups squirreled away, some weeks old, that he had given Ken for review. These follow-up treatments were vital to any dental practice. What the hell was going on? What was the matter with Ken? But Phil decided that this wasn't the right time to bring it up. He'd wait till Monday.

Phil, his girlfriend and Teresa drank the wine. Ken was drinking Jack Daniel's. Ken lit a joint which Phil shared.

After about an hour, Ken brought out a packet of cocaine and set out lines on the coffee table they were sitting around. Although Phil would deny it for a long time, both he and Teresa joined Ken and did a couple of lines.

At two A.M. or so, Teresa and Ken retired. Ken had to be in the office in the morning, and Teresa was meeting Cindy Diaz, one of the "Glitter Chicks" from her high school days, to look at some fabric at a wholesale house in Brooklyn. Phil and Kathy stayed up till about four o'clock finishing the wine and then went into the guest room to sleep. When they awoke, Ken and Teresa were gone.

Ken's Datsun 200SX was on the fritz, so Teresa had taken him to work and then went to pick up Cindy. Her husband was a commercial photographer. He was testing out a new video camera and shot a tape of Teresa and the baby inside and outside the house. Crossing the bridge into Brooklyn, Cindy remarked that Teresa wasn't her usual ebullient self. Teresa explained that she was a little hung over. Her brother had been over the night before, and she guessed she'd had one glass of wine too many. After lunch on the run, she dropped Cindy off, picked up Ken, and drove back to Manalapan.

Around three-thirty that Saturday afternoon, Angela phoned. Teresa had told her that her maternity dresses were ready, and they'd made a date for Angela to come over at five-thirty. She was calling to confirm. But Teresa said that she was tired. She wanted to take a nap. Could they put it off a couple of hours?

"How about seven-thirty?" Angela said.

"Perfect," Teresa said.

Every minute of that evening would be forever etched in Angela's mind. When she, Peter and their daughter Christie arrived, Angela instantly sensed tension in the air. She really couldn't put her finger on it, though. It was as if Ken and Teresa had just had a fight, although Peter would say that he hadn't noticed this.

Angela had brought two Entenmann's Louisiana Crunch cakes. Great, Teresa said. She was starving. While she was napping, Ken had fixed her some supper, "a piece of pork."

"Come on," Ken said. "I made you a whole dinner."

"Well, I'm still hungry."

Teresa put one of the cakes in the freezer and the other on a plate. Angela noticed a partially smoked joint in an ashtray. It must be Ken's, she thought. She knew Teresa didn't like the effect of pot, even in high school.

Ken appeared very hyper. He was holding a Jack Daniel's—at least Angela assumed that was what it was—and while he knew that Peter hardly ever drank, he kept after him to have a drink. And finally Peter said okay, he'd have a "Seven and Seven"—Seagram's 7 whisky and Seven-Up. Ken, slamming cabinet doors, couldn't find any Seven-Up. Was plain soda all right?

That'd be fine, Peter said. But when Ken made it, it was so strong that Peter grimaced after one sip and set the glass down on a table where it remained untouched for the rest of the evening.

Teresa took Angela into the room across from the kitchen to give her the dresses she had finished. It was where she sewed. The room was a jumble what with the washer and dryer, Ken's golf bag, and the weight stand where he worked out.

As Angela went in, she tripped over a dumbbell with weights on it lying on the floor and nearly fell. Ken and Peter were in the doorway. She said, "Jesus, Ken, I almost killed myself on this stupid thing," and he picked up the dumbbell and placed it near the stand.

The two men went into the living room and watched television. Peter said that the deer hunting season was coming on. Did Ken want to go hunting with him? No, Ken said, that wasn't his bag; he couldn't bear the thought of looking into a deer's eyes after he had shot it.

Except for the room where Teresa sewed and another room next to it that was being converted into a second guest room—there was a big roll of carpet padding in it—the downstairs was essentially open space, the kitchen flowing into the dining and living areas.

In the kitchen Teresa put on the coffee and got out plates for the cake. Angela started talking about what fun it had been going to the Poconos last February and how they really ought to do it again after the new baby was born.

Ken had already put Philip to bed. Christie, by now eighteen months old, was getting rambunctious. Ken asked her if she would like to see her little cousin asleep. He brought her upstairs and on their way back, he set her on a step and told her to stay there. Then he got his camera and snapped some pictures. Ken could really be sweet, Angela thought.

As they had the cake and coffee, the talk turned to sex. Angela said that she supposed it was inevitable, that after a while, sex wasn't the biggest thing, that it was other things which counted in a relationship. Ken suddenly said that after the "whopping" he'd given Teresa the other night, she wouldn't be refusing him. Angela glanced at Teresa, but her face was expressionless, and she imagined Ken was simply making a joke, however lame.

Then Teresa remarked that she was going back on birth control pills, but she'd forgotten last month. She'd been late and she had believed that she was pregnant again, but then she got her period.

"You got your period?" Ken said.

"Yes, it's almost over."

Angela never forgot the look that Ken threw at Teresa. If looks could kill, she remembered thinking, Teresa was dead then and there. Instantly, she remembered Teresa telling her that Ken liked to go down on her when she was menstruating.

There was an awkward pause. Christie began acting up again. Angela said, "It's late. We've got to go." Ken did nothing to dissuade her. Teresa said she was really bushed.

Angela helped bring the plates and cups to the sink. The Entenmann's cake was only half-eaten. "Oh, darn it," Teresa said. Ken had put the box in the trash can. "It's just sitting there on top," Angela said. "You can still use it." She wouldn't dream of it, Teresa said, and took out a roll of Saran Wrap and put it on the counter. "Don't bother with the dishes," she said. "They're nothing. I'll do them as soon as you've gone." Angela did not doubt she would. That was Teresa. Everything had to be spotless.

There were two other items that Angela especially recalled. One was that Teresa was never out of her sight for so much as a second that evening, not even to go to the bathroom.

The other was the way Ken behaved as they were leaving. Whenever the Rozeks came for a visit, they would lug in Christie's portable crib, playpen and toys. Normally, Ken never lifted a finger. But now he was running all around, grabbing the crib, folding up the playpen, loading them into the car.

"You sure you've got everything?" Ken said as they were in their car ready to depart.

Afterward, Angela peeked at her watch. It was about a quarter to eleven. She said to her husband, "Gee, wasn't it funny that all of a sudden Ken was helping you?"

"Yeah," Peter Rozek said, "it was like he couldn't wait for us to get the hell out."

# Chapter

# FIVE

The next day, Sunday, November 11, Al and Louise didn't expect Ken and Teresa for lunch. Teresa had said she'd be at the christening party that afternoon for the baby of another of the "Glitter Chicks," Lorraine Taibbi. She was looking forward to seeing the old gang, so many of whom she had been out of touch with. She would fill in Louise on all the gossip when she dropped Philip off on Monday morning before going to work.

But Teresa never showed up at the christening, although the Benignos did not know this at the time.

On Monday morning, nine o'clock and then nine-thirty passed. No Teresa. Louise telephoned the Manalapan house. No answer. Well, she thought, they're on the way.

Phil Benigno, who still lived with Al and Louise while working for Ken and attending night business administration courses at St. John's University, had already left. And in Ken's main office, he also wondered what was holding up his sister and Ken.

About 10:30 A.M. his phone rang. It was Ken.

Phil listened to him in utter disbelief. Ken said that he was on the road. He said that Teresa was spaced out on drugs—cocaine and codeine. She had finally faced up to her addiction and had gone away to seek rehabilitation. He had dropped her off at the People's Express terminal at Newark Airport, and now he was en route by car to his parents in Indiana with the baby. Teresa had wanted that. She knew he couldn't cope with the child by himself and hadn't wanted to burden Louise.

Then Ken changed subjects, as if there were nothing more to say. He instructed Phil to keep an eye on the office, make sure the dentist he'd hired stayed on the ball, and have one of the girls cancel his appointments until he returned on Friday.

Phil struggled to absorb what he was hearing. It was crazy. Okay, he knew that his sister did cocaine sometimes with Ken. But at worst she was an occasional user, like him, like half the kids Phil knew, not an abuser. And the codeine! He knew Ken had prescribed codeine for Teresa after the persistent pain she suffered from the Acapulco assault. But Ken had made out so many codeine prescriptions in Phil's name, telling him simply to bring them back, that Phil had asked him what the deal was. He thought that codeine was a painkiller. Could you get high from codeine? And Ken, giving another version of codeine's beneficence, had said that if you took it long enough, it stayed in your bloodstream and acted almost like a stimulant. He needed it to keep going, Ken said.

"Where did my sister go?"

"She wouldn't tell me. She wants to be alone."

"How the hell could you drop her off at the airport and leave her there like that?"

"Phil, your sister is very strong-willed. You should know that. She does what she wants."

"When did she say she's coming back?"

"Two or three weeks. She said she'd phone in three or four days, when she got settled. Phil, don't forget to have my appointments canceled."

Phil remembered how calm and collected Ken's voice

was, as if Phil were being the unreasonable one, asking all these dumb questions.

"Listen, Phil, one more thing," Ken said. "Teresa doesn't want Al and Louise to be, you know, upset about her drug problem and being left at the airport. She said to tell you to tell them that we decided, the two of us, to go to Indiana for a short vacation." Then, before Phil could say anything more, Ken said, "I'll be in touch," and hung up.

Phil stared at the phone in his hand, watching his hand shake. He didn't know what to do. He had to do something. His mother would be calling the office any second. So he called her and told her the vacation story.

"Just like that, they're going on vacation?" Louise said.

"Yes," Phil said weakly. "Just like that, Ma. That's what he said."

By the afternoon, Phil couldn't stand it anymore. He had to talk to somebody. He phoned Celeste, but got Jeff instead. Celeste was at the gynecologist. Jeff was home because he was working the night shift on the ferry. What was up?

After Phil told him, Jeff said, "Teresa is screwed up on drugs and she went to rehab, and he doesn't know where?"

"Those are his words."

"Phil, your sister went to a rehab? That's not Teresa. You're not making sense."

"I know."

"This doesn't sound right. He said he was taking the baby to Indiana?"

"Yeah. I don't know what to do."

"Did you tell your mother yet?"

"I told her they were on vacation. That was his idea."

"Come on, you have to tell her everything. We got to get to the bottom of this."

"Okay, I will. But I'll wait till I get home. Dad's still at school. Ma's there all alone."

That evening Phil confessed to Al and Louise that the vacation story was a concoction. Al saw Louise turn ashen and slump in her chair. He rushed to get her nitroglycerin pills.

She began to sob. "Acapulco," she said. "He did it to her again."

"Please, let's wait and see," Al said. In his heart, he was thinking that, too, but he was terrified of saying anything that might heighten Louise's stress. At all costs, he had to remain on an even keel.

The phone rang. But it was not Teresa, or Ken either. Lorraine Taibbi was calling. Was Teresa all right? She hadn't come to the christening and there wasn't any answer at her house.

Teresa had taken a trip suddenly, Al said. He did not elaborate. He did not know what else to say. He felt so incredibly helpless.

"That son of a bitch," Al said and picked up the phone again and called the Taylors in Marion. Zach answered. No, Kenny wasn't there. But he was expected. He had been delayed by bad weather. It was snowing in the Midwest. He'd called from around Columbus, Ohio. Zach said that it would be at least another six hours or so before he arrived. Zach did not mention Teresa, nor did Al ask if he knew anything.

"Have him call me as soon as he gets there," Al said.

At 12:30 A.M., New York time, Ken phoned from Marion. The baby was fine, he said. He repeated essentially the same story that he had told Phil. "Teresa was spaced out on cocaine and codeine," he said.

That was impossible for him to believe, Al said.

Well, she had this "continuing drug problem," Ken said, that she had kept hidden from Al because she was aware of his strong feelings about drug usage.

Even if it were true, Al said, he could not understand how Ken could have left her at the airport and driven off without any hint of where she intended to go.

"That's your daughter," Ken said. "You know how she can be."

It was like punching air, Al thought. "I don't care," he

84

said. "It was a very, very bad error in judgment on your part. Inexcusable."

There was a pause. Then Ken conceded that maybe Al was right. It was a snap decision. He had been completely nonplussed when Teresa announced her intentions. Perhaps he shouldn't have gone along with her. There was nothing he could do about it now. His voice took on an optimistic tone. Anyway, he said, she'd promised to call in a couple of days and everything would be fixed.

"I want her reported missing to the police," Al said.

First thing upon his return he'd go to the Manalapan police, Ken said. As soon as he got baby Philip settled in, he would be on his way. Be back home early Wednesday. By then Teresa should have called.

That Tuesday morning Celeste had classes at Staten Island Community College. Although she was a housewife and an expectant mother, she was determined to continue her education, concentrating on English. Someday, she thought, she might be a teacher.

She told Jeff to pick her up at noon. An idea kept gnawing at her. Perhaps Louise was right, that it could be Acapulco all over again, or something like it. Maybe Ken had beaten up her sister, and Teresa in embarrassment and shame was hiding, not answering the phone. Perhaps this whole story had been cooked up to allow her bruises and God knows what else to disappear.

They'd go to the Manalapan house to find out. She knew it was pretty farfetched, but it offered hope. And hope was all she had, hope that it wasn't something worse.

They parked up the block so Teresa would not spot them in case she was inside. They saw Ken's Datsun in the driveway. Jeff tried the front door. It was locked. He remembered that the door from the garage was often left open. And it was.

Fear coursed through Celeste at the thought of what they might discover. The garage door led into the dining area. Straight ahead was the kitchen. They saw the remains of a cake on the counter, a roll of Saran Wrap next to it. That was so unlike Teresa. She would not leave a cake uncovered like that. It simply wasn't her nature.

There was something equally peculiar in the living area. Teresa's key ring was on the coffee table. Teresa would never leave the house without her keys.

They checked the sewing room, where Ken's weights also were, and then the room being renovated. Jeff noticed that some of the old carpet padding on the floor seemed to have been ripped off.

Upstairs, the two bedrooms and the nursery appeared to be in order. In the master bedroom there was a removable panel about two feet by four that led to an attic crawl space. Celeste told Jeff to look inside, and then she shut her eyes in horrified anticipation. But there was nothing.

They went to the backyard, to the pool. It had been covered for the winter. Celeste made Jeff peek underneath it. Again, nothing. She spoke so sharply that Jeff said, "Hey, come on." She couldn't help it. Her nerves were completely frayed just from being there.

Kittens mothered by Teresa's cat Cleo appeared, mewing frantically. Celeste recalled how Ken loathed Cleo. They began calling for her, but she didn't appear. So they fed the kittens.

Celeste phoned Louise. She told her about the cake and the keys.

That afternoon Al took off from his teaching job and went to the local precinct of the New York Police Department to explain his predicament. But the desk sergeant said that he couldn't be of much help. Teresa not only was a resident of New Jersey, but also her husband was the proper individual to file a missing person report.

Later, at home, Al took a deep breath and called Angela Rozek. "We've got a bit of a problem," Al said, choosing his words as carefully as he could. "Teresa's missing. Ken says that he took her to Newark Airport. She needed help and she was going off to get it. He said she was spaced out on drugs."

His voice breaking now, Al blurted, "You were there on Saturday night. Just what went on? If you know anything about Teresa being strung out on drugs, please tell me. We have to know."

Angela listened to him, stunned. She pulled herself together and said, "Uncle Al, nothing like that happened. Believe me, Teresa's not spaced out. She doesn't do drugs that way."

Then Celeste got on the line and described her visit to the house. She told Angela about the cake. Angela bit her lip. Something, whatever it was, must have started right after she and Peter left. She remembered how anxious Ken was to get them out. And after she had hung up, Angela bowed her head and prayed. "Oh, God," she pleaded, "don't let anything bad happen to my cousin, Teresa."

• • •

On Wednesday Al seized upon a ray of hope.

Celeste had spoken to Cindy Diaz, with whom Teresa had spent last Saturday morning. Cindy told her that another of Teresa's friends, Irene DeBlasio, had flown from Newark to Michigan on Sunday on People's Express. Maybe Teresa had gone with her. Besides the Rozeks, Irene and her boyfriend had spent more time at the Manalapan house that summer than anyone. Irene was a hairstylist, and she cut Teresa's and Ken's hair in return for Ken's dental care. Maybe she knew something nobody else did.

Louise called Irene's mother. Yes, Irene had gone to Michigan to visit her sister, who had just moved there. But she was unreachable. The phone hadn't been installed yet. She was supposed to return late Thursday.

There was no word from Ken that day. Finally, in the evening, he called. He had returned at last. He had taken a wrong turn near New Brunswick, got lost, and then was tied up in traffic. He hadn't heard from Teresa. Had they?

In the morning, he'd go to the police. He was worn out. The long drive had exhausted him. He apologized for not immediately coming to see them, but he had to get some rest. He'd be over after he saw the police.

Al told him of the possibility that Teresa had gone to Michigan with Irene DeBlasio. Ken sounded elated. That was great news, he said. Al added that Celeste and Jeff were going to meet her plane the following evening. In that event, Ken said, he wanted to go along.

Al put Louise on the line. After apologizing again for not coming by that night, Ken hesitated and then asked if Louise knew whether anyone had been inside the house while he was away. Yes, she said, Celeste and Jeff had been there to make sure it was all right. Was there something wrong? No, he said, it was just that he noticed that the panel to the attic crawl area was slightly ajar and he was wondering why. Well, she thought, his fatigue certainly hadn't prevented him from checking the house with a fine-toothed comb.

At 9:14 A.M. on Thursday, Ken appeared at the Manalapan police station to report Teresa missing. He did not mention that her absence had any connection with drugs. According to the notes of patrolman David Visconi:

> Husband Mr. Taylor reported to this officer he took his wife to Newark Airport (People's terminal) on 11/11/84 because she told him she needed space. Husband relates she feels pressure as a result of working and family problems . . . Mr. Taylor believes his wife may be in Michigan. Her girlfriend Irene DeBlasio from Staten Island left to visit her sister in Michigan on 11/11/84.

Afterward, Ken picked up Phil at the office. They were going to the airport to see if anyone there recalled Teresa. He had two photos of Teresa, one of them with the baby. He stopped first to buy a six-pack of beer and then cigarette papers. He appeared very jumpy to Phil, who was edgy himself. Ken rolled a joint and lit it. He asked Phil to hand him one of the beers. Phil refused his offer of a beer, but did take a couple of tokes on the joint to try to relax a little.

At the People's Express terminal, Ken showed the photos to personnel at the ticket counter. No luck. They went into a restaurant and tried the cashier and some waitresses, and next to a bar. Still nothing. At a second bar, though, a bartender studied the pictures for a while and said that yes, he might have seen the lady, or one just like her the previous Sunday. Ken seemed almost triumphant at this apparent corroboration of his story.

He got to the Benignos in the early afternoon. When he saw Louise, he started to cry, as if he was now in total union with them, sharing their misery. After he regained his composure, he said he'd been so anxiety-ridden that he hadn't eaten all day. Louise made him a sandwich. When he left, he shook his head sorrowfully and said, "I love you, Mom, and I love Teresa. I don't understand how she could do this to us."

In the early evening he returned to the airport to join Celeste and Jeff as they waited for Irene DeBlasio's plane. He greeted them cordially and with concern. But when they looked at the screen display, there was no flight from Detroit for the time they had been given. Jeff called Louise and learned Irene had already landed and phoned. She had switched to Northwest Orient. She said that Teresa had not been with her, and she had no idea where she was.

As they left the terminal, Ken suddenly said, "How come you guys were at my place?"

Celeste stared right back at him. "We were looking for something," she said. "Anything we could find." He did not reply, but she would always remember the condescending smirk on his face.

In Manalapan, meanwhile, patrolman Visconi ascertained that the airline kept passenger lists for only twenty-four hours. Cops were always getting complaints like this, and inevitably such disappearances were short-lived. And in his log, Visconi now noted, "It appears at this point his wife wanted to leave her family. No domestic violence was involved. This case is being closed until such time as it would require reopening."

• • •

On Friday morning, Visconi phoned Ken and informed him that "under the circumstances, police involvement in the case was limited" and that it was being closed out.

In his office, Ken told this to Phil as further confirmation of his story. He took a bundle of letters and said that he was leaving to treat a patient at the other office and then going home to scan the mail. With all this distraction, he just couldn't concentrate at work.

Later that morning, Phil called Louise and told her what Ken had said about the case being closed. Celeste was with her. Both women were enraged by the news, and together they phoned Visconi, who for the first time heard about Acapulco, how not only the Benignos but the police and hotel security staff in Mexico suspected that Ken was the one who had beaten Teresa, although no formal charges were lodged.

Visconi wrote up a new report for his captain of patrol, Jimmie Potts, and during the regular afternoon briefing at the Manalapan station, it was decided to take another look into the disappearance of Teresa Taylor. A detective, Robert Fausak, drew the assignment.

Around five P.M., Celeste called Visconi and was transferred to Fausak. Celeste was yelling this time. Why was Ken being allowed to walk around? She was certain he had done something to her sister. *Where* was her sister? What was being done to find her? She came on so strong that Fausak was on the verge of hanging up. But beneath her ranting, he sensed desperation. He calmed her and got more details about Acapulco, including a vivid description of Teresa's physical condition. He winced when he heard about Teresa's fractured teeth and the dreadful pain she had endured. He was plagued by poor teeth and he knew that kind of pain. There was nothing worse.

Then Fausak spoke to Al. In his grave manner, Al was even more impressive. He echoed the family suspicions about what had really happened in Acapulco, but candidly said that his daughter always insisted her husband was not her assailant. It gave his apprehension a special ring of truth.

Fausak sat at his desk. He was an avid golfer and he had a big game on tap in the morning, probably the last chance of the season to get in eighteen holes. This case of a missing woman being dropped off at the airport was a little unusual, but in police work nothing, he reflected, was truly unusual anymore. People packed up and walked away all the time, kids, husbands, wives. Originally, he planned to see what developed over the weekend.

Instead, he phoned Ken at home. Could he come by the Taylor house?

Sure, when?

Now.

Well, okay, Ken said, but why? He thought the case had been closed.

You know how it is, Fausak said. There were always loose ends to tie up.

The Manalapan Fausak drove through had mushroomed since he'd become a cop. Although it had no defined center, it was what the newspapers liked to call a "bedroom community." On the north side, developments had replaced farmland. To the south, where the Taylor home was, at 23 Valley Road in a subdivision called the Knolls, you could still find open spaces, but they were vanishing fast. Fausak couldn't afford to live there. He'd been lucky to buy a small condo for himself and his wife Joan just across the township line.

A slim, intense man, then thirty-six, Fausak couldn't remember when he had not wanted to be a cop. He came from a cop family, his grandfather and two uncles had been police officers in Jersey City where he was raised, and his father was a detective for the old Jersey Central railroad. After he was graduated from Delaware Valley College, he applied to the New Jersey State Police. But instead he took a job teaching high school general science. The salary was better than a thousand dollars more a year and, of course, you had weekends off. Four years later, when Manalapan Township elected to form a police department—up till then the state police handled local law enforcement—pay scales had risen and he joined up. He'd been on the job for twelve years, since the department's inception, and was now one of three detectives on the thirty-two-man force. Along with the population explosion had come crime, mostly home and business burglaries and sporadic sexual assaults.

Ken greeted him affably. They sat across from one another at the dining table. Ken said that his wife had been depressed for several weeks because of work pressures, conflicts with her family, and being a new mother. He said that the two of them really hadn't any disputes to speak of. He did not say anything about drugs. His wife had said that she needed "space." When she left, she was carrying her MasterCard and about eight hundred dollars in cash, two hundred of which he had given her. Ken was quite specific about what she had been wearing—a white sweater, a white jacket, Calvin Klein jeans, and black patent leather pumps.

Ken said that he had reported her missing not because of any pressure from her parents, but because she had not contacted him in the promised three days. Normally, she was very good about that.

At Teresa's request, he said that he had taken their child to stay with his parents in Indiana because of her mother's heart condition.

Ken added that there was reason to believe that his wife had gone with a friend to Michigan. Almost as an afterthought, he said that while Teresa had kissed the baby at the airport, she didn't kiss him. Fausak couldn't help thinking that it was such an odd remark to volunteer.

He asked if he could look around the house. Ken said certainly, but why? Oh, Fausak said, sometimes people are so accustomed to their surroundings that they fail to spot an obvious clue.

Nothing appeared amiss downstairs. Fausak observed how well organized Teresa's closet was, shoes neatly placed, the clothes hangers all turned in the same direction. There was a space where shoes had been removed and hangers empty. Everything pointed to a planned departure.

Then in the bathroom, Fausak noticed four toothbrushes in the holder by the sink. "Whose are those?" he said.

The two on the right were his, Ken said, and the other two were his wife's.

Gee, Fausak said, for someone who had as many dental

problems as Mrs. Taylor, it was strange that she hadn't taken them with her.

Don't give it a second's thought, Ken said. She had plenty of them. After all, he was a dentist.

Fausak brooded on his way back to the station. The husband had been too smooth, too quick to come up with an answer for every question. And the toothbrushes bothered Fausak a lot. Whenever he took a trip, his toothbrush was almost the first thing he packed.

At his desk, Fausak composed a missing person bulletin to be sent to New Jersey, Pennsylvania, Ohio, Indiana and Michigan. In his physical description of Teresa, he wrote that her two front teeth were false. The bulletin was transmitted at 11:15 P.M. At the last minute, Fausak added, "Possible foul play involved."

Fausak arrived home about midnight. When his wife asked what had kept him, he said, "I think I've got my first homicide."

• • •

At five A.M. the phone awakened Fausak. It was the duty officer at the Manalapan station. There'd been a response to the bulletin from the Pennsylvania State Police. "They think maybe they've got something," the duty officer said. "I advised them you'd be in at eight-thirty."

Fausak lay there thinking about Dr. Kenneth Taylor. Was Taylor also lying in bed awake, thinking? By eight o'clock, Fausak was at his desk. Actually, there were three additional responses from other states, but they were all requests for more information. Fausak thought about people missing throughout the country.

Then state police corporal Gary Millward from the Reading barracks in Pennsylvania telephoned. He said that the body of a white female, age somewhere between twenty and twenty-five, had been found in a bird sanctuary at the base of Hawk Mountain off Interstate 78, about fifty miles from the New Jersey border. It was a fairly remote area. The discovery had been made by a fellow picking up tin cans two days earlier, on Thursday morning at ten-fifteen—

just about the time Ken had left the Manalapan station after reporting Teresa missing.

The body had been wrapped in grayish padding, the kind used under a carpet, Millward said, and was inside a tan sleeping bag. The victim had succumbed to massive head injuries caused by an unknown blunt instrument. The absence of blood at the site, a roadside ditch, indicated that death had occurred elsewhere.

Physically, there was a match with Fausak's bulletin except for the clothes. She had on a white knit sweater, beige culottes and white pantyhose. There was also a sanitary napkin. The culottes, pantyhose and napkin had been wrenched down over and below the buttocks area to just above the knees. The culottes were torn in back. There was a large amount of Vaseline, gobs of it, in and around her anus and vagina.

"Bad, huh?" Fausak said.

"Very."

The jewelry on the body, Millward said, included a gold Pulsar watch with a black face and band, a wedding band, one starburst diamond earring with the second one missing, a necklace with a gold tooth and toothbrush charm, and a necklace with a gold tag which was engraved, "#1 Sister."

"What about her teeth?" Fausak asked.

One upper front tooth was completely gone from the blows the victim had received, Millward said. As for the other one, there were remains of an original tooth, as if it had been capped.

"I'll get back to you," Fausak said.

The Monmouth County prosecutor's office was ultimately responsible for law enforcement in the county's fifty-three municipalities, and Fausak notified its major crimes unit of a probable homicide case.

Next, he called the Benignos, reaching Louise. Could she and her husband come to Manalapan that morning?

Louise started to cry. "You found her, didn't you?"

Fausak fell back on the technicalities of police procedure. "No," he said. He needed some more information. He started asking about jewelry Teresa might have worn. He had barely mentioned the Pulsar watch when she moaned, "My daughter, oh, my poor daughter."

It was the first time he'd faced a situation like this and he fought his nervousness. Fausak started to dislike Ken Taylor very much. To his relief, Al came on the line. They'd be there at noon, Al said, and suggested that Celeste might be helpful on the jewelry.

Then Celeste said that Teresa always wore a charm she had given her that said, "#1 Sister." "Why are you asking? What do you know?" she said, her voice rising.

"Celeste, I don't know anything for a fact. I'm just trying to get all the information I can."

Fausak called Corporal Millward and said that he would escort family members down for a positive identification later in the day.

When Al and Louise arrived, Fausak took Al aside and said, "We may have to go to Pennsylvania. They've found a body that closely fits your daughter. But we don't know, we have to make sure." Al said he wanted to call his son to accompany him.

The moment Louise heard about Pennsylvania, she broke down. "Louise, maybe it's not her," Al said. "We don't know yet."

"Yes, it's her," she said. "You know it's her. He's no good. He tried to do it before and now he's killed her."

Fausak excused himself and summoned a first-aid squad. He suggested to Al that it might be a good idea to hospitalize Louise. But she would have none of it. Angela and Peter Rozek came in from East Brunswick, and that helped.

Fausak spoke briefly, alone, to the Rozeks. What had Mrs. Taylor been wearing on Saturday night when they were there?

"A white sweater and corduroy culottes, kind of tan-colored," Angela said. "Has someone seen her?"

"It's just that we got a report that she might have been in jeans, Calvin Klein jeans."

"Believe me, Teresa would never travel in jeans. She was too conscious of her hips."

Sitting with the Benignos, Fausak wished that he was a

million miles away. He wished there was something he could say.

Finally Phil Benigno arrived. He embraced his mother, and Fausak heard him whisper, "Don't give up hope, Ma."

Louise went with the Rozeks. Fausak called the local authorities to have an ambulance alerted. Then he and patrolman Visconi drove off with Al and Phil in the rear seat for the two-hour trip. For a while, nothing was said. Then Al started talking about Acapulco, about all of the might-have-beens. It was difficult to say who he was addressing—Fausak, Phil, himself?

After a wordless interlude, Al asked Fausak about when he had become a cop and what was it like, and Fausak spun out his answer as long as he could.

At the Reading barracks, Corporal Millward privately showed Fausak some of the photographs. Fausak shuddered. He'd seen bodies smashed up in car wrecks, but he had never seen anyone beaten like this. He remembered hoping that she hadn't felt anything, and then realized that of course she must have been immediately rendered unconscious. Nobody could have stood up to such savagery.

Millward led them north to a hospital in Pottsville, the medical facility closest to Hawk Mountain, where the autopsy had been performed. Other state troopers were on hand. The body was wheeled into a corridor outside the morgue. The face was uncovered by the forensic pathologist.

Phil didn't move. He started weeping. Al moved closer to the body. He also was crying. "Yes," he said, "this is my daughter." He bent over and kissed her brow.

The pathologist looked at Phil. "Is this your sister?"

"Yes, that's my sister."

Fausak turned away. He had wanted so much for them both to say that no, it wasn't her, it was someone else.

Formalities had to be concluded at the hospital, forms filled out, papers signed, and more of the same back at the barracks. It was nearly eleven P.M. before they began the long, silent return to Manalapan.

Before leaving, Al called Celeste. Jeff answered the

phone. Celeste was at a girlfriend's house. Al told him that Teresa was dead.

. . .

While Fausak was in Pennsylvania, Lieutenant William Lucia, second-in-command of the major crimes unit in the county prosecutor's office, arrived at the Manalapan station for an update. He came with Guy McCormick, one of his best investigators. McCormick would be assigned to the case. Before joining the unit, he had been on the Manalapan force. He had worked with Fausak and got along well with him.

There was an immediate concern. Ken Taylor couldn't be found. Three times that day a patrol car had gone by the house. There was no sign of him or of Teresa's Cutlass Supreme. Nor was he at either of his two offices in Staten Island.

Concern mounted after Fausak reported that a positive identification had been made. They wanted Taylor—and the car. According to Fausak, as soon as the body had been discovered, the state police mounted a roadblock. A witness reported seeing a vehicle resembling the Cutlass near the bird sanctuary. He remembered a single male at the wheel. He also thought that the car had New Jersey plates. He could not recall the numbers, except that he was sure the middle one was "6." The Cutlass's plates were 464 YEE.

Then, around eight P.M., there was a new twist. Peter Vanderweil, a Manalapan police lieutenant, took the call. It was from a man who said he was Robert Negliaccio, a New York City detective stationed in Staten Island. He said that he was both a friend and a patient of Dr. Kenneth Taylor's.

Taylor had phoned him earlier in the day to say that he needed Negliaccio's help in trying to locate his wife. She had left "spaced out on drugs." This was the first time that the New Jersey investigators had heard about any drug use by Teresa.

Negliaccio wanted to know what the current status of her disappearance was. Could he be of assistance?

Everyone's reaction was that this was a fishing expedition instigated by Ken. Negliaccio could be anybody, and even if he were who he said he was, so what?

Vanderweil treated him cautiously. He did not say that a body had been found or identified. The search for Mrs. Taylor was still going on. Did his caller have any idea where Dr. Taylor was?

Well, maybe, Negliaccio said. He'd left a number in the Pittsburgh area where he said he could be reached.

When the number was tried, though, a woman's voice on a recorded message said that no one was there. Fausak was contacted in Pennsylvania and told to enlist the cooperation of the state police. The number was matched to an address, but when the troopers arrived, they found a small, empty office building. There was no Cutlass, nor was it seen in the parking lot of an adjacent apartment complex. It was eventually learned that an out-of-date street directory had been consulted, that the number had been disconnected and reissued, but by then it didn't make any difference.

Shortly after midnight, Investigator McCormick had called Celeste. She shouted, "He killed her, he killed my sister!"

They were doing everything they could to locate Dr. Taylor, McCormick said. He wasn't in Manalapan. Did she have any ideas where he might be?

Try his parents in Marion, Indiana, she said, weeping, and gave him the number.

Zach Taylor answered. McCormick told him that the body of his son's wife had been discovered and that he needed to speak to Ken as soon as possible.

Zach asked if her death had been caused by a drug overdose.

At this point, McCormick said, he really did not have all the details. The last thing he wanted was to scare off his number-one suspect.

Zach said that he would try to reach Ken. He was sure that he was in Pittsburgh to visit his daughter, although he did not have the address. His son loved that little girl, Zach said. He did not say that the only time he and Jean had ever seen her was when they came east for Ken's marriage to Teresa.

• • •

Around one A.M. Fausak returned from Pennsylvania to Manalapan. Al and Phil left for East Brunswick to be with Louise at the Rozeks. A few minutes later, Ken telephoned.

Lieutenant Vanderweil said that he regretted to inform him that his wife was dead—murdered—and expressed his condolences. Ken started to cry. Where had it happened? What were the circumstances? Did they know who had killed her?

They had no leads at the moment, Vanderweil said. That was why his assistance was so urgently needed. It was crucial to reconstruct all of his wife's movements, starting at People's Express. Right then Vanderweil wanted Ken to think that they were buying his story 100 percent.

Give him a couple of minutes to make arrangements, Ken said. He called back and said that he was taking an eight o'clock flight in the morning from Pittsburgh to Newark.

Did he wish to be met?

No, Ken said, he had parked his car at the airport. He would drive in himself. He'd be at the station no later than ten. He hoped he could help.

• • •

It was the second time that week that Ken had been with Marilyn Hope in Pittsburgh.

The week before, when he said he might come out, she had told him that she would be on vacation in Florida with Astrid. When she returned late Sunday night, her answering machine wasn't working. On Monday, she called both of his Staten Island offices. One said that he was on vacation; the other said there'd been an emergency that had caused him to go to Indiana.

On Tuesday morning he phoned her from Marion. He said that he'd been trying to contact her.

"What are you doing there?" she asked.

Teresa had taken off, he said, "all hopped up on coke."

She had gone somewhere to dry out, so he had brought the baby to his mother's place. He'd drive to Pittsburgh in the afternoon.

Well, she said, she was supposed to attend a PTA meeting in the evening. The teachers had gone on strike. But okay, she'd skip the meeting.

Ken showed up around midnight, she remembered. She made him a grilled cheese sandwich.

He said that Teresa's parents wanted him to report her missing to the police. What did she think?

"How can you report somebody missing who says they're leaving?" she asked. "Where did she go, anyway? What did she do?"

He said that he had dropped her off at People's Express in Newark.

"She didn't say anything about where she was going?"
"No."

Then he said that he had a feeling that she was just going to hole up in a hotel somewhere. As a matter of fact, he had told her that he was going home because she would probably change her mind and want him to fetch her.

But he decided to take the baby to his mother's. They had discussed that thoroughly. It was for the best. One thing was sure. It was definitely, absolutely finished between him and Teresa. "Things just didn't work out," he said.

In the morning, Marilyn said, "Maybe you had better report it to the police." And he ought to tell them about Teresa's drug addiction. It would give them a better slant. They'd know what to do.

She recalled that he seemed reluctant. He didn't want to say anything about the drugs because of all the prescriptions she forged that he hadn't done anything about. That could cause him all sorts of problems. He'd think about it.

He said that he would return on Friday or Saturday.

She told him to be sure to let her know. Astrid had a birthday party to go to on Saturday, and she didn't wish to hang around the house not knowing one way or the other.

By two o'clock on Saturday, she was ready to give up when Ken phoned. He was in Pittsburgh at the airport. She reminded him about the party. He said that it was fine with him.

Outside the party, they talked about Teresa. What on earth could have happened to her?

"She wouldn't go kill herself someplace because she thought something's going on between us, because her marriage is falling apart?" Marilyn asked. "You know her. Would she do that?"

"Well, with drugs and stuff, you never know," Ken said. "You never know who she might have gotten mixed up with."

"You mean she might have taken off with somebody because the marriage isn't working, because sexually it wasn't there?"

"I asked her brother about that," Ken said, "and he said absolutely not."

"Maybe," Marilyn said, "she wants you to go searching for her, to show that you care for her. You know how some people are when they're breaking up. They get crazy."

That night they went to a restaurant called Charlie's Place. "We had a lovely dinner," she remembered, "and my daughter was thrilled to death. She was all dressed up, and when we came back, it was late. She fell asleep on the couch, and so did I. He was watching some movie. I woke up and he was putting pajamas on Astrid, and I was laughing because it's hard to put pajamas on a sleeping child. He said he didn't see what was so funny."

After everyone was in bed, the phone rang. She didn't answer, resenting a call in the middle of the night. Then it rang again, and this time she groped for the phone. It was Ken's father, asking for him. She heard Zach say that Teresa's body had been found.

The only way she could describe Ken's reaction was in relation to her own. "I got a sick feeling," she remembered. "I felt like I went dry, you know, and I was drinking water, and I noticed he was drinking water, too. I know I cried, 'Oh, my God,' and he cried. I guess he called the police about coming back, and then his parents were talking about how they were going to get to Newark, and I felt, Oh, my God, how can he get on an airplane by himself, having to go through this kind of thing alone? So I asked him did he want me to go with him and he said, 'Yes,' and I arranged for Astrid to stay where she'd been for the birthday party. I think it was me who thought that well, I could drive him from Newark to the police station and drive the car back to the airport and give the keys to his parents."

• • •

Captain Richard Canneto, who headed the major crimes unit, brought a contingent of investigators to Manalapan to await Ken's arrival. All the top township police officials also were on hand that Sunday morning.

From a station window, Bob Fausak saw the Cutlass pull in shortly after ten A.M. He watched Ken talk to a red-haired woman and kiss her on the cheek, and then saw the woman drive off.

Fausak greeted him in the reception area and told him that he regretted the circumstances under which they had to meet again. Ken acknowledged this with the resigned shrug of a bereaved.

Instead of using an office, Fausak ushered him to one of the interview rooms. It was intimate and intimidating, barely large enough for a small table and three chairs.

Fausak introduced Ken to Lieutenant Lucia, who informed him that he was a suspect. Lucia softened this by saying that almost everyone they were talking to at this stage was a suspect. He started reading Ken his Miranda rights, but Ken waved him off nonchalantly and signed an agreement to be questioned and a form consenting to a search of the Valley Road premises.

Lucia asked Ken if he'd like a cup of coffee. Ken said he would, and Lucia left the room. Outside, he gave Guy McCormick the consent-to-search form. Captain Canneto and two investigators in the prosecutor's office for forensic and technical services were immediately dispatched to the house. McCormick would serve as liaison between them and the interrogators. McCormick also began writing up an affidavit for a court-ordered search in case Ken changed his mind. He had yet to ask for a lawyer. One object of the interview was to keep it going at least long enough to determine if any physical evidence could be turned up.

Fausak could not discern the slightest sign of unease in Ken. He was properly solemn and cooperative, anxious to be of assistance.

When Lucia returned with the coffee, he told Ken that he wanted him to start from the beginning, from the time he had first met his wife. Somewhere along the way, he said, there might be someone who bore her a grudge.

No, Ken quickly said, he couldn't think of a single person he knew who would want to harm Teresa. The only one who was conceivably upset about their relationship was Sal Aurelio, the boyfriend she had broken up with after meeting him. Aurelio, he said, had once hit her and burst her eardrum.

Lucia studiously wrote down Aurelio's name. He led Ken through his courtship and marriage to Teresa. Ken did not mention anything about being married before. Then Lucia questioned him closely about Acapulco. Ken told the same story. He'd never been charged. The police had "extorted" money from him. In the hospital, his wife had been given "massive doses of drugs."

While Teresa had been under "a lot of pressure" after having gone through premature labor along with "problems" with her parents, Ken said that their marriage was extremely happy. There were no serious rifts between them except for his wife's growing drug addiction, which had upset him a great deal. He added that during Teresa's confinement he had to leave his practice to tend to her and that had hurt "financially."

On Saturday night, November 10, when the Rozeks had left, he said that he went to bed not long after midnight. Teresa had not. He awoke around four A.M. and found her still downstairs. She was strung out again. She told him that she realized that she had to do something to clean up her act. She could not take care of the baby. They discussed it for a while, but she was unable to rest. So he went back to bed alone. Around eight-thirty, she woke him up to say that she had to get away. Then he took her to the airport. He was very specific about the jeans she was wearing.

He reiterated that Teresa wanted him to take the baby to Indiana. He left right after four P.M. He could remember that because he had spent the afternoon watching a New York Jets football game.

After that there was a break so that Ken could go to the bathroom. He had remained impressively confident. If Fausak had not met the Benignos, if he had not spoken to the Rozeks and gotten a description of how Teresa was dressed that night, if the body had not been discovered in those same clothes, Ken's version, despite its bizarre aspects, would have been believable. And in the end, he could have said, well, he was wrong about the jeans.

Lucia asked him to retrace all his moves during the past week, to Indiana, to Pittsburgh, then to Manalapan and, finally, back to Pittsburgh.

There was another break for coffee.

McCormick grabbed Lucia in the corridor to tell him they had finally come up with something important at the house. An earring with dried blood on it, a twin of the one Teresa wore, had been found on the garage floor.

Fausak left the interview room. Captain Canneto and Manalapan police lieutenant Peter Vanderweil crowded inside now with Lucia. Canneto had a Polaroid shot of the earring with a ruler alongside it to indicate its size.

"Doctor Taylor," Canneto said, "what do you see in this picture?"

"A ruler."

"No, I mean the object next to it."

Ken peered at the photograph. "A cigarette butt?"

No, Lucia said, it wasn't a butt. It was an earring from a matched pair. It had been discovered in Ken's garage. The other earring had been on his wife's body.

Still, Ken did not crack. He couldn't explain it. He looked closely at the Polaroid again. Maybe Teresa had met somebody at the airport, he said, and they'd come back to the house and that person had killed her, maybe somebody who was into drugs.

That didn't wash, Lucia said. A stranger picking her up at the airport, going back to the house and killing her wouldn't then transport the body somewhere else. "Doc, did you kill your wife?" Lucia said.

Ken denied it. What they were saying didn't make any sense. He was madly in love with his wife. Why didn't they give him the benefit of the doubt?

"Think about it," Lucia said. "Take your time. It'll benefit all of us." For the first time, he noticed tiny beads of perspiration on Ken's forehead. He and Canneto left the room.

Vanderweil remained there. He stared at Ken. "I believe you killed your wife. Maybe there are circumstances we're not aware of."

Ken's eyes started tearing. Vanderweil recalled that he began nodding ever so slightly.

Lucia and Canneto returned, carrying cups of coffee.

Ken looked up at them. His lips were quivering.

After a long pause, he said, "What would you do if you came down the stairs one morning and found your wife giving your five-month-old child head?"

"Doc, is that what happened?" Lucia said.

"Yes."

Then Ken started crying convulsively.

• • •

Lucia allowed him a few minutes to compose himself. Then Lucia said, "I realize it's difficult for you to talk at this time, but we have to have more information."

Under questioning, Ken said that it had happened about eight A.M. when he woke up and discovered Teresa performing fellatio on little Philip. The child, he said, was on the dining area table.

He had started down the stairs when he saw her "doing that to the baby." He was fed up with her drug problem.

He yelled and Teresa ran into the laundry room. He chased her. She grabbed a dumbbell bar and swung it at him in the doorway. He ducked and wrested the bar away.

Then he said, "I gave it to her."

Ken started sobbing again.

"Did you strike your wife more than once?" Lucia asked.

Almost indignantly, he replied, "Of course, what kind of question is that?"

Lucia said that it was necessary to obtain all the facts, however difficult it might be for him to relate them.

Ken abruptly said that he didn't want to answer any more questions. What he wanted was a lawyer.

As he was led out to be photographed, fingerprinted, and put in a holding cell, he kept sobbing, "I just couldn't take it anymore."

# Part II

## THE INVESTIGATION

# Chapter

## SIX

The grisly details would gradually unfold.

In Pittsburgh, when Ken was eating a grilled cheese sandwich and telling Marilyn that things just hadn't worked out with Teresa, her body was in the trunk of the Cutlass parked in front of Marilyn's condominium.

In Marion, the body had been in the trunk all the time that the car sat in the driveway of Ken's parents' house.

The autopsy revealed that there were nine shattering blows to Teresa's face and head. The back of her skull was in three pieces.

Ken had stuffed her in the trunk, cleaned up the blood, put the baby in a car seat beside him, and driven from Manalapan after the Jets game was over.

Before leaving, he called Marion and spoke to his father. He would be coming out with Philip. He'd be there when he got there. Zach wanted to know if something was the matter. He'd explain everything when he arrived, Ken said.

In Stroudsburg, Pennsylvania, he stopped at a Howard Johnson's to use the men's room and to change Philip's diaper. The Dallas Cowboys were on TV. The Cowboys were his favorite team. He went across the street to a McDonald's for a hamburger and fries.

Still in Pennsylvania on Interstate 80, he pulled in for the night at a Holiday Inn. When he registered, the desk clerk asked how many people would be in the room and Ken said, "Three."

"Three?"

"Oh, I mean two," he said. "I don't know what's wrong with me."

The Holiday Inn people were very hospitable, sending up a crib for the baby right away. In the morning, he called Phil Benigno to tell him that Teresa had gone off to rehabilitate herself. It was snowing. He phoned his parents periodically to report his progress. He cut short one conversation with his mother, saying, "I've got to feed Philip. This is a lot more than I bargained for."

When he finally reached Marion, Jean remembered that as he presented Philip to her, Ken said, "Son, you're in safe hands now."

Jean said that she had better change and bathe the baby.

Be sure to inspect his penis and wash it thoroughly, Ken said. That perplexed her at the time; it looked all right to her. Later, she would say righteously that she now understood why he had made the request.

There was an awkward moment when Zach told Ken's brother to get the luggage. Tom carried in a suitcase with Philip's things and an overnight bag of Ken's that were in the back seat. The trunk was locked, he said. He asked for the key.

Forget it, Ken said sharply. That was all the luggage. It was Teresa's car. There was only one trunk key and she had it.

Then he told Jean and Zach how Teresa, drug-crazed, had taken off to seek treatment, leaving him with the baby. He didn't know where she went. They couldn't imagine what it was like to live with someone hooked on drugs.

He said that he intended to stay in Marion for two or three days. But in the morning, after buying Pampers, he suddenly announced that he had to leave. He phoned Zach at work and told him, "I've got to go and find her. It's my responsibility. Maybe she's come back."

He said to Jean that he hoped the baby wouldn't be too much trouble. Jean recalled that he seemed "very depressed, not like himself." She found a twenty-dollar bill in her vanity drawer following his departure. A note was pinned to it that said, "Love, Ken." She was touched by his thoughtfulness.

After spending the night in Pittsburgh with Marilyn, he headed for Manalapan in Teresa's car, now her "hearse," he would say. On Interstate 80, as dusk fell, he said that he spotted a sign for the Hawk Mountain Bird Sanctuary. On "automatic pilot," he turned off the highway and ended up on a narrow, winding road where he dumped Teresa's body.

Continuing on the interstate, he began to contemplate suicide. Life without Teresa wasn't worth living; he would join her. And, he said, when he was inside the garage and closed the door, he connected the pool-filter hose to the exhaust pipe and snaked the hose through a rear window of the car. He turned on the motor, took several swigs from a bottle of Jack Daniel's, and awaited his demise.

Nothing happened. He got out of the car and discovered that the hose had fallen from the exhaust. He shut off the motor. He started having second thoughts about suicide. "Visions" of his children danced through his mind, he would say. It would be irresponsible of him to leave them fatherless.

He went into the house and called the Benignos to say that he was too tired to visit them. He phoned his parents and reported his safe return. No, he said, there was no word from Teresa. Investigator McCormick subsequently determined that he made two other calls that night to the same number in Hartford, Connecticut—to a massage parlor masquerading as a health club for men. According to the Hartford police, clients were required to undress before negotiating their preferences in sex.

Also, that night, Wednesday, despite telling the Benignos

that he was too tired to see them, he did drive to Staten Island after all—to the go-go club featuring naked dancers that he patronized.

• • •

Soon after Ken cut short his interrogation at the Manalapan police station, Zach and Jean arrived in the Cutlass that Marilyn had left at the airport. They had the baby. Fausak and Guy McCormick met them. Fausak's initial impression of them was "Mr. and Mrs. Middle America, well-dressed, well-mannered people." He said that he was sorry to inform them that their son had confessed to killing his wife and was now a prisoner. McCormick told them that the Cutlass would be impounded for evidence and asked for the keys.

They wanted to see their son. Could they?

Fausak passed on the request to Lucia, but Ken told Lucia, "No."

After Lucia personally relayed his refusal, Jean said, "But he has to. You tell him I said so."

This time Ken agreed to speak to them, but only if Lucia were present. They met in the detective's room, where they embraced and Ken was permitted to hold Philip.

He asked them if they had been told about the circumstances surrounding Teresa's death. They nodded. Then Jean said, "Was that why you asked me to check Philip's penis and bathe it?"

"Yes," Ken said, glancing at Lucia, as if to make sure he had heard.

Jean appeared to be mesmerized by one aspect of the case. How could he have driven for so long with Teresa in the trunk? Wasn't he afraid of an accident or the police?

"Mom, I was driving carefully. After all, I had my little boy with me."

He hesitated, as though more was to be said about what he had done with Teresa's body. "I loved her and I didn't want to part with her. I didn't know what to do. I kept her as long as I could. She liked the outdoors," he said plaintively, his voice trailing off. "She liked birds."

Suddenly he appeared angry. Why had they brought the

baby with them? Didn't they understand why he had taken him to Indiana, to Marion?

Then Fausak drove the Taylors to the Valley Road house. Ken was moved to the Monmouth County Jail in Freehold, the county seat. His bail was set at five hundred thousand dollars. Instead of the usual 10 percent deposit, the full amount would be required. He asked for paper and pencil to write letters. He was warned that they would be scrutinized.

In one letter, addressed to "Mom, Dad, Philip and Tom," he wrote, *What I did was done out of disgust for what I saw Teresa doing and when she swung the dumbbell at my head, I lost all control. I had become increasingly disgusted with her periods of withdrawal and associated losses of money as a result of her habit. Please help Marilyn and Astrid understand I only ever wanted the best for everyone . . . I became enraged but only when she swung at me did I touch her. Please use this to help you keep Philip for me. I want you to be his parents as well as TOM. Fight to keep him for me.*

A second letter was to Marilyn and Astrid:

*My Mom & Dad know what happened. I know I can't make it in this environment. I wanted so much for us all to be together. If only I had slept a little longer I would not have seen Teresa doing fellatio on my baby. I'm so sick inside and I really believe I'll be here for a long, long time . . . I truly loved you and I know that you know it. We were on our way but someone still got in our way. Maybe it was wrong from the very beginning. Please give Astrid the best and always let her know just how much I love her. You gave me the greatest gift in the world—a child. Try to let her know how much I love you and her. All my love.*

• • •

He was arraigned on Monday. Zach looked through the yellow pages for lawyers. One, Barry Shapiro, caught his eye. He remembered that Ken's lawyer in New London had been named Shapiro. Maybe they were related, he thought.

As it happened, there was a connection of sorts. Shapiro also resided on Valley Road, although he had never met Ken. When Zach called him, Shapiro already knew about the case. It was on the front page of the region's major newspaper, the *Asbury Park Press*. A four-column headline trumpeted, "Dentist charged with killing his wife and dumping body."

Zach explained the situation, emphasizing what he said was the untold story of Teresa's drug addiction. Shapiro said that unfortunately he'd recently been elected a member of the Manalapan Township Council and thus couldn't accept the case because of conflict of interest. He would, however, appear with Ken at the arraignment.

Ken elaborated on Teresa's drug habit to Shapiro, a youthful attorney with a child of his own. In the three days preceding that Sunday morning, Ken said, she had been so wired on cocaine that she hadn't slept at all. By then she was out of her mind.

There'd be flashbulbs popping around the courthouse, Shapiro said. Ken was to keep his cool. Let *him* do all the talking. He'd plead Ken not guilty. A trial date would be set, and he would be returned to jail. But that was a formality. When Superior Court reconvened the following week, he would request a bail reduction. Because of Ken's obvious roots in the community, he was confident he would get it.

And from what Ken was telling him, there were plenty of mitigating circumstances. Murder was not in the cards, he assured Ken. Manslaughter or even an acquittal was likely when all the facts were known. Temporary insanity just might be the ticket. He told Ken that he'd recommend several defense lawyers. Ken could choose the one he liked.

As a result of Shapiro's bravura performance at the arraignment, the next day's headline read, "Suspect's lawyer asserts slain wife abused infant son." Shapiro was quoted as saying, "I believe that the evidence will show his wife was a drug abuser and did harm to the child, and that precipitated the incident that caused her death."

Zach Taylor's comments to reporters made news as well. "Our daughter-in-law had a real drug problem. It was so bad it was threatening and affecting the baby."

Zach also called Marilyn Hope and told her that what had happened was Teresa's fault. After Ken had found his wife doing oral sex on his son, he went after her. "She picked up a barbell, and tried to hit him, and he hit her with it," she remembered Zach saying.

Then, after his arraignment, Marilyn nervously took a collect call from Ken.

"I don't want you to think I'm a monster," he said. "Do you know what she did?"

"Yes, your father told me."

"My attorney says I have a case because of what she was doing to my son. And she tried to hit me. What would you do if it were your child?"

"I have no idea."

"That's my point," he said.

"Look, I don't know what to believe about anything anymore."

"When this is taken care of, I still want to be with you and Astrid. I still love you. You have to know that. I've been telling you that for months. I'm not just saying it now."

She felt herself beginning to unravel. "All I know is that I want to stay by myself for the rest of my life."

"You're just saying that today."

"I can't believe that you could have come to your own daughter's house knowing what happened. Why are you calling me? They're going to want to know why."

"Listen," he said, "the first time I felt good was now when I called and got a busy signal and I knew I would get through to you. Talking to you gives me strength. You're not implicated in any of this."

"I know I'm not implicated."

"I mean, in case you have any feelings of guilt, you

know, about saying you hoped you hadn't pushed her to this."

"Look, let's get this straight. I said that I hoped she didn't commit suicide because she thought something was going on between us."

Any second, she thought, she'd fall apart. "I'm going to hang up," she said. "God bless you."

"Please, wait. Has anyone, you know, talked to you?"

"Not yet."

"I talked to my lawyer about Connecticut. He said nobody knows about Connecticut. It's off the record. The charges were dropped. It doesn't have to be mentioned."

She remained silent, afraid to say that everything was bound to come out, that she would have to tell the truth.

"I wrote you a letter," he said. "After you read it, if you don't want to talk to me, I won't bother you again as long as you live—or I live. I think about suicide all the time. I told the psychologist here that I can't get the picture out of my mind about what she was doing."

His voice started to quaver. "If you don't want to have anything to do with me," he said, "I'll go to Indiana and live with my parents and raise my son there."

"Good."

Then, suddenly, he said, "They will never keep me away from you and Astrid."

"Just exactly what does that mean?"

"She's my daughter. I'm her father."

"Yes, that's right, you are her father," Marilyn said, bursting into tears. And then she did hang up. The next day she changed her unlisted phone number. It was the last time she spoke to Ken.

• • •

The funeral mass for Teresa was held in her old parish church, St. Charles, on Wednesday, November 21.

In her grief for her dead sister, a month away from having her own child, Celeste clutched that part of Teresa that yet remained, *a part of herself as well*, she thought—baby Philip.

When her father and brother went to Pennsylvania that

Saturday, when the police were saying maybe it's her and maybe it isn't, she had forced herself to believe that it was not Teresa. These things didn't happen to you; they happened to people you read about in the newspapers. Jeff was working the three-to-eleven ferry shift and she had not wanted to be alone that evening, so she'd gone to a girl-friend's house. That had buoyed her spirits because her girlfriend's husband was a New York City cop, and he had talked about missing persons and the procedures which were followed and how more often than not the person missing was found or reappeared.

When Jeff phoned after getting the call from Al, he did not speak to her. He just said, "Tell Celeste to come home," and she had thought that at worst he might be a little annoyed that she hadn't been there to greet him.

One look at Jeff's desolate face was enough. "I'm sorry," he said.

"I knew it!" she screamed. "She's dead. That bastard killed her!"

Celeste bent over her swollen belly, flailing her knees and thighs with her fists, moaning through her tears. She began beating them against the wall. Jeff pulled her away, and she began hammering her fists against him. He did not try to stop her.

Spent, she finally stopped on her own. He helped her to a chair. "Where's Daddy and my brother?" she asked, and Jeff said that they must still be on their way back from Pennsylvania. She thought about her mother at the Rozeks. She had spoken to Louise earlier in the day. "Ma," she had said, "let's wait and see." She thought about calling her now, but she did not know if Louise knew.

"Can I get you something?" Jeff said.

She'd give anything for a stiff vodka, she thought. But she had given up alcohol during her pregnancy. She yearned for a cigarette, but she had stopped smoking as well. "Yes," she said, "some water."

Jeff remembered how she suddenly shook her head and stared wide-eyed at him. "Where is he?" she said. "He could come and kill us all. Did the police find him?"

"I don't know," Jeff said. Her concern was real, he thought. *How* did you deal with a murderer? You didn't know what to expect anymore.

He got her into bed, but sleep was out of the question. "Oh, sweet Jesus," she said, cradling her head against his shoulder. "I hurt all over so much. My poor, poor sister."

She began to weep again.

In the middle of the night, Celeste bolted upright. "Where's the baby?" she said. "The baby! We've got to get the baby! Are you with me?"

"All the way," he said without hesitation. Later he would think how momentous a turning point it was for both of them, and for the rest of the Benignos.

In the morning they went to the Rozeks. Around four in the afternoon, Bob Fausak phoned from Manalapan and said that Ken had confessed. Fausak did not go into any details.

His call was an anticlimax. At the Rozeks the mood had moved from anguish to anger to guilt.

"You know, once it happened, there was no question who did it," Jeff said. "I mean, nobody said, 'Was it Ken?' You said, 'That miserable fuck,' because everyone knew. And all of the anger from Acapulco came out then. Not only the anger that now we knew for sure, definitely, that he had done it to her there, but anger at each other that we kind of went along with a phony story. That we had sidestepped what was staring us in the face, that something of that magnitude had happened at that time, and so we should have been able to prevent *this* and we didn't. Look, I can only speak for myself, but there was a lot of guilt about it. In real life, of course, there was nothing anybody could have done to prevent it. But like, all of these emotions, all of a sudden, they hit you, the fact that Teresa was gone, the fact that we hadn't done anything about Acapulco, the fact that we couldn't even get this bastard in our hands, to choke him ourselves. I'm here to tell you that if Phil and him were in a room at the same time, I wouldn't want to be between them. And Phil, I guarantee you, would be the only one walking out of that room. Like if you saw

Phil sitting there, you'd understand. This was his sister, he loved her so much, they were so close."

In the evening Phil returned with Jeff and Celeste to their apartment. Phil said he was going to lie down in the bedroom. A little later, Celeste said that she was going in to see how he was.

After a while, Jeff, concerned, looked in on them. Phil was on his side facing the wall, knees drawn up, his fingers entwined as if in prayer. Celeste lay behind him, her arms locked tightly around his neck. Both of them were asleep.

The next day, after Ken's arraignment, Celeste called the Manalapan house. Zach answered. "We'd like to see the baby," she said.

At that time she, like the rest of the Benigno family, was unaware of the story Ken had given the police about why he had killed Teresa.

Zach was all cordiality on the phone. "No problem," he said, and a visit was arranged for that evening.

Al and Louise accompanied Jeff and Celeste. At first, both families seemed to be united in tragedy. There were subdued greetings, some tears. Shortly after their arrival, Jean put Philip in his crib upstairs. He was obviously cranky and tired. Although the Benignos did not know it, the Taylors had just returned with him from seeing Ken in jail. They also did not yet know that the murder had taken place in the house, that Teresa's body was dragged right by the sofa and chairs they were sitting on.

Jean served apples for refreshments.

Then Al, addressing Zach, said, "I want you to know that we don't hold you responsible for what your son did. He's a grown man. It's his responsibility, not yours, and nothing is being held against you."

Zach's mouth tightened.

"We're here to discuss Philip," Celeste said.

His face flushing slightly, Zach said, "There's nothing to discuss."

It was at that moment, Jeff recalled, that the battle lines were irrevocably drawn.

"What's that supposed to mean?" Celeste said.

119

"Philip is ours. Kenny wants us to have him and we're going to have him."

*Kenny wants it,* Celeste remembered thinking. This creep murdered my sister, and his father is sitting there telling us what he wants.

"That's my dead sister's baby you're talking about," she said. "There is something to discuss."

"No, there isn't. As soon as we can, we're leaving for Indiana with him."

"When?"

"Thursday."

For once, Celeste restrained herself. She shot a warning glance at Jeff and her parents. They were all on the same wavelength. If they said anything threatening, the Taylors might pack up on the spot and take Philip with them, and nobody could do a thing about it.

"I hope we can see Philip again before you go," Celeste said as sweetly as she could.

"Certainly. Just call first."

Outside, in the car, Celeste said, "They're not normal people. Nothing to discuss! Can you believe it?"

"Look, we lucked out with them telling us what they're planning," Jeff told her.

"We have to do something right away," Celeste said.

The next morning they were at the office of the Benigno family lawyer in Staten Island. He'd have to retain a New Jersey attorney, he said, but don't worry, he would be riding herd on it himself. And on Wednesday, the day Teresa was buried, "show cause" papers were served on the Taylors. A "show cause" order was a swifter remedy than the usual legal motion. It was used in instances of immediate, irreparable harm. At issue, the papers said, was a custody situation concerning a five-month-old child whose father had been arrested for the murder of his mother. "Upon information and belief," there was every likelihood that the parents of the defendant now in control of the child, a legal resident of New Jersey, would shortly remove him from the state's jurisdiction. Pending the outcome of the defendant's trial, Jeff and Celeste asked for custody of the infant.

A hearing on the "show cause" order was set for the following Tuesday, November 27. In the meantime, Zach and Jean were effectively prevented from leaving New Jersey with Philip. They could depart themselves, but not with him.

In jail, Ken reacted in fury. How could Jean and Zach have been so stupid? Al and Louise must have been the prime movers in this, he reasoned. The last person whom he suspected was that "dingbat," Celeste.

By now Celeste knew about the accusation against Teresa that Ken was giving as the motivation for his lethal assault.

Her fury more than matched his.

• • •

Forensic technicians had found carpet padding fibers in the trunk of the Cutlass that matched those in the downstairs room being renovated. At one end of a dumbbell bar without weights, there was a brownish stain. Tests showed the stain to be positive for human blood. The bar was lying under Ken's work-out bench.

So many blows to her head would have caused extensive bleeding, but there was no visible sign of it. Quite a thorough clean-up job, Bob Fausak thought, for a fellow supposedly in the grips of an emotional frenzy.

That same Wednesday night a Luminol test was scheduled. Luminol was a chemical that reacted to the slightest traces of blood no matter how much a surface had been scrubbed, traces that could not be seen even with a magnifying glass. The process was conducted in complete darkness.

Fausak obtained a second search warrant and informed the Taylors. He went out to the house with two forensic experts from the prosecutor's office and two chemists from the New Jersey State Police Laboratory. They waited until it was pitch-black outside. Still, all the shades were lowered in case of a passing car. Fausak instructed the Taylors to retire to their upstairs bedroom and turn off the lights.

The Luminol was in a bottle that looked to Fausak like

the syrup jars in restaurants. It had a spray dispenser on top. "You just spray it," one of the chemists told him, "and let it settle and see what you can see."

The chemists first tried the laundry room, where Ken said Teresa had swung a dumbbell at him. But only a small spot on the washing machine faintly "luminesced." They sprayed the room being renovated. Nothing.

In the passageway outside this second room, though, there was a very obvious reaction, an eerie greenish light suddenly rising from the floor. The chemists tracked it around the corner into the living room area and, retreating slowly now, spraying in front of them, they moved across the floor past the kitchen to the garage door and into and along the side of the garage.

Fausak had never experienced anything like it. He felt as if he were in a sci-fi movie. Initially, there was the same pale green light. It got greener and brighter. It began to glow. And through its luminosity he could see the trail of blood. The trail was solid, but with streaks in it, as though someone had taken a big wet mop and wrung it out and dragged it along the floor. The length of the bloody trail measured some fifty-five feet.

The shimmering glow hung in the air, above Fausak's knees. It had become so bright that he could see the faces of the forensic men and the chemists. He looked up and at the top of the stairs, he saw the ghostly visage of Ken Taylor's father staring down at the scene.

Photographs were taken. Then one of the forensic men switched on the lights. And the trail of blood instantly vanished. It was as if Fausak had dreamed it all.

He asked the chemists, "What if it's a surface, like a table top, and it's Formica, or some kind of plastic that's real smooth, would Luminol work?"

"Sure," he was told. "Nothing's perfectly smooth in this world. There's always a crack or a pore, some minute imperfection that blood gets into. Even if you clean it up, there's a residue that Luminol reacts to, and you saw what happens next."

Maybe, Fausak thought, Ken Taylor's story about his

wife running into the laundry room or the sewing room, the room where his weights were, and picking up a dumbbell bar and swinging it at him before he got it away and gave it to her—maybe all of that wasn't the real story. There was hardly any sign of blood there.

The trail of blood began in the passageway by the entrance to the second room. Maybe he'd gone into the laundry room following some altercation and grabbed the dumbbell bar and went after her.

Later, at the Olde Silver Tavern, a popular hangout a couple of miles down the road from the Manalapan police station, Fausak met with Guy McCormick. McCormick had been busy in the prosecutor's office taking statements from the Rozeks, the Benignos, Jeff and Celeste, Ken's parents and the New York City detective Robert Negliaccio, who had called when Ken dropped out of sight. In questioning Negliaccio, it became clear that Ken was using his relationship with him to find out just what the cops in Manalapan did and didn't know.

"You think he came up with the sodomy stuff at the last minute?" Fausak said.

"No," McCormick said. "I think he had it all worked out in advance if the rest of it didn't fly."

# Chapter

## SEVEN

Paul Chaiet, the first assistant prosecutor for Monmouth County, was a stocky, powerfully built man with a bull neck and an incongruously low voice that really made you sit up when he raised it. He kept in shape jogging and weight-lifting. It was easy to picture him as an outstanding guard in football at Albright College in Pennsylvania where he completed his undergraduate studies. He also had tried for the baseball team, with less success. "I thought I was the next Yogi Berra," he said, "but it didn't work out."

He married a schoolteacher while he was still at Rutgers Law School, and they had two children, a boy and girl. He had always wanted to do trial work and had an affinity for law enforcement. So after a desultory year with a private firm specializing in civil matters, he joined the prosecutor's office as an assistant in 1973. For the past six years, since 1978, he'd been the first assistant, handling major felonies, including a number of homicides.

And he saw at once that Ken Taylor was going to be the slipperiest kind of murder case. *Because there was no motive*. Once you discounted Ken's explanation of what had occurred in the Manalapan house, which Chaiet immediately did, there was no motive to offer a jury, no robbery, for instance, no money at stake, no mistress in the woodpile, none of the usual suspects. There had only been two people in the house at the time. One was dead and the other one wasn't telling the truth, and there was little likelihood that he ever would.

Chaiet didn't have to prove that Ken had killed Teresa. He'd already admitted to that. It was the circumstances of that killing that counted. He had to prove that what Ken was saying wasn't so, that the events that Ken described as having taken place on Sunday morning, November 11, were not the facts, that he had "knowingly and purposefully" murdered his wife.

And a murder conviction was what Chaiet wanted. Any lesser conviction would be an unacceptable defeat, a miscarriage of justice.

The murder of Teresa Taylor was as egregious a case as Chaiet had encountered. The only one that could touch it had occurred in Chaiet's hometown, Oceanport, and it had an especially personal impact. In this case, when Chaiet viewed the victim, a woman with twenty-three stab wounds, he recognized her as the mother of his children's babysitter. The prime suspects were the victim's husband and his girlfriend.

More than a year and a half passed, though, without enough evidence for indictments. Then, in the middle of the night, around three A.M., Chaiet got a call from Bill Lucia in the major crimes unit. The girlfriend had just phoned him from New York City and confessed to stabbing the wife on instructions from the husband. She had apparently broken up with the husband and was sore at him for getting her into this situation.

The girlfriend was brought in and given a deal to turn state's witness. Then a lengthy telephone conversation between her and the husband rehashing the murder plot was recorded.

Chaiet learned valuable lessons from that case. One was

patience. Another was an insight into the sociopathic mind. Polygraphs were not admissible in New Jersey courts. But both the girlfriend and the husband had volunteered to take one in an effort to demonstrate their innocence to Chaiet—and passed with flying colors. Still another was a reminder never to presume what a jury will do. During the trial, the husband continued to maintain that he was not guilty. His defense was he had been entrapped by his former girlfriend in the recorded conversation that became the principal evidence against him.

Chaiet was sure he'd get an immediate conviction. But the jury remained out for hours. He never forgot sitting in his office, playing the tape again and again, trying to reassure himself that nobody could listen to that tape—with all of its blood-curdling details—and not convict for murder. And finally the jury did. The debate in the jury room had been about the relative degree of guilt; who had been the key instigator?

And now in the Taylor case, he not only had this bizarre crime, but also an equally bizarre—and novel—justification for it. He'd never heard anything like it, and that was worrisome. There would be nothing he could hark back to, nothing where he could declare to a jury with appropriate sarcasm, "We've heard that one before, haven't we?"

Taylor could claim insanity, but the old McNaughton rule out of English law on that subject—did the defendant know the difference between right and wrong?—still applied in New Jersey. Temporary insanity was a possibility, but then how *temporary* could it be when Taylor carefully scrubbed down a house in an attempt to wipe out every vestige of the crime, carted the body around the country for the better part of four days, sticking as long as he could to the story that Teresa had gone off on her own for drug treatment? Chaiet was most concerned about verdicts of manslaughter with reckless disregard to life or manslaughter committed in the heat of passion. After all, Taylor hadn't hit his wife in the head one time with a dumbbell bar, he'd done it nine times. Chaiet had seen the photographs, and they were gruesome.

The more he thought about it, the more he was sure that Ken had not just come out of the woodwork. He had to have a history. You didn't just up and do this. Chaiet told Lucia and Guy McCormick in the major crimes unit and Fausak from the Manalapan police that it was essential to comb through Ken's entire past.

"What we do is we find out everything we can about this guy," Chaiet said. "Start with the other wife."

•  •  •

But Marilyn wouldn't cooperate. When Lieutenant Lucia contacted her, she said to talk to her lawyer, a Pittsburgh attorney named Carl Gainor. Then she notified Gainor to keep her out of this. She couldn't shed any light on the "incident." It also seemed that she had a few unresolved problems about Ken, Teresa and herself:

*He said she couldn't understand why I had a house & she didn't, etc., etc., etc.,* Marilyn wrote. *Well, in the first year he bought her a house, car, etc. & was upset that I didn't let Astrid go to his house. Our divorce argument was that he see her in my house. Visits were less frequent, usually after work & he payed [sic] me by signing insurance checks over to me. He was upset with me. Visits were to be on Sundays & apparently his wife wouldn't let him come.*

*Around April last year, Ken started telling me that Teresa was on drugs & stealing money from insurance co's. She went into premature labor at 6 months of pregnancy. So I assumed the drug business was true. He said he wanted to leave her but couldn't until the baby was born & well started in life. He said he was keeping proof of the drug abuse & thefts so he could get custody of the child. After the child was born he wrote a letter expressing sincere regret for any problems he's caused people in his life.*

*It seemed the shoe was on the other foot & Ken had really learned about life, responsibility, caring. Here he was in a situation similar to the one he put me in when he was doing drugs. There were sometimes that he said he was concerned for the safety of his child because his wife just couldn't cope. He said he wanted to leave, get custody of his child & be with his "family" (Astrid & myself).*

*He visited us in Pa. and at that time he told me that she had taken off because she was using cocaine & was going to straighten herself out.*

*You ask if I've changed my opinion of Ken?*

*I've known an extremely gentle man who left me with a note in a tea cannister.*

*I've seen a man who delights in growing flowers, feeds all stray animals & can play for hours with a child, try to take my life.*

*I've heard him say mean things & return with roses.*

*I've heard him express regret for any pain he's caused anyone with a hint that he may not be able to go on living.*

*I've seen this man cry profusely at a sad movie—just months ago. Now I've heard this man's father saying that his son's wife was doing oral sex to her son, Ken went after her & she tried to kill him with a barbell. He then hit her.*

*Have I changed my opinions—?*

*I have no opinions, I'm not a doctor. I'm devastated. I just don't know what to think about anything, anymore.*

Gainor tried to soft-sell Chaiet. Look, she wants to put this behind her, he said. It's been too traumatic. She doesn't believe she can contribute anything. She did not know about the body in the car. She was not privy to anything. She just wants to be left alone.

Chaiet got tough. Marilyn was a critical witness. He couldn't subpoena her directly because she wasn't a New Jersey resident. But he had another avenue, the federal route, under a statute called the Uniform Act to Secure the Attendance of Witnesses. If she refused to talk to his investigators, he would use it to bring her in front of a grand jury, a less pleasant option. "Believe me," he said, "I'm not kidding."

Gainor explained the pros and cons to his client, and she caved in.

On November 27, Lucia and Fausak flew to Pittsburgh

for the interview in Gainor's office. Fausak noticed how cool she was to them, then fidgety as hell. He expected that. What he didn't expect was how quickly Marilyn would give them stunning information, almost in relief, as if all of her pent-up emotions had been uncapped. It happened during the preliminary, sort of getting-to-know-you conversation before a recorded formal statement was taken.

Lucia asked if her ex-husband had ever been physically violent, and, just like that, she said yes, he had tried to kill her once when she was in bed, half-asleep.

Lucia didn't blink an eye, nodding slowly instead, sympathetically, as though what she was saying confirmed something he'd known all along.

"And where was that again?"

"Waterford," she said, her words rushing out. "In Connecticut when he was in the Navy. I reported it to the police."

Stone-faced, Fausak excused himself to call McCormick back in Freehold.

Then they learned for the first time that he had still another former wife.

"Do you know what his previous wife's name, previous to you, was?" Lucia asked.

"At the time? Emily Taylor."

"Are you aware of her maiden name?"

"Oh, I believe it was Latrelle. Yeah."

"Do you have any information regarding their relationship, or any problems that they may have had?"

"Not really. It was just something where he indicated that he had previously been madly in love with some girl. She left him and he felt like he'd never love anybody again like he loved that girl, and he was dating Emily and some other girls. Emily was the first one that was interested in getting married, so he decided when he was twenty-one it was about time, what else would he do anyway? and he got married and he said from the beginning it wasn't right. According to him, they would split up, go back, split up, go back, and at one point she got pregnant and later admitted that she did it on purpose to hold the marriage together, and they agreed to stay together until the baby was born."

"During this time that you had been dating, or that you were married, up to this point, did you have any marital problems?"

"Yes."

"Could you tell me what they were?" Lucia asked.

"When we were married? Well, I just had a feeling that he was screwing around, you know."

She recalled finding an unsigned note to Ken—"Where are you?"—slipped under their apartment door. Then she got crabs. "I spoke to a nurse or I called some dental clinic, and said, 'Is it possible to get crabs working in a clinic?' and she said well, yes, touching these people, you know, you could get them. Now, at another time, I got scabies, which is like little insects that get under your skin, and then it was, well, those are the dirty sailors, but there was some question in my mind."

She wept when she talked about the harrowing night after she returned from visiting her cancer-stricken father in New York and Ken tried to chloroform her.

"You say Ken was examined at the Navy hospital in the psychiatric ward. Do you know the name of the doctor or doctors that examined him?"

"There was a Doctor Smith. I don't know whether he was a captain, it was a Navy rank. I cannot remember his first name. And another doctor, Bill Pettit."

"Did you have any opportunity to have any discussions with them concerning their findings?"

"I went to see Ken and Doctor Smith said, 'Do you really want to see him?' I said yes, and he said, and I don't know if this is in the right sequence or not, 'Why would you want to see him? All he's interested in is doing you in.'

"That scared me, but I thought it was kind of strange that a doctor was talking like that. He also said to me, 'There's plenty of fish in the sea. You're an attractive woman. What do you need with a guy like this?'

"And I did go home. I didn't see Ken. I was upset."

She started crying again. After a break, Lucia said, "Okay, can we continue on with Dr. Smith?"

"Okay. Subsequently, he called me on the phone and said that I had better call the police in regard to this matter because he had to release Ken from the hospital, and he felt that he was a homicidal maniac. If he got out, all he'd want to do is finish off the job. I said to him, 'How come you have to release him, if that's the way you feel?' and it seemed like he wanted me to report it to the police. There was something about that the Navy couldn't do it. I called any number of captains or whatever that I could think of and said how could this possibly be? How could he say this and then say he was going to let him out? I wanted Ken to be taken care of. I figured he was really sick. And yet at the same time I was afraid that he was going to be let out. So I called the Navy chaplain and we sat down and soul searched what to do . . . Consequently, it was reported to the police. I called the police. I told them."

"Now I think you said that there was also another doctor involved, Doctor Pettit. What basically did he tell you?"

"Doctor Pettit said that, as much as I can remember, it was an isolated incident. It was drug-related, and that the diagnosis of Ken was gross lack of adjustment to adult life. He told me that Ken had never dealt with a problem in his life. He gave me an example of constantly putting things in a closet until one day you cannot get any more in and the whole door opens up and everything that has ever bothered you comes out. And that Ken was under a lot of pressure because he was driving back and forth to New York to help me to go see my father and not too much attention was being given to caring about him. He was being left alone. I'm trying to think of what else. Low self-esteem, which he put into a whole. He explained a lot of things that were found at the time this incident took place."

"As a result of this incident," Lucia asked, "did you learn anything about, number one, Ken's drug abuse and, two, his relationship or other relationships he was having with women?"

"Yes. Ken said he had taken three black beauties that

night and was hearing voices, and it came out in therapy that he had been using a lot of drugs. I think they said speed, uppers, downers, whatever, and they found pornography in the wall of the house, like behind the plaster boards."

"Who found it?"

"The detectives. They searched the house."

"Basically, what kind of pornography? Did it involve children?"

"The detectives told me that it was homosexual and heterosexual. One of them said did I want to see it? He said it's just your regular homosexual/heterosexual stuff, so I said, 'No.' It was, I think, in the garbage that there was a picture found of him, like a Polaroid picture, naked from the neck down and also a letter applying to a sex club in New York. He didn't want his name used because he was a dentist, and he didn't want to be involved in homosexual activity if he could help it."

"Did you ever learn of any specific relationships he had?"

"Well, there was one black girl that I know of that I could not believe, he's so prejudiced, and they said that was part of the low self-esteem. What he did was to get involved with people that he didn't even think anything of."

"Did you ever witness Ken using or abusing drugs?"

"The only thing I ever saw him do was smoke marijuana."

"On how regular a basis?"

"Just occasionally."

"You never saw him take any type of pills or take or use another drug, cocaine or anything else?"

"No."

"You said Ken stayed at the hospital for psychiatric evaluation and then moved into Bachelor Quarters on the base."

"Right. He went for group therapy and alcohol abuse courses. The Navy provided us family counseling. We'd meet for lunch, you know, and dinner, stuff like that. We even went, I think we went for dancing lessons. It was all in an effort to get things back to a normal keel. He went to AA sessions. I went to some with him because it was important to understand alcohol abuse. The Navy doesn't deal in drugs, they didn't do drug rehabilitation, they said."

"Did you get back together?"

"What happened is I was still going down to see my father and when things were calming down, I had asked him to go in and feed the cats, or you can stay in the house on weekends while I'm in New York, and it just kind of went from there."

"You said that you and Ken lived in Staten Island for about a year and a half after his discharge. What caused you to separate?"

"Well, I was having difficulty adjusting sexually because of everything that happened in Connecticut, which the doctors had told us would happen. But we weren't making too much progress. At that point in time, I believe he was carrying on with the receptionist in his office."

"Is that Teresa, the same Teresa that is the victim of this particular homicide?" Lucia asked.

"Right. Teresa was his receptionist."

"What was your relationship with him from then on?"

"Well, basically we really tried to keep friendly. I always thought it was a tragedy that we weren't able to work out our problems. I realized I was having problems dealing with what happened to me. It was, like, sad that we weren't able to live with each other after going through all of that, that we just didn't make it."

"After your divorce, did he keep up his alimony and support payments?"

"Well, he did fairly well until he got married. There would be weeks when I didn't get anything. I'd think, Oh, God, how am I going to pay these bills, but then he'd come up with checks, large-amount checks to cover back periods. I would say that basically I've gotten all the child support but I haven't gotten any alimony when you come down to the figures."

Lucia led Marilyn through Ken's marriage to Teresa and the Acapulco "mugging," as Ken had described it. Then he asked, "What was your relationship with Ken after you moved to Pittsburgh?"

"It was still friendly. He still expressed wishes that he had always expressed to be back with myself and Astrid."

"Did he indicate to you that Teresa was abusing drugs, abusing their child, or anything like that?"

"Well, I think it was last year. I remember because it was shortly before I was considering selling the house that he was telling me that she was pregnant and he told me that she had been taking drugs. She was taking codeine, writing out prescriptions on his pads, forging his name, that she was signing his checks and taking money. I figured he must be telling the truth because he said she went into premature labor and I thought to myself that if you're taking drugs, that could do it. But I'm no doctor. I just told him, 'You should really tell her doctor because what about the baby?'"

"Did he ever indicate to you that she ever abused the child?"

"He had just said on different occasions when he was coming over and didn't come that there were extenuating circumstances like, 'You don't know what it's like at home. I'm concerned for the safety of the child.' He was never really specific about it. He just said she doesn't seem to be able to cope."

"In Pittsburgh, on Tuesday, November thirteen, were you visited by Ken Taylor?"

"Was that the thirteenth? Two whole weeks in between, already? Yeah, yes, he came to the house."

"Did you see his car?"

"Yeah, it was parked out in front of my house."

"Did he ever indicate to you in any way that he had any involvement in Teresa's death or disappearance?"

"No."

"Were you ever approached by Teresa's mother regarding any problems you might have had in your marriage with Ken?"

"Well, at the time the Acapulco incident had happened,

she was going on and on that her daughter was brutally beaten.''

"Is there any specific reason why you didn't tell her about the incident in Connecticut?"

"Uh, well, the psychiatrist said it was an isolated incident, a product of his problems at the time and, you know, how could I just say, 'Oh, well, he did this, this, and this, and ruin his life?' I still don't know what happened in Acapulco. They could have gotten mugged. So, you know, I really didn't know how to answer.''

Until then, listening to her, Bob Fausak felt sorry for Marilyn. He didn't after that.

• • •

At the major crimes unit in Freehold, when Fausak phoned him from Pittsburgh, Guy McCormick put in a call to the Waterford Police Department. He was transferred to Detective Sergeant Joseph San Juan. Sure, San Juan said, he remembered the case. How could he forget it?

It was, McCormick reflected, the ultimate unfunny good news/bad news story. The good news was that San Juan had confirmed everything Taylor's ex-wife said. The bad news was that Paul Chaiet couldn't use it. McCormick put it all in a formal report:

The undersigned contacted the Waterford, CT, PD, in order to ascertain whether or not Kenneth Taylor had any contact with that agency.

Det. Sgt. Joseph San Juan said he believed that Kenneth Z. Taylor was a lieutenant stationed at the Groton Naval Base and that on April 16, 1979, Kenneth Z. Taylor tried to kill his wife who at that time was Marilyn Hope.

According to Sgt. San Juan, Miss Hope was in bed when Kenneth Taylor stuck a chloroform soaked sponge in her face and nearly smothered her with it. Sgt. San Juan advised that Taylor was arrested and charged with attempted homicide but the case was later dismissed because Marilyn Hope made an impassioned plea before the Court to have the charges dropped.

San Juan further advised that during the course of their investigation, the police found all sorts of sexual related correspondence. The correspondence was to various smear type magazines and nude photographs of Kenneth Taylor were also discovered. These nude photos were of Taylor's genital area and had been apparently taken by Taylor himself while utilizing a mirror.

This writer was advised by Sgt. San Juan that since the charges against Taylor were dismissed, he is not permitted to send this writer any of his reports concerning the investigation.

He did supply this writer with a name of a female who was believed to be Kenneth Taylor's wife prior to his marriage to Marilyn Hope. She is Emily Latrelle with an Indianapolis, Ind., residence. An attempt to contact Emily Latrelle was made at the number given, but there was no answer.

Chaiet couldn't believe it.

He phoned an assistant in the appellate bureau of the Connecticut Chief State's Attorney, explained why he was calling, and was told that once someone dropped charges in a criminal case in Connecticut, it was over, *erased*.

What's more, none of the investigative documents could be used in another jurisdiction. It was all in Connecticut's erasure laws, General Statutes, paragraphs 54–142a (a).

"Listen, I really need that material. I thought we were all on the same side," Chaiet said, fuming.

"I'm sorry," the assistant state's attorney said. "I wish there was something I could do."

• • •

The same day that Marilyn Hope was being interviewed by Lucia and Fausak, a hearing was held in the Monmouth County Juvenile and Domestic Relations Court regarding custody of Philip Andrew Taylor, age five months, Judge Julia L. Ashbey presiding.

Having prevented Ken's parents from taking Philip back to Indiana, Jeff and Celeste were now asking for full custody. Barry Shapiro, the lawyer who had represented Ken at his arraignment, appeared in behalf of the Taylors. The infant could not be in better, more experienced hands, he argued. Not only did the baby's father, who had not been convicted of anything, desire that he be placed with Jean and Zach, but also his late mother had often declared that she wanted him raised by his paternal grandparents if anything ever befell her and her husband.

Judge Ashbey temporized, ordering a shared custody pending the outcome of Ken's trial. The child would remain with the Taylors at the Manalapan house except from Tuesday at eight A.M. until six P.M. on Thursday when he would be with Celeste and Jeff in Staten Island. The judge also ruled that when Celeste entered a hospital to have her own baby, these visits would cease until her obstetrician forwarded a letter to the court stating she was physically able to care for Philip. The thought that the Taylors would be bringing him to see her sister's murderer tormented Celeste. But at least her certainty that she would never see him again if he were taken to Indiana was no longer a concern, for now anyway.

• • •

Chaiet had no direct interest in these proceedings. Still, he had them monitored in case something pertinent occurred. And it did.

Investigator Barbara Coleman reported that the doctor who delivered Philip testified that there was no indication that Teresa Taylor "had been or was on drugs of any sort when Philip was born."

• • •

For Chaiet, even if Teresa had been on cocaine night and day, it didn't come close to justifying what was done to her. After reading the autopsy findings and seeing the photographs, he had no trouble concluding that if anyone had been deranged by drugs, it was Ken.

The medical language did not begin to communicate the sheer horror of the damage. "MASSIVE HEAD, FACE, AND CRANIOCEREBRAL INJURIES DUE TO BLUNT FORCE TRAUMA," it said. "FRACTURES, COMPOUND AND COMMINUTED, BASE

AND VAULT OF SKULL, BILATERAL, WITH FOCAL EXTRUSION OF BRAIN. ACUTE DIFFUSE SUBARACHNOID HEMORRHAGE, BILATERAL, SEVERE, CEREBRAL HEMISPHERES, BASILAR AND SUBTENTORIAL.''

Ken Taylor had pounded the fourteen-inch-long steel dumbbell bar with its wicked, protruding clamp, like the business end of a hammer, over and over again into her face and head with unbelievable force. Her mouth was smashed in. Most of the blows had struck the left side of her face and head. One had slammed in just above Teresa's left eye below the brow. Another was right above that, in her forehead. Four more surrounded her left ear, one on each side, two higher up. One of them resulted in a bloody gaping wound a full two and a half inches long and half an inch wide, through which brain matter oozed. Three additional blows had been delivered to the back of her head through which more brain matter leaked, penetrating so deep and landing with such ferocity that they shattered her skull into three separate sections.

Still, Chaiet wanted drug screening for codeine and cocaine. The medical examiner in Pennsylvania assigned the task to a nationally recognized bioanalytical toxicology lab headed by a Dr. Frederick Rieders. The report said that 121 nanograms per milliliter of codeine had been found in Teresa's body. There wasn't any cocaine. But there was benzoylecgonine—.04 parts per million—which was a breakdown product of cocaine.

Chaiet called Rieders. He was sure to be a prosecution witness, and it was important to know how he would phrase his findings in plain English.

After talking to him, Chaiet felt pretty good. The amount of codeine, Rieders said, was a normal therapeutic anti-pain dosage.

"Would your findings corroborate or negate a contention that at the time this individual died, she was drug-crazed by cocaine?"

The level of benzoylecgonine indicated recreational, not abusive, use of the drug, Rieders said. Cocaine started breaking down right away, so it was hard to tell whether it had been absorbed the day death occurred. It could have easily been two or three days before. In any event, there wasn't enough to induce a deranged or crazed state.

There was also a .04 alcohol reading. Almost certainly, though, this was due to the body's decomposition.

"That's what you would testify to?" Chaiet said.

"Of course."

On a medical basis, short of no evidence of cocaine at all, it was the best news Chaiet could have gotten. As far as he was concerned, that was it. Still, whoever Taylor's defense lawyer turned out to be, it was a safe bet he'd try to work the cocaine angle for all it was worth. And who knew how this would affect some juror pondering a murder conviction? Hey, she did do coke, didn't she?

On that score, Chaiet couldn't discount the possibility that the defense would come up with a witness or witnesses who would swear that Teresa was addicted to cocaine. Sooner or later, before trial, he'd know that. Under New Jersey discovery statutes the prosecution had to disclose all the tangible evidence it planned to use. But so did the defense.

Chaiet wasn't going to wait around for any surprises. Besides digging into Ken Taylor's past, McCormick and Fausak were to unearth everything they could about Teresa. From then on, they worked together on nearly every investigative aspect of the case.

Like Fausak, Guy McCormick, then thirty-six, round-faced with no-nonsense eyes, came from a cop family. His dad had been in police work for forty-one years before retiring as chief of detectives for Monmouth County. Married with two sons, Guy had been dogged about improving his professional capabilities. He had started out as a dispatcher with the Manalapan police while pursuing a degree in criminal justice at Trenton State College. After becoming an investigator in the prosecutor's office in 1977, he continued his studies, earning an M.A. in public administration. By now, five years in the homicide division, with fifty-odd murder cases under his belt, had given him a less than salutary view of the human condition.

From the beginning, he found Ken's explanation of the events leading to her death not only ludicrous, but typical despite its grotesque details. Suspects in cases like this always reverted to type. As soon as they confessed, they trotted out a reason to exculpate themselves, to try to make themselves look better.

What did fascinate McCormick was the defendant himself. He hadn't encountered such dark reaches of the soul before. This wasn't a guy you instantly sensed was bad. On the surface everything was rosy. Ken was a professional man, charming, a dentist with a promising future, a nice house, a nice wife whom he claimed to love, a new baby boy, and suddenly all the information you're beginning to develop about him is totally contradictory. McCormick realized that he was dealing with truly unfathomable evil.

The first thing he and Fausak did was to check all the pharmacies in the Freehold and Manalapan area and along the Route 9 corridor leading to the Garden State Parkway and the New Jersey Turnpike into Staten Island. They found a number of codeine prescriptions, usually Tylenol #3, for Teresa. Others were for Phil Benigno—five in all—and for a Tom Taylor, Ken's brother. Neither cop then knew that Tom had a drug problem of his own and had visited Ken and Teresa.

Angela Rozek had already said that Teresa confided to her that Ken did cocaine and that she occasionally joined him. Then they interviewed Irene DeBlasio.

"What is your relationship to the deceased, Teresa Taylor, and how long have you known her?"

"Good friends, around twelve years. Until she started going out with Ken Taylor. Then I really didn't see her. We kept in touch once in a while. Then when she got back from Acapulco, I went to see her in the hospital. She wrote me a letter after she got pregnant. I called her and we began our friendship again. I would cut her hair and Ken's, and he did my dental work. I went to the baby shower that was held in her house. Then we, my boyfriend and I, started hanging out there on Sundays and would sleep over."

"When was the last time you saw Teresa Taylor?"

"Monday, November fifth. I went to the office for a dental visit. I told them not to make an appointment for the following Monday, as I was going to visit my sister in Michigan, and was going to be gone four or five days. I told them I was leaving Newark Airport early Sunday morning and was flying People's Express."

"After the office visit, when you told Ken and Teresa of your trip, did you see or speak to Teresa at all?"

"No."

"After arriving home from Michigan, did you speak to Ken Taylor?"

"Friday morning, I called and woke him up, around nine A.M., just before I went to work. I was worried and called, and asked if he'd heard from Teresa. He said no. During our conversation, I asked if maybe she had recalled Acapulco and her attack and he said, 'I don't know, why do you ask?' He said everyone thought she was with me, and so did he. He just didn't seem worried on the phone. I haven't spoken to him since."

"How often, and how many times, have you visited and stayed the night with the Taylors?"

"Six to eight times, the past three months."

"Did you ever see Ken Taylor assault Teresa, or see any indications that she had been assaulted?"

"None whatsoever."

"To your knowledge, did Teresa ever use or abuse any type of narcotic drugs?"

"She used to take diet pills all the time, and was on pills from the doctor during her pregnancy. She also was on codeine because of her teeth."

"The times that you stayed overnight at Teresa and Ken's house, was there any type of drug used socially?"

"Just once. There was cocaine there when we arrived. My boyfriend and I brought some marijuana with us. Ken and he smoked it, but Teresa wasn't offered because she didn't use it. Ken had cocaine. We were watching 'Star Search' and I asked Teresa to ask Ken if he had any cocaine to buy. She did, and later there was cocaine on the table. Ken didn't give it to us. It was just on the table. My boyfriend gave Ken fifty dollars. All of us, including Teresa, did the coke.''

"How many times, while at Ken and Teresa's house, did you all use cocaine?"

"One time. It was either the second or third visit."

"What led you to believe that Ken Taylor had cocaine, or could get cocaine?"

"Because he was a dentist, a doctor."

"On your other visits to the Taylor residence, or to the offices on Staten Island, did you observe Teresa or Ken using any type of drugs?"

"Just drinks. Teresa drank light, not a lot. That night we all got drunk—that night being when the cocaine was on the table."

"In your twelve-year association with Teresa, have you ever seen her under the influence of alcohol or drugs?"

"We would drink socially when we went to clubs, prior to her marriage. I never saw her use any drugs, just the ones for diets, as she worried about her weight."

"Did Teresa ever indicate to you any problems with Ken and their marriage?"

"None. She had mentioned to me that with the baby, the house and the business—that they had a lot of financial pressures."

"Did Teresa ever indicate to you any of her more intimate problems?"

"Just one time. The past month or so, my boyfriend mentioned that we were having sexual problems. Teresa mentioned that she had the same thing, and Ken just smiled. The remark was to the effect that I didn't want to have sex as often, or at all."

"Are you aware of the incident in Acapulco and what occurred?"

"I didn't recognize her in the hospital in Staten Island, she was so badly beaten and bruised. Later, the first time my boyfriend and I went over to her house, she brought out pictures from Acapulco and spoke at length about the incident. She said they had gone out for dinner, got boisterous at the table, and Ken advised he felt that Teresa possibly had insulted one of the waiters, and that's why someone got even with them. Ken went on to say that possibly the sliding glass door to the room was unlocked, and that they were both sleeping, and someone came in and hit them over the head. Teresa said that she recalled a pair of bare feet but nothing else."

Irene DeBlasio was going to make a hell of a witness, McCormick thought. Matter-of-fact, perfect pitch on truth. She didn't have to volunteer that one-time cocaine snorting. Put this together with the toxicology report and what Angela Rozek had said, and it was an ideal antidote to any defense claims that Teresa had been drug-crazed—and abusive to the baby.

* * *

You could not have found a better, more caring mother, Cindy Diaz told them. Teresa was always on the phone reporting little Philip's progress. Like Irene, Cindy had known Teresa since they were teenagers. They had drifted apart somewhat after Teresa met Ken, but she never saw Teresa doing drugs. Besides the Rozeks, Cindy was the last of Teresa's friends to see her alive on Saturday, November 10—in the morning when they'd gone shopping in Brooklyn.

"Did Teresa ever indicate any problems that she had with Ken?" McCormick asked.

"No, not really. Only that they had money problems." Cindy hesitated and then she said, "It seemed like she was afraid to get Ken upset. Like being late." That day after they got back from Brooklyn, Teresa had said, "I've got to go. I'm going to be late. If I don't pick him up on time, Ken will kill me."

They had been running behind schedule, Cindy said, because her husband had videotaped Teresa and the baby.

McCormick perked up at that. What was the tape like? Could he have a copy?

She hadn't seen it yet herself, but yes, she'd ask her husband for a dupe.

It was one thing, McCormick thought, to have testimony about what a lovely mother Teresa was. But she would remain an abstraction to the jury. This way, the jurors could actually see her as a person.

Cindy Diaz also supplied the name of Teresa's old boyfriend, Sal Aurelio. When questioned, Aurelio still seemed miffed that Teresa had dropped him, but he said that during the two years they had gone together, he had never known her to do cocaine.

In Brooklyn, an abrasive Dr. Irwin Azar said that he had fired Teresa because she "talked back" to him. He was unaware of any drug problem with either Ken or Teresa. In his last weeks at the dental center, Ken was having federal tax troubles. Ken's explanation for having stolen thousands of dollars in cash and checks from the center was that he needed money to cover expenses for his honeymoon in Acapulco. If Azar never saw Ken Taylor again, it would be too soon.

In Staten Island, Dr. Ronald Avis, Teresa's next employer, said that she'd been a first-rate hygienist who brightened up the office. No problem of any sort.

Avis's partner, Dr. Stanley Weinstein, thought that Ken was an "undesirable individual." According to McCormick's notes, Weinstein had additional comments:

> Dr. Weinstein recalled Kenneth Taylor coming into the office to see Teresa and from his office he would call different pharmacies and order prescriptions quite a bit and that Weinstein felt that Teresa used to pick up these prescriptions. This is one of the reasons he never trusted Kenneth Taylor. He also advised how on one occasion after Teresa Taylor resumed work and recovered from her injuries in Acapulco, Mexico, Kenneth was going to perform some dental work on Teresa Taylor at Dr. Weinstein's office, but Teresa was very apprehensive about letting her husband perform it and she would not let it occur. Dr. Weinstein believes that Teresa Taylor was frightened by Kenneth Taylor.

Besides reporting that Ken had wanted Teresa to have an abortion, Ann Toppino, the hygienist who worked with her in the Avis office, also said that Ken and Teresa once had a big fight that left Teresa terrified "because of this look in his eyes." At the time, Ken was still renting his Staten Island apartment.

The landlord of the two-family house recalled that Ken and Teresa regularly had "loud arguments." On one specific occasion after considerable yelling, the landlord's son said that he heard "something or someone" being thrown against a wall followed first by silence and then apologies from Ken.

Fausak canvassed neighbors in the Knolls development in Manalapan. Had they seen or heard anything unusual?

One housewife on an adjacent block remembered screams coming from the general direction of the Valley Road house which woke her up in the middle of the night. She looked out the window but didn't see anything. Her husband confirmed her story. A second husband and wife, four houses up Valley Road, also heard the screams. Neither family phoned the police. They thought someone else would do it.

Nor could they pinpoint the exact date. It was either two or three weeks ago, close to a weekend. Two weeks would have put it around the time of the murder.

The weekend before, Ken and Teresa were to attend a Sunday gathering at the Benignos. That same night Irene DeBlasio and her boyfriend planned to come by. But Teresa called to cancel. She said Ken had slipped in the bathtub and hurt his ankle. Yet on Monday, when Irene went in for dental work, he seemed fine.

Dr. John Bobinski, a dentist Ken had hired for his new practice, said that he really didn't know much. While he worked in one of the offices, Ken was in the other. Ken and Teresa seemed like a happy couple, both devoted to the baby.

Other employees in the two offices, all women, cited Teresa as being a "good mother." One, a young Vietnamese, reserved praise exclusively for Ken as a caring father. It seemed that she was trying to find something detrimental to say about Teresa, McCormick thought, but couldn't quite do it. He wondered if Ken had a relationship with her.

Everyone, however, had the same version of Acapulco. Intruders had broken into the room, knocked out Ken, and beat Teresa.

• • •

At 11:44 A.M., December 7, the call came into the Manalapan police station while McCormick and Fausak were on the road interviewing. The caller, "a distraught female," according to the dispatcher, asked for "the detective or whoever is taking care of the case about Teresa Taylor." She refused to give her name.

The station's reel-to-reel recorder was activated and the call was switched to Captain Jimmie Potts.

"I was calling about that man, you know, who killed his wife. Kenneth Taylor. We were on vacation in Acapulco when they were there. The newspaper didn't say . . ."

"I'm sorry. I can barely hear you," Potts said.

". . . that you know, he beat her up."

The connection was bad. Potts thought about asking her to call back. He decided not to. There was real tension in her voice. He could lose her for good. "Yes?" he said.

"On their honeymoon. In Acapulco."

"Yes?"

"We were at the hotel. There was a big scandal about him."

"Yes?" Potts said. The woman's voice had a slight accent, but because of the connection, he couldn't place it.

"And I really wanted to know what is happening to him. I mean, he killed his wife."

"Okay. The case is still developing. Could I have your name, please?"

"No, I don't want to leave my name. I have a family."

"I understand," Potts said. "But you understand, too, that your information could very possibly help us."

"Well, I just, uh, you know, I was wondering if he could get away with this? You know, it bothers me."

"I don't know what you mean, 'get away' with it?"

146

"Well, is there going to be, you know, any punishment for what he did to her?"

"Are you talking about the Acapulco thing, or the—?"

"I am talking about the girl, Teresa!"

"I know," Potts said. "But is it Acapulco, or the murder?"

"The murder. The thing in Acapulco—you know, I stayed there with my kids and my husband. All I know is that the girl at the front desk told me that Teresa didn't want to prosecute. She was hurting and he had told people at the hotel that there were four men who broke into the room, or two men. Then we found out the truth that he did it . . . that, you know, he beat her all up on her honeymoon."

Potts sensed the tension in his own voice now. The woman on the other end of the line was getting close to what she was really calling about. The thing was to keep her talking.

"You were staying at the hotel at the same time?"

"Yes," she said.

"And what month is this?"

"This is July, nineteen eighty-three. The second week in July."

"Yes."

"We rode to the hotel from the airport with them in the van. We were the only others, my four kids, my husband, and I. And then we invited them to our room, you know, for a drink because it was their honeymoon. We drank a toast to their wedding."

Her voice started to falter.

"*Yes!*" Potts said.

Finally, it came.

"We didn't see them after that," the woman said. "Then when we were leaving, he was in the lobby with the policemen and he called my name. I looked up at him and I saw his growth of beard. I asked him what happened. He said he had been in jail for four days. He said, 'We had a fight.' And, you know, I just thought that he had a fight with people in Mexico, in a bar or something. But then he started saying, 'My wife, she's in the hospital,' and I said,

'What did they do to her?' He said, 'No, not them, me. We had a fight and I beat her.'"

Oh, boy, Potts thought.

"I was wondering if you knew this," she said.

"Okay, let me speak to you a second here. What you are telling me is very, very important. It could mean all the difference in the trial. Can't you please let me talk to you person-to-person, so you could give me a statement on this? It's extremely important."

"I'm afraid."

"There's no need to be afraid. He's still in jail."

"He's in jail?"

"Yes, he's not out."

"But I'm afraid, though. He could be running around loose."

"He's not going to run loose. There is no need to be afraid."

"No?"

"I'm positive," Potts said. "I'm married myself and I would tell the same thing to my wife."

"You know, if something happened and he got free . . ."

"He won't hurt you, believe me. Right now, all he's interested in is getting out of this thing. But you know, every little bit is going to help. What you're telling me would certainly help."

"Let me think about it. I want to talk it over with my husband."

"All right," Potts said. He could feel the sweat running down inside his shirt. "I'm not trying to force you into it, of course, I'm not. And you know that, ah, look, it could be a thing where the prosecutor could take your statement and he might not have to use you on the stand. This information could be background and it would certainly help in the trial."

"What do you mean?"

"Well, you know, I don't know for sure what's going to happen. I don't have a crystal ball. But let's suppose they say, 'Well, gee, this is an isolated incident,' right?"

"It's what?"

"An isolated incident when he hit her, you know, with a blunt instrument. Well, now we can show there is a pattern and your statement where he said, 'I did it'—that could be important. Really, you ought to bring that forth."

"I really want to."

He had her, Potts thought. Just a little more coaxing. "Okay," he said, "I don't want your last name. What is your first name?"

Then it was back to the beginning. "Oh, I don't want to say it. I think I'm really afraid . . . It's just terrible, awful."

"I know. That's why you ought to give a statement. All I'm asking is your first name."

"I wonder about the young girl's parents. They didn't mention anything about her mother. Is the mother alive?"

"Is the mother alive? Yes, she's alive. Yes."

"Oh, they must be going crazy. Because the newspaper said that the little boy, their little child, was given to his parents."

*He* was the one going crazy, Potts thought. "Well, that's a matter for the courts," he said.

"I know, but I would think . . ."

"Sure. I know what you mean."

"It's so terrible. I have a daughter, twenty-three."

Potts grabbed at that. "So you know what this mother is going through?"

"Yes, it's terrible, horrible. Maybe he needs help. But he shouldn't be allowed to get away with this."

"Well, we don't want him to get away with it. Whether it's help he needs or whatever, I don't want him to get away with it either."

"I'll call you back in a couple of days."

"Let me have your first name so I'll know who I'm speaking to."

"I'd rather not. What is your name?"

"Potts. Captain Potts. With two t's."

"You know how I feel. I'm just afraid."

"I assure you there's no reason to be afraid. Even if he got out on bail, he'll only want to save his hide. He's not that dumb, you know, that he'd try to harm somebody."

"Let me call you back."

Potts resigned himself. It was the best he would get. The thing now was to try to make sure she would do it. "All right," he said, "when would you call me?"

"By next week, I promise. Tuesday or Wednesday."

"And you won't give me your first name?"

This time, there was a pause.

"Sorayda," she finally said.

"Sorayda? What is that?"

"It's a Spanish name."

"Ah, Spanish. It's very pretty."

"Thank you."

"Okay, Sorayda, my first name is Jimmie. I hope to hear from you."

Potts decided to make one last attempt. He invoked the name of Kitty Genovese, a young woman who was walking home one night in Queens, New York, when she was attacked and stabbed to death. It triggered an enormous scandal. Potts explained what happened. People in buildings all over the neighborhood heard her screams for help. Yet not one called the police. "They didn't want to get involved," he said.

"Oh, that's terrible. I know what you are saying. I wish I could have helped that young girl, Teresa. But she's gone now."

"You can still help her, Sorayda. And others, too. If he were left to go free, he may repeat something like this again, and what's the next person going to do?"

"Yes, he could do the same thing."

"And I would like to think that somewhere, some way, Teresa is crying for justice. Can I come over and speak to you?"

"I'll call you back."

There was a finality in her voice now. "Okay, please do," Potts said. "Thank you for taking the trouble to call me now. I really appreciate it. I'll wait for your call on Tuesday, maybe even Monday if you can."

But the call never came.

# Chapter

## EIGHT

On November 28, ten days after he had come into the Manalapan police station, Ken retained Jack Venturi, a thirty-three-year-old defense lawyer with a brash, boyish charm.

He was the third candidate who had been recommended by Barry Shapiro. The other attorneys, both older, were too authoritarian for Ken's taste. Venturi recognized at once, however, that Ken desired major input into the defense strategy, and he made it clear that while he would give him his best advice, Ken would ultimately decide what avenue to pursue.

Ken liked the fact that he and Venturi were close in age, which led to an easy rapport. He liked how Venturi said at the outset that there was "no way" the state could obtain a murder conviction. He liked the idea that Venturi was from New Brunswick in Middlesex County, not Monmouth, so Venturi wouldn't have to "kiss any courtroom ass." And he especially liked learning that Venturi not only was the father of a young daughter and son, but also that his own marriage was on the rocks.

He immediately told Venturi about Teresa's drug habit. She was insatiable, he said. When she got high, she would do big amounts of cocaine—one to two grams, even more. All that Thursday, Friday, and Saturday, during one of her binges, her *fatal* binge, she had not slept at all. He said that she was an intensely sexual woman in normal circumstances, so Venturi could imagine what her sexuality was like doing coke. But nobody could know what it was like to experience the shock of seeing what she was doing "to our son."

According to Venturi's notes, Ken said, "Then it hit me, all of it. Her forging prescriptions, signing medical insurance checks and cashing them, using our money for cocaine and codeine. She couldn't care for our son when she was high. She used to beg me to do it for her—'Please, Ken, I can't handle it when I'm high.' I shouted at her, 'What the fuck are you doing?' and she ran, and I went after her, and she came at me with the dumbbell bar and I hit her."

Venturi said, "Maybe she was just kissing the baby. You're certain she was doing that? You weren't imagining it?"

"I know she was," Ken said. "I saw it. Her head was bobbing up and down. What else would make me do something like this?"

Granted that Ken wasn't undergoing a grueling cross-examination, Venturi still found his demeanor impressive. He appeared to speak more in resignation than anger. "I loved her," he said.

As far as Venturi could see, the willful and knowing elements for murder in the New Jersey criminal code weren't there. Manslaughter was the likely outcome.

He sketched out the various scenarios. Aggravated manslaughter—defined as reckless indifference to life with a high probability that death would result—carried a twenty-year sentence, with a "hard ten" with no time off for good behavior. But it was a far cry from the mandatory thirty years without parole—or the death penalty—that would result from a murder conviction.

There was also reckless manslaughter—which was the

same as aggravated, except it incorporated the possibility instead of the probability of death, and had a ten-year sentence with a hard five. And, finally, manslaughter committed in the "heat of passion," induced by provocation. There was some sentencing leeway here—a ten-year maximum, but with a chance for as little as three years. Privately, Venturi thought that a successful reckless manslaughter defense, considering what had occurred, would be a win. Proving heat of passion would be a real triumph, but he believed he had a chance based on the combination of drug use, problems in the marriage, seeing what Ken said he saw Teresa doing, Teresa then attacking him with the dumbbell bar—all of it arguably sufficient provocation to "arouse passion."

In the Monmouth County Jail, Ken said, "What else?"

Suddenly it began to dawn on Venturi that Ken wasn't interested in mitigating factors leading to a lesser sentence. He wanted to get off completely. To be found not guilty of anything.

"Temporary insanity."

Ken bridled instantly. "I don't want that," he said. "I am not insane. I have no problems in that regard." He reacted as if personally insulted by the suggestion.

Venturi attempted to explain that legal and medical insanity were not quite the same, although, of course, there would be some overlap.

But his client was adamant. Later he learned that Ken had rejected one of the other attorneys because of his insistence on temporary insanity as the only workable strategy.

Well, Venturi said, there was self-defense. And the defense of a third party, the child.

Ken leaned toward him, smiling. "That's what I want," he said.

There was a problem, though, Venturi said. The moment Ken had taken the dumbbell bar away from Teresa, self-defense no longer existed.

Staring right at Venturi, Ken said, "I was under a lot of pressure. I was disoriented when I said that to the police, *if* I said it. But there were *two* dumbbell bars. You have to understand. I was mad as hell when I yelled at her from the stairs. She looked at me, bug-eyed. She tore off through the kitchen. I chased her into the laundry. I saw a flash, a blurred movement. She swung a bar at me and I tried to get out of the way. She got me in the shoulder. I lost my balance and fell on my back in the doorway. She pounced on me. She was pounding my chest. There was another bar holding the door, like a doorstop. I reached over to my left and grabbed it. I rolled out from under her and got to my feet. She charged at me with her head down, like she was going to butt me or something. I hit her in the head. She's like dazed. She came at me again, and I hit her again. That's all I remember. That's the truth.''

Surveying Ken's tall, muscular frame, Venturi said, "I have to tell you, it won't be easy to establish this."

"Sometimes the truth is hard to believe," Ken said.

Venturi wished he had never mentioned self-defense. He should have maintained that this was a manslaughter case, period, and gone from there. But if he had, he was sure he would not have been retained. And Jack Venturi wanted this case. The fee was very good—$20,000 down plus an initial $5,000 for expenses, $15,000 more if the indictment was for capital murder, a $10,000 bonus for a ten-year sentence with a three-year minimum, and an additional $5,000 for a straight acquittal or an acquittal by reason of temporary insanity. And it was a high-profile case, at least locally, the kind that defense lawyers coveted, especially one, like Venturi, who had been practicing on his own for less than two years.

The book on him in the northern New Jersey legal community was that he was smart, thorough and resourceful. A slender, well-groomed man, unfailingly polite, an avid skier, and skilled in Tae Kwon Do, a Korean version of the martial arts, he seemed to have a way with juries. After one trial, a juror said to him, "A lot of us thought your client was guilty, but we liked your style, so we gave you reasonable doubt." "Jack comes off as the sort of fellow a mother would want her daughter to marry," a lawyer who had observed him in the courtroom said. "Excellent body language."

Unlike many defense attorneys, Venturi had never been a prosecutor. And there was nothing special in his background—his father was in the scrap steel business—to direct him toward criminal law. But when he was still a kid, he read *The Story of My Life* by Clarence Darrow, and after that, he never wanted to do anything else. He devoured everything he could about the great attorney. He couldn't remember the number of times he'd journeyed to see revivals of *Inherit the Wind,* the play dramatizing the famous Scopes trial which pitted his hero against William Jennings Bryan over the right to teach the theory of evolution. He never forgot that Darrow's victory, with its far-reaching consequences, rested on what was derided at the time as a "technicality."

Venturi grew up in New Jersey. After his graduation from New York University Law School, he clerked for a Newark Superior Court judge who primarily handled criminal cases, then joined the Public Defender's Office. Next, he was recruited by one of the state's most prominent law firms before striking out on his own. Since then, he had enjoyed a string of notable successes. In the prosecution of a major marijuana smuggling ring, his client was the only one to be acquitted. He also got an acquittal for a police sergeant accused of attempting to maim a drug dealer, who had claimed that the sergeant was trying to shake him down. And in the face of a battery of high-priced legal talent and expert witnesses, he had recently won a seven-hundred-thousand-dollar liability action against the Ford Motor Company.

Now he would be defending Ken Taylor. The case wasn't of the magnitude of a Scopes trial. But in one of the most notorious crimes in Chicago's history, the thrill killing in the 1920s of a boy named Bobby Franks, Darrow also had saved the defendants Leopold and Loeb from certain execution on the grounds of temporary insanity.

Personally, Venturi did not believe that Teresa was sodomizing the baby. His instinctive feeling was that if cocaine had been involved, both of them were doing it that night and that something explosive had happened, a fight of some sort that escalated out of control, probably grounded in something sexual that his client wasn't prepared to talk about yet. Still, for Jack Venturi, that didn't constitute murder.

All right, he told Ken. For now, self-defense would be their strategy. But prudence demanded that it be reconsidered once the evidence the prosecutor intended to use was obtained through the discovery process. He wasn't ready to totally abandon either manslaughter or, for that matter, an insanity plea. When they knew precisely where they stood, Ken could make a definitive decision about how he wanted to proceed.

"That's fine," Ken said, smiling again, a rather satisfied smile, Venturi thought—as if pleased that he had succeeded in convincing Venturi of the rightness of his cause, as if that was all that really mattered.

Then as Venturi was leaving, almost as an afterthought, Ken said, "There was an incident in Connecticut with my ex-wife they might try to bring in. It was an assault and battery. She refused to have sex and I tried to scare her with some chloroform. But the important thing is that she dropped the charges, so I don't really see what they can do."

It was always the same, Venturi remembered thinking. You never got the whole story at first. But if the charges had in fact been dropped, this didn't sound like much. He wondered, though, what other booby traps might lie ahead.

The next day he filed a notice in Superior Court for a reduced bail of one hundred thousand dollars.

• • •

On December 3, five days after Venturi was retained, Cindy Diaz and her husband were stunned to receive a letter from Ken:

*I've wanted to write to you but my grief and sorrow have prevented me from communicating. I chose you because Teresa and I thought very highly of you and felt you knew* us and how we felt about each other. Teresa and I had a great relationship. We truly loved each other. We loved our son more than life. This is a tragedy beyond anything I've ever known.

I am not at liberty to discuss what happened or what caused the whole situation. I can say that Teresa had family problems which in my mind led to her excessive drug habits . . . I can't be specific although I wish I could to clear up many of the questions concerning our relationship. Unfortunately this can not be discussed until my trial.

Another matter that several people keep throwing out is our honeymoon. What happened is exactly as Teresa and I explained it to everyone. I have an investigator who will prove this as it seems her family wants to try to use this against me. I've lost my wife and my life will never be the same. Teresa and I were blessed with joy and happiness and closeness that people just don't find in this world. The judge, jury, prosecutor and my lawyer will settle the case and in that I put my trust . . . but another issue is at hand which is a total miscarriage of justice.

I'm not asking for help but understanding and the Truth! Celeste is trying to take my boy! Her caring for my son is beyond my wildest imagination. Teresa told me and all her friends how much she objected to her mother and Celeste caring for Philip and how poorly they cared for him with improper feeding, sleeping etc. You both know Teresa was opposed to this. As you surely recall TERESA asked my parents to come from Indiana the week she gave birth because she didn't want her family hanging around getting in the way and screwing up the works. My parents love my son like their own, they truly love him and can give him the best of care. Yet in court Celeste and Louise acted like their relationship with Teresa was the best possible and we all know how unjust and untrue that is.

If not for me please try to understand for Teresa and my son. You will not have to do anything except answer to this fact that Teresa did not want Celeste and/or Louise caring for our son. Now that Celeste is going to have a child I can just imagine the horror show of her trying to take care

*of 2 babies. And YOU KNOW which one of the 2 babies
would get her attention as well as I do. I'm distraught. I've
lost my wife and now these people are trying to take my
son.*

*Once again the facts WILL be brought out at the trial,
all of the facts, so please keep a clear head about that but
do try to consider my request in behalf of Teresa, myself
and Philip for his custody until my trial is over . . . I'm
sure you have mixed emotions so just forget about me and
think of Teresa and our son. If I have rambled on I can't
help it. God bless you. Merry Christmas.*

*P.S. I hope I have read you correctly and can trust
you in this matter. Your confidence here will be most
appreciated.*

Cindy read the letter in utter disbelief. She was revolted
by Ken's references to his "love" for Teresa and how he
had "lost" her. She fervently hoped that he was right when
he wrote that "his life would never be the same," but not
in the way he meant it.

But what appalled her more than anything was that not
one of his premises in the letter was accurate. Teresa had
never put down Louise and Celeste as he described. Sure,
Teresa had complained about her mother, just as *she* would
complain about her own mother, and Celeste was always
the "kid sister." But it was Ken who had really put them
down, calling Louise a "disaster," characterizing Celeste
as "airbrained," and saying, "I don't know where she's
coming from."

What was he up to? Was he trying to convince himself of
something? Scramble *her* brains? Change black into white?
There had to be some reason, she thought. When she
showed the letter to her husband, he said, "Is he crazy?"

• • •

Jean and Zach told Venturi that they didn't know all that
much about the "incident" in Connecticut, but they confirmed that Marilyn had not in fact pressed charges and
that the case was dismissed. He could confirm this with
Ken's attorney in New London, Max Shapiro, who, Zach

proudly noted, was the law partner of L. Patrick Gray, the director of the FBI under President Nixon. Ken had succumbed to work and domestic pressures and too many pills. It had been "merely a bout of marital discord." Both Ken and Marilyn underwent counseling and everything appeared to be fine until Teresa entered the picture.

Prior to the current "incident," Jean said that she had never heard anything about Teresa and cocaine. She had always found her a "sweet, loving girl." It was shocking to think that she had driven Kenny to this. "He couldn't have been himself. He loved her deeply. *That* was his normal self. He wouldn't intentionally hurt her."

Then she said, "At least twice while Teresa was nursing the baby, Philip 'spaced out' due to drugs in the milk from breast-feeding. And several weeks ago Teresa was 'stoned' and dropped him from the couch." Although Jean was not an eyewitness to these events, she stated them as facts. She added that possible cocaine sources for Teresa were "a girlfriend who visited the home frequently," her brother, Phil, and "Kenny's dental office employees."

Zach said that efforts should be launched to dig into Teresa's background and past associations. He was sure that there was plenty of dirt. Venturi replied that he had hired a private investigator.

In a follow-up memo to Venturi, after visiting Ken in jail, Zach now recalled signs of Teresa's drug addiction:

*Ken and Teresa visited our home in Marion—Labor Day weekend with the baby Philip.*

*It was very noticeable Teresa had some kind of problem. She would sniff frequently, drank black coffee, smoked cigarettes, had headaches and ate very little food. Went to bed frequently.*

He also suggested that she had lesbian inclinations:

*On one occasion at a ballgame my wife was in the front seat of our car with Philip and Teresa was in the back seat. She began to stroke my wife's hair and complimented her on how smooth it was and that my wife should put color on it and she kept stroking my wife's hair and talking nice to her. Jean asked her to stop.*

*When we were here in June and my wife was taking care of Philip and Teresa—one day they were going shopping. My wife had on a green checkered short suit with hose. My wife said, "I should change clothes. It doesn't look good for an older person like me to go out and look like this." Teresa said, "Young or old, you look good to me."*

What this had to do with anything only became evident to Venturi when he received discovery material from the prosecutor's office.

One of Guy McCormick's first investigative steps had been to subpoena records on telephone toll calls made from the Manalapan house beginning Saturday, November 10, through Sunday, November 18, when Ken confessed to killing Teresa.

McCormick determined that Ken had made two calls to a massage parlor in Hartford on Wednesday night after having disposed of Teresa's body in the Hawk Mountain Bird Sanctuary, calls that Ken would deny making, insisting that it was a billing error.

But the records also disclosed that early on Sunday, November 11, about three hours after Angela and Peter Rozek had seen Teresa alive for the last time, twenty-six other calls were made from 2:23 A.M. to 5:48 A.M. They had been placed repeatedly to San Francisco, Los Angeles, Beverly Hills, Santa Monica, Las Vegas, Chicago and New York City. Some of the calls to the same number were made in rapid succession, a minute or two minutes apart. McCormick dialed them all. A few had been disconnected, but most were still operational. All but three were pornographic hot lines featuring women spinning sexual fantasies. The remaining calls were to a whorehouse in Manhattan where available services were described and prices quoted.

Since there were only two adults in the house at the time, McCormick assumed—correctly—that Ken would claim Teresa had made the calls.

McCormick also ran a financial check on Ken. Even though his income was $110,000 annually, he was unable to obtain normal commercial or personal credit. He also had an outstanding debt of about $26,000 to the Navy Federal Credit Union. McCormick wondered how much of it had gone up his nose.

• • •

The grand jury convened on December 14. Paul Chaiet's principal witness was Lieutenant Lucia. Chaiet led him step-by-step through the events from the time Teresa was reported missing until Ken arrived at the Manalapan police station. The crucial part of his testimony came after he described how Ken finally broke down and admitted killing Teresa and said that he had seized the dumbbell bar from her and hit her with it.

Then, as Chaiet expected, a grand juror said, "There seems to be an indication that she had a drug problem."

"Well, that's what Doctor Taylor says," Lucia answered.

"According to him?"

"Yes, ma'am."

Chaiet interjected. "He told us she was using drugs."

"He said she was a drug addict?"

"I don't know about addict. She had some problems with drugs. We have a continuing investigation and we have, I would guess, established that she did use drugs on occasion. To what extent she used drugs we're not sure. Isn't that correct?" Chaiet said, addressing Lucia.

"That's correct."

Another grand juror said, "Did you ever check his story out? Or wasn't that necessary, about where he said he had been—to Pittsburgh and back?"

"You have been to Pittsburgh?" Chaiet said to Lucia. "Is that correct?"

"Yes, sir."

"You've interviewed his former wife?"

"Yes."

"You have taken an extensive statement from her?"

"That's correct."

Chaiet, uncertain about whether he would ever secure the documentation he needed, did not mention Connecticut.

• • •

The following Friday, the grand jury again convened. After the forensic evidence had been presented, including a graphic description of the fifty-five-foot trail of blood revealed by the Luminol test, Zach Taylor took the stand.

Almost immediately, Chaiet addressed Teresa's alleged drug abuse.

"Following their marriage in July of nineteen eighty-three, how often had you visited them in New Jersey or Staten Island?"

"The next time we saw them after the wedding was when the baby was born . . . That was in June of 'eighty-four. We were here for ten days."

"And then you went back to Indiana?"

"Yes, sir."

"Prior to her death did you again see them?"

"Teresa and Kenny and the baby, they visited us Labor Day weekend. They were there for two days."

"During your visit to the house in Manalapan, did you observe any drug use by Teresa or by your son at that time?"

"No, sir."

"Were you personally aware of any drug use at any time by Teresa Taylor? Through your own observation."

"Not personally, not through observation. If you mean actual taking of drugs or—"

"Taking drugs, seeing her under the influence of a drug?"

"On the Labor Day visit, we noticed something was different. But my wife and I, I am saying we, we didn't know what the problem was."

"When you say noticed something different, what do you mean, noticed something different?"

Zach repeated almost verbatim what he had volunteered to Venturi after visiting Ken—that Teresa smoked, drank coffee, had headaches, and spent a great deal of time in bed. "She seemed to be just, I don't know how to explain it," he said, "really kind of a different person."

162

Chaiet snapped, "All right. Did you ask your son about that at that time?"

Zach shifted uncomfortably in the witness chair. "No, not that I recall, no, I don't think so."

Then, for the first time, the grand jury heard about Acapulco. "Now, were you aware of a problem that Teresa and Doctor Taylor ran into on their honeymoon in July, nineteen eighty-three?"

"Somewhat, yes."

"When you say somewhat, tell me what you know about what happened in Acapulco, Mexico."

". . . To the best of my recollection, Kenny said that, Kenneth said that the room was broken into and that he was knocked out, he was dazed and he started to come to, and then he was knocked out.

"When he awoke, there was glass, I think he said glass, on the floor from a broken lamp. He saw his wife, I don't recall whether he said that she was on the floor or still on the bed or what, but his first thought was that she was dead. She had been beaten and cut and he called the front desk, I guess, I am not sure whether he called the front desk or the police, or whatever.

"When they came," Zach Taylor said, "they took them both to the hospital, as I understand, and Kenny was released and he was arrested by the Mexican police."

Chaiet turned away from Zach, looked at the grand jury and looked back at him. "Her injuries, would it be fair to say, in his relating the story to you, were more severe than his?"

"Yes."

"The information that you related to us just now, is this your recollection of what you were told by your son, your best recollection?"

"I would say yes. But I have a difficult time because Mr. Benigno said things to me on the phone. All of this conversation is on the phone."

"Between you and your son?"

"Yes."

"Did you talk to your son about the fact that he was

held by Mexican authorities and what happened? What did he tell you about that?"

"He just told me that he was arrested. And that he was put in jail and apparently in Mexico they don't feed the prisoners. He wanted some food and one of the guards said, 'I'll get you food for fifty dollars.' He got a cup of coffee and a roll . . . I don't know exactly when they released him. But he got out by paying a five-hundred-dollar fine to a Mexican policeman that just stuck it in his pocket, so to speak."

"That's what *he* told you?"

"Yes."

"What did Teresa tell you about the assault? Did she tell you she knew who did it? Did she give a description of the people who did it?"

"Teresa said she did not recall anything. She saw no one, absolutely no one . . . First she was on the bed asleep and then she was in the hospital. Maybe even unconscious in the hospital."

Chaiet then took Zach through Ken's explanation of why he had brought the baby to Indiana. Periodically, Chaiet would interject, as he had concerning Acapulco, "Is that the story your son told you?" and Zach, increasingly red-faced, answered, "Yes."

Finally Chaiet asked what Ken had said to him at the Manalapan police station on Sunday, November 18. "What did he tell you about what happened with Teresa?"

"When we went into the room where he was, I believe Mr. Lucia was with us and—he, I really don't recall what he told us except that—I honestly can't say what he told us. I am trying to think here whether the police told us what he told them."

"I am asking you what your son told you . . . I want you to use your best recollection. I realize this is difficult for you and you're under oath. But it would seem you should be able to remember a conversation with your son in an incident where he is telling you about the death of his wife."

"Okay, I believe he said that he woke up on Sunday

morning and started down the steps and he looked down and saw his wife performing oral sex on the baby. And he yelled at her. She got up and ran. He ran after her. And she swang [*sic*] at him with a, what I would call, a dumb-bell, which is a piece of work-out equipment, and at that point in time, that's as far as he could talk."

(When Ken got his copy of the grand jury proceedings, he starred and underlined this last sentence and scrawled in the margin, "Good. STOP." He also wrote, as if it were a reminder to himself, "Defendant crying, emotional.")

• • •

Chaiet hadn't planned on introducing Acapulco. Unlike some grand jury proceedings that wound up being mini-trials, this one was fairly cut-and-dried. The only issue was whether there was probable cause to believe a murder had been committed, and Lucia's testimony took care of that.

Acapulco had been an impulsive decision, a hunch more than anything. Chaiet only knew of the suspicions of the Benignos and the anonymous phone call. Still, he thought it might be a good idea to place it on the record. It went right to the issue of Ken's credibility. If he had lied about one thing, why not another? And the moment the grand jurors got wind of a previous act of violence between the Taylors, they sat straight up in their chairs.

Chaiet had already decided not to seek a capital murder indictment. He was not a strong advocate of the death penalty, mostly because of his reservations about its deterrent effect. If he had it his way, the ideal punishment would be life without parole. In Taylor's case, under New Jersey statutes, conviction called for a mandatory thirty years, which, considering the defendant's age, added up to practically the same thing.

In New Jersey, execution was by lethal injection. But since the U.S. Supreme Court had legalized the death penalty, to date not one had occurred in the state. And there were other practical considerations. Without any assurance that either Connecticut or Acapulco would be part of the trial, getting a first-degree murder conviction presented enough problems. Chaiet did not want a jury wrestling with the death penalty as well. If a debate started over that, the elevator could start dropping through the various levels of manslaughter, and who knew where it would stop?

The indictment was returned on Friday, January 4, 1984. Jack Venturi told reporters, "Doctor Taylor is naturally very upset and depressed. But on the whole his health is good and he is looking forward to a trial date to exonerate himself."

• • •

In his motion to reduce bail, Venturi emphasized the importance of having his client immediately available for the preparation of his defense, an effort now being severely hampered by incarceration that served no real purpose. The defendant was established in the community and would not leave the court's jurisdiction. He was the recipient of a U.S. Navy scholarship, which was awarded after a thorough investigation that attested to his "outstanding" background and character. He had never been convicted of a crime. He had achieved professional success in both his military and civilian careers. He was financially responsible, having faithfully provided support to children from two previous marriages. His wife's death had occurred only after his client saw her abusing their baby "in a sexual manner and while he was being attacked by her with a deadly weapon."

Venturi was surprised by the vehemence of Chaiet's Certification in Opposition. This time, not bound by rules of evidence which apply in a trial, Chaiet did introduce Connecticut. Based on interviews by his investigators, the defendant not only had seized the dumbbell bar from Teresa and "gave it to her," but also had attempted to kill his second wife while she was sleeping. He was a violent man and a threat to those he came in contact with.

Chaiet's certification charged that Kenneth Taylor's three marriages had been marked by irresponsibility, violence, and financial problems. His investigators had learned that the defendant abandoned his first wife when she was on the verge of giving birth, had never seen their child, and was thousands of dollars in arrears in child support. It noted Ann Toppino's statement that Ken once tried to persuade Teresa Taylor to have an abortion.

The defendant not only had stolen money from previous employers but also owed the Navy Federal Credit Union some twenty-six thousand dollars. If he got the opportunity, there was every indication that he would flee the court's jurisdiction.

After the court documents became public, the revelation about Connecticut was big news. The headline in the *Asbury Park Press* was, "Alleged killer tied to another attack."

On his copy of the certification, Ken circled Chaiet's name and wrote, "ASSHOLE!" He told Venturi it wasn't fair. Chaiet was treating *him,* "a formerly happily married, devout family man who had survived a freak encounter with destiny," as though he were a serial killer, a "Ted Bundy or Richard Speck or Charles Manson." He begged Venturi, "Get me out of here, please. I want to be a free man!" His fourteen-man cell block was a "squalid, filthy, cramped hovel." There was "no privacy, constant noise, one shower stall, terrible food and no physical contact"— as he put it—"with loved ones."

Venturi did his best.

He countered that his client denied telling the police that "he got the dumbbell away from his wife and 'gave it to her.' "

Furthermore, "Upon information and belief, Dr. Taylor did see his first wife twice after he separated from her and he saw his daughter. Dr. Taylor did pay child support. There are canceled checks showing [this]."

As far as Connecticut was concerned, Venturi declared that "the charges were dropped against Dr. Taylor because there was not sufficient evidence to proceed with the charges.

"In reply to the statements of Mrs. Ann Toppino, upon information and belief, Teresa Taylor never got along with Mrs. Toppino very well. Teresa told Dr. Taylor that Mrs. Toppino's husband, also a dentist, would bring cocaine and sell it at Teresa's place of employment to the employees.

Also, Dr. Taylor was very happy when Teresa became pregnant. It was Teresa who was not happy because her mother and sister both said she should not get pregnant so soon after the incident which occurred on her honeymoon in Acapulco. She was too unstable from the incident to have a baby."

In regard to Chaiet's allegation that the defendant absconded with funds from the Fulton Family Dental Center, Venturi declared, "There was a profit-sharing plan, and, therefore, the money was not stolen."

And any debt burdening the defendant had been for Teresa's benefit: "Following the incident that occurred in Acapulco while he and Teresa were on their honeymoon, Teresa was very unstable. Dr. Taylor felt it would be much safer if they moved away from the Brooklyn, New York, area. Dr. Taylor therefore borrowed from the Naval Credit Union to open his own offices and capitalize his business, and he and his wife moved to New Jersey.

"For all of the foregoing reasons," Venturi submitted, "it is respectfully requested that Notice of Motion for Reduction of Bail be granted."

Venturi's motion was denied.

He then requested an adjournment of the February 19 trial date. "This is a murder case," he wrote, "that requires extensive preparation and investigation. My trial schedule is busy throughout the winter into April and there is no way I can be adequately prepared for this case before May."

A new date was set for May 20.

Paul Chaiet was delighted. He still had a great deal of investigating to do himself.

In jail, Ken railed on about Chaiet—calling him "that pig of a man!" To his mother and his brother, Tom, who had come to Manalapan after Zach returned to his job in Marion, he said, "A murder indictment is one thing, but a conviction is something else. Don't worry. I'll beat this yet."

# Chapter

## NINE

Al Benigno gave the letter to Chaiet. Dated September 13, 1983, it was from Las Brisas in response to Louise's request for information about the beating Teresa had received—the same letter that Louise feared confronting her daughter with, afraid that it might cause Teresa to pack up with Ken and leave for good.

Signed by the executive assistant manager, it said:

*I have just received a copy of your letter addressed to Dr. Ortiz.*

*The answers to the questions in your letter are as follows: The approximate time Mr. Taylor telephoned regarding the incident was 9:30 P.M., at which time he used the expression "attack, attack," and the Assistant Manager who received the telephone call reported him as panting as if he had been doing a lot of exercise.*

*The Assistant Manager and the Security man, together with the bell captain, went to the room immediately and found it in a terrible state with broken bottles, blood stains*

169

*on the walls and your daughter lying on the floor on the side of the bed nearest the telephone; it appears she had been trying to reach the phone, but didn't make it. According to our records your daughter was taken to the hospital between 20 and 30 minutes after the initial call.*

*Unfortunately, your daughter was in no condition, in fact she was unconscious, to make a telephone call to you that night. Whether she tried prior to the incident, we do not know.*

*As you may know, Las Brisas is not open to the public, strangers cannot get into the hotel without the knowledge of our Security Department. In addition to this, there was a security man on duty in the area of your daughter's room and he would have seen anyone entering or leaving the casita and would have stopped them if they were not guests of the hotel. We are convinced that the injuries your daughter sustained were caused by someone in that room and not by someone outside it.*

*I am sorry to have to be so frank, but all indications lead the police to believe that Mr. Taylor was responsible.*

*I understand from Dr. Ortiz that he will be sending you the medical report from the hospital. The police report is basically the same as I have set out above. The only addition I can make is that Mr. Taylor was released because your daughter did not, or could not, sign a complaint.*

In early January, right after the indictment was returned, Reyes Quinones, a Spanish-speaking investigator in the major crimes unit, spoke by phone to Dr. Esteban Ortiz Pavon, the attending physician at Las Brisas. According to Quinones:

The Dr. stated that he had been notified of an attack which had occurred within the room of the Taylors in which Mrs. Teresa Taylor was just about killed . . . Mr. Taylor had stated they had been attacked but once questioned by hotel security and local police, Mr. Taylor admitted that he was the perpetrator and Mr. Taylor allegedly signed a release form releasing the hotel of any liabilities. Dr. Ortiz Pavon stated that from the beginning he and the authorities realized that the attacker was Mr. Taylor and not an outsider.

Dr. Ortiz Pavon further stated that Mrs. Taylor for reasons unknown would not press charges against her husband. The Dr. feels that she would not because she did not want to see her new husband go to jail. Dr. Ortiz Pavon stated that he would send this investigator a copy of his report and would attempt to obtain a copy of the local police report. He feels, however, since Mrs. Taylor would not sign a complaint, that there are no official police records.

Quinones then reached Gabriel Santoyo, the Las Brisas security director, who put a Miguel Lugo on the line. Lugo had been on the scene the night of the assault:

Lugo stated that on the day in question, he responded with ten other officers to the Taylor quarters . . . Mr. Taylor was apprehended and transported to a local police station where, after approximately 12 hours of interrogation, he "unofficially" admitted that he was the perpetrator that had assaulted his wife.

This investigator requested to know if a formal police report was prepared on the aggravated assault and I was informed that once Mrs. Taylor came to her senses, she refused, stating that they were on their honeymoon, she loved her husband and did not want to see him go to jail.

Then Santoyo gave Quinones the name and number of the police precinct chief. Santoyo said he was a personal friend of the chief's. Be sure to use him as a reference.

Despite repeated tries, Quinones was unable to reach the chief. It seemed that he was off in the mountains somewhere chasing crooks. At last Quinones got through to the deputy chief, whereupon events took a mystifying turn. After Quinones explained that he was calling at Santoyo's suggestion, the deputy chief said that he "could not help" because Santoyo had been transferred from Las Brisas and no longer was in charge of security there. Quinones was about to say, "So what?" when the deputy chief hung up.

Baffled, he called Las Brisas. To his astonishment, Santoyo got on the phone right away. Santoyo said that he had no idea what was going on. "Obviously, I have not been transferred," he said, "and the police have made no attempt to reach me." In any case, Santoyo said that he would be happy to supply all of the hotel's own investigative reports if Quinones wrote a formal request to the general manager at Las Brisas. A copy should be sent to the resident manager as well as to him.

Quinones said he would dispatch them promptly.

By now it was January 31.

• • •

In the meantime, Detective Bob Fausak drew the additional assignment of trying to track down the anonymous female caller who claimed to have been at Las Brisas and heard Ken admit that he had beaten Teresa—*if* she existed.

After listening to the tape, Fausak believed that she did. She'd talked too long and expressed too much concern in too cultivated a voice for a simple crank call.

He made his own call to Las Brisas seeking a list of reservations for the week Ken and Teresa were there. A horrified spokesman replied that the essence of a great luxury hotel like Las Brisas was privacy. Releasing a guest list could ruin its reputation.

Then Fausak learned that Las Brisas was owned by an American company, the Westin hotel chain headquartered in Seattle. When he called, he was informed that the only person able to help was the chain's senior general counsel. He was on vacation, unreachable. Then he was ill. Aware of the difficulties Quinones was experiencing, Fausak started wondering if the counsel's illness might have a diplomatic side to it.

But eventually they were in contact. The same privacy issue was raised. There had been well over five hundred guests at Las Brisas during the week in question. Who knew if somebody was with somebody else's wife or husband? A lot of very important people stayed there. The counsel conjured up an avalanche of lawsuits.

Look, Fausak said, this was a major murder case. If necessary, a subpoena would be issued. The counsel said that he doubted a wholesale fishing expedition would stand up in court. And in any event, it would take a long time. He wanted to be of assistance, however. Couldn't Fausak be more specific?

Fausak decided to take a chance. A survey of press clippings after Ken Taylor's arrest showed that outside of local media coverage and coverage in eastern Pennsylvania, where the body had been found, the most prominent article had been in the tabloid afternoon daily, the *New York Post*. It featured photographs of Ken, Ken and Teresa, and little Philip with a screaming headline that said, S.I. DENTIST ACCUSED OF BEATING HIS WIFE.

Fausak said he'd settle for reservations made from the tri-state area—New Jersey, New York, and Pennsylvania. The Westin general counsel agreed because of the "extraordinary circumstances of the matter you have under investigation," with the condition that Las Brisas would not be identified as the source if any guests were contacted.

There were twenty reservation slips. Fausak saw them for the first time on January 31, the same day that Quinones was mailing his request for investigative reports from Las Brisas. He combed through them, searching for the name, "Sorayda." It wasn't there.

• • •

In his office, Paul Chaiet took stock. He had two perfect building blocks for a willful murder case. Ken Taylor had tried to kill his second wife in Connecticut. Except, as it now stood, he could not use the evidence. And he had a witness who could testify that Ken Taylor had savagely assaulted Teresa in Acapulco. Except that he did not know who or where this witness was.

Chaiet determined to focus on Connecticut. His repeated conversations with an assistant state's attorney in Connecticut finally opened the door a crack. While the records would remain sealed, his investigators could speak to the Waterford cops.

Chaiet had another thought as well. Since Ken Taylor had been on active duty at the time, there must have been some inquiry conducted by the Navy. He told Guy McCormick to look into it. McCormick knew a special agent in the Naval Investigative Service (NIS) who was stationed right in Monmouth County, at the nearby Colts Neck ammunition depot. For once, there were no obstacles. The agent said that he would launch a file search immediately.

* * *

On February 15, McCormick and Fausak met in Waterford with the two officers who had been on the case, Sergeants Joseph San Juan and Joseph Faldman. The ground rules were that McCormick and Fausak could take notes from what was read to them, although in reality they did considerable reading themselves.

According to these records, Marilyn had called the police late in the afternoon of April 18, 1979, the day after Ken tried to chloroform her. They basically confirmed what she had told Fausak and Lucia in Pittsburgh.

But it was other aspects of the investigation in Waterford that revealed at least the nature, if not the genesis, of the unfathomable evil McCormick had perceived in Ken Taylor.

One of the first persons the police had talked to was Lieutenant Commander Ronald C. Smith, the Navy psychiatrist who initially treated Ken. He had described Ken as "homicidal" and had urged Marilyn to bring charges against him:

> Dr. Smith advised that Kenneth Taylor had told him that he had planned to kill his wife after he figured out how to use the chloroform. He further advised Dr. Smith that he took the chloroform from the ship he was assigned to, USS *Fulton*. Taylor had carried it off the ship a couple of days before, carrying it in his briefcase. Taylor had done this because of marital problems he no longer could tolerate.

(The actual Waterford police report would state:

TAYLOR told us he is presently married for the second time. He has been divorced from his first wife for several years. He told us his second wife is four months pregnant. He wanted to get out of the second marriage but was afraid to because of pressure from friends and family . . . he is afraid of people saying, "I TOLD YOU SO.")

Dr. Smith advised the investigating officers that in his opinion there was no doubt the incident was planned and that Kenneth Taylor knew what he was doing. He said that he had never seen anyone plan so "calmly and coolly" to murder someone and carry the plan out. He could not find any mental or physical disorders which would cause Taylor to act as he did.

In an interview two days after the attempt on Marilyn's life, Ken corroborated the events of April 17:

Kenneth Taylor advised investigating officers that at approximately 0100 hours, April 17, things started to rush through his mind and he thought of killing his wife. In the past he had thought of it but he never attempted to carry it out. He decided to use chloroform. He wasn't sure if it would kill her but if it did not kill her, it would render her unconscious and then he could suffocate her.

. . . Taylor further advised investigating officers that he did not know where the chloroform came from or how he got it in the house. After the struggle ended [his conscience having gotten the better of him], he put the sponge in a Ziploc bag and told his wife to call the police. He called the Lawrence and Memorial Hospital to advise that he was under the influence of drugs and needed help. The hospital advised that since he was in the Navy he should contact the base hospital. Kenneth Taylor also advised the investigating officers that before he attempted to kill his wife, he had taken three black-colored capsules but refused to say what they were or where they had been obtained.

Then, to their amazement, McCormick and Fausak learned that Ken had actually enumerated seven reasons why he wanted to murder Marilyn.

They were:

1. Verbal abuse from his wife.
2. Lack of respect from his wife.
3. The fact that his wife chose to retain her maiden name after marriage.
4. Lack of affection.
5. Sexual abstinence.
6. Belief that his wife may be bi-sexual.
7. Statement by his wife that if she bore a boy child, she would prefer to see the boy gay rather than athletic.

Ken had been interviewed on April 19, two days after he was admitted to the submarine base hospital. That evening he phoned the Waterford police. He said that he was worried that his wife might discover some obscene material he had hidden in his clothes closet. "She's been through enough," he explained.

A search warrant was obtained and executed the same night. In fact, earlier that day, Marilyn had turned over some pornography she found in a garbage can which included a nude photo of Ken from the neck down. She also had found a letter folded in the headband of his hat from a "Gary" to "Ken" that was "homosexual in content."

The Waterford police then seized more salacious matter including another photograph of Ken's genitals, a stack of Polaroids of naked women, and correspondence to and from various "swinger-type magazines."

In a memo pad on his desk written in his own hand were the same seven reasons for doing away with Marilyn that he had verbally given the cops when he was first interrogated. The list was dated April 17. Ken must have written it minutes before he went into the bedroom with the chloroform-soaked sponge.

• • •

The Waterford police files reflected the bitter dispute that erupted between Dr. Smith and his immediate superior, Commander W. F. Pettit, on how to treat Ken. It came to light in a call to Smith by Detective Paul Liparulo:

> During this conversation, Dr. SMITH told Detective LIPARULO that Dr. PETTIT had just returned from vacation and had taken over the case involving TAYLOR.
>
> Dr. SMITH told Detective LIPARULO that he still remains very strong concerning his examination results of TAYLOR and that TAYLOR is homicidal and not in any way insane or mentally distorted. TAYLOR should face criminal prosecution. SMITH said he is more than willing to appear in Court on this matter.
>
> Dr. SMITH said that since TAYLOR is an officer in the Navy, Dr. PETTIT had taken over the case and he (Dr. PETTIT) is conducting a "coverup" concerning TAYLOR. Dr. SMITH said that Dr. PETTIT had told him as well as other hospital personnel that nothing in fact is wrong with TAYLOR.
>
> Dr. SMITH said that Dr. PETTIT'S only treatment planned for TAYLOR is out-patient care and no formal hospitalization. Dr. SMITH told Detective LIPARULO that Dr. PETTIT felt that he (Dr. SMITH) should not have participated in the investigation with the police.

It all became academic when Marilyn eventually withdrew her complaint. McCormick and Fausak couldn't help dwelling on the might-have-beens for Teresa had Dr. Smith prevailed.

With the abrupt suspension of the Waterford investigation, many inconsistencies were left unresolved. Among the most significant was that while Ken claimed not to have been himself because he had taken three black beauties—a potent form of speed—in the hours immediately preceding the murder attempt, "There was no indication of drug use or Taylor's being under the influence of drugs at the time he was admitted to the submarine base hospital. Urine specimens were taken on April 17, the admission date, and the results were negative for drugs."

And there was a hair-raising footnote. After he had confessed to trying to kill his wife, Ken's main regret was that "many years of education and schooling would now be wasted."

• • •

Ten days after his trip to Waterford, McCormick got Ken's file from the Naval Investigative Service. It included a narrative clinical summary by Dr. Pettit that essentially absolved him:

HISTORY. This 30 year old married Navy dentist with 2 years 10 months continuous active duty presently stationed aboard the USS FULTON was admitted to Navy Submarine Medical Center, Groton, Connecticut, on 17 April 1979 after evaluation in the Emergency Room. Dr. Taylor and his wife were brought in by a Navy chaplain whom they had called.

Dr. Taylor indicated that on the day of admission while at work he drank twelve cups of coffee. In addition, that evening, he drank an additional eight cups of coffee and took three "Black Beauties" (each tablet containing 10 mgs. of amphetamine and 10 mgs. of dextroamphetamine). He indicated that he had also smoked one or two joints of marijuana.

As the evening progressed, he noted feelings of a "driving sensation," feelings like wanting to "stand in a corner," and a feeling that his head was expanding. Over the next several hours he noted progressive restlessness, irritability, tenseness, palpitations and anxiety. He went to his spare bedroom to study for his [Florida] board examinations.

During that time, he noted progressive intrusive homicidal ideation towards his wife and experienced hearing a voice from within himself telling him to kill her. After a period of 1½ hours of struggling with these impulses, he indicated that he soaked a towel with chloroform, went to where his wife was sleeping and held the towel to her face. When she reacted to the towel, there was a brief struggle and he indicated that he suddenly became more fully aware of what was happening and what he had done. He and his wife prayed together.

Afterwards, they began seeking means for him to get to the hospital. He denied previous plans to kill his wife. He denied plans for behavior or the disposal of her body should he have killed her.

He indicated that he took two "Black Beauties" on Saturday, three "Black Beauties" on Sunday and the additional three "Black Beauties" on the night prior to the alleged incident. He indicated that approximately three weeks prior to that, he had taken two "Black Beauties" one day, followed by three "Black Beauties" on the next day and on the third day three additional "Black Beauties." It was on that day during an argument with his wife that he struck the refrigerator, breaking a metacarpal bone in his right hand. He indicated that this was an option to hitting his wife.

He denies regular amphetamine use, though indicating that he had taken them infrequently to study for major dental school exams. He admitted to Valium use, 1–2 tablets a day for approximately one year while in dental school. He had experimented with LSD on two occasions and for a period of time in dental school had taken 50 mg. Seconals about twice a month.

In addition, he had taken cocaine on two occasions in 1976. He admitted to the regular use of marijuana, one or two joints on a regular but not daily basis since approximately 1971. He indicated that he used marijuana as a way of releasing anxiety and tension. He admitted the use of coffee, 10–12 cups a day, on a regular basis and smoking 2–3 packs of cigarettes on a daily basis.

He gave his alcohol history as: first drink, age 17; first drunk at age 18. He indicated in 1975 he had a car accident while under the influence of alcohol. He admits to drinking about twice a week, 2–3 drinks and becomes drunk about once a month. He indicated that he required the equivalent of about one pint of whisky to become drunk.

Dr. Taylor admitted to progressive marital discord over the previous two months. He indicated that he had experienced feelings of lack of respect and lack of affection from his wife. He indicated that he has marked difficulty in expressing his feelings and a marked fear of having verbal arguments with people, especially his wife.

PAST HISTORY revealed he is the oldest of three children from an intact lower middle class family. He admitted to severe nail biting at 8–9 years of age during a time his younger brother became the center of his father's attention. He did well in grade school but had difficulties in 7th grade when he broke his foot. He graduated from high school and was vice president of his senior class. He lettered in basketball, football and baseball. He graduated from college and attended dental school by working part time and attending dental school part time.

He married initally during his junior year in college and was divorced after a year of separation in October, 1974. He married his present wife December, 1974.

He described his father as a 52 year old industrial engineer who is a quiet man, a hard worker and proud. He indicated that he got along well with him but that his father's level of interest in him seemed proportional to his athletic achievements. He described his mother as a 52 year old housewife who is "overly concerned about making everyone happy." He indicated that she "dominates in subtle ways" and tends to be very interfering with his life.

MENTAL STATUS EXAMINATION. At the time of admission he was described as "quite calm, collected, oriented." Initially, the patient was started on 5 mgs. of Stelazine a day and Artane, 2 mgs. 4 times a day [tranquilizers], with the diagnosis of acute psychotic reaction secondary to drug abuse.

He was initially under the care of Dr. Ron Smith, LCDR MC USNR. On 20 April 1979, Dr. William F. Pettit, CDR MC USN assumed primary care of the patient after the patient's request for a change of physician.

Over a period of 6 days hospitalization, the patient became more aware of his difficulty in dealing with his emotions in an appropriate and effective manner. He indicated increased realization that he tended to hold things in and had difficulty finding adaptive outlets for the expression of his feelings. He appeared actively motivated for treatment and read a book on feelings within 24 hours after receiving it. He appeared motivated for individual and group therapy and showed marked insight into his difficulties.

He is not felt to be drug dependent. There is no evidence of psychosis or clinical depression. He denied suicidal and homicidal ideation.

A final report by Dr. Pettit included the test results of the Minnesota Multiphasic Personality Inventory (MMPI), which is designed to provide a comprehensive profile of an individual's personality adjustment range. According to the report, it revealed an "essentially unremarkable pattern" for Ken. "The MMPI profile suggests no evidence of neurosis, psychosis or character disorder."

Dr. Pettit continued:

My general impression is that this man has chronic difficulty in dealing directly with his emotions and tends to allow things to build to where he experiences chronic tension and anxiety. A great deal of his difficulty in expressing his feelings directly is secondary to his tremendous need for acceptance and fear of rejection.

In addition, my impression is that the alleged incident was the result of a combination of factors which had built to explosive proportions:

1. Growing discontent with his marital relationship, accompanied by feelings of "total emptiness, hopelessness and helplessness" with regard to his marriage.
2. A growing feeling of lack of respect and appreciation from his wife.
3. Fear of loss of his parents' respect and their relationship if his marital relationship failed.
4. Chronic anxiety related to his inability to express emotions and frustrations in an effective, appropriate manner.
5. More recent feelings of abandonment related to his wife's absence due to her father's sickness.
6. Toxic effects of nearly 3,000 mgs. of caffeine in combination with four days of sympathomimetic tablets culminating in transient homicidal impulses.

During the two weeks' period of time since his discharge from the hospital, the following has been noted:

1. The patient has actively participated in group and individual therapy.
2. No evidence of alcohol addiction. Even so, Doctor TAYLOR, upon my recommendation, will begin attending a 36 hour course on alcohol education on 15 May 1979. He and his wife at this time plan to attend the course together.
3. He and his wife have sought out couples' therapy from a civilian therapist and will begin this in the near future.
4. Over a 14 day period he has taken approximately 14 tablets of Stelazine for anxiety and tension. He has denied recurrence of homicidal ideation. His mood and mental status are normal and appropriate to his present life situation.

It is the opinion of the Medical Board that the diagnoses are:

1. Acute toxic drug reaction (amphetamines, caffeine and marijuana) with transient homicidal impulses.
2. Situational adjustment reaction of adult life with severe marital maladjustment.

It is the recommendation of the Medical Board that LT TAYLOR be placed on six months limited duty during which time he should attend group therapy one or two times per week and individual therapy as deemed indicated. Short-term use of anti-anxiety agents to be utilized as seen fit. He was also encouraged to markedly reduce his use of caffeine. In addition, he has been encouraged to gradually initiate a physical exercise program to heighten feelings of self-esteem and for the relief of tension.

LT TAYLOR has been informed of the findings of the Board and does not desire to submit a statement in rebuttal.

The "Medical Board" consisted of Pettit and Smith. Both were signatories to the final report, although Dr. Smith would later declare that he had no choice.

The report—based on a key premise that aberrant drug abuse had largely caused Ken's assault on Marilyn—went up the chain of command to the Navy's central personnel files, where it lay forgotten until McCormick's query. It was dated May 14, 1979.

Nearly a month elapsed before—on June 11—lab tests which had been requested by the Naval Investigative Service showed that no drugs, including amphetamines, were evident in Ken's system the night he was admitted to the base hospital. By then, apparently, it no longer mattered.

• • •

The NIS inquiry, conducted separately from the psychiatric evaluation of Ken, concentrated on possible drug use by him and other personnel on the base with whom he was in regular contact. A dozen officers and men were interviewed. Ken himself "declined to make any statements on the advice of retained legal counsel."

The chief of the dental unit said that Ken had been "informally" cautioned about his continual fraternization with "enlisted persons."

One sailor, who had returned to civilian life, admitted buying marijuana for Ken. The rest denied knowing anything about Ken's drug use or marital status and refused to waive their rights. Two enlisted females were named as having had affairs with him. Both denied any "romantic links."

Confidential informant NL-P-1, who is in a position to provide reliable information, was interviewed. NL-P-1 related personal knowledge of SUBJECT's frequent use of marijuana and occasional use of amphetamines. NL-P-1 is aware that SUBJECT purchased illegal drugs from enlisted crew members aboard the USS FULTON. NL-P-1 related that the SUBJECT frequently smoked marijuana during lunch hour and as a result would treat dental patients while under the influence of marijuana.

And buried in the NIS files, almost a throwaway line, was a notation:

"It appeared that the SUBJECT prescribed codeine on numerous occasions when the treatment did not require it."

The Naval Investigative Service closed its books on Ken Taylor with a teletype to headquarters: THE CHARGE OF ATTEMPTED MURDER AGAINST SUBJECT WAS DISMISSED IN SUPERIOR COURT, NEW LONDON, CT, WHEN SUBJECT'S SPOUSE DECLINED TO TESTIFY AGAINST HER HUSBAND . . . CT STATE LAW REQUIRES THAT IN THE CASE OF A DISMISSAL THE RECORD IS SEALED. NIS FILES CONTAIN NO ADDITIONAL INFORMATION PERTINENT TO THIS INVESTIGATION.

• • •

After reviewing the Navy records, Paul Chaiet told McCormick to locate Dr. Ronald C. Smith. If the defense resorted to an insanity plea, temporary or not, he'd be a crucial witness. Chaiet allowed himself a small satisfaction. Let the defense call the other psychiatrist, Pettit. Let Pettit explain how Kenneth Taylor's "lack of self-esteem" prompted him to savage poor Teresa.

Chaiet also knew he would have to redouble his efforts to obtain the original copies of the Waterford police files. Even if he couldn't introduce them because of what he considered Connecticut's inane legal restrictions, he counted on putting the cops and Marilyn Hope on the stand, and he did not want any factual slip-ups in questioning them about what had occurred during the early morning hours of April 17, 1979.

• • •

In the Monmouth County Jail, Ken told Jack Venturi, "You've got to keep Connecticut out of this. I did that one. But I didn't do Acapulco. I swear to you, that's the truth."

# Chapter

## TEN

Ken loved Jack's idea. Venturi was going to bring in the eminent psychiatrist, Dr. Robert L. Sadoff, as an expert witness for the defense. In one of the most famous murder cases of the 1970s, Sadoff had appeared on behalf of Jeffrey MacDonald, the Green Beret doctor accused of slaughtering his wife and children. At the time, Sadoff had said that in his opinion MacDonald was incapable of committing such a crime.

Sadoff was a recognized authority in the use of sodium amytal, popularly and inaccurately labeled a truth serum. If the testing went badly, Venturi did not have to provide the results to Chaiet under the rules of discovery. Like polygraphs, sodium amytal tests were inadmissible in New Jersey courts to determine guilt or innocence, on the grounds that they had not been established as "scientifically reliable." Ironically, case law stemmed from a conviction that was reversed after the prosecutor claimed a defendant had to be guilty because he refused to submit to the barbiturate.

The problem was that, as with polygraph tests, a true sociopath could manipulate the "truth." Or, as Dr. Sadoff made clear to Venturi, "It should be noted that people can lie under the influence of sodium amytal and they can also fantasize and give answers that are not reflective of objective truth. Mostly, the person may believe that what he is saying is true, but it may not be verified by the facts of the case."

In criminal matters, Sadoff said he used sodium amytal exclusively to recapture lost memory when a defendant had amnesia regarding a particular event. While his score was not perfect, he "usually" enjoyed success. Still, he acknowledged that there was no standardized measurement for the test. Interpretation was left up to the individual "operator or physician conducting the interview," and the unfortunate fact was that the results were not accepted by all psychiatrists.

Privately, Venturi was hoping that Sadoff would find that Ken was loony. That way, he believed that he could get the test in at the trial as a "diagnostic aid," which the New Jersey Supreme Court had ruled allowable. And it was a hedge against another possibility. Defendants that Venturi successfully represented gave him high marks. Those in prison were less kind. He could easily see Ken appealing a murder conviction on the grounds of incompetent counsel for not exploring a temporary insanity defense.

A preliminary psychological examination was completed by an associate of Dr. Sadoff's on January 25. The sodium amytal session was set for March 6. Ken could hardly contain himself. "You'll see," he told Venturi.

• • •

Before then, though, Venturi had a whole new set of problems. Some of the discovery evidence from Chaiet had arrived. Topping the list were the sex phone calls the night Teresa was killed, calls that had gone on until almost six A.M.

Venturi had to hand it to Ken. Nothing appeared to faze him. "Look," Ken said, "I didn't want to tell this to the police or anybody. Even you."

The events of that night weren't quite as he had said thus far. He just hadn't wanted to hurt Teresa any more than necessary.

Around midnight after the Rozeks had left, he said he told Teresa, "I'm going to bed. You should come to bed, too. You haven't slept."

According to Venturi's notes, Ken reiterated that Teresa had not slept since Thursday. She'd been snorting coke, working on a half ounce of it that she had gotten from her brother. He cited the police interview with Cindy Diaz as proof. Teresa had gone shopping with Cindy on Saturday morning. Cindy confirmed that she "looked like shit." And Teresa at least admitted that she was hung over, right?

"I told her to come to bed. She said, 'Well, I'm going to do a little bit more coke and then I'll come to bed.' I said, 'Teresa, you do a little more coke, you're not coming to bed till you wear down.'

"I said the hell with it, I'm going to bed. I wake up about two, two-thirty. Teresa's not in bed. I go across the hall. The baby's asleep. Okay, I take a leak. I hear Teresa on the telephone downstairs. So I go to the top of the stairs and I said, 'Who the hell are you talking to in the middle of the night?' She says, 'Come on down here, I want you to listen to this.'

"So I go down and listen, and she's got a phone sex thing going. She's a very sexual girl, granted, but she's never gone this route. Where'd she get the numbers? Jeff and Celeste had been over, and Jeff left a *Hustler* magazine with all these numbers. The magazine was on the table.

"A female was talking sex to her, okay? She said, 'I'm going to dial another number.' Sometimes it was a tape and sometimes live, mostly tapes. Then Teresa wants to have oral sex with me while I listen to this on the phone. Okay, I said, whatever. I can say I had an orgasm while this went on and I hung up and went back to bed.

"I woke up again, about seven I would say, and the first thing was Teresa wasn't in bed. The baby's not in bed. I went to the top of the stairs and looked down and saw what I saw."

This time, Venturi decided to push Ken a little harder. The autopsy had shown that gobs of Vaseline had been smeared in and around Teresa's vagina and anus. What about that?

Ken didn't miss a beat. While Teresa was performing fellatio on the baby, he said, "She's got her hand between her buttocks. Her culottes were down. Not down to the floor or down to her knees, but down, half of her ass is showing. I know it flashed on me that second that I noticed that she had her hand between her buttocks. And I saw what was going on on the table and I ran to the bottom of the stairs to make sure I saw what I saw."

How could Teresa have run so quickly to the laundry room with her panties and culottes at mid-thigh?

Well, she did, Ken said.

Not your best, Venturi thought. Then Venturi brought up something else. At the time Teresa's body was discovered, the culottes were ripped open in the back, all the way along the seam of one leg, as if someone had tried to tear them off her.

When he had seen them, Ken insisted, the culottes weren't ripped. They were *unzipped*.

Other discovery material included the interview with Marilyn Hope about Ken's attack on her and the subsequent meetings between McCormick and Fausak and the Waterford cops.

Ken said, "First, they say they can't give out any information because the charges were dropped. The case was sealed. Then they go ahead and do it. How can they? You have to object."

Also included were the evasive, conflicting reports that Reyes Quinones had received from the Acapulco hotel security people and the local police—and the anonymous phone call Captain Potts had received from a "distraught female" about a fight between Ken and Teresa at Las Brisas. All Venturi had seen at that stage was a one-page memo by Potts that said, "The caller was finally coaxed into giving her first name which she provided as 'SORAYDA' (her spelling)."

"Who's this Sorayda?" Venturi asked.

"I don't know," Ken said. "I'll try to think."

• • •

On the evening of March 6, Ken was driven a few miles from jail to a hospital in Neptune, New Jersey, for the sodium amytal procedure.

After assuring Ken of confidentiality, Dr. Sadoff said, "Dr. Taylor. Ken, can I call you?"

"Yes."

"Good. What I'm going to do is give you just a little bit of an injection at this point, as a test dose, to see if you have any reaction. I assume that you will not because you told me that you are not allergic to medication."

"That's correct." Ken, in a short-sleeved shirt and slacks, was lying on an examination table, a video camera trained on him, his face turned to his right, toward Sadoff.

". . . You may tend to inject words that you don't mean and have slips of the tongue, but that's all right. We'll all be aware that it's the effect of the medication and not you."

"Okay."

With brisk confidence, Sadoff said, "I'm going to have you relive the experience of the death of your wife and also have you relive other experiences. And by 'reliving,' what I mean is to have you actually be there, rather than telling me about it in narrative. I want you to see what's going on, look around you—"

"Okay."

"—and that way you'll actually experience what happened. What'll happen is, you may have some emotional reaction to it and that's all right. And you might shout or scream, you might cry, you might do a lot of things. Again, that is all right. Okay, I'm slowly injecting it. Are you feeling any numbness yet on your tongue?"

"No, not yet."

After asking about his childhood pastimes and his family, Sadoff said, "Did you have a favorite?"

"My brother."

"What's he like?"

"Tom was a very good person," Ken said. That was

why he wanted the baby to be in Tom's custody—with his mother—while awaiting trial after his father had to return to Marion.

"Tell me something about your mother."

"There again, a very good person. I don't know. She's a religious person, but she's very strong in the family. She tends to try to keep the family together. She's very good with children. That's another reason I wanted her to have my son."

"How was she with you, growing up?"

For the first time, Ken paused. "Uh, very patient. Very understanding, loving, caring."

"Were you her favorite?"

"I would say so."

"How did she show it?"

"Well, she didn't show it in any other way than just what I picked up. I know she was very proud of me for what I did with my education. She told me she was disappointed with my brother not doing anything with his education."

"Are you disappointed with him, too?"

"I am."

"And yet you trust him enough to take care of your son?"

"Oh, yes. The problems we had were just problems. That's all they were. Man to man. But we always discussed it."

". . . How old were you when you had your first sexual experience?"

There was no discernible change in Ken's demeanor. He said that if Sadoff meant intercourse, he was around sixteen or seventeen and that it was "fine."

"Have you had any negative sexual experience, or have they all been pretty positive?"

Sex had been "positive" even with Teresa, he said, even "knowing what we know."

"Knowing what we know about what?"

"Maybe . . . maybe she was a bit over-sexual, but I didn't see that as a problem."

"By over-sexual, you mean what?"

Ken appeared to be searching for an answer. "Oh, she, let's see. Well, the bit with the telephone calls."

"That was her idea?"

"Yes."

Jack Venturi, sitting in the examining room out of Ken's line of sight, kept waiting for the moment when Ken would start "reliving" these events—showing the emotions that Sadoff had predicted. But as Sadoff took Ken through all of the woes and heartaches of Teresa's supposed drug addiction—indicating at one point that the baby had become "high" from Teresa's milk—he remained completely laid-back, conversational, his only body movement to cradle his head with his left hand to make himself more comfortable on the pillow.

Finally, when Sadoff asked about Acapulco, Venturi was sure there'd be some turmoil. But Ken, recalling the break-in by unknown intruders, remained dispassionate. The only new element he added was that he had glimpsed two men in the room. "When I got up to look around, I was kicked in the back of the head. I saw the man that kicked me and I saw a man across the room from the waist, maybe mid-chest to mid-thighs. That's all I saw." The way he said it, it was as if he were describing something that had happened not to him and Teresa, but to another couple.

"How's my pulse?" Ken asked.

"Normal, regular. Seventy, seventy-five."

Then Venturi listened in amazement as Sadoff introduced the night that Ken had attempted to chloroform Marilyn Hope. Although Ken had confessed to at least three Waterford cops, to a Navy chaplain, and to two Navy psychiatrists that he tried to kill her—had actually written down seven reasons why he wanted to do so—he now told Dr. Sadoff, under the influence of sodium amytal, that his intent was to rape Marilyn, not kill her. "We were in our fifth, maybe sixth year of marriage," he said. "She had become completely frigid and considered me a pig. A male pig. I had had sexual relationships, affairs if you will, with numerous of the girls in the Navy. That night I took the chloroform, put it on a sponge and put it to her face, tried to render her unconscious and rape her.''

Ken looked a little drowsy. His voice had begun to slur slightly. He had already tried out the rape version on Venturi. Maybe it's what he really believes, Venturi thought. Maybe he is nuts.

But then Ken made a small slip. He said that he had immediately called the Waterford police. "I said, 'You must send policemen after me. I've attacked my wife.' They said, 'Is she hurt?' And I said, 'No, apparently not.' And they said, 'Well, in that case, we cannot send the police.' So I called the chaplain.'' Unfortunately, Venturi noted, it was on record that the police weren't notified until the following day when the Navy psychiatrist Smith urged Marilyn to report the assault. And Marilyn, not Ken, phoned the chaplain.

Only when Sadoff began to discuss the night of Teresa's death did a dramatically different twist in the sequence of events unfold, totally different from what Ken had told the police in Manalapan, different even from what he had elaborated on with Venturi. Now Ken was saying that for a good part of the time, on November 11, he was not asleep at all, but had been up—with Teresa.

". . . At about two-thirty, I woke up to urinate. I said, 'Teresa, what are you doing still up?' She says, 'Well, I've been high and I'm just getting high. I'm going to come to bed pretty soon.' At seven-thirty I woke up. No. Excuse me. At three-thirty I woke and she was still up. At three-thirty we began these, what I call sex calls on the telephone. She wanted me to talk to a woman and have the woman talk to me while my wife performed sexual acts on me.''

"What kind of sexual acts?"

"Not intercourse. Oral sex. Petting and one time, anal sex.''

Hearing this, Venturi thought about Teresa's ripped culottes. He remembered his gut reaction that something explosively sexual had taken place, something that got out of control.

"On you?" Sadoff asked.

"Yes, while the woman was talking to me. This lasted approximately three hours. I think you have a telephone bill that will last [*sic*] that amount of time. List the amount of time."

"From three to about six?"

Staring vacantly into space, Ken said, "Can he understand me?"

"Sure," Sadoff said.

"Okay. Of these telephone calls. She used her credit card. She asked me to do the calling. She was embarrassed. For whatever reason, I don't know. She used [*sic*] a telephone call with her credit card. So I did. Two people would not accept the fact that it was her card. I said, 'Fine, we'll call someone else.' Thereafter I went to bed. Four-thirty. At seven to seven-thirty, I'm guessing more seven-thirty, I woke. My wife was not upstairs. I looked in my son's room. He was not there. He was not asleep. I thought, She's downstairs changing her [*sic*] diaper. So I went downstairs and this is when I couldn't believe my eyes."

"I want you to be there."

"I am."

"Can you be there?"

"I am."

"What do you see?"

"I am. I'm at the stairways. I believe there's eighteen stairs." Ken raised his left hand and gestured vaguely with it, then cradled his neck again. He had some trouble articulating. "Orange carpet, white whales. Right whales . . . rails. I walked two-thirds of the way down the stairs and she didn't see me. Now she's got good ears. She hears sounds all night. And wakes me. I say, 'Teresa, that's just the house settling in or expanding. There's nothing to it.'

"What happened here? Oh, this is the night my wife was killed," he said, his voice quite calm. "I got halfway down the stairs and I said to myself, 'I believe my wife is doing fellatio on my son.' I got to the bottom of the stairs and I was convinced. I said, 'What the fuck are you doing?' She looked at me very glassy-eyed, very—her eyes were red.

Very glassy-eyed. Drug-crazed. She had probably done a gram of cocaine that night. A gram of cocaine.

"She had her culottes pulled down. And now I did not know this at the time, but I have since been informed at the autopsy, that she had smeared Vaseline all over her buttocks, her anus and perineum. Now she was fellating my son on the table and trying to put her fingers into her anus or rectum, anus or vagina, I don't know."

He paused. "She looked at me, as I said, and ran—scurried—her skirts and pantyhose were down. I've been questioned on that. Okay, how fast can a woman run with her panties down? She scurried. Across the hall, approximately twelve to fifteen feet across the room into the hall and then into the laundry room. I picked my son up off the mat, because I knew he would fall over, and put him in the baby bed."

Ken took a deep breath and slowly exhaled. His voice got lower. "I followed by wife to the laundry room and she tried to kill me. She tried to kill me. She swung a set of dumbbells at my head. I've since been informed that they are twenty-five to thirty pounds, which is not surprising. She was five-seven, uh, two-three, but she was strong."

He yawned. "I didn't know if she would try to render me unconscious, knock me out, which is the same thing, or run in and hit my son. So I fought. I went down, somewhat. I grabbed the barbell that was waiting [sic] by the door to hold the door open as a doorstop. I picked up the doorbell [sic] and I hit her in the head. She fell to the floor. I fell to the floor. And I slumped against the floor. It was like I hit the wall and then just slid down. Moments, probably twenty to thirty moments later, I came out of what I call a robot or trance-like stance. A trance-like stance. After that, I had become a robot. I check my wife's vital signs and she had none. She looked like she was in bad shape. Apparently, she was in bad shape. Apparently, I hit her more than once. Apparently, the autopsy report says nine, uh, skull fractures."

Throughout this, Ken's tone stayed very matter-of-fact.

Sadoff urged him to try to recall more. "*Try* to be there. You hit her. With the barbell?"

"Yes."

"How many times do you remember hitting her?"

Ken cupped a hand over his eyes, as if in reflection. "Twice. And she fell. I hit her once and I hit her on the way down, and she fell."

"Do you remember hitting her more than that?"

"No, sir."

"Is that the first time you remember twice? Usually you say once."

". . . The second time was when she was falling, grabbing at my leg as if to punch me, claw me or trap—tackle—me."

"Have you ever told anybody you hit her twice?"

"No, sir . . . I think I told my lawyer."

"Because he told me you hit her once. Can you remember hitting her a third time?"

"No, sir."

"Fourth time?"

"No, sir."

"You think you did or do you think you could have given her nine skull fractures by hitting her twice?"

"No. I believe I hit her more."

"Why don't you remember?"

Ken did not respond. He pursed his lips and frowned. He scratched an ear.

"What happened that you don't remember?" Sadoff asked.

"Well, it's not that I don't remember. It's just that nine cumulated fractures could come from three blows."

"Why couldn't it come from two blows?"

"It could. I'm just saying the odds are better that they could come from three."

"Or they could come from nine blows. Do you think you hit her nine times?"

"They were all in the same area."

"All in the same area? So a couple of good swings might have given her nine fractures. You didn't have to hit her more than twice, did you?"

Ken sighed deeply. "I—I don't know."

"Well," Dr. Sadoff said, "you remembered everything else up to that point in great detail."

"I know she was breathing."

"She was what?"

"Breathing."

"She was breathing. And you know you hit her. You remember hitting her twice?"

Ken yawned again. He did not answer.

"Why do you think if you hit her a third time or fourth time," Sadoff coaxed him, "that you wouldn't remember?"

"That I wouldn't?"

"Yes."

"You mean with this medicine in me?"

"Now, yeah. Even now, if you'd hit her a third time, suppose she's lying on the ground. You take that barbell and you keep smashing her and smashing her. Wouldn't you remember?"

"I don't believe so . . . I have dissected skulls and I know where the bones come into each other. And I know that a fracture here," Ken said, pointing at his head, "is most likely going to fracture two or more bones."

"So you could have hit her only twice."

"That's very possible."

"Okay. Then you went into some kind of trance?"

"Yes. I remember slumping against a door."

"What was on your mind when you hit her?" Sadoff persisted. "What were you thinking? What was going on?"

"I was thinking, I've saved my life and my son's life. I did not know she was dead until I came out the trance."

"Did you intend to kill her?"

"No."

"What was your intent?"

"My effect—my intent—was to defend myself."

"Against what?"

"Against the attack that she was doing to me with the swinging of the doorbells [sic] on my head."

"How did you save your son's life?"

"I knocked her in the head and removed the doorbells."

"What makes you think she would have harmed your son?"

"She was already harming my son."

"How?"

The slurring in Ken's words was more evident. "By performing fellatio on him."

"That's harmful to him. How'd you feel—"

"It's not harmful physically, but I can just imagine the child's complex later in life when he goes to his mother for fellatio."

"—How did you feel when you saw her fellating your son?"

"Berserk," Ken said, his face expressionless.

"Berserk? Why should that make you so berserk?"

"Because I knew she was high. A few hours before we had these phone sex—while she was doing that to me and having me and the woman on the other end. I just thought, This is enough. This *really* is enough."

Sadoff waited for a moment and then said, "When you told me how you saw her doing this to your son, you didn't sound as though you were berserk. You were just describing it very calmly to me. But in fact you got very upset?"

"Yes."

"Why aren't you upset now, talking about it?"

"I am. But I think I'm sodium amytaled out."

"When you talk about it without the sodium amytal, do you get more emotional?"

"Yes. I usually get emotional and tear."

"You're crying a little bit now. You were somewhat emotional."

"I cried a lot with Doctor Cook [Sadoff's associate]."

"Did you? Why?"

Ken smiled. "Boy, you have a way with questions. He mentioned my daughter. My daughter and I were very close. The fact that I can't communicate with her—can't call her. I can't write to her. I can't see her. Can't hold her. I can't play with her."

"You seem to have more feeling about her than you do about your son?"

"No, that's not true."

Then Dr. Sadoff asked, "Do you know of any other mother who has ever fellated her son?"

Ken's voice was slurring even more as Venturi leaned forward to hear the answer.

"Yeah."

"Who?"

"A sleazy couple. In Ohio."

"People you knew?"

"Yeah."

Quickly—perhaps too quickly in the view of another psychiatrist who has seen the tape—Sadoff said, "Anybody in your family?"

"No."

"Did what you saw between your wife and your son bring back any memories about you and your mother?"

Clearly impacted by the sodium amytal now, lids heavy, Ken said, "Yeah, because she had done it to me that night."

"Not your wife. I'm talking about your mother."

Ken appeared to gather himself. His voice rose. "My mother? *No.*"

"This is your son's mother doing it to him. Did you have any feelings at all about your mother at that time?"

"No. None whatsoever."

Venturi had wanted questions that might buttress a self-defense strategy and Sadoff said, "The harm that your wife did to your son by fellating him was one thing. Did you think she was going to harm him physically as well?"

"Not until she ran into the laundry room and picked up the barbells [sic] and tried to kill me."

"Did you think she might do something to him?"

"I thought that if she rendered me unconscious, she would kill him."

"Why? Why would she do that?"

"Teresa was very strung out. We're talking months—of cocaine and codeine."

"Okay, how do you account for that trance-like stance that you said you had?"

"I think I was not believing, but believing. Not being able to believe my wife was dead. That she had been so good to my son. Except for the fellatio. And my wife had been so good to me."

"When did you come out of that trance?"

"Three hours."

"Three hours?"

"Not even. Two hours."

"Two hours. When you came out of it, what did you do?"

"First, the very first thing I did was walk to see if my son was in the infant seat, and he had fallen asleep. Then I hurried back to my wife and she had no pulse."

"She had no pulse? What were you feeling at the time?"

"Well, I know I had hit my wife in the head, uh, twice, and I believed she was dead."

"What did you do?"

"What did I do? I wrapped her in a carpeting pad that's used for carpeting. I brought her to the car and put her in the trunk of the Oldsmobile. I decided to take my son to Indiana and then come back and either one of two things: turn myself in, report what had happened, or kill myself."

In Marion, he said that he said, "Look, my son, you're safe with your [*sic*] mommy."

Why, Sadoff asked, had Ken driven around with Teresa's body for so long?

"So long. Because it was cold and the body gases were not starting to smell a lot."

"Why didn't you bury her?"

"I didn't want to leave her."

"Why not?"

"I loved her. What happened was just a freak. We were so happy together. I had been married three times. I knew what hell was in marriages. I knew what the problems were. We just didn't have those. We were best friends at first. We were totally supportive of each other and very loyal."

"So you kept her as long as you could?"

"Right."

"Why didn't you kill yourself?"

"I tried . . . I began thinking of my children, my parents, my family. They don't deserve this. They've lost Teresa. Losing me is not going to help. I'll take my chances. I'll go to jail."

Finally, Sadoff said, "Anything you want to tell me or ask me that I didn't ask you?"

And Ken said, "I wanted to know, and I think Jack [Venturi] mentioned this to me . . . that there was a psychosexual problem or possibility with me."

"With you?"

"Yeah."

"With respect to what?"

"Well, I don't know. I didn't know how to understand that. I'm not a homosexual. I've never raped anyone. I attempted to rape my second wife. I have not been with children. I've been with two women. I've never been with a man."

"Two women at the same time?"

"Yes. But I don't know what that means—psychosexual possibility in relation to me."

"I'm not sure we can answer that right now."

"Well, okay, let's face it. I had the Acapulco thing, I had this thing, I had the chloroform."

"The Acapulco thing you said was people who broke in."

Ken's eyes had been shut. They opened immediately. "That's right," he said.

"So if that's true, there's no psychosexual problem, is there?"

Ken nodded. "Right."

"Okay," Sadoff said. "I think that's enough. Are you tired? You think you'll be all right?"

"I could sleep," Ken said.

• • •

Dr. Sadoff took Venturi aside. This was about all they could get, he said. But he could state right now that Ken was not legally insane, temporary or otherwise. He knew what he was doing. Sadoff said that he would put it all in

201

his report, of course. Venturi had no doubt he would. Sadoff was getting two thousand dollars plus expenses for the examination.

It was just as well to cut it off, Venturi thought. One thing was sure. Paul Chaiet would never get to see this tape. Chaiet would have a field day with it—Ken's denial, despite all the Connecticut records to the contrary, that he had tried to kill Marilyn; Ken's new admission that he had been up for hours with Teresa in the Manalapan house; the anal sex that night; the way he had suddenly linked Acapulco with his violent acts in Connecticut and Manalapan. Venturi could hear Chaiet in court. Just what *is* the truth, Dr. Taylor? What is it that we're supposed to believe? Would you mind giving us a road map?

What bothered Venturi the most, though, was the whole ambiance of the videotape—how flat and emotionless Ken had been, with no sense of reliving anything.

In any event, the test was now irrelevant. Without an insanity plea, the tape could not be introduced. Venturi hoped that if Sadoff wrote the right kind of report, perhaps he could bring in elements of it without mentioning the use of sodium amytal.

After resting and being permitted to view the tape, however, Ken was elated. He was vindicated! The tape backed up everything he'd been saying about what Teresa was doing to the baby, how she had attacked him. He kept pressing Venturi. Wasn't that so?

Venturi didn't want to get into a debate. At last he ventured that perhaps Ken had been a little too cold, like an "ice man."

Suddenly, Ken's eyes hardened, his body went rigid. But he didn't say anything. There was only that stare.

Then Venturi got a letter from Ken laced with repressed anger.

*Jack,*
*After the interview on Wed 3/6/85 I understand some things about my case and my personality. Until the last 2 years I was not "cold" as you and others are describing*

*me. There are several reasons for this. First of which is I*
*have had a very tumultuous and tough adult life. I've had*
*a lot of pain, hurt and disappointment. I've seen a hell of*
*a lot and I've lived a hell of a lot. I've been through some*
*times that could change the toughest of individuals. I'm a*
*strong person but I've been through so much hell that I've*
*become hardened. I can handle pressure and I always*
*have. I have always been the clutch performer but over the*
*years all these clutch performances have worn the edge*
*and flattened my personality.*

*I can handle pressure just as always but I've become the*
*"ice man." I love my family and children like nothing else*
*and more than ever. In all of the athletic events and teams*
*I've participated with I've always and consistently been the*
*clutch performer and I've always provided. In the Navy my*
*captain depended on me to carry the load for the clinic.*
*There were times when he said I saved his ass by carrying*
*the load and keeping "production" while our staff was cut*
*into half and we still got the work done.*

*In Brooklyn I worked 60 hours a week, managed 10 girls,*
*four dentists, the "books" for the office and trained the*
*dentists as well as did at least one half of the entire patient*
*load. It was hell but I did it. (Dental school did a number*
*on me also—I'd rather discuss that issue than write about*
*it.) In fact, I'd rather discuss the whole thing so I'm going*
*to stop writing. I've seen and done so much that I know*
*why I've hardened.*

A memo accompanied the letter. It was written in big
block letters, almost as if Ken had been stabbing the paper
with his pen:

COLD?
I. AS A HOSPITAL ORDERLY—
   1. 3 ALL NIGHT "DEATH" WATCHES (2 OF THESE PEO-
      PLE DIED WHILE I WAS "WATCHING" THEM).
   2. WALKED INTO ROOM TO TAKE VITAL SIGNS AND
      FOUND PATIENT HAD DIED WHEN I BEGAN TO
      TAKE PULSE.

3. I HAD TO TAKE 4 *BABIES* TO THE MORGUE WRAPPED UP AND PUT THEM IN THE FREEZER WAITING AUTOPSY (4 SEPARATE OCCASIONS).
4. ASSISTING A SURGEON IN SURGERY—
   HE DID NOT TELL ME WHAT HE WAS DOING. HE TOLD ME TO HOLD THE BOY'S (16 YRS) LEG. HE PICKED UP AN INSTRUMENT AND AMPUTATED THE BOY'S LEG FROM THE THIGH. I WAS LEFT HOLDING THE LEG. HE LAUGHED!
5. I HAD TO CARE FOR A QUADRIPLEGIC (29 YEAR OLD MAN), TURN HIM, CLEAN HIM, HOLD URINE BOTTLE FOR HIM.

II. I'VE HAD WOMEN COME TO ME—IN THE NAVY (OFFICERS' WIVES, ENLISTED WIVES, DENTAL ASSISTANTS, PATIENTS, ETC. ETC.)—AND DO EVERYTHING FROM ASKING ME TO TAKE THEM TO ACTUALLY WALKING INTO MY ROOM AND TAKING OFF THEIR CLOTHES. I HAVE HAD A COMMANDING OFFICER OF A SUBMARINE ASK ME TO TAKE HIS WIFE WHILE HE WAS OUT TO SEA. I HAVE BEEN BOMBARDED BY WOMEN IN SO MANY WAYS I BECAME COLD. I COULDN'T BELIEVE THE NUMBER OF WIVES AND OTHERS, GIRL FRIENDS, ETC., WHO CAME ON TO ME. I REALLY DIDN'T LIKE IT. (THEY CAME TO MY HOUSE!)

IF I APPEAR TO BE COLD, MAYBE I AM. *BUT* THERE IS A REASON FOR EVERYTHING.

I HAD A LOT OF SLEAZY TYPE GIRL FRIENDS. DRUGGIES, GO-GO GIRLS AND EVEN 2 HOOKERS. THEY WOULD PICK ME OUT. 6 DIFFERENT TIMES GO-GO DANCERS ASKED ME TO TAKE THEM OUT AFTER THEIR JOBS WAS [*sic*] FINISHED THAT NIGHT.

I TOLD DR. COOK ABOUT A HITCH-HIKER WHO PRACTICALLY RAPED ME. SHE WAS GORGEOUS. THIS JUST DOESN'T HAPPEN TO PEOPLE.

2 AIRLINE STEWARDESSES (SEPARATE INCIDENTS) PICKED ME UP ON FLIGHTS (NOT INCLUDING MARILYN HOPE). EACH ONE GAVE ME A NOTE—ONE TO MEET HER IN INDIANAPOLIS AND ONE TO GO TO THE BACK OF THE PLANE WITH HER.

JACK, IF I APPEAR COLD, THERE ARE GOOD REASONS.
III. THE 2 BROKEN MARRIAGES TOOK A LOT OUT OF ME.
LOSING ASTRID WAS DEVASTATING. THAT LITTLE GIRL
LOVES ME. I CAN'T THINK ABOUT HER WITHOUT TEARS
COMING TO MY EYES.
IV. DRUG ABUSE—NO EXPLANATION NEEDED.
V. TERESA—

Abruptly, Ken's handwriting changed to script.

*She was the epitome of what I wanted. She was by no means the most attractive woman I had. She was chubby. Teresa was so good to me and loved me so totally. We were best friends. We were best lovers. She was the one woman I could have lived a lifetime with. Teresa and I could say anything to each other and do anything together.*

*After all the bullshit with women, I finally found the one woman I loved as a person. We were partners. We were friends, lovers, spouses, business partners, parents, homemakers, etc. etc. Jack, I've lost her. The one woman, the one person, my best friend, is gone. She's dead. You wonder why I'm cold?! I could have spent my entire life with her and been forever happy.*

*Yes, I'm cold. I've lost my wife, my profession, my daughter, and now people are trying to take away my son. I have memories and nightmares that would put most people in a strait jacket but I continue to function. Yes, I'm cold but I love my family and children. I want to have a simple life caring for my family and giving them the best I can. I want my freedom and need it. Now that I'm certain about what happened, I know for sure I'm okay.*

*P.S. I could go on and on about the experiences and situations in my life that have hardened my exterior but I think you get the message.*

Venturi also had asked Ken for his comments concerning many of the people McCormick and Fausak had interviewed. Checking them off one by one, he wrote back that they were all either dope addicts themselves or liars.

• • •

But on one score at least, Jack Venturi knew that Ken was absolutely correct. To avoid a murder conviction, Connecticut had to be kept out of the trial.

Right then, Venturi more or less forgot about Acapulco.

# Chapter

# ELEVEN

On March 11, five days after Ken's exposure to sodium amytal, Paul Chaiet now decided to send McCormick and Fausak to Acapulco. Reyes Quinones went as their interpreter.

On the face of it, Connecticut would seem to be all Chaiet needed to show a pattern of deadly, knowing and purposeful violence by Ken that culminated in Teresa's murder. But he was determined to leave nothing to chance. Ken Taylor had to be put away for the rest of his meaningful life, and whatever that took, Chaiet was prepared to do it.

Nearly a month had passed before the Las Brisas security log concerning the alleged assault on Ken and Teresa was received and translated by Quinones. As soon as he read it, Chaiet knew he had to pursue the matter. One report noted that while Teresa was lying in a "pool of blood," her husband "did not appear injured." Another said, "Mr. Taylor had a tiny cut that did not look that it could be caused by a blow." A third observed that the bed in which Ken claimed he and Teresa were asleep was "still made up."

For use in the trial, all of this had to be followed up.

And there was something else. No reports from the local police had been forwarded. Chaiet warned McCormick to be diplomatic about the five-hundred-dollar payoff Ken claimed to have made to get out of jail. The tortured body of a missing American drug enforcement agent named Enrique Camarena had just been found in Mexico, and the U.S. press was filled with stories about corrupt Mexican police.

Quinones had made arrangements for the three of them to stay in the same room—casita 249—that Ken and Teresa occupied. First thing on their arrival, Quinones called the elusive police official he had vainly tried to reach by phone from New Jersey, Comandante Alvaro Gutierrez Mendoza. But Gutierrez was still unavailable. This time he was said to be hot on the trail of some bank robbers. No one could predict when he'd be back in the office.

They then interviewed Gabriel Santoyo, the Las Brisas security director. According to McCormick's notes:

Santoyo advised that he was at home when he received a call asking him to respond to the hotel. He was also asked to summon the police. He related that when he got to Room 249, there were several persons present. Taylor was sitting on the balcony and Mrs. Taylor was within the room. Santoyo recalled having a hotel employee, identified as José Romero, ask Taylor why he had assaulted his wife and with that Taylor became somewhat excited and began to yell. Mrs. Taylor was taken to the hospital and Taylor was taken away by the police.

Santoyo was later asked if there had been any incidents involving intruders around the time of the assault on Teresa Taylor on July 14, 1983. He advised that since he has been with the Security Forces at Las Brisas—for the past five years—there have only been two incidents of such assaults, one in May, 1984, the other in June. In both incidents, the perpetrators were apprehended. Santoyo advised that in 1983 there were 192 reported thefts at the hotel. It is believed that most of these thefts are committed by certain employees, but unless they are caught in the actual crime, the union they belong to protects them from being fired.

Chaiet had wanted a complete rundown on the hotel's security setup. Santoyo took the investigators on a tour. McCormick was impressed—three twenty-two-man shifts a day, five mobile patrols and a foot patrol covering a perimeter chain-link fence.

McCormick and Fausak also questioned Miguel Lugo, who was in charge of security that night. According to Lugo, he immediately called in both the incoming and outgoing guard shifts and assigned some forty men in all to scour the area around casita 249. The hotel's main entrance was locked:

> Taylor was outside the room on the balcony with José Romero. Lugo went on the balcony and had Romero ask what occurred. Through Romero, Taylor stated that one individual wearing blue pants had entered the room and hit him while he was lying on the bed sleeping.
>
> Lugo stated that he was very suspicious because at that time everyone including Taylor believed Mrs. Taylor was dead and that Taylor was not upset. Lugo reentered the room and went over to Mrs. Taylor. He placed his hand on her chest and felt a slight heartbeat . . . Lugo went back to the balcony to have Romero tell Taylor that his wife was still alive and that an ambulance had been summoned. Taylor just sat there emotionless and remained emotionless even after Mrs. Taylor started to moan and call out for help. Lugo went to her and attempted to comfort her. After doing so, Lugo had Romero ask Taylor for a better description of the assailant. Taylor responded that "he was like you," indicating that he was about the same size as Lugo. Lugo had Taylor stand and related that he could not understand how an individual the size of Tay-

lor could have been assaulted by anyone as small as himself.

Lugo examined Taylor and observed fingernail scratches on the inside of both of Taylor's forearms. He also noticed a small, very slight reddish mark on Taylor's forehead, but did not observe any other injuries on him. Lugo added that he recalled that the Taylors had received room service at approximately 9:30 P.M. and that some of the food had been eaten before the assault had occurred at about 10:30 P.M.

The doctor arrived and attended to Mrs. Taylor who was taken to the hospital. When she was being taken out, she began to moan in pain and ask for help. Taylor made no attempt to comfort her.

The next day McCormick and Fausak solved the mystery of the red-haired woman who visited Teresa's hospital room when Al Benigno was there. She was a guest of the hotel herself, a bilingual Texan who'd been pressed into service by the Las Brisas reservations manager, Valentino Nada, to help obtain a release from the Taylors.

Nada confirmed that Ken was brought back to the hotel by police on July 18—the day Ken said that he had paid the five-hundred-dollar bribe—and that his belongings, which had been placed in a vault, were returned to him. That was all he knew about it, Nada said.

Nada gasped when McCormick showed him a photograph of Teresa's smashed face after her body was discovered in Pennsylvania. Nada thought it had been taken at the hospital. That was exactly how she had looked then.

Like Nada, Dr. Ortiz Pavon, who initially attended Teresa at Las Brisas, also thought it was a picture taken at the Acapulco hospital. According to Ortiz, when he first entered the casita, Ken was lying on the floor between the room and the balcony:

The doctor attended Kenneth Taylor first because without observing any trauma to his body, he believed that Taylor might have been shot. The doctor was unable to find any signs of injury that would have rendered him incapacitated. He then turned his attention to Teresa Taylor who was sitting slouched on the floor in a corner of the room.

Dr. Ortiz advised that Mrs. Taylor appeared dead. She was covered with blood. There was blood all over the walls, as well as on the floor where she was located. Mrs. Taylor's pulse was weak. She was given immediate attention for her eye and a deep gash in her throat. Teresa Taylor had been beaten up so badly that she had defecated herself.

He advised that he did notice an odor of alcohol on Mrs. Taylor's breath, but he failed to notice the same on Taylor because he was only with him a short time. He also advised that he did not know whether or not Mr. and Mrs. Taylor may have been under the influence of drugs.

While he was in the room treating Mrs. Taylor, Taylor was placed in a chair on the balcony by security people who were speaking to him. He said that Taylor acted very calm and cool during the incident.

. . . A couple of days after the assault, Dr. Ortiz related that he went to the Centro Medico Hospital to pay a courtesy call on Mrs. Taylor. He said that Taylor was there with her and that when the doctor asked her what had happened, Taylor appeared to become frightened. Mrs. Taylor said that she preferred not to discuss it. When Mrs. Taylor's father arrived at the hospital, Taylor again became frightened—that he was nervous and shaking and repeatedly asked the doctor when his wife would be able to travel.

Mrs. Taylor's father asked Dr. Ortiz Pavon what had happened and the doctor stated that he really did not know. He was afraid of a lawsuit if he had given his opinion that it was Taylor who assaulted his wife. Mrs. Taylor's father then said that they wanted to leave the hospital as quickly as possible, so the doctor transported them to the airport.

McCormick and Fausak sensed that many of the hotel employees they were questioning were fearful of somehow saying the wrong thing, something that might put the hotel in an unfavorable light and cost them their jobs. This occasionally made them sound hesitant and imprecise. But not José Francisco Romero, an assistant manager who had been on duty that night. Romero was the witness they'd been hoping to find. He not only was forthright and fluent in English but also had a vivid recollection of events from the moment when, manning the switchboard, he heard the words, "attack, attack." The caller, he said, was "definitely a male," his voice "weak," almost as if he were "faking" it.

Romero commandeered a jeep. With another assistant manager and a security guard, Romero drove along a roadway and hurried down a flight of stairs that led to casita 249 and an adjoining one, 250, which was then unoccupied. He rang the bell and heard moaning inside the room. It seemed to be right on the other side of the door. The door was double-locked. He told the guard to radio for assistance. He went around the casita and down an incline to a wall that enclosed the pool. Lights were on in the room and on the balcony. From his vantage point, he spied Ken lying halfway out of the balcony door, his head at the top of the steps descending to the pool. He was moaning.

Scared, Romero retreated to the roadway stairs for perhaps ten minutes until security reinforcements arrived. He returned to the pool wall. Ken no longer was on the balcony. Romero scrambled over the wall followed by several guards:

> Mr. Romero stated that as soon as he got into the room, he smelled blood and excrement. He observed Taylor now lying on the floor of the room by the bathroom. Taylor was clothed in a short-sleeved shirt and yellow swimming shorts. He appeared in a daze. The shower stall door was open and the water running. His legs appeared wet.
>
> Romero then turned to the corner of the room where he saw Teresa Taylor on the floor covered with blood,

wearing a pink baby-doll type nightgown. The floor under her was covered with blood. There was a broken green glass water bottle on the floor, as well as broken glass on the bed. Romero advised that the sheets to the bed had been turned down, but the bed did not appear as though anyone had been in it.

Romero went outside until a doctor arrived. The entire area was searched by hotel employees, both on foot and in jeeps, but no one was discovered. Taylor was brought to the balcony where Romero translated for Captain Lugo of the security force. Lugo asked him to ask Taylor where he was from, how he had come to Las Brisas, what the name of his wife was and what his profession was. Taylor answered all these questions correctly, to the point and without hesitation.

When the police arrived, Romero said that he continued to act as an interpreter. Ken volunteered a possible suspect. While he was shopping with Teresa in Acapulco that afternoon, they were approached by a boy trying to sell them jewelry. They rebuffed him and the boy became angry. He said that it may have been the boy who came into the room and assaulted him, hitting him "over the head with a green glass water bottle." He described the boy as being Mexican, about eighteen, wearing jeans and a red shirt.

Romero said he went with the police and Ken to the station where Ken kept to his story about an intruder. The police also tried to question Teresa at the hospital, but she was "incoherent."

In room 249, the bathroom and dressing area were to the immediate right. Beyond this, also to the right, was a king-size bed. Past the bed was a sliding door to the balcony. To the left was a minibar, a round marble table, and chairs.

Except for a shattered glass lamp, the broken water bottle, and the spread now on the bed, Romero said the layout was the same as it had been the night of July 14.

A heavy green water bottle—like the one that caused the most damage to Teresa, the one that Ken had cited among other items that he might have been hit with—was on the minibar in the corner of the room farthest from the balcony door. Was that where water bottles were normally placed? Yes, always, Romero said. That was interesting, McCormick thought. These supposed intruders were so well prepared that they had to creep past the bed, past Ken and Teresa, to obtain a weapon to attack their victims.

McCormick and Fausak asked Romero to help them recreate the scene that night. McCormick and Romero went outside. Fausak lay on the floor by the door inside the room and moaned. Yes, Romero said, those were the moans he'd heard. Fausak moved to the balcony door where Romero first saw Ken and moaned again. From outside the front door, the moans couldn't be heard. Romero estimated that it had taken him about three minutes to get around the casita where he saw Ken on the balcony. Then, ten minutes later, he actually entered the room and found Ken on the floor by the bathroom. The sequence was repeated with the shower on and off. The results were the same. For a guy who claimed to have been knocked senseless, McCormick thought, Ken had been pretty active.

As if he were Teresa, Romero cowered against the wall away from the bed in a fetal position, hands up, trying to ward off blows. Both cops stared at each other. Both had the same thought. Fausak said it first. She must have known who her assailant was, that it was her husband.

McCormick and Fausak had only lately become aware that battered wives quite often returned to their brutalizing husbands or refused to press charges against them because of shame, humiliation, guilt and fear. Hadn't that been the case with Marilyn Hope? However incomprehensible it was to him, McCormick decided that it was also true of Teresa.

Fausak had another notion. Maybe the trauma of the awful beating Teresa suffered had wiped out her memory of it. There were plenty of case histories on that score. He recalled some of Teresa's friends mentioning that she had started hearing "voices" about Acapulco. Maybe it was all coming back to her. But Fausak realized that he would never know. Nobody would.

•   •   •

Despite repeated phone calls to Acapulco police headquarters by Quinones, Comandante Gutierrez remained unavailable. The hell with it, McCormick told Quinones. Gutierrez was obviously ducking them. They'd go down there unannounced.

Fausak stayed behind to diagram and photograph the area around the casita, check out the placement of guards and the frequency of security patrols.

Casita 249 was located below a hotel roadway. The concrete wall around the private pool it overlooked was about three feet high. Beyond the wall, toward Acapulco Bay, was a ten-foot cyclone fence topped with barbed wire. From the fence there was a sheer rock drop of approximately fifty feet to a public road.

Fausak drove along the road and surveyed the cliff. Anything was possible, he thought, but it would have taken Spiderman to scramble up there. If someone had anticipated a cache of thousands of dollars in the casita or, say, the Hope diamond, it might have been worth a try. But even the valuables that Ken claimed were missing were hardly the stuff for a daredevil climb like this. And, according to Romero, neither the closets nor drawers in the room showed any signs of having been rifled.

• • •

Sure enough, Comandante Gutierrez was behind his desk when McCormick and Quinones arrived, ushered in by his ravishing secretary. If Gutierrez had really been away, McCormick couldn't help thinking, she might have been the reason.

McCormick did not mention the difficulty in contacting him. Nor did Gutierrez, a rather short man with a bland round face and alert black eyes. Of course he recalled the savage beating of the American woman at Las Brisas, he said. As a matter of fact, he had gone to the hospital to speak to her. And, almost as if challenging McCormick to dispute him, he added that Señora Taylor out of gratitude for his concern gave him her watch, which he in turn had given to *his* wife.

It was clear, Gutierrez said, that the assailant was the

husband. During one of his hospital visits, he himself had heard Taylor "apologizing" to his wife for what he had done.

Treading lightly, McCormick inquired why charges had not been brought against Ken. Ah, said Gutierrez with a shrug, it would have been different had a Mexican been involved. But since this was purely an American affair, the realities of the tourism business demanded that the aggrieved party sign a complaint. After all, Gutierrez pointedly said, who needed a "bad press"? Because Mrs. Taylor had refused to file charges, no police reports were on record.

McCormick asked if he could talk to some of the men who had been on the scene. No problem, Gutierrez said, and McCormick at last got what he'd been after. Armando Vallarino, a bilingual officer specializing in tourist problems, had conducted the interrogation of Ken at the jail. Over lunch at the best restaurant McCormick and Quinones could find, Vallarino said that during hours of questioning, Ken kept insisting that two "terrorists" dressed in black with black masks had assaulted and robbed him and his wife. Finally, Vallarino said he said to Ken, "Don't make a fool of me." If anyone was going to be beaten to a pulp under those circumstances, it would have been "the man," not the woman. "You are lying," he told Ken and slapped him. McCormick got the impression that it was a pretty good smack. After that, Vallarino said, Ken looked at him and confessed that he had a fight with his wife, but that she had started it.

Vallarino also said that the American consular agent for Acapulco, L. J. Bon Urbanek, had come to the jail. The next day McCormick visited Urbanek. For McCormick, Urbanek personified the stuffy striped-pants State Department type always being caricatured in cartoons. Urbanek said that he only "vaguely" remembered the incident. That was a little odd, McCormick said. Were that many Americans beaten that badly in Acapulco? Hadn't the victim's father telephoned Urbanek at least twice? And wasn't it true that Urbanek had been to see the husband?

Urbanek stiffened. He'd have to clear this with the embassy in Mexico City. He excused himself, returning several minutes later with the smug air of a man who knew his bureaucracy. Before any information could be released, a formal request in writing had to be forwarded to the Department of State in Washington.

"You ever work for the State of Connecticut?" McCormick asked.

"What?"

"Never mind," McCormick said.

After interviewing members of the hospital staff and obtaining a sworn deposition from Vallarino—Comandante Gutierrez declined to provide one—the three investigators returned to New Jersey with assurances from Vallarino, Romero, and Dr. Ortiz that they would testify.

In his Freehold office, even Paul Chaiet was ready to concede that a case against Ken for murder was just about buttoned up.

• • •

As yet unaware of Chaiet's Acapulco foray, Jack Venturi got a testy note from Jean Taylor. After the birth of Celeste's first child, a girl, the Monmouth County Juvenile and Domestic Relations Court not only had restored baby Philip's shared custody between the Whites in Staten Island and the Taylors in Manalapan, but also had given Celeste and Jeff an additional day. It was simply outrageous, Jean wrote. Each time the baby was returned to her, he had a severe diaper rash. Obviously, Celeste was an unfit mother who didn't know how to care for an infant, who didn't have the slightest interest in cleanliness.

Venturi should see how "Kenny's" eyes lit up with joy when she brought Philip on her daily visits to jail and how upset he was about what was happening to *his* son.

This was news to Venturi. His client, presumably with weightier issues on his mind, hadn't mentioned it.

Zach also wrote an angry letter to Venturi, demanding to know why nothing was being done about "smearing Teresa's character." Venturi promptly replied, "Please be advised that I do not know anything about this."

In retaining a private detective agency, Venturi had, of course, counted on some evidence of Teresa's past drug abuse turning up. That was critical in establishing her behavior on November 11. But no substantiation could be found to verify Ken's claim that she was addicted to cocaine, or anything else for that matter. She appeared to be a loving, generous person. The worst that could be said about her was that she had a temper, hardly grounds for killing her.

Couldn't Ken supply any names? He had, he said. There was Cindy Diaz, Irene DeBlasio, the Rozeks, Teresa's old boyfriend, and her brother. They were all lying. Venturi pressed him. How about *his* friends? He didn't have any. He hadn't had time to socialize. He'd been too busy building his practice.

The picture wasn't totally bleak, though. Following the sodium amytal session, the analysis Venturi received from Dr. Sadoff was better than he had dared to hope. It said in part:

> . . . *I find he is currently without psychosis and that he is not mentally ill. He does not require psychiatric treatment. He is mentally competent to proceed legally in that he knows the nature and consequences of his current legal situation and can work with counsel in preparing his defense.*
>
> *With respect to his state of mind at the time of the death of his wife, it is my opinion that Dr. Taylor was in such a state of mind that he believed that his wife was having fellatio with their son and that she posed a significant threat of harm to the son since she had been under the influence of drugs and alcohol and that he found her "crazed with drugs." Furthermore, his state of mind was affected by her attack upon him, knocking him down with one of the barbells kept in the laundry room. He believed both his life and the life of his son were in danger at the hands of his wife. He reacted instinctively by picking up the nearest object in order to stop his wife from harming him and harming his son, too. He hit her with the object*

*and his recollection even under sodium amytal is that he hit her only twice with the door weight.*

*There is no indication that Dr. Taylor was McNaughton insane at the time of this occurrence and there is no indication that he was hallucinating or distorting his perception. He is consistent in his reports about her attack on him and on the baby. In my opinion, he acted to protect himself and his son from serious bodily harm or death at the hands of his wife who was under the influence of drugs and acting irrationally.*

• • •

Now he could at least put Sadoff on the stand as an expert defense witness concerning Ken's state of mind. If he stipulated that there would be no reference to the use of sodium amytal, he didn't see how the court could refuse him. Sadoff's credentials were impeccable. After all, he'd just been the main witness in a widely publicized appearance before a New Jersey legislative commission weighing changes in the McNaughton insanity test—knowing right from wrong. Sadoff testified that the test was fair, that it was a tougher standard than those of many other states, and he had carried the day.

As soon as Ken read Sadoff's report, he saw it as the certain key to his acquittal. All the hostility he had displayed after Venturi's "ice man" remark vanished. In his new euphoria, he wrote to Venturi: "IF THE STATE SENATE PUTS SO MUCH CONFIDENCE IN DR. SADOFF'S OPINION, THEN THE LOCAL COUNTY ASSISTANT PROSECUTOR, JUDGE AND JURY SHOULD HAVE CONFIDENCE IN HIS STATEMENTS CONCERNING ME. I THINK THE JURY SHOULD BE VERY MUCH IMPRESSED WITH HIS CREDENTIALS AND CREDIBILITY!"

A flurry of excited memos from Ken followed:

*JACK,*
*After reviewing initial discovery, digesting the report concerning the sodium amytal interview and knowing what's true and what is not true, I have drawn certain conclusions. There are several false statements being made, especially*

*by my in-laws, which we will not be able to prove as false. The way I see it, it's their word against mine.*

*(1) I didn't have them fill prescriptions and give them to me. Any precriptions written for them were for them.*

*(2) Teresa abused my prescription writing privilege. I did write numerous prescriptions for her.*

*(3) I did not use drugs in my office during working hours. I did cocaine after work on several occasions before I left to go home.*

*(4) Acapulco is a total frame by the Mexican police and Las Brisas hotel security to cover their asses against a law suit. Jack, I tell you I did not do it. Any and all statements to the contrary are false and fabricated to protect the hotel against liability.*

*(5) Agar & Sutton—I told you from the beginning that I did steal from them and I told you why I did it.*

*(6) The sodium amytal depicts the incident at my home with Teresa. Anything to the contrary either comes from a) false witnesses and b) pressure and/or disorientation when I made my statement to the police concerning the manner in which Teresa was struck.*

*(7) Disposition of Teresa's body and all actions and/or statements concerning the incident that I made are all efforts on my behalf to stall the eventual and inevitable discovery, so I could make my "goodbyes" to Marilyn and Astrid as well as ascertain my son's health and safety in the custody of my Family.*

*Anything else in the additional discovery will be what it is and I'll give you an honest evaluation of the material.*

• • •

Among the "false witnesses" that Ken railed against over and over again was a Joseph Shamonsky, a man he had never met, who lived near the Hawk Mountain Bird Sanctuary. Shamonsky had been questioned by the Pennsylvania State Police in one of the roadblocks that had been thrown up in the area the morning after Teresa's body was found. He reported seeing a vehicle in the sanctuary about twenty minutes after midnight. Like Teresa's Cutlass, the car was two-toned with a white top. It had New Jersey plates and Shamonsky remembered that, like Teresa's, a "6" had been one of the numbers. The solitary male driver, he said, appeared to be unfamiliar with the road.

Although Shamonsky was the most marginal of witnesses in the investigation, his name popped up repeatedly in police summaries, and every mention of him seemed to drive Ken into a frenzy. "Not true!" Ken wrote. "This witness is in error," he wrote another time. "LIES!" he scribbled in a memo to Venturi.

At best, it simply meant that Ken might have returned to Manalapan before leaving Teresa's body at Hawk Mountain. What made it all the more bizarre was that his explanation of where he had actually gone—to a go-go dance joint after telephoning the Benignos, his parents and a massage parlor in Hartford—hardly enhanced his character. But he insisted, "There were two blond dancers that evening. The owner will confirm this! Ask Lori the barmaid if I was there. I'm certain she'll remember. We talked!"

It was as though Ken had finally unearthed a factual flaw in the case against him, however inconsequential, and wouldn't let go of it, like a dog with a bone.

• • •

He appeared fixated by Hawk Mountain:

*Statement was made that the area where Teresa's body was found is heavily wooded. I realized this fact also. However, my intent was not to hide her body. In my confused state I wanted to leave her at this sanctuary as a place of peace and natural beauty, knowing she would be found soon. I had said my goodbyes, left our son with my mother and father and was then prepared to return home and end my life.*

• • •

On March 20, with the trial date two months off, he wrote to Venturi:

*Jack,*

*I want you to be aware of 2 cases that have come down here.*

*First, Joe Mulvahill. I sent you an article concerning this guy. He killed his wife. He knocked her out with a baseball bat and then drowned her in the bath tub. He got a 10 yr flat for manslaughter.*

*Second, Joe Taylor. 27 yr old State Trooper. He knew his girl friend was cheating on him. He went to her house, took his pistol with him and broke in the door. He shot the man twice and his girl friend once. The man died. He got 20 yrs. with a 10 yr stipulation for manslaughter.*

*In light of these two cases and in light of the sodium amytal results, I have to feel better than these two guys. All I want is to be a loving parent. I know you're doing your best and I pray my self-defense will let me walk out of here.*

* * *

Venturi had tried to nudge Ken toward a defense of manslaughter committed in the heat of passion. The stumbling block was always the likelihood of some prison time. Now Sadoff's report had made Ken even more obstinate. Wasn't sodium amytal the "truth serum"? Hadn't everything he'd said under the barbiturate been precisely what he had said all along? The sodium amytal *proved* he was innocent.

Venturi didn't seem to be able to get through to him that lacking an insanity defense, there was no chance of citing the sodium amytal procedure. One thing was sure, Venturi thought. He had a client with a remarkable facility for not hearing what he didn't want to.

If he got Dr. Sadoff on the stand, what Venturi hoped to do was focus narrowly on how Ken "reacted instinctively" when he saw Teresa performing fellatio on the baby and then was attacked by her. That way, he could establish the provocation and subsequent passion that rocketed him out of control.

The last thing he wanted was to delve into the business of the two dumbbells. Venturi could see Chaiet salivating over this. Unfortunately, the one without weights was the one with blood on it. The other dumbbell, the only one Teresa could have used, had the weights in place, and they came to thirty pounds. Well, Ken had said, "she was a lot stronger than you'd think." Maybe so, but Venturi wasn't eager to dazzle jurors with that proposition. Besides, it opened up another delicate question. Why didn't a man as big and as strong as Ken simply take the dumbbell from her?

So far, Venturi had emphasized the advantages of a defense based on heat of passion. Now he tried a negative approach—ticking off all the problems inherent in a self-defense strategy. The autopsy report said that Teresa's shattered skull had nine separate fractures. Even if he argued that this did not necessarily mean there were nine blows, it surely indicated there had been more than the one, possibly two, that Ken recalled. Venturi had been researching this question. Five blows was about the best he could expect the medical examiner to grant in cross-examination. "In a nutshell," Venturi told Ken with as much irony as he could muster, "even five is a bit excessive, you know, for self-defense." And to claim he had gone into a "robot-like trance" would be too much for a jury to swallow.

Venturi wanted to say, "Look, dummy, you're paying me to save your ass, so listen." He wanted Ken to say, "Okay, I just went batshit when I saw what she was doing and I don't know how many times I hit her because I just was out of my mind at that point."

But the words had to come from Ken. Venturi couldn't write this script for him. The canon of ethics aside, he wasn't about to risk Ken—or his parents—coming back at him in an appeal if it didn't work out, asserting that he had caused his client to commit perjury.

Venturi told Ken, "Think this over carefully before you tell me anything. We'll discuss it again in a couple of days."

But Ken remained mesmerized by his sodium amytal performance. He was sticking to his trance story.

223

# Chapter

# TWELVE

On April 15, Paul Chaiet, after weeks of cajoling, at last got copies of the original Waterford police files concerning Ken's attempt to kill Marilyn. A covering letter from a Connecticut assistant state's attorney warned about the state's erasure laws. None of the documents could be directly introduced in Kenneth Taylor's murder trial.

Chaiet didn't care. He could now subpoena Marilyn and the cops involved and question them with confidence.

Included in the documents he received was a letter from the superintendent of a state psychiatric center, Fairfield Hills Hospital, who had been retained by Ken's attorney. The contents of this letter, above all else, had persuaded Marilyn not to press charges.

Nothing would appall Chaiet more:

*Examination revealed a depressed and anxious-appearing white male who was clearly cooperative and in every respect attempted to be helpful during the interview.*

*It was my impression that during the examination he was altogether truthful with me.*

*Other than the aforesaid depression and anxiety, Lt. Taylor showed no gross psychopathology other than responses and history which made it clear he suffered to a substantial degree from a passive, submissive, dependent personality (which is not a major psychiatric disorder even though it accounts for a person's lifestyle). In addition to the above, Lt. Taylor gave a history of both alcohol and amphetamine abuse.*

*The Lieutenant conveyed to me that on the night of the crime he was not only depressed and extremely resentful of his wife but had been abusing amphetamines and claimed that that night he heard a voice telling him to kill. According to his story, he did attempt to chloroform his wife. She pleaded with him, he interrupted his activity, subsequent to which they both prayed. Through a chain of misadventures he ultimately wound up in a base sick bay where a psychiatrist, who examined him briefly, purportedly made a statement to the wife that [he] might repeat his assaultive behavior and allegedly recommended that a complaint be made to the police. On the other hand, subsequent to this examination, the Lieutenant was seen and treated by a more senior psychiatrist on the base and in fact remains in treatment at the time of this examination. Further, that not only has the "injured" wife returned to live with the accused but also they embarked on a course of marital therapy at the recommendation of the base psychiatrist.*

*It became apparent through the interview that the Lieutenant has an extremely long history of being unable to deal with women and has never been able to properly handle feelings of fear and rage. His rage at the real or fancied humiliation from his wife was dealt with by helpless rage and ultimately this abortive assaultive act. It should be stated that on one occasion in a rage he struck a wall with his hand rather than strike his wife, which to me indicates some degree of control. Further, that though under the influence of controlled substances at the time of the act, he was able to regain control of his behavior and abort his attempt.*

It was the last sentence of the letter, however, that Chaiet found so sickening:

*I should also state that in view of the treatment in which he has already embarked and the new insights and personality changes which have begun that the possibility of his repeating assaultive behavior is virtually non-existent and that in this instance on the one hand incarceration would not help and on the other hand further psychiatric treatment on an ambulatory basis would restore this young doctor to his intended role as someone beneficial to society.*

Along with the Connecticut files, Chaiet got good news from Guy McCormick. A fruitless hunt had been going on for Dr. Ronald C. Smith. Apparently the Navy recorded the wrong social security number when he was discharged from active service and McCormick couldn't find him listed with the American Psychiatric Association in Washington. Finally, after several false leads, the Naval Investigative Service located him in Huntington Beach, California. In ill health, he had given up counseling, but had no trouble remembering Ken. After a phone conversation with him, McCormick wrote:

Dr. Smith advised that he was the first one to treat Kenneth Taylor before Mr. Taylor went under the care of Dr. William Pettit. Dr. Smith advised that Kenneth Taylor had informed him that he had in fact been planning to kill his wife and that he had been stealing chloroform from the ship he was on.

Dr. Smith advised that Taylor had informed him that he was planning to kill his wife because she was not responding to him sexually and that he was getting more response from sexual-related ads that he had placed in "swinger-type" sex magazines. Taylor also advised that his wife was a constant nag.

Dr. Smith informed this writer that Mr. Taylor had even brought in several of these sex magazines and showed him the ad he had placed as well as a nude picture of himself that he sends out. Dr. Smith advised that Kenneth Taylor had bizarre sexual ideas and that Taylor was sexually perverted. Dr. Smith related that Taylor had advised him that he would dress in his wife's clothing and masturbate.

Then, in reviewing his reports, McCormick realized he never followed up on the videotape that Cindy Diaz told him her husband had made of Teresa and the baby on the Saturday morning before Teresa's death.

"Oh, my God, I forgot, too," Cindy told him. The next day, when McCormick picked it up, she also gave him a xerox of the unnerving letter she and her husband had received from Ken shortly after his arrest, the one that had asked their help in preventing Celeste and Jeff from sharing in the custody of baby Philip.

McCormick took the tape home first to view it. It was everything he could have wished for. His wife Anne was crying before it was over. It showed Teresa, young and attractive, completely oblivious to the camera, kissing and cuddling Philip, her love for him unmistakable.

"That should take care of what kind of a mother she was," McCormick said after he ran it for Chaiet.

"Yeah, if we can get it in." Chaiet knew that Venturi would bitterly resist its admission into evidence. The tape really carried an emotional wallop.

•   •   •

McCormick kept brooding about all the sex phone calls from the Manalapan house during the dark morning of November 11, 1984. If Ken ever took the stand, no psychic powers were required to predict what he would claim—that a drug-crazed Teresa made them.

He asked the Benignos if Teresa had ever been away for an extended period, visiting them or any of her girlfriends. No, the only times they could remember was when she was having pregnancy problems and, of course, when she went into labor.

So then McCormick took a flyer and subpoenaed Ken's telephone records during the last months of Teresa's difficult pregnancy. And he got a match. The night of the murder, three calls were to a whorehouse in Manhattan. The same number was called on another night, June 11—when Teresa was still in the hospital, only hours after she had given birth.

McCormick began to regret that Chaiet wasn't going for the death penalty.

• • •

In late April 1985, a month before the trial was scheduled to begin, McCormick and Fausak interviewed Emily Latrelle in Indianapolis. The Waterford cops had spoken to her by phone during their investigation, but she said that while her former husband had temper tantrums and demanded her "undivided attention and affection," he had not been violent to her.

When McCormick tried to reach her, her number had been disconnected. He contacted the Indianapolis police and received a call back from the principal of the school where Emily was teaching. The principal said that Emily had not seen Ken for ten years and was very distraught about being dragged into this. Was it really necessary to interview her? McCormick replied that he was sorry, but it was a murder case and the prosecutor had to get every scrap of information he could about the accused.

Through a local attorney she hired, arrangements were made to meet with her at Indianapolis police headquarters. She had dark brown hair and a healthy body. She was dressed in a high-necked blouse and skirt and wore practically no makeup or jewelry. She kept her hands folded on her lap. If Fausak had to come up with a one-word description of her, it would have been "nice." She looked like, well, a school teacher, Fausak thought.

McCormick asked, "How long has it been since you either heard from or saw Mr. Taylor?"

"I haven't seen or heard from Mr. Taylor since the time of our separation in June, 1974 . . . I first met him when we were both students at Ball State University in Muncie, Indiana."

"How long were you married to Kenneth Z. Taylor?"

"Somewhere between four and five years."

"Could you please explain the circumstances surrounding your eventual divorce from Mr. Taylor?"

"During my marriage to Kenneth Taylor, he began to become involved in drugs and was seeing other women. Near the end of our marriage, he met a gal, I believe her name was Marilyn Hope, whom he went out with and when I was nine months pregnant, we separated and were divorced later that year."

"Could you please elaborate about Mr. Taylor's being involved with drugs?"

"During our marriage, Kenneth Taylor and I went to several parties during college and there was pot being passed around, and we would smoke. Then, as the years of our marriage grew on and I began to work and become the breadwinner, and the people I associated with were quite different than the people he was with, he wanted to continue this kind of experience. I was really not very interested. At that time I could begin to see that we were starting to go apart and had differences. Near the end of the marriage, approximately six months before we had separated, he had stored in the spare bedroom closet of our apartment three large garbage bags of pot or hashish, or whatever it was. I went into a fit of rage and they were removed immediately. Then later on, another month or two, when I was home from work ill, and he did not expect me to be there, he came in with several large quart-size plastic bags full of pills, and again I went into a rage."

"What was Mr. Taylor's occupation at this time?"

"Full-time dental student."

"You mentioned that you were the breadwinner."

"I was a teacher."

"Were you supporting the two of you?"

"Yes, I was."

"Was there any indication that he was going to leave you?"

Till then, her voice had remained flat, matter-of-fact. Now Fausak could sense the tension in it.

"Ken and I were having differences," she said, "but

there were no plans for us to separate. I came home one day and he had packed his bags and moved out."

McCormick asked, "What was your physical condition at the time that your husband left you?"

"I was nine months pregnant."

"Emily, has there been any contact with Kenneth Z. Taylor since the birth of your daughter?"

A hand came off her lap, fluttering aimlessly. "I have not seen Kenneth since he left that one day in early June, 1974," she said. "He did file for divorce later on that summer or that fall . . . There was no need for me to be present at the hearing since Kenneth was the one who filed. He was ordered to pay twenty-five dollars a week in child support. He did pay very inconsistently for the first two or three years. The child support would come to me in strange amounts, like thirty-two dollars, forty-nine cents or one hundred twenty-two dollars and two pennies. Those kinds of checks were being sent. Somewhere along the second or third year, I hadn't received any child support for some time. I attempted to contact Ken while he was in the Navy and did speak with him very briefly on the phone, for maybe a minute or two, concerning payment of the support. I have filed for contempt of court on several different occasions."

"Did Mr. Taylor display any indications that he was upset or unhappy with your pregnancy?"

"Uh, early in the pregnancy, before I had gone to the doctor to find out for sure, Ken indicated at that time a lot of delight. He told many of his friends that I was pregnant, seemed to be very happy and pleased with the idea we were having a child. Throughout the remainder of the months, he really did not show any affection toward me one way or the other."

She looked at McCormick as if he might have an answer. "He didn't, you know, show any extra consideration because of the pregnancy," she said, "but also I can't say that he neglected me during that time, either."

"Do you recall any particular occasion where there may

have been a physical altercation between you and Mr. Taylor?"

"Only after we separated. I was speaking to his parents one evening on the phone. They wanted to speak to their son and I informed them that he had moved out, that he had decided, evidently, that he no longer wanted to be married. They asked where he was staying. I gave them the telephone number of a friend I believed he was with. They said that they would call him and get back to me. Later on in the evening, they did call and did say that he was coming over and to expect him shortly. When Ken came into the apartment, he was very angry, the most anger I'd ever seen him display. He picked up a basketball and threw it at a rocking chair and broke the back of the chair."

"Emily," McCormick said, "could you please tell us if you have been contacted or received any correspondence from either Mr. Taylor or members of his family in regard to this current case and the charges pending against him?"

She shifted uncomfortably in her chair. She gazed into space, then at her lawyer, then back to McCormick.

"Yes," she finally said. "I have received a couple of different letters from his mother. Kenneth's mother, I guess, has tried to keep me informed of the happenings involving her son. She wrote to me about the woman he was married to, the now deceased Teresa Taylor, and gave me some of her background, whereby she stated Teresa had been involved in drugs since she was approximately fifteen years old and was a person who had become very sick with sex. She stated to me that she, Teresa, had made telephone calls on the night before the murder—many different long distance telephone calls where she would talk to a sex line by phone. She stated that the bottom half of her body, or from the waist down, was covered with Vaseline and this was something to do with her sexual perversion that she had gone off into."

McCormick and Fausak stared at one another. McCormick said, "Emily, at this point, is there anything else that you would like to add?"

"No."

As they were leaving, McCormick felt compelled to say, "You were lucky he just left you."

"Yes," she said. "I know."

Afterward, Fausak said, "That's some mom he's got."

"Yeah," McCormick said. "I wonder what her apple pie's like?"

• • •

On May 1, with the trial scheduled to begin in three weeks, Chaiet received disturbing news. He was depending on the testimony of José Romero, Dr. Ortiz Pavon, and officer Armando Vallarino to bring Acapulco into the trial. According to Reyes Quinones, Romero was still coming. But Ortiz was begging off. Not only was he the physician for Las Brisas, but also for several other hotels in Acapulco. He couldn't afford to take the time off. Worse, Vallarino said that obtaining a visa, making travel arrangements, being apart from his family, and losing salary was too much for him. He sent his regrets.

Vallarino's testimony was essential. He was the only available witness who could testify that Ken had admitted assaulting Teresa.

"He knows we'll reimburse him?" Chaiet said.

"Yes, sir," Quinones said. Chaiet told him to get ready to return to Acapulco. Then he called in Fausak. Now the mystery woman "Sorayda" became the center of attention. With everything falling into place, with Vallarino, a cop, presumably available to provide evidence, she had wound up, as Fausak put it, "sort of on the back burner."

"Find her," Chaiet said.

Sifting through the reservation slips was like scanning tea leaves. The problem was that if it hadn't been a crank call, the woman had obviously changed her mind about coming forward. If Fausak started blindly phoning all the names on the slips, there was nothing to prevent the person who made the call from denying it and nothing he could do about it.

Fausak kept reviewing the tape. It didn't help that the connection had been bad to begin with. But perhaps the sixth or seventh time he listened to it, he caught something that hadn't registered before—the woman had said she'd been at Las Brisas with her husband and kids.

Wait a minute, he said to himself. He remembered a show on television, "Lifestyles of the Rich and Famous." The guy had said that Las Brisas was one of the top ten hotels in the world for romance. It catered to newlyweds, to couples on a second honeymoon, to husbands and wives with a lot of bucks and a yen to get away for a few days. It wasn't a place where you'd expect "families" to stay.

Fausak went back over the registration slips. This time he found one that said "Mr. & Mrs. L. Peraino & Family," the only one with that notation and the only one that reserved two rooms, 510 and 511. The home address was in the affluent Long Island suburb, Locust Valley.

There was the name of a Long Island travel agency on the bottom of the slip, and to make doubly sure he was right, Fausak phoned the agency and asked to speak to the manager. He said, "My name is Bob Fausak. I feel a little silly calling, but maybe you can help me out. I was at Las Brisas last year—in July—and I met a family named Peraino. We had drinks and so forth, and I'd like to contact them again, but I've lost their address."

"Oh, yes," the manager said. "Louis and Sorayda Peraino. Lovely couple. They use us often. They went down there with their boys, I believe. Great boys."

"That's them."

"I'm sorry, though. I can't give out their address. But if you drop us a note, I'll see that it's forwarded."

"I'll do that. I appreciate it."

The home phone number was also on the registration slip. Fausak dialed it.

"Mrs. Peraino? Sorayda Peraino?"

"Yes."

Fausak identified himself and said that he was calling about the call she had made to Captain Potts the previous December 7 concerning the murder of Teresa Taylor.

"You are mistaken. You are mixing me up with someone else."

"I know you are the same party. I know you were at Las Brisas when Teresa Taylor was there."

"No, no. I tell you, you are wrong."

"Mrs. Peraino, I have to inform you that your call was recorded. Your voice is identical to the one on the tape. It is very important that you speak to me."

There was a pause, and then she started to cry. "That poor, poor girl. Why did he do it to her?"

"This is one of the reasons we need your help."

"Is he still in jail?"

"Yes. He will be going on trial very soon."

There was another pause. That was really why she had called, she said. To find out where he was. She couldn't believe it when she read the article in the *New York Post*. She had wanted to come forward. "But I discussed it with my husband and he said the police must already have the evidence if he'd been arrested and is in jail."

She was nervous enough as it was. Fausak didn't want her to know that, at the moment anyway, she was the key to proving the Acapulco assault.

He said, "We have other witnesses. But we need all the corroboration we can get—you know, to verify everything. How did you happen to meet Teresa Taylor and her husband?"

They met in the van coming in from the airport, she said. "We learned that they were newlyweds. We invited them to our suite the next night and we had champagne to celebrate their marriage. They stayed for about an hour, and we talked about getting together later in the week. But we never did," she said, starting to cry again.

"Yes?"

"I was in the lobby," she said. "We were getting ready to check out when I saw him—Ken Taylor—in the lobby. He was with two men, detectives I think. They were in civilian clothes, but he said they were police. He was disheveled. He said that he had been in jail. He and Teresa had been drinking, and she bit him on the ankle and he hit her. And knocked her teeth out, and that he was a dentist and they wouldn't let him treat her."

"Did he say anything else?"

"Well, that he might need money to get out of jail."

Sorayda Peraino's sobs were uncontrollable now.

"Thank you, Mrs. Peraino," Fausak said. "I'll be in contact with you again."

• • •

He phoned Chaiet at once. "Sorayda," he said. "I found her."

Fausak could tell how excited Chaiet was, not by the tone of his voice—Chaiet always maintained a very low-key level—but the way he hopped on every answer. Usually, when you answered something he'd asked, he would kind of weigh it before going on to the next question.

"What did she say?" Chaiet said, the words tumbling out. "What did she say about Taylor? And then what? When are you going to see her?"

"I just said I'd be in contact again," Fausak said. "She was real jumpy, but she didn't say no."

"Get together with McCormick," Chaiet said. "Go see her."

When Fausak called her back, she was reluctant, but finally agreed to receive them. On May 7, Fausak and McCormick drove to the Locust Valley home. It was big and white with pillars in front, a sweeping lawn with huge old trees, a carriage house, a swimming pool and a tennis court. Rich and gorgeous, Fausak thought.

Sorayda Peraino turned out to be extremely attractive. She had long black hair and wore a gray silk dress with a double strand of pearls around her neck. Fausak figured she was in her mid-thirties. He was astonished to learn that she had sons and daughters in their twenties. Her husband was at her side, older, an obviously prosperous businessman who owned a chain of discount stores retailing electronic equipment and home appliances.

She reiterated how she and her husband first met the Taylors. Then McCormick asked her, "When did you next encounter either Kenneth or Teresa Taylor?"

"On the last day of our week's stay, I saw Ken Taylor. It was in the lobby of the hotel. He was standing on line with two Mexicans. I believe they were Mexican policemen. That's what Ken Taylor said. Ken had seen me in the lobby and called my name. He told me he had to get his money, to get bail to get out of jail, and asked me would I lend him some money if he didn't have enough.''

"What did Ken Taylor tell you regarding his situation?"

"He told me, 'We had a fight.' I thought he meant in town, and I asked, 'Where's Teresa?' He said, 'She's in the hospital.' I still thought they had a fight with someone in town. And I asked what hospital was Teresa in and he began to tell me that he and Teresa had fought. He told me that they wouldn't let him see Teresa, that he had knocked her teeth out, and they wouldn't let him fix her teeth, that he was a dentist.

"He went on to say that she had bit him on the foot, and 'I hit her,' that they had been drinking and had a fight. After I walked away, upset, I spoke with a Mexican lady, who worked for the hotel, and she told me that it was terrible what happened to his wife, that he had called and said that four Mexicans had broken into the room, and he did admit to the police that he was the one that beat his wife up. The lady said it was terrible what he had done to her on the honeymoon."

"Do you recall Kenneth Taylor saying anything while at your suite when they came over for the honeymoon drink?"

"He was very quiet, but while Teresa was saying something about his being a dentist, and them being married, and speaking about clothes she had purchased, he replied, 'Now that she's my wife, I'll straighten her out.' "

"Anything else you can recall at this time?"

"The only thing is how bubbly a person she was, and how quiet he was. He did tell us that he was a Vietnam veteran during our conversation."

McCormick could see how tense she was becoming and cut off the interview. They'd gotten what they wanted. Fausak had brought a typewriter and transcribed her statement on the spot. Sorayda Peraino read and signed it. Her husband, present throughout, signed as a witness.

"I won't have to be at the trial, will I?" she asked. "I don't believe I could do it."

"I really can't answer that," McCormick said.

* * *

"She'll be a fantastic witness," McCormick told Chaiet. "She's intelligent, cultured, and she doesn't have a stake in any of this."

"Is she willing to testify?"

"I think you're going to have to talk to her yourself."

* * *

In the Monmouth County Jail, Jack Venturi said to Ken, "Remember telling me the name 'Sorayda' didn't ring a bell? Well, her whole name is Sorayda Peraino. Any bells now?" Then Venturi gave him a copy of her statement to McCormick and Fausak.

After he read it, Ken said, "Yeah, now I remember. She was that weird crazy bitch we met down there. This is all shit. *Why* would I tell her that? Jesus Christ, Jack, even if I had beaten Teresa, would I go around saying it? Give me a break. The woman is certifiable. Why would I say I was a Vietnam veteran?"

The next day Venturi received a memo from Ken that wasn't quite so dismissive of Sorayda Peraino:

### SORYADA [sic]

*Upon arriving at the hotel with my escort of 5 policemen, I noticed Soryada in the lobby near the reception desk. When she saw me, she exclaimed, "What happened to you, Ken?"*

*I was in bad shape. I was filthy, dirty and very shaken from no food, clothing change or shower for 4 nights. I had not shaved and in short I looked like a bum from sleeping on the floor of the jail as there were no beds or mats to lie on.*

*I told her I had to pay the police $500.00 to let me go see Teresa. The police (one on either side of me) stood behind me slightly. The other 3 police were scattered about the lobby: one talking to the man at the reception desk and the other two talking to hotel employees (2 maids).*

*I told her Teresa had been beaten badly and that I had been hit on the head, cut on the arms, hands and also cut on the foot. I told her the police had told me Teresa had broken teeth from her beating and that I wanted to be able to at least repair the damage to her teeth and try to make her comfortable.*

*I told her the police had taken me to jail to cover up for the hotel security deficiency. I told her the police had not charged me with anything as I had not done anything, just that they wanted to lay the blame on me instead of damage their reputation with their tourist trade.*

*At that point, Mr. Nilo Lopez, who was at the reception desk, came to me and took me to an office where all of our belongings were located. From there I could see that two police who were standing near me were talking to Soryada. (She spoke Spanish and therefore these 2 "police" explained to her in Spanish their version of the story.)*

*Upon viewing our belongings, I noticed that we were missing the tri-colored gold bracelet, a gold cigarette lighter and my Cross pen that had been stolen by the police captain, Gutierrez Mendoza. After meeting with Teresa in her hotel [sic] room, I discovered she was missing 2 pair of earrings and her diamond engagement ring.*

*There was an insurance claim made with USAA insurance in San Antonio, Texas. Because the items were not individually insured, we were paid a lump sum of $500 allowed for stolen jewelry. (I believe it was $500. I valued the total loss at $2,500, as I recall.)*

Then Ken, having unburdened himself about the missing jewelry, appeared to retreat from his harsh comments to Venturi about Mrs. Peraino:

*Soryada was in an excited state trying to check out of the hotel and appeared to be upset. She spoke fluent Spanish and did seem to like both Teresa and I. I feel certain that she misunderstood me and got the "official version" from the police.*

Venturi assigned his own investigator to talk to her. At least he needed to know how firm she was in her story. But the investigator reported that she refused to see him. That was unsettling. Now Venturi knew he had two big problems—Acapulco as well as Connecticut.

Venturi again moved for a reduction in Ken's bail from $500,000 to $100,000, with a provision allowing him to post 10 percent of it. He argued that the prosecution's case was gravely flawed. The police allegation that his client seized a dumbbell from the deceased and struck her with it was false. His client "instinctively picked up" a different dumbbell while under attack. As evidence, he cited a "truth serum" examination of his client by a psychiatrist who was "world-renowned," who "has administered this very test on hundreds of occasions."

Furthermore, the defendant not only was a homeowner in the community and in the midst of a custody battle over his ten-month-old son, but also had every expectation of being found innocent.

Chaiet's response was brief. They'd been through this before. The defendant's story was basically the same, Dr. Sadoff's "opinion" notwithstanding. The finding in the first bail hearing was "reasonable." On the eve of the trial, "It would seem foolhardy to allow the defendant an opportunity to flee the jurisdiction."

The judge appointed to try the case, Michael D. Farren, denied Venturi's motion. Citing Ken's lies about putting Teresa on a plane and then changing his story when her body was found, he said, "I think the proofs are very strong for a conviction." He added that since sodium amytal or the "truth serum" would be inadmissible in a trial, he didn't see why it should be admissible in a bail hearing.

At the Monmouth County Jail, Ken fractured his ankle in a pickup basketball game. He was transferred to the jail's medical wing.

"It's better there," he told Venturi. "There's more freedom."

# Part lll

## THE
## TRIAL

# Chapter

# THIRTEEN

On May 8, the day after Fausak located Sorayda Peraino, Venturi officially notified Chaiet, "Be advised that Dr. Kenneth Taylor intends to claim defense of self-protection and protection of another."

That surprised Chaiet. He'd always thought it would be manslaughter in the heat of passion. If Ken ever took the stand, he wondered how Venturi was going to explain away the dumbbell that was bloodstained, the one without weights, with only its wicked clamp. How could Teresa, with little upper body strength, have been able to swing the only other dumbbell, loaded with thirty pounds of weights, at Taylor?

Still, the critical element in this defense, like the others, was "state of mind." Which was why prior instances of Ken's violent assaults were so critically important to prove. When Judge Farren, in denying bail reduction, said that there was probable proof for a conviction, he didn't specify what kind of a conviction.

Venturi moved to keep both assaults out of the trial. The

decision one way or another would set the tone for the rest of the proceedings, would, in fact, presage victory or defeat for the defense. Venturi figured that if he could exclude Connecticut and Acapulco, the big hurdle left would be Ken's cover-up lies after he had killed Teresa. The argument there, of course, was that he had panicked.

Farren set the hearing for May 10.

He was a hard read. A cherubic-faced man, regarded as either highly intelligent or very shrewd depending on your politics, he had been prominent in Republican party affairs. He was an assistant in the prosecutor's office when Chaiet started there. After that he entered private practice and later became the assistant county counsel. When a Republican, Thomas Kean, was elected governor, he appointed Farren to the Superior Court. This was his first big trial.

Venturi was counting on Farren's caution about making decisions that might invite a higher court reversal. To exclude Connecticut, Venturi would rely on Rule 55 of the state's Rules of Evidence, which essentially provided that evidence that someone had committed a similar crime on a specified, previous occasion was inadmissible in order to infer or prove a defendant's disposition to commit the crime then being adjudicated.

Chaiet expected Venturi to trot out Rule 55, so he asserted another ruling, Rule 48, which provided that Rule 55 could be preempted to prove other issues of fact including motive, intent, plan or knowledge. "Intent" was at the heart of it, he argued.

The attempted murder of his second wife was "highly probative" of the defendant's later, fatal attack upon Teresa Taylor. Both were "sparked by mounting marital pressures." In Manalapan, Ken admitted, "I just couldn't take it anymore." In Connecticut, he had "complained of marital problems which he could no longer tolerate."

In Acapulco, the assault on the victim showed the defendant's "malicious intent in the present matter." The fact that it occurred at another, earlier time "is of no consequence." What was important was that it did happen. He was prepared, Chaiet declared, to present "competent witnesses . . . who were privy to the situation as it then existed and comments made by the defendant regarding same.''

Neither previous act, he emphasized, was being offered to prove the defendant's disposition to commit the "present offense," but to "prove motive and intent and refute the defendant's claim of self-defense.''

So, in the end, after all the months of detective work, the painstaking gathering of facts, the tracking down of witnesses, the chances of a murder conviction would hinge on narrowly interpreted technicalities about the admission of this evidence.

Farren reserved his decision.

Then, on May 15, he dropped a bombshell. He disallowed the introduction of Connecticut, citing Rule 55.

Chaiet was stunned—and steaming. Clearly, the connection was there. First, one wife and then the next one, rationalized by bizarre explanations from Taylor. That was the real relationship, Chaiet thought. But there was nothing he could do. Farren was obviously worried about the legalities. In an instant, half of Chaiet's case, designed to show that Ken's self-defense plea was a sham, had been thrown out.

Perversely, Farren left the door open on Acapulco. He wasn't going to decide that until the trial. His ultimate decision would rest on "clear and convincing evidence" that Ken had savaged Teresa on their honeymoon.

Venturi told his investigators to redouble their efforts to talk to Sorayda Peraino. And if Chaiet brought up any cops from Mexico, he'd hammer them on the payoff Ken had made.

The trial date, scheduled for May 20, was postponed to give everyone a chance to regroup. Judge Farren announced that jury selection would commence on May 28.

For reporters covering the courthouse, a case that had once appeared fairly cut and dried was suddenly too close to call. The headline in the *Asbury Park Press* was, "Defense Says Wife Caused Her Death by Attacking First.''

As soon as he got back to his office, Chaiet immediately dispatched Reyes Quinones to Acapulco. He wanted the Mexican cop, Vallarino, of course, but he also wanted Quinones to try to convince Dr. Ortiz Pavon to change his mind about testifying. Chaiet wanted to show the jury the horrible photographs of the dead Teresa's battered face, then he wanted to show them to Ortiz and have the jury hear Ortiz say that they looked just like Teresa after her beating in Mexico.

But two days later, Quinones reported that it looked hopeless as far as Ortiz was concerned. He would not jeopardize his position with the various hotels he serviced as an on-call physician. The word on Vallarino, however, was all good. Quinones had gotten him his visa and settled on an expense advance. They'd be flying out the next afternoon. Then Quinones called back. He'd managed to get Vallarino to the airport when he suddenly refused to board the plane.

"He says he can't do it," Quinones said. "He's afraid."

"Of what? Being asked about the money Taylor paid?"

"Yes, I'm sure of it."

By now the furor in the media about the link between the murder of the U.S. drug agent—Enrique Camarena—and corruption in Mexican law enforcement had reached new heights.

"What's the atmosphere down there?" Chaiet asked.

"Hostile. Very hostile," Quinones said.

"Then the hell with it. Come on back before something happens to you."

Chaiet had Fausak and McCormick set up a meeting with Sorayda Peraino at her Locust Valley home. The moment Chaiet laid eyes on her, he realized how impressive a witness she could be. And just the way she held her husband's hand, he saw at once the conflict within her—her desire to have Taylor punished and her almost palpable fear that he would strike back at her.

Fausak remembered how Chaiet's physical presence, already imposing enough, seemed to fill the room, his voice low, authoritative, comforting. "I can understand your apprehension," he said. "I have had many similar cases, and I can assure you that not one witness of mine has ever suffered retribution of any kind. Information about where you live, or anything else of a personal nature, will not be asked."

Fausak could sense that her husband, listening to Chaiet, was more at ease than before. He squeezed his wife's hand encouragingly.

Chaiet said, "I must tell you that if justice is to be served, your testimony is extremely, vitally, important. It is your civic duty."

"Why me?" she said. "Do I really have to?"

Chaiet could have issued a subpoena. He didn't mention it. He wanted her to come voluntarily. "You are the only means we have," he said, "to show that Kenneth Taylor beat his wife in Mexico." He stared at her. "Mrs. Peraino, there's a dead woman up there somewhere looking down at us, at you, who wants you to tell nothing more than the truth. She is calling out for help. Somebody has to help her."

"What would I have to do?"

"You will have to come to court twice. The first time will be to let the judge hear what you have to say. And depending upon the judge's ruling, if he decides to admit it into evidence, you will have to testify again in front of the jury. Kenneth Taylor's lawyer will cross-examine you, ask you many questions, but if you tell the truth, as you will, there's nothing to worry about."

"Somebody from his lawyer, some investigator, has been trying to see me. I refused."

"Mrs. Peraino," Chaiet said, "you don't have to talk to anyone you don't want to, including me."

"Thank you."

That's it, Fausak thought. Even if she hadn't said so outright, she was going to testify.

"We'll let you know when," Chaiet said. "Detective Fausak will come for you and drive you down and back."

Then, in Freehold, Chaiet's secretary put in a call to the State Department's Bureau of Inter-American Affairs. He already had sent two letters asking for any information that the consular agent in Acapulco, Urbanek, might have filed about Teresa's beating. There had been no response.

"We're processing it," an Ivy League voice said. "The Mexican Desk has been contacted."

"Goddamnit," Chaiet said, "this is a murder case. Let's get on with it."

• • •

Chaiet hadn't decided which Benignos he would have testify. For sure, Al. And Teresa's brother, Phil. But he was going to have a serious talk with Phil first.

Dr. Frederick Rieders, the toxicologist who worked on Teresa's autopsy report, would testify that Teresa had been a user but not an abuser of cocaine. That was hard, medical evidence. Still, there had been cocaine residue in her body, and Jack Venturi wasn't going to let it slide by the jury. Chaiet had to confront this before Venturi did.

For Chaiet, the most likely time Teresa did cocaine consistent with Rieders's findings would have been on Friday night, November 9, when Phil and his girlfriend visited the Manalapan house. Questioned initially by McCormick and Fausak, Phil said that Ken was the only one who had ingested cocaine. Chaiet didn't buy it.

He summoned Phil to his office—with Al.

Chaiet said, "We have to know the truth about any drug use by you and Teresa. It's going to be raised by the defense and if you care about justice being served, I have to know everything, and I don't think I do. Exactly what happened on November ninth when you and your friend were over there?"

McCormick remembered glancing at Phil's father. Al had his eyes fixed on his son.

"Let's begin at the beginning," Chaiet said. "What time did you arrive?"

"Around ten, ten-thirty."

"And you stayed overnight, is that right?"

"Yes."

"And then what? You said you brought some wine, two bottles."

"Yes, me and Kathy drank most of the wine. Teresa had two or three glasses. Ken drank straight Jack Daniel's. He smoked a joint. I smoked a little of it."

"What time was this?"

"I'd say about eleven."

"What were you doing?"

"Just sitting on the couch and talking, you know. I think Teresa was showing us a photo album."

"What else?"

"Taylor brought out some coke, a packet."

"Who used it?"

Phil hesitated. His eyes teared. "Myself and Teresa and him."

"Had you ever seen Teresa use cocaine before?"

"Yes. Once."

"How about Kenneth Taylor?"

"I saw him do it all the time. Even in the dental office."

Phil said that Ken and Teresa had gone to bed around two A.M. He and his girlfriend stayed up until four watching a movie on television. When they awoke in the morning, Ken and Teresa had left the house.

Chaiet believed him. In their investigation, McCormick and Fausak hadn't been able to find any evidence that Phil was either a big user or dealer in drugs as Ken claimed. He could have stuck with his original story, but he was willing to admit the truth in front of his father. That couldn't have been easy.

• • •

Jack Venturi noticed in one of McCormick's Acapulco reports that the consular agent there said nothing could be released on the Las Brisas assault without State Department clearance. Funny there hadn't been anything more on this.

So on the off chance it might be useful, he made his own request, simply addressing his letter to the Department of State, Washington, D.C.

He promptly got a reply from the Information and Privacy Coordinator, Foreign Affairs Information Management Center. There would be a fee. Surprised that he had even gotten this far, Venturi sent a fifty-dollar check.

He also contacted three different toxicologists to see if they would refute Rieders's testimony. Ken had been harping on it continually as the trial approached. And to Venturi, it did seem to defy logic that the amount of cocaine in Teresa's body could be accurately measured after so many days of decomposition, a body practically devoid of blood. He sent Rieders's analysis to the toxicologists and then spoke to them by phone. The news was bad.

All three said that on the basis of what they'd been given, they agreed with Rieders and would so testify. It still didn't make sense to Venturi. He called one of the toxicologists again, S. K. Niyogi in Philadelphia, who had come highly recommended, and asked him to take another look. A lot was at stake here. Niyogi said he would, but he didn't think it would make any difference. Well, okay, Venturi thought, he'd have to appeal to the jury's common sense. No matter what an expert claimed, Teresa had been dead for too long. Too much time had elapsed and an unknown amount of the cocaine could have easily dissipated before they finally got around to doing the toxicology.

Then Ken volunteered thumbnail sketches of the Benignos as potential witnesses.

Al Benigno, he scribbled, "could be the toughest as he is the most intelligent." He "went to Mexico to bring us home and saw firsthand the corruption and police behavior and said he knew Teresa and I were mugged. YET now he has turned on me because he knows the Mexican cops will stick to their story about me beating Teresa, etc., etc." He added that Al also had once invested money in a business venture and when his partner lost it, he "tried to have his partner killed!"

Ken didn't see Louise as being very dangerous on the stand "except to create sympathy for Teresa." He said, "She says that she made me a sandwich after I came back from Indiana. She doesn't say that she insisted on making me the sandwich."

Phil was a "no-good thug and dope dealer." Teresa

"begged me to give him a job to get him out of drugs." Phil also had threatened him. "Jack," Ken wrote, "you've got to get this in to show how prejudiced he is." During one of the shared custody nights when Celeste and Jeff had his son, he called from jail to see how the baby was, and Phil answered and said, "KEN, I'M GOING TO KILL YOU. I SWEAR TO GOD I'M GOING TO KILL YOU."

Nothing, however, appeared to drive Ken into more frustrated fury than Jeff and Celeste. "JEFF WHITE—calm but not intelligent. Jeff can 'lie' very well but should be easy to manipulate and confuse. When first married, they sold coke for their income . . . CELESTE WHITE—very stupid woman. Very easily confused. Very confusing in her explanations. Can be very easily manipulated to sound like she's confused . . . I can't overemphasize how confused and how excitable this woman really is. She is also very emotional and has literally no common sense. She is a pathologic [*sic*] liar."

At least something had dissipated, Venturi thought—the cool, almost eerie confidence Ken displayed when they first met. A last exhortation came from him on the eve of his appearance in court:

*Jack,*
*Before we go to trial I want to let you know something about me that we will have to deal with. I did not beat my precious wife on our honeymoon. I did not at anytime or anyplace sell cocaine. I loved Teresa more than I love living. She meant the world to me and now my world is gone. Anything else you want to think about me, and God knows you have enough, okay, but just know what I state above is true. I'm guilty of certain accusations, I'm not pure and you know it. But believe me, I loved Teresa. I'll do anything to protect my children and I did not sell cocaine.*
*I realize this will be a very difficult case. God bless you for your skills, effort and concern.*

He signed it formally. *Dr. Kenneth J. Taylor.*

• • •

Jury selection took two days. Sixteen jurors, twelve men and four women, were impaneled. The final twelve to deliberate a verdict would be chosen by lot. Over the winter, media coverage had been extensive and generally anti-Taylor, Venturi thought. He questioned prospective jurors on how closely they had followed the case. He challenged anyone who said that they had read or heard about Las Brisas—or Connecticut, even though Judge Farren had excluded it. He searched for anyone who'd had a bad experience with dentists, and found two examples. He tried for younger jurors who might have a passing familiarity with the drug culture, its ups and downs.

Chaiet sought solid, middle-class citizens with a strong sense of right and wrong, and he wanted men who could put themselves in Ken's place when Teresa was supposedly attacking him. In the end, both Chaiet and Venturi got a mix they could live with. Chaiet was philosophical about juries. Betting on them was a fast way to go broke. Still, he was confident of winning, especially if he could bring in Acapulco.

During his opening statement on Thursday, May 30, Chaiet's normally quiet demeanor disappeared, his voice now raised dramatically in scorn and outrage. They were gathered in this court, he said, to render judgment on a "brutal, senseless" murder. "I will call upon you for a murder conviction for this defendant because that's what he committed when he smashed the head of Teresa Taylor into pieces on November eleventh, nineteen eighty-four."

Kenneth and Teresa Taylor had met, married, and had a baby boy. "It could have been, should have been so right, but it turned out so wrong."

He had viciously bludgeoned his wife. He "cracked open" her skull with a dumbbell bar. She had succumbed to massive head injuries and fractures, "nine of them in all." He carefully cleaned up a house splattered with her blood. With his wife's body stuffed in the trunk of a car, Chaiet said, he carried the infant to Indiana. And for a week, he tried to cover up his crime. He lied to his wife's family. He lied to his parents. He lied that his wife was addicted to drugs and left him voluntarily because she needed "space." The jury would hear of twenty-six phone calls of a sexual nature that night when the defendant claimed to have been asleep.

He dumped his wife's body, her culottes and pantyhose pulled down to mid-thigh, her sweater blood-soaked, in a Pennsylvania ditch. And what did he do the night before he finally reported to the police that his wife was missing? He went to a go-go saloon to watch topless dancers perform.

At that, Venturi was on his feet, demanding a mistrial. Judge Farren waved him off.

And where was he when members of his wife's family were identifying her corpse? He was in Pittsburgh, visiting his ex-wife.

The jury would hear, Chaiet said, that as Manalapan detective Robert Fausak pursued his investigation into the disappearance of Teresa Taylor, at the urging of her family, he found the defendant at home, "calm, businesslike, not overly worried."

It was only after many hours of police interrogation, and being confronted by growing evidence against him, that the defendant broke down at last and admitted what he had done. Even then, Chaiet continued, he fabricated a "sordid" story that his wife, crazed by cocaine, was sexually abusing her baby and attacked him with a dumbbell bar when he tried to stop her. A toxicology study, however, revealed just a minimal amount of cocaine in her body. And how did he "defend himself"? By his own admission, he had seized the dumbbell bar from his wife and then beat her to death.

He quoted Ken as saying, "I just couldn't stand it anymore. She was stealing my prescriptions and taking my money." The state would prove that this plea of self-defense, along with everything else, was baseless. As he spoke, Chaiet had been moving closer to the table where Ken was sitting. Now he jabbed a finger inches from Ken's face. "This perverted tale," he cried, "is just that. A perverted tale by a sinister and calculating mind."

* * *

In preparing his opening statement, Venturi had written himself a reminder: "I don't have the flair for drama as Mr. C. does."

Nonetheless, he couldn't resist one sally. The jurors, he said, would be removed from the courtroom from time to time while "lengthy arguments" took place. It would be because "I anticipate in this case what I call the kitchen-sink prosecution of Doctor Taylor, and that is that the state will try to introduce into evidence anything it can, including the kitchen sink, in order to arouse your passion, your sympathy, your prejudice and inflame you against Doctor Taylor."

Chaiet shouted an objection.

"I will sustain the objection," Judge Farren said. "Mr. Venturi, please confine your remarks to what you contend is the position of your client."

"That is our position, your honor."

"I understand that is your position. The prosecutor objects to the position. I sustain the objection."

Venturi thought he got a couple of smiles and some sympathy when Farren rebuked him. Then he reverted to his basic themes: "Sadness, grief, loss. Be sure to speak in sorrow. There are no winners here."

Dr. Taylor, he said, was guilty of terrible mistakes. He was guilty of obstruction of justice, of "giving false information to the police." But he was not on trial for that. He was being charged with murder.

"I could see during the prosecutor's opening," he said, "that some of you were sitting there uncomfortably, knowing that you are in the presence of a man who took the life of another human being. I can understand that, and I would be, too, if I thought for one second that this man, Doctor Kenneth Taylor, was a murderer. But the evidence will not show that."

Venturi slowly approached the jury. "You see, ladies and gentlemen, this is not a murder. This is a family tragedy."

He said, "The marriage was not a trouble-free marriage, but there was a loving, caring relationship between the two of them, and one of the problems during the marriage was Teresa's abuse of cocaine and codeine. And also alcohol.

"That night, the night of the incident, Teresa was unfortunately using all three of those substances. During the course of that evening, Teresa could not and did not sleep. Doctor Taylor had awakened from his sleep, and the doctor and Mrs. Taylor had marital relations that might, in some circumstances, might be considered unusual.

"When he awoke that morning, and he walked down the stairs, he saw something that was just shocking and unbelievable to him that the prosecutor referred to in his opening. And it was shocking and unbelievable because Teresa Taylor was such a good mother. He could not believe his eyes. He did yell and scream and he did chase her into the weight room, the sewing room, the extra bedroom, but he did not take any barbell away from Teresa. As he saw her, she was in a crazed state. For whatever reason, she was acting crazy, irrational."

There was another barbell, Venturi said. "She was not a weak woman by any means. We are not talking about heavy barbells here. We are talking about small dumbbells, and when he went into that room, he was confronted with her coming at him with one of those barbells. She hit him on the shoulder with it and knocked him on the floor. And on the floor, acting as a doorstop, was the other barbell, and fearing serious bodily harm, not only to him, but his baby boy, he instinctively reacted and picked up that other barbell and started swinging it at Teresa.

"He remembers at least two blows, maybe more," Venturi said, but "at some point, he blacked out." When he came to and found her dead, he "panicked."

Yes, Dr. Taylor made up a story and stayed with it for too long. "He did not want anybody to know what he had seen. He did not *want* to tell that perverted tale referred to by the prosecutor."

The only issue, Venturi said, was whether the state can prove Dr. Taylor guilty of murder "beyond a reasonable doubt" or "whether he is not guilty because, at the time of this incident, he was acting in imminent danger of serious bodily harm to himself and his baby."

• • •

The trial was adjourned till Monday.

The headlines were good, Jack Venturi thought. One had Ken "forced to fend off wife." Another said, "Dentist claims wife sexually abused child." Could be the jury was seeing it that way, too.

Over the weekend, when Jean and Zach visited Ken in jail, Jean said, "How could Jack let that awful man say those terrible things about you?"

"I don't know, Mom. Did you see his pig eyes? He's an animal. He'll do anything to hurt me. Please pray for me."

# Chapter

# FOURTEEN

On Monday morning, June 3, Venturi began building a record for appeal. He wanted Farren to remove himself as judge because of his prejudicial pretrial comment, reported in the media, that the "proofs are very strong for conviction."

Farren declined.

Jean and Zach brought the baby to court. He instantly drew the attention of photographers and TV crews. Chaiet objected. It was a cheap maneuver to get "sympathy" for the defendant.

Venturi argued that his client's parents had come all the way from Indiana to attend the trial. To do that on the days they had custody, they had no choice except to take him with them. "I have no objection," Farren said, warning Zach, though, that a "courtroom was like a church when the pastor is speaking, or something." Any disruptive outcries and the baby had to go.

Things grew testier between Venturi and Chaiet when Venturi moved to let Dr. Sadoff testify without any reference to sodium amytal. Venturi had already entered a letter from the psychiatrist saying that the barbiturate "should never be used in order to prove the guilt or innocence of individuals but, primarily, to help recapture lost memory."

Sadoff wrote that in three previous cases he had "testified on the results of the sodium amytal as a general conclusion about my evaluation and examination of the individual, without mentioning specifically the sodium amytal." In his opinion, as it concerned "Dr. Taylor," there "was a proper response to the sodium amytal and material was recalled that had not been remembered without [its] use."

Chaiet resisted. He could not effectively cross-examine Sadoff without viewing the videotape. Venturi had promised to deliver it, but had reneged so far. Moreover, Chaiet said that he might call his own psychiatrist to the stand who also would have to see it.

Farren gave Venturi two days to make up his mind. Either Chaiet got the tape or no Sadoff.

• • •

Chaiet's initial witnesses were cops and technicians who testified about forensic evidence—which included a description of the body when it was found, the blood on the dumbbell without weights that was introduced as the murder weapon, and the bloody fifty-five-foot drag marks that the Luminol test revealed in the Manalapan house.

Chaiet asked a Pennsylvania state trooper named Eugene R. Taylor about the padding Teresa's body was wrapped in. "There was separate padding for the head?"

"There was a smaller piece of some padding, yes sir."

(In his trial notes, Ken wrote: *Jeez. Was really worried about protecting her after I killed her. What the hell kind of logic is that? LUNACY, that's what, you dumb, big, stupid clod! Well, shit! At least the jury knows I wanted her body protected. After I killed her? OH, BOY, Jack. WHY DIDN'T WE SEEK TEMPORARY INSANITY???)\**

---

*This and other parenthetical, italicized observations by Ken Taylor on the following pages were taken directly as written from his trial notes or his comments on the trial transcript.

There was also a multi-colored towel next to the body, Trooper Taylor said.

*(Towel? Holy Christ! A towel? Why did I put a towel inside the padding? Must have been one of the towels to wipe up the blood on the walls and floor. What did I do with the rest of the towels? Good question, asshole! What a fucking mess this is.)*

"All right," Chaiet asked. "You did not find blood at the scene?"

"No, sir."

"Okay, did you look?"

"Yes, sir."

*(SIR, SIR. WHY DON'T YOU KISS HIS ASS WHILE YOU'RE UP THERE, TAYLOR. TAYLOR? WHAT A NAME FOR THE STATE'S FIRST WITNESS.)*

Chaiet's main witness that day was Dr. Richard Bindie, the Pottsville pathologist who had conducted the autopsy. Venturi objected to the introduction of photographs showing Teresa's hideously battered face and head. Not only were they unnecessarily in color, but, he said, they had been enhanced with a "reddish tint" that made them all the more revolting and, indeed, the jurors were visibly shaken when they saw them. Chaiet said that the doctoring claim was ludicrous. Farren turned Venturi down. He asked for a mistrial. Duly noted and denied, Farren said.

*(OF COURSE YOU SELF-SERVING SLOB. WHY NOT? WHY NOT DIG HER UP WHILE WE'RE AT IT?)*

In the dispassionate voice of a man who had performed more than fifteen hundred autopsies, Bindie said, "I first examined the back of the body. The anal area and genital area were examined first. I observed a marked amount of ointment, white sticky material, about the buttocks, around the anus and vagina and on the menstrual pad. This material resembled Vaseline to me."

"Could you describe the quantity of it?"

"It was a copious amount. It was globulous—globs stuck on the hair and on the pad and on the skin and inside the orifices."

Bindie said, "There was a torn pair of tannish-colored

corduroy-like culottes. They weren't in place at the waist. They were pulled down to the mid-thigh level. There was a zipper in the posterior area that was torn. There were focal blood spots to the front."

*(I should have changed her clothes before I moved her. Goddamnit, I couldn't even bear to look at her. Too late to cry now. Stupid. You fucked up!)*

"What is focal?"

"Focal means in one or two places."

". . . Now, during the course of your autopsy, did you find a number of lacerations to the head area?"

"Yes."

"And could you tell us the number of lacerations that you found?"

"I found nine lacerations."

Chaiet led him step by step, photograph by photograph, through Teresa's fatal wounds. "This was a six-centimeter laceration—which is about two and a quarter inches in length," Bindie said. "This was an open, gaping laceration and the underlying skull was exposed and I could—one could observe the inside of the cranial cavity and see the brain. There were loose fragments of the brain on the surface."

Bindie said, "Yes. This is a chromo-colored photograph of the left eye area and the forehead and demonstrates a close-up view of lacerations one, two and three."

Chaiet asked, "Now, did you find any evidence of past injuries on the body?"

Before he could answer, Venturi approached the bench. "Judge, everybody, and including defense counsel, would like a break. My client is getting a little upset."

Then he objected to any reference to past injuries. They weren't relevant "to any findings in connection with the death of Teresa Taylor." No one had any doubt what he had in mind—the looming issue of Acapulco.

Chaiet kept a straight face. To complete the record, he had to have a complete rundown on the victim's external physical condition. "This jury is not going to decide this case because she had a scar on her neck," he said.

"All right," Judge Farren said. "I will overrule the objection. I'll permit the testimony of the doctor as to what his findings were when he conducted the autopsy of the decedent. If she had a fractured leg, he would be permitted to testify to that . . . I will also caution the jury at this juncture that we don't know what caused these other injuries, and they're not to speculate."

Boxed in, Venturi said in that case he'd just as soon skip it. "I'd rather no further attention be drawn to this by such an instruction."

Almost all the evidence of prior trauma inflicted on Teresa's face about which Bindie testified was a result of the Las Brisas assault. Venturi still had no idea what Farren would do about letting *that* in. Chaiet, with nothing to lose, was betting that he would admit it.

Then Chaiet asked, "Now, in going with your general review of the body, did you find any more of that Vaseline-like substance?"

*(VASELINE your ass Chaiet! WHAT GIVES with your obscession* [sic] *with vaseline already?)*

"There was a marked amount of Vaseline-like ointment material present in the vagina and also the inguinal arc and pubic hairs and the hairs were described, as I said, matted together. They were all stuck together by this ointment."

"Okay. Anything else significant about your general observations of the body?"

*("The body"!! Lord have mercy. They're going to bury me behind this.)*

"There was early—an examination of the external aspect, early signs of decomposition, skin slippage where the skin like peels off with little pressure and greenish discoloration at the abdomen, which were signs of decomposition."

*(THAT DOES IT. I just bought a 30 YEAR BID. Slipping skin, green abdomen—turn out the lights, this party's over. This jury is sick to their stomach. I'm finished.)*

The autopsy had revealed a .04 alcohol content in Teresa's corpse. In his opening remarks, Venturi had singled out alcohol as one of the substances she abused the night she died.

"Now," Chaiet said, "associated with decomposition of the body—of a body—is alcohol formed?"

"Yes."

"Now, could you say whether or not within a reasonable degree of medical certainty that this point-oh-four percent reading could be consistent with that decomposition?"

"Yes, I could say that. I have an opinion."

"What is that?"

"That it's consistent with decomposition rather than change."

"Rather than the ingestion of alcohol?"

"It is also consistent with ingestion of alcohol."

"Oh, it is? In this case, do you have any opinion as to which it is?"

"Yes."

"Okay. And what is your opinion?"

"I found evidence of advanced gas in the blood vessels and throughout the system, indicating fermentation was taking place, or decomposition. I could attribute it to decomposition."

Venturi objected. A proper foundation had not been laid. Opinion wasn't medical certainty.

Judge Farren interjected, "Are you testifying within a reasonable degree of medical probability that the amount of alcohol found in the body was due to decomposition as opposed to ingested alcohol?"

"Yes, I am."

Farren told Chaiet to proceed.

Once more Chaiet returned to the presence of Vaseline, and the ripped culottes. But it was difficult to prove that profound sexual perversion played a part in Teresa's death. There was no evidence of sperm.

Like Venturi, Chaiet was convinced that something explosive had occurred that night. His theory was that Ken had murdered Teresa in a rage after being rebuffed by her. He knew that cocaine could trigger intense desire and then just as easily prevent performance. He believed that all of the phone calls to sex hot lines were made by Ken "in some sort of a frenzy" after Teresa was dead. It made sense out of the senseless. Connecticut had shown the "bizarre sexual way" Ken's mind worked. "It's my feeling that he killed her and then made the calls," he told Guy McCormick.

Chaiet had no way of documenting this, of course, so given the absence of sperm, he did what he always did when faced with the unknown. He'd bring it up first, beat Venturi to the punch if the defense tried to make something out of it, at least demonstrate to the jury that it was really of no consequence as far as the defendant's guilt was concerned, perhaps even set jurors to wondering *why* wasn't there sperm in such an explicitly sexual context? Besides, the more he thought about it, Chaiet wouldn't put it past Ken to claim that Teresa dialed the calls as part of some kinky sex play with him which she had initiated.

"Now, first, as regards to spermatozoa, could you tell us what tests you did, and the results?"

"I prepared smears from the vagina, from the anal area and the oro cavity, and the results were all negative for spermatozoa."

"All right. Now, if you accept for the moment, Doctor, that the death in this case occurred on November eleventh of nineteen eighty-four, and the body was found the fifteenth of November, and you did your autopsy on the sixteenth, if there was sexual activity prior to death, immediately prior to death, within a reasonable time of the death of this person, and then you had the intervening time before you did the—before you did these tests, would you expect to find spermatozoa?"

"Yes."

"Could you tell us why you expect to find it?"

"Spermatozoa are cells that are present in semen. They are male sex cells that fertilize the egg and when a person—if ejaculation occurs, and semen is deposited in the vagina, say, and the evidence of semen is spermatozoa, what we find—if that person—in a dead person, spermatozoa can be found for several days after death because there is no gravity mechanism or drainage mechanism to rid the body of this spermatozoa and it's possible to find identifiable spermatozoa many days after death."

"And how much before death would intercourse with ejaculation have had to occur to find that?"

"About a day . . . providing douching or bathing didn't take place or providing—depending upon the activity of the subject, too."

"You found none?"

"No."

"Would the presence of that Vaseline substance have any effect on your ability to find the spermatozoa?"

"No," Dr. Bindie said.

"Now, Doctor, as a result of your examination of the body, the autopsy, as a result of the history of this matter, and based upon your training and experience, do you have an opinion, within a reasonable degree of medical probability, as to the cause of the death of Teresa Taylor?"

"My opinion is that Teresa Taylor died of massive cranial cerebral injuries secondary to a blunt force trauma."

"Could you just briefly review your autopsy findings?"

"Objection," Venturi shouted.

"I'll sustain that objection," Judge Farren said.

• • •

In his cross-examination, the best Venturi could do was to wring an acknowledgment from Bindie that the number of blows Teresa had received might have been "six or seven" instead of nine. So he tried another tack.

"And if there was a door frame, or the edge of a door frame exposed, and the head was forcibly thrown back into the edge of that door frame, that could possibly cause one or more of the lacerations that you referred to—is that correct, sir?"

"I would think it would be unlikely to get that extensive a fracture of the skull underneath the laceration."

"Unlikely, but not impossible, depending upon the force of the head snapping back?"

"Yes, anything is possible."

During the sodium amytal procedure, in his latest version

of the events of that night, Ken had said he'd engaged in oral and anal sex with Teresa at her behest. If he ever took the stand in his own defense, he was sure to repeat it. So, because of the sperm issue, Venturi focused on an enzyme called acid phosphatase, a component of semen. Hadn't it been found in Teresa?

"Yes, very low levels."

"But there were findings of same?"

"Yes."

". . . And you also indicated that the acid phosphatase activities would have decreased during decomposition—is that correct?"

"Yes."

"And there was a severe amount of decomposition in terms of this examination, correct?"

"Yes."

"So that one could assume that if there was examination at an earlier point in time, there would be a higher level of acid phosphatase activity?"

"Yes."

Then Venturi zeroed in on Teresa's alcohol content.

"Now, you rendered an opinion that the finding of alcohol was not inconsistent with alcohol being used—is that correct?"

"It's inconclusive either way. That's what I think I said."

"So that if Doctor Taylor told the police that his wife was using alcohol that evening, that would not be inconsistent with your findings?"

"No, it would not be inconsistent."

Venturi remembered how the jury took that in. It was vital that Teresa be perceived as a willing accomplice to the events of November 11, events that spun out of control.

But then, in his redirect questions, Chaiet picked up on the alcohol.

"I'm a bit confused. When we talked about a point-oh-four percent alcohol reading, it was my understanding that your opinion was, within a reasonable degree of medical certainty, that the reading was a result of decomposition. Am I correct or am I wrong?"

"Yes, that was my opinion."

"Okay, defense counsel then asked you a question about whether it would have been consistent with the consumption of alcohol and your answer was yes. I don't understand the two."

"I meant that without knowing any other facts, the level of point-oh-four would be consistent with the intake of maybe one or two drinks, or the decomposition. When these other facts came out, I said decomposition."

"So that in this particular case, the autopsy of Teresa Taylor, you're telling us that point-oh-four percent is the result of decomposition?"

"Yes."

"Now, the low level of acid phosphatase in the body. If there was a high level, it would break down during decomposition?"

"Yes . . . we have this contaminating Vaseline, whatever that substance is, that could inactivate some of the enzymes. There is a lot of factors."

"Let me now get—if there were no semen in the vagina, the anus, then would it necessarily have to break down from those higher levels?"

"This level we got could be a normal level. It's not diagnostic of anything."

"All right. So what you're telling me is from the acid phosphatase that you got in the body, you can't tell us anything about whether or not this person had sex shortly before her death?"

"No, I can't."

"Okay. So we've got to completely discount the acid phosphatase?"

"Yes."

"As far as the spermatozoa, you found none?"

"Yes."

• • •

Venturi thought he'd muddied the waters. He was certain of it when Chaiet suddenly and angrily approached the bench, complaining that during Bindie's testimony, Venturi's client had been "constantly shaking his head in agreement or disagreement. I ask the Court to request counsel to have him not react to witnesses."

Venturi said, "I think it's humanly impossible. He's on trial here for his life."

"Let me interrupt," Judge Farren said. "He's not on trial for his life."

"Well, he's here to be in jail for the rest of his life . . . He can't sit there—it's incredible for him to sit there as some kind of robot."

"To tell you the truth," Farren said to Chaiet, "I don't find him doing that to impress the jury. I think it's a gut reaction to the testimony. I'm going to ask Mr. Venturi to indicate to him that he's not to try to impress the jury with his nodding or the shaking of his head and let it go at that."

"Sure, no problem," Venturi said.

The local headline was: "Head injuries killed victim."

So what else was new? Venturi thought. It could have been a lot worse.

• • •

On the trial's second day, Chaiet put Linda Jankowski, a state police forensic chemist, on the stand to testify about the blood found in the house and car trunk. There also was "human blood" on the dumbbell without weights; none on the one with them. And again, before Jack Venturi could do it, Chaiet asked about the condition of the blood sample taken from Teresa's body.

"It was putrid."

"What would be the effect of that in doing the various tests?"

"That could have a great effect on many of the enzymes. It makes it very much more likely to get no reaction or any conclusive results on some of the enzymes."

*(It screws up the results Linda. We concede the blood on the earring, on the padding, etc. are Teresa's. BUT that putrid blood sample must have given poor results for drug analysis.)*

267

In his turn, Venturi went right to the alleged murder weapon.

"Now, the blood on the dumbbell was human blood but no further testing was done—is that correct?"

"Yes."

"So there was no comparison of that blood with either Teresa Taylor's blood or Doctor Taylor's blood?"

"Correct."

But in redirect, Chaiet raised the possibility that, like the rest of the house, the dumbbell had been wiped clean and that only a "trace" of blood was left on it.

"And the only thing you could tell about that from the sample is that it was—"

"Human blood."

"And that there was just no more to use?"

"Correct."

· · ·

Angela Rozek testified about the visit she and her husband made to the Manalapan house on the night of November 10.

"Now," Chaiet asked, "were you with Teresa and the defendant at all times during that night?"

"Well, Teresa and I were in the dining room and Ken and my husband were sitting in the living room, but it's one big room. We were all in plain view of each other."

"While you were there that night, were there any arguments?"

"No"

"Did you have anything to drink?"

"No, just coffee."

"Did you observe whether or not Teresa Taylor had anything to drink?"

"She just had coffee."

"What about your husband? Did he drink anything?"

"He had a mixed drink."

"And did you note whether or not the defendant had anything to drink?"

"Yes, he did."

"Did you note the use of any controlled, dangerous substances?"

"No."

"You did not see Teresa Taylor use any drugs?"

"I did not."

"Okay. Could you tell us how Teresa Taylor was acting during that period of time from seven-thirty to ten-thirty?"

"Just her normal self."

"And what's normal?"

"Just like anybody else would. Just sitting around having coffee, talking. Nothing unusual."

"Was the baby up while you were there?"

"Yes."

"Have you seen her care for that baby?"

"Yes, I have."

"And could you tell me how she cared for that baby?"

"Very well."

*(God rest her soul. Teresa I'm so sorry, this has all been so unnecessary.)*

The jurors could see for themselves how physically imposing Ken was. Chaiet wanted them to hear how Teresa compared to him in size, how absurd it was that he could have feared for his life that night.

"Do you know how tall Teresa was?"

"She was about five three."

"And weight?"

"It's hard to say. Teresa was very deceiving in her appearance. I would say she weighed between one-thirty-five and one-forty . . . Teresa had a weight problem. She used to dress herself to hide it, you know, to deceive everybody as to how she had big hips."

*(Precisely why she wouldn't swim in our pool. NOT once, NOT ONE TIME did Teresa use the pool. What a shame. What a goddamn shame.)*

"Okay. What about, you know, up top, the arms—"

"She was small. She had a small bustline and chest, you know."

"And could you tell us anything from your observations of her about her physical strength?"

"Teresa was not—I don't think she was a strong person.

She might have been as strong as me. That's not very strong."

After a subdued, hesitant start, Angela was proving to be a surprisingly potent witness. So far, there was little Venturi could do about it. Then Chaiet asked if there had been any discussion about what Teresa had eaten for supper that night. Venturi was immediately up, objecting. It struck at the heart of Teresa's allegedly cocaine-crazed condition. Cocaine was an anorectic drug. Anyone high on cocaine would not want food.

"Basis of your objection?" Judge Farren said.

"Calling for a hearsay statement."

The jury was excused.

Chaiet said that he not only intended to question Angela about Teresa's meal, but also about the conversation Teresa had with Angela when she said that Ken did cocaine and she occasionally joined him. Again, Venturi objected. Angela could say all she wanted to about Teresa doing cocaine, but nothing about Ken's use of the drug.

Chaiet argued that the autopsy already had revealed remnants of food in Teresa's stomach. "My other argument," he said, "is that in defense counsel's opening to this jury, he said that Teresa Taylor was crazed with drugs, alcohol, codeine, cocaine . . . and how all of a sudden this problem manifests itself on one particular night. I think that the defendant's drug use is part of this case, just as Teresa Taylor's use of it is, and that's why I think it's admissible."

Farren agreed with Chaiet. The fact that Teresa had eaten something was already in evidence. As for the use or nonuse of drugs, it was "part of the mosaic of this particular offense, or alleged offense, in the light of the opening statements of counsel."

When Angela resumed the stand, Chaiet said, "I believe I asked you a question whether or not Teresa Taylor told you what she had for dinner that night. Did she?"

"Yes."

"And what statement did she make to you?"

"That she had pork."

"Did she tell you what time they had dinner?"

"No."

"Okay. You indicated to us that you observed no drug use in the house that night. Is that correct?"

"That's correct."

". . . Now, did you ever have a conversation with Teresa Taylor concerning cocaine?"

"Yes."

"All right. What did she tell you about the use of cocaine?"

"That they did use cocaine."

"They, meaning?"

"Her, Ken."

"And did she indicate to you how often she used cocaine?"

"On occasion, she said."

"On occasion?"

"Yes."

"But again, you saw no drug use that night?"

"That's right."

"Did you see any indication that anybody was under the influence of a drug that night?"

"Not at all."

"During the course of your conversations with Teresa that night, did the topic of sex come up?"

"Yes, it did."

Venturi objected.

Out of the jury's presence, Chaiet said he intended to introduce Ken's "whopping" remark.

Venturi argued that it would be prejudicial.

Farren ruled, "It's not hearsay. It was made the evening that allegedly she died at the hands of the defendant. The position of the defendant is that although he allegedly committed the act, he did it to protect himself in self-defense. I think it is relevant. I don't think it carries the degree of prejudice that it should be excluded."

Chaiet continued. "I'm not interested in the details, but in a general way what were you discussing? What was the sexual conversation?"

"We were discussing the difficulty of having sex while you were pregnant."

"Did the defendant say anything or chime in?"

"Yes, he did . . . He turned around and he said that Teresa wouldn't refuse him after the whopping that he gave her the other night."

"What did she say to that?"

"Nothing. She just looked at him."

"What did you say?"

"Nothing."

Then Chaiet showed Angela Rozek a photograph of the room where Teresa sewed, where Ken's weight stand also was.

She testified that it was basically the same as it was when she went in to view the maternity dresses the night Teresa died.

"As you see," Chaiet said, "there is—in the photo there is a weight there and a little barbell there. Do you recall the exact position of those weights on Saturday night?"

"I remember this weight was right around there. I almost tripped on it when I looked at the outfit that was hanging on the weight bench."

"You say this weight, the dumbbell that has—"

"Right."

"—that has some weights on it?"

"Right, right."

This was the dumbbell Teresa would have had to use, and Chaiet said, "You don't know if it was in that exact position?"

"I don't know if it was exactly there, but it was on the floor."

"It was in that area?"

"In that area, because I tripped over it."

"Do you recall whether or not that particular room had a doorstop or a weight used as a doorstop?"

"No, I don't remember."

"You don't recall it?"

"I don't."

Once more, before he concluded his questioning, Chaiet

made sure to invoke an image of Teresa that was the antithesis to that of someone supposedly high on cocaine.

"During the course of that evening, did Teresa indicate to you how she was feeling that night?"

"She was tired."

"She said she was tired?"

"Yes."

"And did she tell you why she was tired?"

"She was up late the night before with company."

• • •

Venturi could not shake Angela's ingenuous manner despite the acerbic, accusatory tone he adopted.

She was Teresa's cousin, wasn't she?

"Yes."

She had testified that she and her husband and Teresa and Ken were "in plain view" of each other that evening. Were those her words or words that the police might have suggested?

"You can see each other," she said. "The back of the love seat is basically part of the dining room. It sectioned it off."

"I understand that you could see each other, but what I'm asking, the phrase 'plain view,' was that your phrase?"

"It's my phrase."

Hadn't Teresa bathed the baby that night? She had no trouble lifting him in and out of the tub, was that right?

"That's right."

Teresa would also have to pick up the sewing machine and move it around when she sewed, wouldn't she?

"I don't know. I don't sew."

That "whopping" remark that Ken allegedly made, was it serious or light-hearted?

"I thought it was a joke." The way Angela said it, though, it sounded as if she didn't think it was so funny anymore. Venturi tried again.

"You took it as a joke. Is that right?"

"Uh-huh, right," she said, almost mockingly.

"And Mrs. Taylor didn't say anything to you at all that evening about being beaten by her husband. *Is* that right?"

"That's right."

Did Teresa say *why* she was tired that night?

"She said she was up late the night before with her brother and his girlfriend."

"Did she say that she had done cocaine with them that night?"

"No, she did not."

"Did she say she was hung over?"

"She just said she was tired."

"Did she say she was up until about four A.M.?"

"Yes."

"And you were in the sewing room and you observed some weights on the floor—is that correct?"

"That's correct."

"Do you remember if it was like it was in the picture, one with weights on and one with weights off, or if it was both with weights off, or if you only observed one set of weights?"

"I only saw the set of the weights that's on the weight bench and the one that's right at the foot of the weight bench on the floor."

"With the weights on?"

"With—with the two little weights on, right."

"Did you pick them up and move them?"

"No."

"When you were there, you said you tripped over it."

"I tripped over it, but I didn't move it. I was pregnant. I didn't lift anything."

"Did Teresa pick it up and move it out of your way?"

"No."

Then Venturi moved toward the jury box, turned back toward Angela and said, "Have you ever used cocaine?"

"No."

"I have nothing further," he said, hands raised in exasperation, as if this were the last straw in an endless series of falsehoods.

• • • •

*(Rieders is going to be dangerous, potentially damaging. Another scientist, but this scientist is a toxicologist.)*

The issue would be central to self-defense—Teresa's purported drug-crazed state.

Dr. Frederick Rieders was in his late fifties, bow-tied, hair falling over his forehead, shoes scuffed. He had the slightly bemused air of a man you could expect to find at home in a lab filled with test tubes, slides and microscopes, and had been certified as a chemical toxicologist for fifteen years, the last five as a forensic toxicologist as well.

He'd been chief toxicologist for the Philadelphia Medical Examiner's office before becoming the laboratory director for National Medical Services, a private group that serviced coroners and medical examiners across the country, along with assisting physicians in diagnosing illnesses of mysterious origin.

"Toxicology," he explained, "is the study of the harm that foreign chemicals can do to animals or man or other systems. That is what the laboratory works at in determining what analyses to do, performing those analyses and interpreting their results."

At the outset, Chaiet brought up the fact that there was practically no whole blood in Teresa to be tested.

Yes, Rieders said, the testing requested for cocaine and codeine had been conducted using bloody fluid taken from her chest cavity and from "vitreous fluid"—fluid from the eye. But it didn't matter. While there was a certain lag time in transference from the bloodstream to other parts of the body, "vitreous fluid," lacking good blood samples, was "much less subject to putrefaction change than other fluids in the body—except for urine, of which none was found in this case."

Had the presence of codeine been detected?

It had.

"Now, in reference to your finding of codeine, can you tell us what type of drug codeine is?"

"Codeine is used to relieve pain. It also has the ability to depress the central nervous system and, as a matter of fact, can put someone to sleep and thus is classified as a narcotic analgesic, not narcotic in the legal sense, but narcotic as a sleep-producing pain reliever."

"Could you tell us about the level of the drug that was found?"

"Well, what I can tell you is that this is a concentration which you would expect to find in the circulating body fluids . . . in an individual that has taken a dose—a normal analgesic dose between half a grain and one grain. So it is well within the therapeutic pain-relieving range for codeine which also has some sedating properties."

"All right. When you say that, does it mean that if I had a particular problem, this would be in line with the pre-scribed amount a doctor would give for the pain?"

"Yes."

". . . Now, Doctor, in your opinion, again with probable certainty, would this level of codeine by itself cause one to behave in a drug-crazed manner?"

"No. Codeine is not a stimulant. It is a depressant drug, and pharmacologically and physiologically I do not expect it to produce any type of stimulation. Rather, sedation and drowsiness."

Chaiet returned to the level of alcohol evident in Teresa's body. What was his opinion of the .04 reading?

"My reasonable certain opinion is that this reading of alcohol in the chest fluid, while no alcohol was found in the vitreous humor, is due to a postmortem putrefaction change. A low concentration of alcohol, such as this, is not uncommonly formed in the course of putrefaction from the fermentation of sugar-type molecules in the body."

Chaiet paused. He shuffled papers. He looked at the jury and then back to Rieders.

"Now, did you also check for the presence of cocaine?"

"Yes."

"And did you find any cocaine?"

"No."

"What did you find when you checked for cocaine?"

"I did not find any cocaine. However, the request was specifically for cocaine, and knowing that cocaine is changed by the body into another substance quite com-monly and normally, we also performed a separate and inde-pendent analysis for that substance, which is called benzoylecgonine, a metabolite or breakdown product of cocaine, and we did find that breakdown product, that metabolite in the specimen—point four parts per million.''

"Now, tell us about, uh, benzoylecgonine. I never could pronounce it.''

"Benzoylecgonine itself has no pharmacologic activity. It's not a stimulant, not a depressant. In this particular case, the analysis shows no presence of cocaine around the time this individual died, but only that at the time the autopsy was done and specimens were taken, the inactive microtransformation, or breakdown products of cocaine, was present—showing that that individual at some time prior, which could be many hours prior, to her death, had used cocaine. Therefore, benzoylecgonine was present. So that is the direct evidence of the analysis and that is as far as it goes.''

"All right. This is—what you're—aren't you saying at the time that she was killed, the cocaine had already broken down into this by-product?''

Venturi objected, trying to undo the rapt attention that Rieders's testimony was getting from the jurors about the metabolic workings of the famous drug. The question was leading the witness.

"I'll permit it,'' Farren said, who seemed as intrigued as everyone else. "Go ahead. Overruled.''

"No,'' Rieders answered. "I cannot say that. The only thing I can say is that I cannot know whether at the time she was killed there was any active cocaine present in her. At the time the analysis was performed, the only thing present was the breakdown product. Whether this breakdown occurred prior to death or after death, I cannot tell *per se*. I have only evidence for presence of benzoylecgonine, which is an inactive substance.''

"In other words, you don't get high from that inactive substance?''

"You don't get high on anything from it. It has no effect.''

"The effect of taking cocaine lasts how long?''

"In general, the ordinary one hundred milligram recreational-use dose has a significant stimulatory effect for a period of approximately one hour. In some cases, somewhat longer."

"Okay," Chaiet said. "Based upon benzoylecgonine that you found, can you say anything about the amount of cocaine ingested?"

"Well, yes, I can, and that is, at the most, if cocaine had been used shortly before this person was killed, and the cocaine had reached a certain level in the blood by the time the person was killed, and the cocaine subsequently broke down after death and all turned into benzoylecgonine—which is an unlikely situation, as I will explain to you shortly—then this might have been at and around the time of death what you might call a recreational dose, for lack of a better term, that an individual would use in order to feel good, to be stimulated by it and to feel on top of the world . . . a pleasant excitement, but not the aggressive hallucinatory derangements that occur when heavy cocaine is used."

Rieders went on to explain that cocaine started to break down immediately upon being inhaled, swallowed, or injected. But even if it had all been cocaine in Teresa's body at the moment she died, there still wasn't enough to produce anything approaching "drug-crazed behavior." Indeed, he said, the residue of cocaine was less than half the usual recreational amount if she had ingested it just before she was killed.

• • •

Like an illusionist, Venturi would attempt diversions in an effort to undermine Rieders's testimony.

Was the toxicologist aware that "this young woman" had started her menstrual cycle?

"I don't believe I was. I certainly didn't take it into consideration."

So Rieders didn't know what effect this might have had on her personality?

"No, I do not."

Well, had he ever heard of PMS—premenstrual syndrome?

"Yes, I've heard of it."

278

Wasn't it a condition "well-documented medically?"

"I suppose so," Rieders said with a dismissive air. "It's not a toxicological problem, you know."

Venturi was pleased by that. Maybe the female jurors would not be so amused by Rieders's condescension.

And how about postpartum depression? Was Rieders aware that Teresa sometimes suffered from *that?*

"No. Again, you know, it had no bearing on my considerations."

But wasn't it a fact that when people were depressed "a lot of times cocaine is the drug of choice, so to speak?"

Chaiet objected, and Farren told Venturi, "He's a toxicologist. I don't think that's within his field of expertise."

Okay, Venturi said, but cocaine was a stimulant, wasn't it?

"That's correct."

"And in your expertise, and in your study and in the literature that you've read, you have studied why people use cocaine, what has led them to use it, is that not correct, sir?"

"I've read some of that literature, but to a limited degree because what makes people do things is a psychiatric question rather than toxicological."

Venturi persisted. Wasn't there a correlation between "depression and the use of cocaine?"

"Objection, Judge," Chaiet said.

"I'll overrule the objection."

"It's a recreational drug," Rieders said with obvious annoyance, "and certain people will use it perhaps, particularly if they are depressed."

Venturi let that sink in before moving on to the vitreous fluid which was used for most of the sampling. It was a poor sample, correct?

"I fully agree [but] it's still a sample," and, he reiterated, it was "much less subject to putrefaction change than other fluids in the body, except for urine."

Was Rieders aware that there wasn't enough blood in Teresa "to even get a complete blood typing of all the blood factors?"

"I didn't see that. It didn't concern me, really."

Venturi pursued another angle. Cocaine was often mixed with other ingredients to increase profits. Had the cocaine residue in Teresa's body been screened for the presence of methamphetamine—speed—or another hallucinatory drug, PCP, commonly called angel dust?

No, it hadn't, Rieders said. But methamphetamine was no more potent than cocaine. As for PCP, he declared, "I have not encountered it in any of the mixtures that we have analyzed for police departments, which are by the thousands, a mixture of cocaine with PCP. It's theoretically possible. In my experience, no."

Venturi kept trying. But it *was* theoretically within the realm of possibility, and it hadn't been screened. Was that so?

"That's correct," Rieders conceded.

Then Venturi conjured up a new mix of aberrant drug use. Did codeine depress the central nervous system and act as a sedative?

"Among other things, yes."

"Now, for example, heroin is also a strong depressant, isn't that a fact?"

"Moderately strong. No stronger a depressant—it's no more potent than codeine."

"No more potent?"

"Not as a depressant."

"Than codeine?"

"No."

"You've heard of heroin and cocaine being used together?"

"Uh-huh."

"It's been highly publicized about John Belushi. They call it a speedball and—"

Chaiet was on his feet, objecting.

Even Judge Farren was taken aback. "Mr. Venturi, we're not going to get into John Belushi's death, are we?"

"No, sir."

"All right."

"Just by way of analogy," Venturi said.

When Rieders told Farren that he was aware of what Venturi was talking about, the judge allowed the cross-examination to continue.

"And the point of these two items together is to complement them and get a greater high or a greater feeling?"

"Judge," a frustrated Chaiet said, "I'm going to object as to relevance."

"Sustained. Is there evidence," Farren said, "that this in fact was used by the decedent?"

"Not as to heroin, Judge. We're getting the heroin in as an example, an analogy to the codeine, about which he testified heroin is not as strong."

"We're getting too speculative," Farren said. "Unless you're going to represent to me that this was in fact ingested by the decedent prior to death."

"No, no, no. Nothing like that."

"We're getting too esoteric," Farren said wearily. "He's a toxicologist and pharmacologist. And unless you're going to tie it in, I'm going to sustain the objection."

"Let's tie it in then," Venturi said.

"When you say tie it in, tie it into this decedent. We're not going to have this jury speculate that this decedent ingested something esoteric like a speedball or whatever it might be. Unless there's going to be some proof from you that she did—"

That was, Venturi hoped, exactly what they were speculating about, along with premenstrual syndrome and postpartum depression and the fact that there was evidence of cocaine and codeine in Teresa's system. "Well," he said, "you've heard of people using codeine—"

"Mr. Venturi," Farren said, "you don't seem to understand."

"I'm moving to something else, Judge. I'm out of there."

"Okay, fine."

Addressing Rieders, Venturi continued, "You've heard of people in your experience, in the literature, doing codeine because of the numbness it can produce and cocaine because of the stimulating effect it gives them as a complement to each other and to get both aspects of a high, is that correct?"

". . . The combination made them feel good, whatever that may mean. That's very subjective, and that's precisely what they're referring to. They felt good, trouble-free and at peace with the world."

"But one of the things that can occur when these two things are used together, because they counteract each other, is they could tend to cause confusion—is that correct?"

"They can cause confusion independently of each other and in their interaction, that confusion may well remain confusing . . . a misrepresentation of what is going on around the person."

Then Venturi overreached. Couldn't this also have led to a "drug-crazed state"—the one that "the prosecutor" was so bent on ridiculing?

"What I consider, and what generally one considers, a drug-crazed state means that it's an aggressive state. And at these levels, with these drugs from the drugs themselves, not a likely occurrence in my opinion . . . It depends very much on the individual. Cocaine would tend to excite. Codeine would tend to reduce excitement. So you can't say what a little bit of each would do."

Venturi decided that he had gotten as much mileage out of this as he could. "I have nothing further," he said.

\* \* \*

At the Monmouth County Jail, Jean and Zach Taylor arrived with a change of clothing for Ken's next day in court, a white shirt, blue tie and a navy blue suit with a light blue pinstripe—in line with the sober dress that Venturi had advised him to wear. Venturi had also suggested rimless glasses to enhance further the image of a mild-mannered dentist. But Ken balked at this. He'd feel too uncomfortable with them.

Now he was beside himself. On the intercom, behind the glass that separated him from his parents, he raged about the *putrid blood*. Had they listened to that testimony? How could any tests have been made with *it?* And did they hear that "weasel-eyed" Farren say that he wasn't facing life in prison? What did Farren think thirty years without parole was? Why hadn't Venturi found a toxicologist? *Why* hadn't they pleaded temporary insanity?

Zach, his voice cracking, said, "We've just got to hang in there, son."

Jean's mind seemed to be elsewhere. This was the period of the week when the baby was with Celeste and Jeff. It simply wasn't right for them to have him, she kept saying.

Don't worry, Ken told his mother, he'd fix their wagon.

• • •

Ken already had lashed out at Venturi as well for not pushing more on the putrid blood sample. Venturi reminded him that the testing hadn't been based on it, that it was futile to get into a medical dispute with a medical expert. But, as usual, his client hadn't listened to what he did not want to hear.

Everything considered, the day threatened a knockout punch, but that hadn't happened. Venturi figured that his commonsense approach—suggesting that too much time had elapsed, an unknown amount of cocaine must have dissipated before they did the toxicology—had had an impact. And certainly it had come across that Teresa was less than angelic. She did cocaine, no question about that. He wouldn't allow anyone to forget it in his summation.

Venturi took particular heart that as he was heading for his car, several jurors were in the courthouse parking lot, and they hadn't tried to avert their eyes or otherwise avoid him. "Good night, Counselor," they'd all said quite pleasantly.

# Chapter

# FIFTEEN

On the third day of testimony, Wednesday, June 5, Chaiet guided Lieutenant Bill Lucia through the litany of lies that Ken told in the Manalapan police station to explain Teresa's disappearance.

"... Now, would you tell us what happened at three-oh-two P.M. when you walked back into the room?"

*(I remember that moment very clearly. I was finally surrendering. I was at the end of the rope, no hope in sight.)*

"I looked at Doctor Taylor," Lucia said. "He seemed somewhat in deep thought at this time and somewhat upset, and he looked up at me and he said, 'Sit down, I want to tell you something.' I said, 'Okay,' and I sat down ... He said to me, 'What would you do if you came downstairs one morning and found your wife giving your five-month-old baby head?' With this, he broke down and started crying."

"And following that, did you try and question him more?"

"Well, yes ... We gave him a little bit of time, and he

went on to say at that point she swung a dumbbell at him. He got it away from her and 'gave it to her.' ' "

"And the words 'gave it to her,' " Chaiet asked, raising his voice, "are those your words or his?"

"No. 'Gave it to her' are his words."

*(a BOLD-faced, detestable, state-prosecution-serving LIE.)*

"Continue."

"Okay . . . I then asked Doctor Taylor some more specific questions as to what had actually taken place. He indicated in response that he was tired of her drug problem. That it happened on a Sunday morning, around eight A.M. He was upstairs sleeping previously . . . He saw her 'doing that to the baby.' He screamed. She ran into the laundry room and grabbed a dumbbell. She swung it at him. He ducked and got it away from her."

"Did he say where he was when that happened?"

"At that point, he just indicated that he was in the doorway of what he referred to as the laundry room. As I stated, he said he ducked and he grabbed it from her and he hit her with it. I then proceeded to try to establish how many times he had struck her. His final response was that he had hit her several times with this dumbbell bar."

"Several times?"

"Yes."

• • •

Venturi went right at Lucia.

Wasn't it a fact that the defendant was very emotional, his lips "quivering"?

"Yes, sir."

"So it took some minutes for him to compose himself before he could talk again—after his initial statement to you?"

"I would say it was more intermittent."

"But when he was saying it, he was still in this emotional state of crying and physically trembling and quivering, as you described?"

"Yes, sir."

"For instance, you stated that what he said to you was

that she ran in the room, swung a dumbbell at him, and he got it away and gave it to her—is that correct?"

"Yes."

"Is it not possible," Venturi then asked, measuring his words carefully, as if the truth was at last being revealed, "that he said that she ran in the room, swung at him, and then *he got away* and gave it to her?"

Lucia hesitated. "No, that's a—I recall basically that's what he—those were his exact words, what he said to me. I was paying very specific attention at that time. Obviously he was going to tell me something I had been waiting a long time to hear."

Venturi stared at Lucia. "Was a tape recording made of this statement?"

"No, sir."

"Was there a stenographer in the room at the time when he was making these statements?"

"No, sir."

"So there is no transcript of the statement?"

"No, sir."

"Was there a typist in the room?"

"No, sir."

Venturi walked away from Lucia toward the jury, shaking his head in theatrical disbelief. "No more questions," he said.

• • •

Chaiet put Manalapan police lieutenant Peter Vanderweil on the stand to corroborate Lucia's testimony. At the time of the confession, Vanderweil quoted Ken as saying, "I just couldn't take it anymore. She was taking my prescriptions and stealing my money. I just couldn't take it anymore."

Vanderweil also said he heard Ken admit that Teresa was in effect defenseless when he struck her, that after seizing the dumbbell bar from Teresa, "I gave it to her."

Then Venturi renewed his attack.

"At the time Doctor Taylor arrived that morning, he was already a prime suspect in this homicide. Correct?"

"He was a suspect, yes."

"*Was* there any other suspect?"

"No, not at that point."

"And there were two law enforcement officers there to question him at the same time that others went to his house?"

"Yes."

"There was a lot of activity by a lot of people that morning—isn't that correct?"

"Yes."

"Yet no one got a tape recorder or got a court reporter there to talk—when he came in to talk that morning, even though they knew he was coming in."

"That's correct."

"By that afternoon, by one-fifteen, there was additional information [Teresa's earring on the garage floor] that had been developed, right?"

"Yes."

"And the whole nature of Doctor Taylor's interrogation had changed?"

"I don't know what took place prior to me getting there, but we continued along the same lines as the interview in the morning."

"And nobody got a tape recorder to tape the statement, or a typewriter to type it, or court reporter to record it?"

"That's correct."

"And by this point that afternoon, Doctor Taylor was no longer *a* suspect—*he was the key suspect,* correct?"

"That's correct."

• • •

Paul Chaiet—the smoldering animosity between him and Venturi clearly felt in the courtroom—strode toward Vanderweil.

"Lieutenant, could you tell me the practice in taking statements prior to requesting that a written statement be put down or a statement recorded? Could you tell me what your practice is in interviewing a suspect in Manalapan Township?"

"Objection," Venturi said. "Could I be heard at the sidebar?"

"Overruled," Judge Farren said. "Go ahead, Mr. Chaiet."

Chaiet continued, "Could you answer that question, please?"

Vanderweil said, "With any suspect in any investigation, you conduct a verbal interview. You reach a point, hopefully, sometimes you don't, but you reach a point where the suspect admits to whatever you're investigating. You still gather information after that. You continue to gather it . . . you let the suspect tell his story until you reach a point where you feel you have enough information, that you have all the facts available. Then you go back—have either a stenographer or recording device, and go over the statement again."

"So you know where you're going?"

"Exactly."

"Now, other than your practice, would there have been anything that prevented you from tape recording this statement?"

"No."

• • • •

Chaiet called Cindy Diaz.

Instantly, with the jury absent, there was another angry exchange between Chaiet and Venturi. Chaiet said he was going to show the videotape that Cindy's husband had made of Teresa and the baby on Saturday morning, November 10.

Venturi furiously objected. It was a cheap tactic. And it had no relevance.

Not so, Chaiet said. From the very beginning, the defense had made an issue out of the decedent's care and concern as a mother. The jurors had every right to view her relationship with the infant. They also had a right to observe her physical stature.

Farren ruled for Chaiet.

Venturi moved for a mistrial.

"You may proceed, Mr. Chaiet," Farren said.

Chaiet asked Diaz about Teresa's "care of the baby, her actions with the baby?"

"The baby meant everything to her. Everything was the

baby. That's all she spoke about was—she'd call me up and said, Oh, the baby's doing this now, he's moving his head. She was telling me all the things she bought for the baby's room even before the baby was born. Then after that, she's telling me about a little scale she bought and every day she'd weigh him to see how many pounds he gained, but she was—that baby was everything!''

The videotape was played. It ran about ten minutes. Seated at the prosecutor's table, Guy McCormick didn't look at it. He'd seen it enough. He watched the jurors instead. From the moment Teresa's smiling face appeared, they kept their eyes glued to the screen. And when it was over, he saw how solemn their faces had become. A couple of the jurors were even daubing at their eyes with tissues. It was as if Teresa had been resurrected. Right then and there, McCormick thought that Ken Taylor had had it. He'd bet the farm on it.

Chaiet also believed that any advantage Venturi had gained from Ken's confession not being recorded had now been wiped out. Chaiet wasn't happy that no transcript was available, but Lucia had told him that there just hadn't been time for it. It was difficult enough to break Taylor, and when it happened, it was sudden. They were about to bring in a tape recorder, he said, when Taylor abruptly cut off the interrogation and demanded a lawyer. Chaiet had decided not to pursue any of this. It would only complicate matters. Better to be forthright. Standard procedures had been followed. Besides, Venturi could only suggest some impropriety. For Lucia's—Vanderweil's—testimony to be directly contested, Ken would have to take the stand in his own defense. And if he did, Chaiet had plenty to ask him.

The tension continued. During Jeff White's direct testimony, he described the scene in the Newark Airport parking lot after he, Celeste, and Ken had vainly awaited Irene DeBlasio's return from Michigan.

''As we left,'' Jeff said, ''and were going to the car— I don't know, he made a face, like a smirk—this is my interpretation—like he had just gotten away with something.''

Venturi jumped up, objecting.

"I'll sustain," Farren said, and then to the jury, "I want you to disregard it. When I say disregard it, I don't want you to forget it. I want you to disregard it. I want you to remember that if someone brings it up while you're deliberating, the judge told us to disregard this alleged smirking, 'like he just got away with something.' Don't forget, remember not to use it. All right, go ahead, Mr. Chaiet."

"Okay, just describe his facial expression."

Jeff replied, "I would say it was like smirking."

*(JESUS! He said it again. I'll bet my last dollar Chaiet orchestrated the whole thing.)*

Then, in cross-examination, Venturi asked if it was not a fact that Jeff and Celeste were in a custody battle over the baby "against Doctor Taylor and his parents . . . and in contesting that custody, did you not say to a probation officer that Doctor Taylor's parents shouldn't have custody because they've already raised one murderer?"

"No, sir. I never said that."

Well, Venturi shot back, displaying a piece of paper, "Does this refresh your recollection?"

"What is it?" Judge Farren said.

"It's a Monmouth County Probation Department report."

Jeff said that he didn't need to refresh anything, that he had never made the statement, period.

"All right, Mr. Venturi," Farren said. "He doesn't need any refreshed recollection."

Livid, Chaiet went to the bench. He had not been given the probation report that Venturi had just been flourishing.

"You don't have to yell, Mr. Chaiet," Farren said. "I'm right next to you. Mr. Venturi, why wasn't a copy of that supplied to Mr. Chaiet?"

"Judge . . . if that was not photocopied and sent out to him, then I apologize."

"Apologies don't carry the ball at this juncture. We're in the middle of a trial and he doesn't have this information. Mr. Chaiet extended himself with regard to discovery with you and I would certainly hope that you're going to reciprocate."

Well, Venturi countered, what about the rap sheets on

the prosecution witnesses that he had requested to see if any of them had criminal records?

Farren sighed. "Mr. Chaiet at the commencement of trial indicated that he didn't have any in his possession with regard to certain witnesses. They were ordered and he'll supply them to you. As you know, discovery is a two-way street, Mr. Venturi, and after that last witness with the statement that was not supplied to Mr. Chaiet, I'm not happy with that at all. As I indicated before, I just don't want to see that happen again."

Then, after the jury was dismissed for the day, Farren inquired about Dr. Sadoff. Was Venturi going to hand over the sodium amytal tape to Chaiet and call the psychiatrist as a witness? "You were to decide by four o'clock today. I would think perhaps you have made your decision. I know it's five minutes to four. You don't need the extra five as to whether you're going to use him or not."

*(Pompous, fucking asshole!)*

Still smarting, Venturi said, "You would perhaps be correct. We have made a decision."

"And that is?"

"Not to."

"Not to? All right. Fine. Anything else, Mr. Chaiet?"

Nothing really, Chaiet said. He wasn't surprised by Venturi's decision about the tape. From the moment Venturi started getting cute about its submission, he sensed there must be quite a bit in it that Venturi didn't want known.

His first witness in the morning, Chaiet said, would be Marilyn Hope.

• • •

Farren saved his big news for last. Time permitting, he would begin evidentiary hearings the next day on the admissibility of Acapulco.

• • •

In a brief meeting with Venturi, Ken did not argue about Sadoff again. They'd hashed it over and over. As though reading his mind, Venturi had said that if Ken were ever to raise charges of incompetent counsel, letting Chaiet have the tape would be a great place to start.

Not even the prospect of Sorayda Peraino on the stand bothered Ken the way the news about Marilyn did. Supposedly Connecticut was out of the case, but suppose somehow she mentioned it?

"Don't worry," Venturi said. "I've spoken to your ex-wife and her lawyer. She's a little mixed up, but she doesn't intend you harm. You should have stayed with her."

• • •

They did not speak when she entered the courtroom dressed in a charcoal gray suit over a white blouse, but he was certain he had caught her eye momentarily.

*(Maybe I'll come out of this with a minimal sentence to serve. Then what? You know I'm going to come back to see my girl, my sweet Astrid. What have you told her? Did you tell her I'm DEAD? Sick? In jail? Ran away? WHAT?! What DID you tell her, Goddamn you, Marilyn.)*

Chaiet originally subpoenaed her for her testimony about Connecticut. And he actually traveled to Pittsburgh to see her. It had not gone well. She had come off flaky, very nervous and emotional, even fearful, as if *she* were somehow on trial for having married Ken. By the time the Pittsburgh session was over, Chaiet could feel the waves of antipathy from her for forcing her appearance.

Questioning her about Taylor's attempt to chloroform her, of course, would not have presented much of a problem. He had all the investigative reports, knew precisely what to ask and what she would have to answer. When that was no longer in the cards, he briefly considered not calling her at all. But at least, through her, he could establish firsthand that Taylor had spent the night with her while Teresa's body lay stuffed in a car trunk outside. Let the jury contemplate that.

Chaiet objected to a Bible prominently displayed in front of Ken at the defense table. He wanted it removed. Then it turned out that Marilyn had given it to Venturi to give to Ken. Farren overruled the objection. The jury was "sophisticated" enough to handle it.

*(Fuck you Chaiet, you sniveling, pouting spoiled fuck.)*

She began weeping almost with her first answer—that

yes, she knew the defendant, Kenneth Taylor, and, yes, she was his second wife.

In the end, treating her almost as a hostile witness, Chaiet managed to get her to admit, "Ken and I discussed the possibility of getting back together from the very first day we separated."

Had he ever mentioned that Teresa was stealing money or checks from him?

"Yes, that she was writing out prescriptions for herself on his pads and signing his name and falsifying some dental insurance forms to get back more money than was right."

*(WHY DID YOU SAY THAT? JEEZ, HE DIDN'T EVEN ASK!!!)*

"Did he talk to you in regard to whether or not he should stay with Teresa?"

"That's hard to answer."

*(Excellent. Bust his butt. You're driving him up the wall.)*

"Could you tell us as best you can recall what statements he gave you or said to you about whether the marriage would work?"

"Well, there were some problems . . . He said that she had been taking drugs . . . He said that it might not work with these problems."

"Okay. Did he mention anything to you about Teresa Taylor's ability to care for the baby once it was born?"

"Well, again there was a reiteration of the drug problem. He felt she had an inability to cope with caring for the baby."

"Did he give you any specifics in regard to that?"

"No."

"Did he ever discuss possibly getting custody of the baby?"

"Yes."

*(OH SHIT, MARILYN. WHY DID YOU SAY YES? YOU WERE DOING SO GOOD, SO DAMN GOOD.)*

". . . And did he indicate what he was doing to support the position that he would be entitled to custody?"

"I'm trying to get this part straight in my mind."

Chaiet turned toward the jurors with a shrug, inviting

them to share his frustration. He thrust a document at her. It was a copy of a letter she wrote to her lawyer, Carl Gainor, when she first attempted to avoid testifying. Gainor had forwarded it to Chaiet in the hope that it would convince the prosecutor to call off the dogs. "Does that refresh your recollection? You wrote that, did you not?"

"Yes."

"And what did the defendant say to you, if anything, about the child and about staying with Teresa?"

"He wanted to get custody of the child."

"Did he indicate whether or not he wanted to leave Teresa?"

"Exactly indicate?"

"What does it say there? What did you write?"

"You want me to read it?"

"No! I want you to tell me."

"He wanted the baby well started in life and established."

*"Before what?"* Chaiet demanded.

"Before he would leave," Marilyn said, her voice barely audible.

Chaiet moved on to Ken's arrival at her home, Tuesday, November 13, two days after Teresa's death, a day before he would dump the body in the Hawk Mountain Bird Sanctuary.

"Could you describe his emotions while he was with you on Tuesday night to Wednesday afternoon?"

"Nothing unusual."

"Was there anything different that you noted?"

"You mean just in normal activities, was he different?"

"Right."

"No, nothing that I noticed."

*(?YOU JEST SURELY, MARILYN!)*

And how, Chaiet continued, did the defendant conduct himself when he returned to Pittsburgh the following Saturday?

"I want to say normal, regular . . . concerned, but regular."

"Concerned about Teresa?"

"Yes, I guess—yes."

"He wasn't crying or emotionally upset?"

"No."

Chaiet wanted to remind the jury about all the Vaseline found smeared on Teresa's body, the culottes ripped down the back. "Do you recall any discussion of his sexual relations with Teresa?"

Venturi yelled, "Objection! To the form of the question and also its substance . . . First of all, the form is very leading. Second, a discussion of sexual relations, whether he was or wasn't having sex, is irrelevant and immaterial and very highly prejudicial. It has nothing to do with motivation. It causes the jury to speculate."

Judge Farren hesitated. He started to sustain Venturi, then reversed himself. Venturi had introduced the subject himself. "If I recall your opening, Mr. Venturi, you told the jury that they engaged, ah, in some sort—you were sort of vague, about some kind of different sex on the evening in question."

Chaiet repeated, "Did he make any comments to you concerning sexual relations with Teresa Taylor?"

"Okay . . . some remarks were made that he wasn't sexually interested, something about the drugs."

"Now, during the early morning hours of Sunday [November 18], did you receive telephone calls?"

"Yes."

"And what did you hear? What do you recall hearing?"

"Well, mostly what I recall was that they found Teresa's body. She was dead."

Marilyn Hope dissolved in tears. A five-minute recess was ordered.

Afterward, Chaiet didn't let up. "Were you in a position to see the defendant when he heard that news?"

"I was on the extension phone."

*(RIGHT NEXT TO ME IN BED IS MORE ACCURATE, BUT THANKS JUST THE SAME.)*

"Now, did you eventually—and I'm sure you did—confront the defendant?"

"Yes."

"And could you describe his emotions at that time?"

"His emotions?" she said. "How he looked?"

"Yes."

"Stoned. He wept some and then stopped and then wept some more and tried to figure out how to get back to New Jersey."

"And did you go with him?"

"Yes."

"And when you got to New Jersey, the gray Oldsmobile was in the parking lot?"

"Gray—his car was there."

"And on the trip on the plane and driving to Manalapan, did you have discussions with him of what happened to Teresa, or how she was killed?"

"Well, I may have said a lot of things, but there wasn't too much discussion because Ken would get very upset. And then I just tried to be quiet because that would upset him more."

"And when you said he got upset in the car, on the plane, would he show that?"

"He was crying," she said, crying.

Chaiet said, "That's all I have, Judge."

• • •

Venturi smiled at her. "On cross-examination," he said, "I get to ask what's called leading questions. Hopefully, that will make it easier."

"Mr. Venturi," Farren said, "we don't need any instructions. Pose whatever questions you have to the witness."

*(LAY DOWN AND REST YOUR BIASED ASS, YOU POMPOUS ASSHOLE!)*

"Mrs. Hope, when Ken would talk to you about Teresa, it was not unusual for him to confide in you because you had a very close relationship—is that true?"

"We always tried to stay real friendly, yes. I always considered us friends."

"And when he would talk to you about her, he would tell you that she's not a bad person. She just has this problem. Isn't that what he would say?"

"Oh, yes."

296

"And he was not trying to malign her. In fact, he was very protective of her, wasn't he?"

"I'd say yes. You mean gossip—malicious gossip? I don't ever recall Ken doing that about anybody."

*(THANK YOU. HANG IN THERE, NOT MUCH LONGER NOW.)*

"And in terms of her taking care of the baby, when he would say she had problems coping, that was in reference to when she was using drugs—is that correct?"

"I believe so."

"In fact, there were times that he couldn't make his visitations and you would ask why, and he said it was because Teresa couldn't make it up in the morning, and he had to take the baby to the doctor, and so forth. Things like that?"

"There were some occasions, you know, he'd leave work."

"And he never said he was definitely going to divorce Teresa, definitely going to leave her, definitely going to go back to you, or anything of that nature, did he?"

"Definitely, specifically? I couldn't say definitely. No."

"And, in fact, the time that he was most upset and concerned and indicated that he wanted to leave . . . was when Teresa went into premature labor."

"Yes, I do remember that."

"And she was on her back for about three months and there was a time after that when she was also weak, and that's the period of time that he had no sexual relations with her. Do you recall that?"

"I, uh, don't know when it was."

"And after the baby was born . . . when he came out to see you, that's when he indicated that things were getting better in the relationship, that she was getting better with the baby? It was during that time that these remarks were made to you, wasn't it?"

"Well, it was—yes, back and forth."

She looked as if she were going to fall apart again, and Venturi quickly asked, "And at some point, did he discuss with you her not understanding the money situation, that he had to pay alimony, he had to pay child support, things

of this nature, and that she couldn't understand why you
had a house and she didn't have one?"

"Oh, yes. It was . . . because they were married a short
time and she wanted to know why she didn't have a
house."

*(NO LOVE LOST BETWEEN MY WIVES FOR SURE.
LET THERE BE NO MISTAKE ABOUT THAT.)*

"Thank you," Venturi said. "That's all I have."

*(She didn't help me, but she didn't hurt me except a
couple of times. She could have hurt me. Maybe it's her
way of saying, "I'm sorry" and "goodbye." Will I ever
see her again? Now there's this bitch Peraino.)*

• • •

That same morning Detective Bob Fausak drove to Long
Island to pick up Sorayda Peraino.

Chaiet had called her the night before. He regretted the
short notice. She still sounded tense, but she said that she
would be ready. "Good," Chaiet replied. "I can't tell you
how important this is for justice. For Teresa."

She was dressed in black and framed by her black hair;
Fausak couldn't get over how stunning she was. And now
she seemed much less nervous. Perhaps it was the presence
of her two sons, tall, dark-haired, good-looking young fel-
lows. One of them kept saying, "Mom, you're sure you
don't want us to come?" and she said, "No, it will be all
right." The other son said to Fausak, "What do you think?
Should we go?"

Fausak said, "It's really up to your mother. I'll bring her
back. That's no problem." But she said, "No, no, I'll be
fine," and he thought, That's a real good sign.

They were going down a winding road, a shortcut she
directed him to, when he spotted a car barreling up behind
them, headlights flashing. He stopped. Now what?

It was the two sons. "Mom, we're coming," the one
who looked older said. "That way, we can drive you
home." Despite her protests, she seemed pleased. Even
better, Fausak said to himself.

In the car, on the way to Freehold, she told Fausak that
she had never been in a courtroom before. What would

happen? "Well, you go in there, you know," he said, "and they'll have you place a hand on the Bible, and you'll raise your right hand and swear to tell the truth, and that's what you'll do."

She started talking about how she first met the Taylors, and what had happened in the Las Brisas lobby, how shocked she'd been to hear what Ken said to her. Three times she said, "That poor, poor girl. Why did he do this to her? Who could do such a thing?"

Fausak again thought how marvelous a witness she would be. She was so consistent—her statement to him and McCormick, what she said to Chaiet the second time, the phone call she had made to the Manalapan police station. It was always the same.

He sat with her outside the courtroom. Then Chaiet came by and spoke to her briefly. He explained again that this was going to be a hearing without the jury present to decide whether she would be allowed to testify. It had nothing to do with her personally. It was a legal question. He would ask her exactly what he'd asked her in her home. All she had to do was to tell what she remembered.

Fausak was impressed at how calm and reassuring Chaiet was with her. Because he would be a witness, Fausak had not been at the trial. McCormick, though, had told him how Chaiet was really seething—about some of the tactics Venturi had used, but especially about Taylor, how Taylor kept giving this hard stare to prosecution witnesses, and had even tried it on Chaiet himself. Once, McCormick said, Chaiet had finally whirled on Taylor and said, "Something bothering you?"

On the stand, she kept her eyes fastened on Chaiet. Ken might as well not have been in the courtroom. As she related her story in a firm, well-modulated voice, every trace of her previous timidity disappeared. After Ken had told her in the hotel lobby that there had been a fight and that Teresa was in a hospital, she declared, "I said, 'What happened to her?' and he said, 'You see, the fight was between us in our room . . . You know how it is. We had a few drinks and we got into a fight . . . I knocked her teeth out.' And he said, 'They won't let me see her. I want to fix her teeth. I'm a dentist.' "

• • •

Chaiet concluded by discussing her anonymous phone call.

"Could you tell me, please, why you made that call?"

"I had bought a New York newspaper, and I saw the picture of him. I read the story. I just felt very, very bad. It bothered me that I knew he had been very violent to her in Acapulco."

"What was your purpose in calling?"

"He was saying he was never violent to her, and I knew that he had been."

". . . And did you give the officer your full name?"

"No, I did not. Only my first name."

"Just your first name. Now, did you indicate to the officer whether or not you would call him back?"

"I said I would think about it and call him in a week or so."

"Did you?"

"No."

"Why was that?"

"I was, in a way, afraid to come forward at first."

"Why were you afraid?"

"Because of the violent nature of this case. What had happened to Teresa."

"So that's why you didn't call?"

"I wanted to. I knew it was my duty. It was just that I had to think about it."

• • •

Without the reaction of a jury to worry about, Venturi challenged her relentlessly in tones that went from sarcasm to incredulity. Somehow he had to rattle her, bully her if he had to, get her confused, catch her in contradictions, try to ferret out some hidden motivation. But nothing worked.

"Mrs. Peraino, do you speak Spanish?"

"Yes, I do."

"And when you were on line there to check out, do you recall that being July eighteenth?"

"Either the eighteenth or seventeenth, I believe."

"And do you recall the two people who looked like policemen . . . did you speak to them?"

"I just told them how nervous I was about what I was hearing."

"Did you tell them *what* you were hearing from Doctor Taylor?"

"No."

"You were talking to them, telling them how nervous you were about what you were hearing?"

"I said, 'I'm very upset about what this man is saying.' "

"About what *he* was saying?"

"Yes."

"Were they talking to you and telling you what they were accusing him of doing?"

"They just told me that he was in jail for four days."

Venturi leaned toward her. "But they didn't tell you that he was in jail for four days because they said that he beat up his wife and that he knocked her teeth out?"

"No, they didn't."

As loudly as he dared, Venturi demanded, "That wasn't the police that told you that, was it? That was Doctor Taylor that told you?"

"Yes."

"And when Doctor Taylor told you that, you knew he had done something very wrong? Isn't that correct?"

"I felt he did."

"You knew he had done something very harmful, correct?"

"Well, wouldn't you feel that it was harmful?"

*"Judge!"*

Farren tried, with some difficulty, to maintain a stern judicial visage. "Mrs. Peraino, let me just caution you here. You don't make statements, you don't inquire of counsel. If you don't understand the question, you indicate that to me and I'll have him rephrase it. Okay?"

So, Venturi pressed on, "You knew he had done something very, very harmful—correct, *ma'am?"*

She refused to be intimidated. "Yes, because he told me he did."

"He had done something that you thought he should be punished for?"

She flushed slightly. "No, it wasn't my—I wasn't judging him. I was just shocked."

"You thought it was very wrong and you were shocked and upset?"

"I was upset and shocked."

"And there were two policemen there, is that right?"

"Yes."

"And you didn't tell them what this man had just told you?"

"No."

"And this man, who just told you about all these wrong things he had done, then asked you for money so he could get out of jail?"

"No, he said that first."

"He said that first?"

"Yes."

"First he asked you for money before telling you what he did?"

"He said something to the effect, 'If I don't have enough money, could you help me out?' Because he was going to his vault, whatever they call them, in the hotel, to get money to bail himself out."

"And then after asking you for money, in order to persuade you to give him money, he told you he had beaten up his wife?"

"No, no. He wasn't trying to persuade me to do anything."

"He was not? He asked you for money but he was not trying to persuade you to give it to him. *Is that what you're saying?*"

"Right." There was considerable defiance in her voice.

• • •

Venturi attempted a new approach.

"When you met them at the airport, you befriended Teresa Taylor more than him—is that correct?"

"No, that's not correct."

"Well, you said [in direct testimony] that you spoke mostly to her."

"No," Sorayda Peraino insisted, "I said she was more of a talkative person."

"He did not talk to you?"

"He talked to me. Not very much."

"Well, your opinion of her was very high from the time you first met them, wasn't it?"

"It was just an opinion about anyone I would meet who I thought was nice and pleasant."

"I believe you described her as friendly and bubbly?"

"What stands out in my mind was a happy person. She seemed bubbly, yes, in her manner of speech."

"And your opinion of Doctor Taylor was not as high?"

"I had no opinion. I just remember that he was very quiet and didn't talk much."

"Didn't do anything to insult you?"

"No."

"But he was withdrawn and would not talk to you that much?"

"I already said that," she said, her irritation hard to miss.

Venturi hoped it would cause her to blurt out something he could use. He returned to the scene in the lobby when she encountered Ken.

"Now, when you were standing on line there, you said that he was unshaven, had dirty clothes, had lost weight? It was visible to you that he had lost weight?"

"Yes."

"And these two men that were policemen, were they right next to him on either side?"

"Yes, from what I remember."

"And you didn't talk to the policemen first? You talked to him first?"

"Yes."

"The first thing he did was ask you for money, if he didn't have enough, right? That was his first statement to you?"

"Well, he explained what he was doing on line. Yes."

"And he said he'd been in jail four days?"

"Yes."

"Did he say he told the police that he had done this?"

"I don't remember talking about that."

"So, when you say he told you these things, for all you know, he never admitted it to the police?"

"I don't even know why he was telling me."

"But you didn't tell them what he had told you?"

"No, I was trying to get away."

"You did talk to them?"

"I don't remember what I talked to them about. I was just so stunned."

•    •    •

Venturi tried still another gambit, suggesting that her words were perhaps not her own, that her testimony had been artfully manipulated by the prosecution. Hadn't she refused to speak to one of his investigators, "a man named Kurt?"

"I don't recall his name . . . Someone called and said that they had something to do with Doctor Taylor's lawyer."

"And did you refuse to talk to him?"

"No, I didn't. I just told him—first of all, he talked very fast. And it was hard to understand what his conversation was in relation to."

Venturi couldn't resist. "Excuse me," he said, "you have no difficulty understanding English, do you?"

"Do you think I do?"

"Ah, Mrs. Peraino," Farren said, "again, please don't ask questions. He's asking whether or not you have any difficulty understanding English."

"No, I don't."

"So," Venturi continued, "did he ask to talk to you and did you refuse?"

"I just told him that I might talk to my attorney about it."

"Did you ever tell him that Investigator McCormick told you not to talk to anybody?"

"No, I did not."

"Did he ever ask you for your attorney's name and you refused to give it to him?"

"I did say that, yes."

". . . And you did speak on May twenty-second with Investigator McCormick, didn't you? In addition to May seventh?"

"I believe so. Is that the date? I can't remember dates."

• • •

Right from the beginning, when he first learned of the mystery-woman phone call in the discovery papers, Venturi had allowed himself to believe that she would never be located. It seemed so unimportant at the time, especially after Ken initially told him that he didn't even remember her. And now here she was, in the witness chair in front of him, more damaging, in person, than anything he had bargained for.

What made him so angry was not her testimony in this hearing, but that it might be ruled admissible in the trial. To Venturi, as a defense attorney, it offended his whole concept of the law. It didn't matter whether or not Ken had beaten up Teresa in Acapulco—by then, Venturi had little doubt that he had—it was that it would completely obviate the possibility of a fair trial. It simply had no business being introduced. It was blatantly unfair, so violently prejudicial. That was the argument he would have to use with Farren.

He began to think how clever Farren had been. Farren had thrown out Connecticut. And suddenly he was going to allow in the Acapulco assault if "clear and convincing evidence" was presented that the defendant had committed it.

But as far as Connecticut was concerned, you couldn't ask for anything more clear and convincing. Venturi could just see this on appeal—how favorably Farren would be viewed in his evenhanded administration of justice. Talk about a Mexican standoff! The irony was that Acapulco appeared infinitely more harmful than Connecticut. He'd bet that Chaiet hadn't counted on this either. All you had to do was track his discovery material. Until practically the last minute, the emphasis had been all on Connecticut.

During a short break, Ken whispered that her testimony was colored by what hotel employees had said to her. They'd had it in for him because of his many charges of lousy service.

Venturi gave it a try. It was the only thing he had left.

"Now," he asked, "when Doctor and Mrs. Taylor met you in your room for drinks, you were saying how wonderful it was in Mexico and at Las Brisas—is that correct?"

"Yes."

"Doctor Taylor didn't say how wonderful it was, did he?"

"If I remember correctly, he said it was nice there."

"He didn't complain about the hotel?"

"No."

"He didn't complain about the people who worked there?"

"No."

"He didn't complain that the service was poor?"

"No."

"I have nothing further," Venturi said.

• • •

When Sorayda Peraino came out of the courtroom, Fausak, waiting in the hall, remembered her total transformation—"blood boiling, the smoke just coming out of her ears."

"Who does he think he is, that lawyer?" she sputtered. "Trying to make me look like I don't know what I'm talking about and that I'm a liar. And that Ken Taylor," she went on, the way he stared at her as she was leaving. "Who does he think he is, looking at me with that look?"

She said, "You tell Mr. Chaiet that if he needs me again, he doesn't have to send anyone. I'll be here."

"I'll be sure he gets that message," Fausak said. "And thank you."

• • •

Chaiet's next witness was Al Benigno.

Chaiet took him through the anguish of discovering what had happened to his daughter and his flight with Celeste to Acapulco. Speaking slowly and precisely, Al faithfully conveyed Ken's version of what had occurred in the room that night, choking up briefly when he described his first sight of Teresa in the Centro Medico Hospital and later when he recounted Dr. Ortiz Pavon's initial fear that she had bled to death. "When he discovered that she was alive, he told me he didn't give her any chance of pulling through. He said it was strictly a miracle of God that she did."

Then, before Venturi could do it, Chaiet asked Al if he had continued to question his daughter about her memory of the events at Las Brisas.

"Yes, I did, several times after that, especially since she was beginning to have flashbacks of some things. I would say, 'Teresa, anything come to mind? Do you remember anything?' And she said, No, she did not remember."

"But she did tell you it wasn't Ken?"

"Yes. She said it wasn't Ken," he replied, shaking his head in bewilderment.

• • •

Al Benigno had supplied Chaiet with four photographs of Teresa during her recuperation at Staten Island Hospital. They were marked for identification and Chaiet showed them to him.

"Yes, this is of Teresa lying in bed. Her face is badly swollen and bruised . . . That one again shows Teresa with a bandage over her eye. Her teeth are all badly damaged, broken, the way the other pictures were."

"Now, do these four photographs accurately represent her facial appearance?"

"No, they don't."

"They don't?"

"No—well, they accurately show her appearance at this time. She was much worse in Mexico."

Chaiet thought he saw Farren flinch a little as he examined the photos. If Acapulco were allowed in, the jurors would also see them. Chaiet had wanted Dr. Ortiz Pavon to testify that he had mistaken the death-scene pictures of Teresa for ones taken while she was still in his care.

Now Chaiet didn't need Ortiz. The jurors could make the comparison for themselves.

• • •

The hearing was adjourned until Monday.

As he had been throughout the trial, Ken was returned to the relative freedom of the medical wing in the Monmouth County Jail where he had been since breaking his ankle playing basketball. Although the cast was off, he insisted that the ankle was still troubling him and the doctor let him stay put.

That weekend a guard he had been cultivating dropped by to chat. The guard was a young guy, far friendlier than the usual run of guards, and recently divorced. Their early talk was about women, what a pain they were and how you couldn't do without them.

At first, the guard had been cheery about Ken's chances. "Hey, Doc, a professional man like you, you'll beat this, no problem." Lately, he'd become more pessimistic. "Boy, I'd hate to see you spend the rest of your life in the can." That was an ominous sign, Ken thought. He wondered if that was what everyone was saying around the courthouse.

And now the guard said, "I hear that the hearing's not going so good," and "Boy, thirty years to life. I wouldn't want that for you."

"You think you could help me? Do anything to get me out of here?" Ken said.

"Well, you know, let's talk. It'd take some money."

"I have some property."

"Yeah, what?"

"All the stuff in my house."

The guard reflected for a moment. He had a new girlfriend, he said, who was after him to get rid of all the junk left over from his marriage. She wanted a new sofa, things like that, but with his alimony payments, it was tough. "What would you say the stuff was worth?"

"Twelve thousand, easy." Then Ken said, Why didn't he see for himself? He'd alert his parents about a visitor who might be interested in making some purchases.

On Sunday, after going to Valley Road, the guard came by again and said, "Okay. What would you want from me?"

He wasn't sure yet, Ken said. "Let's wait till the trial's over. See what happens."

"Right," the guard said, "you never know."

# Chapter

## SIXTEEN

On Monday, June 10, after identifying photographs and diagrams of the casita and the area surrounding it, Bob Fausak described the hotel's security set-up. In his professional opinion, Fausak said it was "highly unlikely" that a break-in could have occurred like the one the defendant claimed. A mountain goat might scale the cliff below the casita, but not much else.

Chaiet then put on José Romero, the assistant manager who received Ken's call about the attack and who first entered the casita to find Teresa crumpled in a corner.

When he flew in from Mexico, Romero had asked Guy McCormick what he was expected to say.

"Just answer the questions. What you saw. What you remember."

"That is all?" Romero said. He seemed dumbfounded at what apparently appeared to him to be a novel approach to justice.

After getting a graphic description of Teresa's condition from Romero, Chaiet asked about any visible injuries on Ken.

There were scratches on his arm, Romero said, and he recalled a cut on one finger.

"Did he have any bruises or cuts on his face?"

"Not on the face, absolutely."

"What about his head?"

Romero pointed to the right side of his own head at the hairline. "Here. A little bump."

"Was it cut?"

"No, just a bump. A little bump."

"No blood?"

"No blood."

• • •

Romero was followed by Derek Gore, a Las Brisas executive. Tall, white-haired and very British, he also doubled as the British counsel in Acapulco. He had volunteered to come, primarily to protect the hotel's reputation.

From the start, Gore was a problem, complaining that he had to share a room with Romero. There was nothing to be done, Guy McCormick told him. The prosecutor's office budget was severely limited.

On the stand, Gore characterized himself as a "trouble-shooter" for the hotel. He said that 193 thefts were reported in 1983 when the Taylors were there, but none involved a physical assault—in fact, in the fifteen years he'd been associated with Las Brisas, there had never been an assault remotely comparable to the one Teresa suffered.

Then Gore overplayed his hand. He brought up the release Ken and Teresa had signed, one that he had prepared and personally witnessed, which absolved management of any responsibility for Teresa's injuries.

Finally, Venturi had an opening. Clearly, Gore had not at any time been to the hospital after Teresa was taken there, and Teresa never went back to the hotel before being taken home. Twice he got Gore to repeat that he had witnessed the signatures.

Chaiet did not get into it. Obviously, Gore had "witnessed" the release when it was returned to him. It wasn't right, but in real life it happened all the time. Chaiet saw where Venturi was going. If Gore was lying about this, why not everything else? And by implication, why not all of Chaiet's other witnesses? But that would require quite an imaginative leap. Actually, Chaiet was comforted by Venturi's attack on Gore. It showed what bad shape the defense was in. Gore, after all, was only window dressing. What he said or didn't say had nothing to do with the testimony of the one witness who counted—Sorayda Peraino.

• • •

That afternoon, Venturi called five witnesses for the defense: Sister Donna Campbell, a nun who had tended to Teresa during her premature labor at St. Peter's Hospital; Nicholas Gujdice, a Valley Road neighbor; Dr. John Bobinski, a young dentist Ken had hired for his practice; and two women, a receptionist and an assistant, who worked in the office. All essentially testified that either Teresa never implicated Ken in the Acapulco assault or that Ken and Teresa, separately or in tandem, said the assault was committed by unknown intruders bent on murderous mayhem.

• • •

On Tuesday morning, Venturi called Ken to the stand.

All through the trial, Ken had been saying that if he only had a chance to tell his story, everything would change. In this hearing, without the jury present, it was as good a time as any to find out how he would stand up under Chaiet.

Venturi got his answer. And it wasn't the one he wanted. Within minutes, Ken was bursting with rage. You could feel it pulsing through the courtroom. The kind of incoherent rage, Venturi thought, that could cause a man to bludgeon his wife to death in a matter of seconds.

Without preamble, Chaiet said, "I want you to tell me exactly what you said to Mrs. Peraino when you were there getting your clothing, baggage or whatever?"

"I told Mrs. Peraino, after she asked me what was wrong, she said to me—no! I told her I needed five hundred dollars to get out of jail."

"Did you ever say there was a fight, 'we had a fight'?"

"No, sir."

"The only conversation you had with her was about money?"

312

"Yes."

"Did she ask you about your condition, what's the matter with you?"

"Yes. I told her that I had been in jail for three or four days."

"She didn't ask you why you were in jail?"

"I told her that the police had held me and said that I had beaten my wife. And that they wanted five hundred dollars to release me."

"Now, you told her that they were holding you because you had beaten your wife?"

"She said *they* said that I had."

"And when she said that, what did she do?"

"It was at that point that she asked the officers what happened."

Chaiet said, "Now, when did you first meet her?"

"Monday, July eleventh."

"Where?"

"At the airport."

"Did you have a conversation with her?"

"There was a group conversation on the way to the hotel."

"Did you talk to her?"

"Yes, I did."

"What do you recall saying?"

"I believe I mentioned there were problems. It seemed that we were all being herded around like a bunch of cattle at the airport. The luggage was not on our bus. That we were on our honeymoon. Just general conversation."

"Did Teresa talk to her?"

"Yes."

"Who was Mrs. Peraino talking to more, you or Teresa?"

"Teresa."

"And then you met for a drink?"

"On Tuesday evening we went to their room for a drink before we were supposedly to go out to dinner . . . We stayed only a short time. I would say thirty minutes."

". . . Do you recall Mrs. Peraino asking you where Teresa was?"

"When?"

"When you were in the line with the Mexican authorities."

"No. I told her that Teresa was at the hospital. That they would not let me go see her unless I paid the money."

"She didn't ask where Teresa was? That was coming from you?"

Ken glared at Chaiet. "Yes."

Chaiet moved closer to him. "Did you tell her that you had knocked her teeth out?"

"No, sir, I did not."

"Did you say anything about drinking? That there was a fight?"

"No, I did not."

"Now, you told Mr. Romero that you were asleep in the room?"

"That's correct."

"From that point on, when you were asleep, you tell me what happened."

"I heard a sound and I got up to walk to the balcony to see if I could see anything."

"Were the lights on or off?"

"Off."

"The room was entirely dark?"

"Yes."

"The patio light was not on?"

"The patio light, to my recollection, was on."

"Then what happened?"

"I was walking back to the bed when I was struck."

"You were walking back to bed when you were struck?"

"I was getting into bed. As I recall, I had almost gotten onto my stomach."

"Almost on your stomach?"

"Right."

"Were you lying down?"

"Nearly," Ken said. Venturi could see his body tensing.

"Nearly?"

"Yes."

"And where were you struck?"

"On the right side of my head in the back."

"The right side of your head in the back? Point where. Show me."

Ken looked as if he would spring out of the witness chair at Chaiet. To break the flow, Venturi objected to Chaiet's "constant repetition" of his client's answers.

Judge Farren said, "I won't tell Mr. Chaiet how to ask his questions. I will ask him to slow down a little. All right, show him where you were struck."

"Right here," Ken said, glowering.

"Right there?"

"Yes."

"Were you cut?"

"No."

"You were not cut? Okay, did you see what you were hit with?"

"Something heavy."

"Something heavy? What was it? What do you recall?"

"I recall that I saw stars."

"You saw stars?"

"Right."

"What's the next thing you remember?"

"I was dragged by my feet from the bed onto the floor."

"That's the next thing you remember?"

"Yes."

"Who was dragging you?"

"I couldn't see. I had just been struck on the head. All I could see was stars."

"Could you tell whether it was one person, two people, *three* people in that room?"

"I believe two people."

"Two people? What do you base that belief on?"

"Because, as I was dragged on the floor and tried to get up, I got a glimpse of the person across the room on the other side of the bed."

"Describe that person to me," Chaiet said. He was as close to Ken as he could get.

"All I could see of that person was basically from the mid-chest area down. I saw a person that had on what appeared to be jeans. All I could see was his shirt."

"What was on the feet?"

"I couldn't see the feet. He was on the other side of the bed."

"You could see that as you were being dragged?"

"*No*. As I was trying to get up after I had been dragged."

"Then what happened?"

"I was either kicked or struck. I believe I was kicked because I felt something on my head different. It felt like possibly a sole of a shoe or a sandal or a sneaker. Something like that."

"And where were you kicked?"

"Lower neck . . . right here."

"What's the next thing you remember?"

"I woke up and found my wife in a pool of blood."

"What did you do?"

Ken hesitated. "Other than my first reaction of horror and shock?"

"I didn't ask you what your reaction was. I asked you what you did."

"I took her pulse to see if she was alive."

"And then?"

"I phoned for help."

"Then?"

"At that point I believe I sat by the phone for a moment or two and then I tried to get to the balcony to see if I could see the intruders."

"What happened when you got on the balcony?"

"I was very woozy and I fell down again. Apparently fainted."

"You apparently fainted? What's the next thing you remember?"

"Getting up, going back into the room, going to the shower to wash myself off."

"When you say wash yourself off, why?"

"Because there was glass and blood on my legs."

"So you attempted to wash yourself off in the shower?"

"I tried to arouse myself, revive myself."

"Then what happened?"

"I heard another knock at the door and I fainted again."

"You *fainted* again?"

"Yes, I was very woozy."

"You were woozy?"

"Yes, from being struck."

"Do you have any scars or cuts back there from being struck?"

"I never said I was cut . . . there was a lump on my head."

"A lump?" Chaiet said. "A little lump?"

*"Little?* Let's describe the lump. I would say it was about the size of a golf ball."

". . . Were you treated at Staten Island Hospital for the cuts on your legs?"

"No, they were minor cuts. There was no treatment for them."

• • •

Judge Farren asked Ken, "How tall are you?"

"I'm six feet one."

"And what's your weight?"

"Approximately two hundred pounds."

Oh, boy, Venturi thought.

Then he addressed Farren. "In discussing the burden of proof that has to be applied here, I would respectfully suggest that the standard of clear and convincing evidence almost approaches that of beyond a reasonable doubt . . . proof must be obvious, positive, plain and certain . . . evidence must be such as to leave no room for speculation."

The testimony of Al Benigno and José Romero, he said, was "all consistent" with what the defendant said. But Derek Gore "was proven to have made false statements to this court about the circumstances surrounding the signing of the release . . . Doctor Taylor did not sign the release in the presence of Gore . . . Teresa Taylor never spoke to, never met, never saw Gore . . . Mr. Gore's job—to put it bluntly—is to cover the hotel's rear end."

As for Sorayda Peraino, she was "confused." Everything

she said that was allegedly said to her by "Doctor Taylor wasn't said to her by him, but by the *police*."

Venturi did not wish to linger on Peraino. "Judge, it is inconceivable, it is totally inconceivable that Teresa Taylor would want to remain alone with him, with this man, in a hospital room by herself, in the condition that she was in, *if* for one second she believed—thought—that he had anything to do with what happened to her. There is no way she would embrace him."

• • •

Once again, everything hung on New Jersey's Rules of Evidence. The hearing was being held under Rule 8, which covered questions of admissibility—in this instance whether the exception in Rule 55 could be invoked which would allow the introduction of a previous crime involving the same husband and wife. The presiding judge was allowed wide latitude.

"All right, gentlemen," Farren said. "We have concluded testimony, as required by Rule Eight, with regard to the proposed introduction of evidence of a prior act, alleged prior act I should say, of the defendant upon the victim in Acapulco in July of nineteen eighty-three."

He noted that Rule 8 case law put the burden of proof on the prosecution, that the state "must establish that this particular incident occurred by clear and convincing evidence."

With an eye on the appeals process, he delivered an exhaustive review of the testimony of all the witnesses, paying special heed to Derek Gore's disputed testimony. "Mr. Gore indicated that he prepared the letter of release that was executed by Mr. and Mrs. Taylor. And the letter of release, as indicated by Mr. Venturi, obviously was prepared for purposes of protecting the hotel [but] there has been no testimony to refute the fact that it was signed voluntarily by Mr. and Mrs. Taylor."

And in the end, Farren declared, "I found Sorayda Peraino to be a very credible witness. I find that she had no interest in the outcome of the case. She had no axe to grind with this defendant. And, actually, I gleaned that she really didn't want to participate in this particular proceeding . . . So it wasn't as if Sorayda Peraino read about this incident in the newspaper and then decided to jump into the fray and help to establish the guilt of the defendant. That is not the case. She was very reluctant to get involved in this particular situation and testified that the only reason she did get involved is because she felt it was her obligation.''

Farren lauded Al Benigno. ''I find the testimony of Mr. Benigno to be absolutely credible, despite the fact that he is the father of the decedent victim. He presented himself as a very credible witness with a good recollection, well aware of what was going on. No doubt he was concerned about his daughter, but he didn't embellish on statements made to him by the defendant. It could have been very easy for him to say that Teresa 'told me' that Ken did it. Certainly no one could contest that statement by Mr. Benigno, because Teresa is now dead. But he didn't say that. He said that Teresa said, 'I don't know what happened.' ''

Then, looking straight at Venturi, Farren said, ''With regard to Mr. Taylor's testimony, I don't find it to be credible. The one area of testimony that jumps out at me is the conduct of this defendant following the alleged attack. We have an individual who is on his honeymoon, allegedly deeply in love with his wife. We also have an individual who is a dentist, who is trained in medicine. That's his specialty, medicine, taking care of the sick and those in pain. His version is that he got up off the floor, crawled over, he said, to his wife. Took her pulse, bearing in mind that she is in a fetal position with her head on the floor and her knees on the floor. According to Mr. Romero, she was covered with blood. She was in a very bad condition.''

Shifting his gaze to Ken, Farren said, ''According to the hospital records, she was in a real bad condition. She is absolutely devastated around the head, pulverized, apparently by a broken bottle or with a bottle that eventually broke. There was glass in her eye, in one of the medical reports.''

Farren's tone grew more scathing. ''And what does *he*

do? He takes her pulse, then gets up and looks on the balcony. He claims he fainted, then went inside to take a shower to wash himself off, while his wife is lying by the side of the bed dying. And he never assists her. He never puts her on the bed. He doesn't try to put cold compresses on her head. He doesn't try to stop the bleeding. He doesn't do anything. He goes in and takes a shower."

*(YOU BASTARD. I DID NOT TAKE A SHOWER, I PUT WATER ON MY—FUCK IT, IT'S IN.)*

"I also do not find and do not accept his testimony that he was struck in the head and knocked unconscious. We have an individual six foot one, two hundred pounds, who has a negligible, if that, bump on the head. If there were intruders breaking into that casita, those intruders, I find, would be far more interested in physically incapacitating Mr. Taylor than Mrs. Taylor."

Citing multiple precedents that would support his decision, Farren said, "The standard of clear and convincing evidence falls somewhere between the ordinary civil standard of the 'preponderance of the evidence' and the criminal standard of 'beyond a reasonable doubt.'

"I find the proposition of the defense that this incident was caused by intruders is a possibility. However, I do not find that it was a probability. As a result, I have a firm belief and conviction as to the truth of the allegation and the testimony of this particular incident as represented by the state."

He looked at Chaiet for the first time. "I will therefore permit the testimony of this incident in Acapulco to be presented to the jury."

Ken, white-faced, instinctively looked back at Jean and Zach.

Jack Venturi moved for a mistrial. "It would seem," he said acidly, "that this court had its mind made up after the testimony of Sorayda Peraino and that was that."

"That is absolutely not true," Farren told him.

• • •

The hearing lasted two days. When the trial resumed on June 12, all the witnesses at the hearing repeated their testimony in open court. Farren cautioned the jurors that if they believed the defendant had assaulted his wife in Acapulco, it not mean that "if he did it in Mexico, he must have done it in Manalapan." They were to weigh it solely in their deliberations as to Ken's "state of mind" when Teresa was killed. The issues here were his "intent" at the time and his claim of "self-defense for himself and his son."

Venturi listened in helpless fury. There was no way the jury would not be persuaded by the admission of this new evidence.

He moved again for a mistrial based on Farren's instructions. Self-defense was not an issue in the Acapulco assault. But if the jury decided that Ken had committed that assault, it would inevitably conclude that he had "a violent character, a violent personality." In effect, he could kiss self-defense good-bye. Throughout the hearing, Venturi charged, Farren had displayed a "pro-prosecution, anti-defense bias."

Now it was Farren's turn to do some glaring. "There has been no bias, passion or prejudice toward anyone in this case," he said. Then he denied the motion, although he further instructed the jury, "You are going to have to determine in your deliberations whether or not the state has proven the defendant guilty beyond a reasonable doubt of purposely and knowingly causing the decedent's death. Purposely and knowingly goes to a person's intent. Mr. Taylor says I didn't intend to kill her. I was acting in self-defense and the defense of my son. So you see the issue of Acapulco goes only to the question of intent, self-defense, not to establish that he is a bad person. If you find that this event did occur and he did it, it has nothing to do with trying to indicate to you that he's bad, that he's disposed to commit crimes. You cannot use it for that purpose."

*(SO, HOW DOES ACAPULCO, EVEN IF I DID IT, RELATE TO 11/11/84, 16 MONTHS LATER?)*

• • • •

All that remained was whether Ken would be sworn in.

And on Thursday afternoon, June 13, Farren asked Venturi, "Is Mr. Taylor going to testify?"

Ever since the Acapulco hearing, lawyer and client had been arguing about it without any resolution. Venturi decided to stall. He would need a continuance till Monday so that he could confer with Ken about some records that were late in arriving from Chaiet.

Annoyed, Farren sent the jury out. "What records?"

Telephone records, pharmacy prescription records, Venturi said.

Farren said, "The records are not of such a magnitude as to warrant a continuance."

Chaiet joined in, "I submit that there is not a lot of critical information here."

That, Venturi retorted, was in the "eye of the beholder."

(In fact, Venturi had plenty to worry about. Ken had claimed that many of the codeine prescriptions rounded up by McCormick and Fausak were forgeries of his name. He accused Phil Benigno of these forgeries. But the New Jersey State Police forensic lab concluded that despite some variations in style and form, the signatures were genuine.)

Farren said, "I find it difficult, if not impossible, to believe that you have not decided by the seventh or eighth day of this trial whether you're going to put Doctor Taylor on the stand."

"Well, without being able to review this material with Doctor Taylor, without being given any time, we can't make an intelligent decision about his testifying."

"It is two-thirty," Farren said. "We're going to take a five-minute break. When I come out at twenty-five to three, you give me your decision."

(JACK IS ELATED! FERRAN [sic] HAS SET HIMSELF UP FOR A MISTRIAL.)

Exactly five minutes later, from the bench, Farren said, "Mr. Venturi?"

"Your honor, at this time, with all due respect, I once again renew my motion for a mistrial based on the prejudice of this court against the defendant, Doctor Taylor . . . it's in effect putting a gun to our heads in terms of making the most critical decision in the case. Whether or not to testify."

"As I've already said," Farren snapped, "we started this case on May twenty-eighth and it now comes down for the defendant to testify or not to testify. I'm denying your application for a mistrial. I'm also denying your motion to continue the matter until Monday."

"Judge, I've discussed this matter with Doctor Taylor and, while he indicated that it was and has been his wish to testify, he would abide by my advice and not testify."

"You've discussed that with Doctor Taylor?"

"During the five-minute break that we had, yes."

The flush slowly crept up Farren's cheeks. "Mr. Venturi, since you're attempting to make a record, let me also put on the record that I've been inquiring of you for some time whether Doctor Taylor was going to testify . . . So when you put on the record you've had five minutes to discuss this with him, it's not fair to this court. You're not being fair at all with this court!"

Venturi wondered if he'd gone too far. The whole thing was a gamble. But this could look awfully good on appeal.

"Doctor Taylor," Farren said, "is it your position that you're not going to testify in this matter?"

Ken answered the way Venturi told him to. "Yes, Your Honor. I originally had wanted to testify in my behalf, but on my attorney's advice, I've decided not to."

Farren glanced at Chaiet. "Do we have any rebuttal?"

But Chaiet wanted no part of this. "I would assume that the defense would rest," was all he said.

Almost without warning, it had gotten out of hand. Somewhere inside Farren, ego and caution were locked in mortal combat. Farren settled a baleful gaze on Venturi. Finally, jaw muscles twitching, he said, "I don't want to put Doctor Taylor in a position where he cannot tell his side of the story . . . So what I'm going to do, I'm going to reverse what I have indicated. I will give Mr. Venturi a continuance until Monday morning at nine o'clock."

He ordered the jury back in. "Ladies and gentlemen, that is going to conclude the testimony for today. As I've indicated to you, Friday is a separate schedule for me. So we will continue until Monday, at which time we may have additional testimony. You're coming up to a three-day weekend. Please don't discuss the case. Don't read any newspapers about the case. You're discharged."

With that, Farren stalked off the bench.

• • •

It was a conspiracy, Ken told his parents. Had they watched how Farren and Chaiet were ganging up on him, framing him?

If only he hadn't talked to the police without a lawyer that Sunday in Manalapan, Jean said. Why did he do that?

"I don't know, Mom. I can't answer."

That Peraino woman should never have been allowed to testify, Zach said. It was incomprehensible to think Ken would say anything to her like what she said he'd said. *Why* in the world would he do it?

None of them appeared to see any link between the twin puzzlements.

They took comfort that everything would be reversed on appeal. The hearing on Acapulco should have been decided before the trial, not during it. The judge had told the jury not to read anything about the hearing. "That was a bunch of baloney," Zach snorted. And the autopsy photos, for certain, were "doctored." Even the court reporter had told him, Zach said, that in seventeen years of trial work, he'd never seen photos "so bright."

The videotape of Teresa with the baby should never have been admitted. It was "inflammatory," Zach said. "No one had suggested that Teresa wasn't a good mother." His face flushed in sudden memory. Why hadn't Venturi followed through on his promise to dig up dirt on her?

Yes, Jean said. "She wasn't like she appeared." And Venturi should have done more to show that what took place wasn't "premeditated." She'd told Venturi, "It was just that something always happens to you to trigger you off."

"Jack doesn't want me to testify," Ken said. He had a mind to, though. He wanted the jury to see him as a "man," not the "defendant," not the "ultimate creator," as he put it, of the "body."

For sure, Jean said, if he was claiming self-defense, he would have to defend himself. The entire First Baptist Church of Marion was praying for them. The pastor himself had telephoned. For Ken, too, of course.

• • •

On Saturday Venturi met with him.

Ken had an idea. Chaiet would be badgering him on the stand, demanding to know what the truth really was, and Ken would "innocently" blurt out that if Chaiet wanted to know the truth so much, why weren't the jurors being allowed to see the tape of the "truth-serum" interview he'd voluntarily undergone? Okay, so the judge would cite him for contempt or whatever, but the jurors would hear this. It would "pique" their curiosity, make them wonder what was going on, what was being kept from them.

Aghast, Venturi found himself saying that this was a real trial, not a television show. No magical intervention was going to save the day. There was still a chance to avoid a murder conviction if Ken didn't testify. If he did, he could forget it.

In the hearing, Venturi said, Ken at best had come off cold and calculating in his responses. At worst, his body language conveyed "kind of a dark, ruthless and violent demeanor." Chaiet had gotten to him. Afterward, the judge had characterized Ken as totally unbelievable. If it came down to it, what did he think Farren would say to the jury when Chaiet finished cross-examining him?

Ken's statement to the cops, as damaging as it was, still couldn't be cross-examined. Chaiet would cut him up, and it would go on and on. Ken could not make the statement any better—his knowledge, intent and awareness of what he had done after Teresa died, why he gave different stories about what was going on between them, why he put the body in the trunk, why he went to Indiana with it, how he could have stopped over to see his ex-wife, why he left the body in Pennsylvania. None of it would wash.

And there were all those sex phone calls.

Was Ken going to switch his story from innocent sleeper

through that night to his new version on the sodium amytal tape of orgiastic oral and anal sex?

"They were made on her credit card," Ken said. "I didn't have any credit cards."

Venturi could just see Chaiet circling in on that—that by then Teresa was already dead.

• • •

Venturi was right. Chaiet was itching to get at Ken, especially about the phone calls. That weekend, in preparing a possible cross-examination, Chaiet was pretty sure that in the last, lengthy batch of telephone records he'd dispatched to Venturi, neither Venturi nor Ken noticed that one of the numbers called the night of Teresa's death also had been dialed from the Manalapan house when she was still in the hospital after baby Philip was born.

• • •

In the Monmouth County Jail, Ken abruptly told Venturi, "Okay, Jack, whatever you say. I don't give a shit."

Coming away, Venturi decided that his client really hadn't wanted to testify. It was all shadow boxing. Some six months ago, when they first met, it was all about acquittal. Now all Ken wanted was to beat a murder rap any way he could.

# Chapter

## SEVENTEEN

In his summation, with acquittal seemingly out of the question, Venturi needed every edge he could think of to avoid a murder conviction.

Concentrate, he wrote in his notes, on what the state's case really amounted to: "suspicion, speculation, innuendo."

And "apologize."

The last couple of days he hadn't been getting any positive feedback from the jury. No more pleasant greetings from jurors in the parking lot after his incessant bickering with Chaiet and Farren, all the times the jury had been removed from the courtroom, mostly because of defense motions and arguments.

And while the charge was murder, and the defense was self-defense, he had to nudge the jury off that and into considering manslaughter.

He flashed the jury his boyish smile.

He wanted to thank them for their attention. "It was hard because you were in and out of here a lot. A lot of legal argument went on when you weren't here . . . And I'm sure you can understand that during a trial things happen, things come up, voices get raised . . . Some things happen that you might regret and wish didn't happen. But I'm sure you can understand that it was done in defense of my client, Doctor Taylor. Don't hold that against him.''

His client, on *his* counsel, had not testified because the state had not met the burden of proof beyond reasonable doubt on its indictment of murder. "We considered each juror very carefully and among the things you undertook to do when you took your oath is to decide the case solely upon the evidence and nothing else."

Do not let "suspicion, speculation or innuendo enter your deliberations"—especially innuendo, "because innuendo is an implication based on a negative image of this man that the state has tried to maintain in connection with its proofs."

Venturi paused.

There were other "lesser" offenses involving manslaughter that the jury would also have to consider, such as "aggravated manslaughter" or manslaughter committed "in the heat of passion." The judge would instruct the jury about them. But there, too, the burden of proof was on the prosecution.

He reminded the jury that he had never said Teresa was in a "drug-crazed" condition. "I said she was in a 'crazed' state." Many elements came together to affect her behavior the "terrible night" of her death. Codeine for her pain. Cocaine to counter the numbness from codeine. Her diet pills and "other drugs not screened for" in the autopsy. "No sleep." Her menstrual period that was just beginning. Her "bouts of depression."

The toxicologist brought in by the state testified that Teresa Taylor's body showed a "normal recreational dose" of cocaine. "What is a normal, recreational dose? A quarter of a gram? A gram every so often? Two grams over a weekend night? The point is there's no such thing. *It depends upon the person.* He said these levels were so low, so low. How can it be said they were so low after five days' postmortem analysis? Does that jibe with common sense? You know, when experts come in and testify, they are witnesses for a party. Doctor Taylor is not a Klaus von Bülow. He doesn't have unlimited funds to go all around the world to get experts. But you, ladies and gentlemen, don't leave your common sense, fortunately, outside the doorway of this courtroom."

Venturi evoked the "shocking and unbelievable sight" that confronted Ken. "Can you imagine the rage of the father?" he asked. ". . . I'm sure the prosecutor will point out to you that my client is a fully developed, strong man. That Mrs. Taylor was five foot three. You have to use your common sense and look at the situation through the eyes of the person who was there. Ask yourself whether detached reflection can be expected in view of a raised dumbbell. Whether *detached reflection* can be expected if that person in her state got past you to your baby. You have to ask yourselves that question through the eyes of a father in fear for his baby."

Afterward, it was "horrible," he said. "It's obvious the body was wrapped up, taken away, put in a trunk. Things were cleaned up. It's not denied. It doesn't make you like this man. It doesn't make me like him. It doesn't make anybody like him. But it doesn't make it murder . . .

"His concern was to buy time, to deliver his son safely to his parents. What's the first thing he said when he handed his son over? He said, 'Son, you're in safe hands now. You're safe now.' That was his concern as a father."

He gestured toward Ken, who was weeping. And when the body was found and Ken Taylor turned himself in to the police, Venturi said, "What did they do to preserve what was going to be his statement? Nothing! No court stenographer to take little notes, no tape recording . . . How different it would be if it was 'he got away' rather than 'he got it away.' He may have said that, but we'll never know beyond a reasonable doubt, will we? They heard what they wanted to hear, not what was said."

Even if Ken had said it, "I submit to you that while there is no self-defense and no self-protection of another under those circumstances, the state has still proven nothing more than either reckless manslaughter or manslaughter under reasonable provocation in the heat of passion."

Venturi became indignant. "I told you in my opening that the state would introduce evidence only designed to paint this man as some kind of evil person, some kind of monster. And they tried that with respect to the Las Brisas frame-up that occurred on the honeymoon in Acapulco . . . the quote minimal injury unquote to Doctor Taylor." Anyone familiar with martial arts knows that a kick to a vital area like the back of the neck cuts off the "circulation of blood to the brain."

Chaiet had had enough. "There is no testimony about that," he shouted.

Farren said, "Mr. Venturi, there is no testimony with regard to the inner workings of the brain, knockouts, martial arts, et cetera. Just confine your remarks, please, to the testimony."

Where were the Mexican policemen, Venturi demanded, who would say that "Doctor Taylor ever admitted laying one finger on his wife? You all heard Mrs. Peraino testify. None of the things that she says he said are corroborated anywhere. Where did it come from? Why in God's name would he tell her he beat up his wife if he wants money from her to go see his wife? Does this make any sense at all?"

This, he cried, was the "kitchen sink" prosecution the state had resorted to. "As I stated in the beginning, this is not a case of murder, ladies and gentlemen. It's the case of a family tragedy. Doctor Taylor, whether he ever spends a day more in jail or the rest of his life in jail, cannot win. He will always be haunted for the rest of his days by what has happened. I place Doctor Taylor's fate in your hands."

• • •

Paul Chaiet's voice boomed through the courtroom.

"Teresa is dead. She can't talk to us. And Taylor is a liar. So when you go into that jury room, there will be some unanswered questions. But there should be no mystery, no mystery at all, that this was a murder and this defendant is the murderer.''

Chaiet said, ''We've heard about an incident in Acapulco and an incident in Manalapan. In both cases, Teresa was the victim. In both cases, the defendant's explanations strain our common sense and understanding to the utmost.''

In Manalapan, ''We heard that he got up at eight o'clock, came downstairs, and observed Teresa having fellatio with the baby. When he saw that, he screamed and she ran to the sewing room, the weight room. He went after her and she attacked him. Perhaps,'' Chaiet said, pointing at Ken, ''she was upset that he intruded into her sex play with a five-month-old baby. But he says she attacked him. And when she attacked him, this five-foot-three woman, he took that barbell from her and he gave it to her.''

In Acapulco, ''We heard about a confrontation with intruders. And if there was a confrontation, it was Teresa who put up the battle, not this six-foot, two-hundred-pound defendant. When you use common sense and reason, you don't even have to consider the testimony of Sorayda Peraino . . . But what possible motivation could she have to come in this courtroom and lie to us? How can you be mistaken when you've had a conversation with a man who you've met on his honeymoon and he tells you that he's knocked his wife's teeth out?''

Chaiet retraced Ken's actions after the murder. In Pittsburgh, his ex-wife described him as appearing ''normal'' before he ''dumps'' Teresa along a Pennsylvania road. ''Is this the 'family tragedy' we've heard about?''

He walked around the defense table and stood behind Ken. ''Can you imagine the man who would take the sister and brother of his murdered wife to Newark Airport with photos of her, show them around, take them into bars, and wait for a flight he knew she would never be on? And then go to the Benigno house and say 'I'm hungry' to Mrs. Benigno, and she would feed him and he would say, 'Thanks, Mom.' '' Chaiet's voice dropped. ''A cold, calculating, devious liar.''

Admittedly, he said, Teresa was using drugs. ''We know

from what was in the autopsy and the toxicological test that there was a small quantity of codeine and a breakdown product of cocaine found in the body. But in all those stories we've heard, where is the bizarre activity? All of her friends testified that she had no difficulty taking care of the baby. You've seen the videotape. She was working. She told Cindy Diaz, 'Yes, I've got a hangover.' That night Angela Rozek was over to the house. Teresa seemed tired, but fine. A normal night. Where is the bizarre activity?''

Nothing had angered Chaiet more than Jack Venturi's references to a "kitchen sink" prosecution. Chaiet was sure that the jury was with him now, and now he let Venturi have it. "We have seen Taylor shed tears in this courtroom, at one time consoled by the defense counsel. I submit to you that the only tears this man has shed are because he's in this courtroom facing what he's facing. And he can turn those emotions on or off like the faucet on that kitchen sink we're supposedly using to convict him.''

Chaiet said, "There was no fellatio. There was no self-defense. Why did it happen? What triggered it? I don't know. Why the Vaseline? I don't know. What time? He says eight A.M. I say I don't know because doesn't it seem strange that Teresa was found in the same clothes she had on at ten-thirty at night, with a watch, a bracelet, with earrings, with her necklaces?

"But what do we know? We know that there is no reason in the world for this twenty-five-year-old woman to be dead. For the baby to have no mother. For her parents to have lost a daughter. And *if* there is no reason for her death, then there is no reason why this defendant should not be held accountable for her murder . . . I ask you to find this defendant guilty of murder, because that's what he did to Teresa Taylor.''

As Chaiet finished, Celeste, sobbing out of control, had to be helped from the courtroom by her father.

*(HA! CELESTE'S BIG MOMENT!)*

• • •

In his instructions to the jury, Judge Farren defined the five possible verdicts it could reach under New Jersey law. All, he said, fell under the umbrella of "intent"—the "design, resolve or determination with which a person acts." All had to be proven beyond a reasonable doubt.

The indictment was for murder—"The unlawful killing of one person by another purposely or knowingly." Purposely meant that the accused had the "conscious object to cause death or serious bodily injury resulting in death." Knowingly meant that he was "aware" of what he was doing.

"Such things as the place where the act occurred, the weapon used, the location, number, nature of wounds, and all that was done or said by the defendant preceding, connected with, and immediately succeeding the event leading to the death of the decedent are among the circumstances to be considered."

While the state was not required "to prove a motive," Farren said, the absence of motive could be considered.

The jury also was required to dwell on three types of manslaughter even though they were not in the indictment.

First, and most serious, was aggravated manslaughter, when a person "recklessly causes the death of another person under circumstances manifesting extreme indifference to human life." Extreme indifference, he said, "does not focus on the defendant's state of mind, but rather on the circumstances under which you find he acted."

The second was reckless manslaughter, when "a person consciously disregards a substantial and unjustifiable risk that will result from his conduct."

Third was manslaughter committed in the heat of passion from a reasonable provocation. "Provocation in law," Farren said, "must be such as, in the opinion of the jury, would probably throw the mind of an average person of ordinary self-control into a state of uncontrolled rage or anger. The provocation must be of such character and so close to the act of killing that for the moment the defendant could not be considered the master of his own understanding."

Finally there was a verdict of not guilty on the grounds of self-defense. "The defendant states that he acted in self-defense and also in what we call the defense of others; in this particular case, the defense of his young child . . . You must decide the following issues: A, did the defendant, Kenneth Taylor, reasonably believe that he was in such immediate danger of actual or pending bodily harm as to believe such a present danger could only be repelled by use of defensive or protective force? B, did the defendant use a level of force in his self-defense which he reasonably believed was necessary? C, did the defendant reasonably believe that the force used or about to be used by the other person, Teresa Taylor, was unlawful?"

• • •

The jury retired at three-thirty that afternoon to commence its deliberations.

Ken was taken to a holding cell in the courthouse basement. Chain-smoking, cursing Chaiet and Farren and Chaiet's "pigs," he paced back and forth, seven paces from one end of the cell to the other. A dreaded future closed in on him. Would he be pacing like this for the remainder of his life?

It was close to six o'clock when a guard came in and told Ken to put on his jacket and tie.

"What is it? They've decided already?"

"No, the jury's confused about something," the guard said. "They want to ask the judge some questions. Hey, Doc, maybe you'll get lucky."

Reporters packed the courtroom. Ken saw the set faces of the Benignos, the drawn faces of Jean and Zach.

After the jurors filed in, Farren told them he had received their request for "redefinition and clarification" of four possible verdicts—murder and the three degrees of manslaughter. Because the hour was late, he was dismissing them for the night. He'd do it in the morning.

"You think they're thinking manslaughter?" Ken whispered to Venturi.

"Yes," Venturi said. Who knows? he thought.

Chaiet didn't know either. His mind went back to another time, to that other murder case, when he sat hunched over a tape recording that indisputably proved cold-blooded murder, wondering what the jury was doing, why it was taking so long.

Only Guy McCormick remained supremely confident. "It has to be murder," he told Bob Fausak. "They just want to be sure they've got everything buttoned down."

\* \* \*

Back in his holding cell, Ken stopped pacing. The jury wasn't just thinking about murder. They were confused! He remembered the chagrin on Farren's face. Thank God, he thought. *Hallelujah!*

At eight A.M., the jurors resumed deliberating. At ten o'clock, they requested more instructions from Farren. In addition to redefinition and clarification, they wanted specific examples from previous trials. He wasn't going to give them that, he said. It would divert them from the case at hand.

Then he went through the possible verdicts again. He spent most of his time trying to delineate the difference between aggravated and reckless manslaughter. Elated, Ken concluded that Farren believed the jury was focusing on manslaughter.

It got down to a difference "in degree," Farren said. "Reckless manslaughter is the same as aggravated manslaughter without the phrase 'under circumstances manifesting extreme indifference to human life.' So you can see it's a degree lower." The operative wording was "disregard of a substantial and unjustifiable risk" in causing death.

Good, Ken thought. It still sounded confusing.

\* \* \*

This time, though, Ken was in the holding cell little more than an hour before his guard said, "They've got a verdict."

Venturi saw it right away. When the jurors came in, none of them looked at him—or Ken.

"We find the defendant guilty as charged," the foreman said.

Later, Venturi learned that the first vote was nine-to-three for murder. The three holdouts had wanted some form of manslaughter.

\* \* \*

In view of the mandatory thirty-year sentence Ken was looking at, Chaiet asked that his bail—"with no percent"—be doubled to a million dollars.

Farren said he would raise it to $750,000. Sentencing was set for September 27, 1985, at nine A.M.

Venturi said in a press interview that undoubtedly an appeal would be filed based on the "cumulative effect" of the admission of three pieces of evidence: the Las Brisas assault, blown-up color photographs of the decedent enhanced with a "red haze," and the videotape of Teresa playing with the baby.

Chaiet said he wasn't surprised that there would be an appeal. "If you were facing thirty years without parole, you'd probably appeal too," he said.

Zach Taylor remained in the courtroom, tears streaming down his face. Jean exhibited no emotion. When they left, they refused comment.

Reporters crowded around the Benignos.

Louise Benigno was quoted as saying that Ken deserved the death penalty.

Al Benigno said, "There's nothing to celebrate. There are no winners here."

• • •

The next day, Jack Venturi received a note from Ken:

*JACK,*
*Thank you for what you could do. I am so shocked by this verdict. I was there, I no [sic] what happened and why it happened. Does my panic and depression over my wife's death mean I am a murderer? Jack, I was not guilty in Mexico. Chaiet and Ferron [sic] were totally wrong to introduce this flaccid "evidence."*

*It's over. It's too late now and nothing can be changed, at least for now in the very near future. I will be in touch. Please do your very best to assure my son goes where Teresa and I wanted him to be in the event of such a tragedy as this—with my parents. That is the only trade-off that will make any sense to me now. God bless you in your endeavor. It means the entire world to me.*

*Thanks again—I know you did your best and had my best interests at heart.*
*Sincerely, Ken*

Two pieces of mail pertaining to the case also arrived that day. One, accompanied by a bill for services, was a formal report from the Philadelphia toxicologist, S. K. Niyogi, unequivocally confirming that "Teresa Taylor was not under the influence of the stimulant effect of cocaine ('crazed with drugs') during the time of her death."

The other was from the State Department. While all of Chaiet's official efforts to get a report from Washington regarding the Acapulco assault were fruitless, Venturi's Freedom of Information request—along with a check—now produced results, however unwelcome. Enclosed was a signed report by the consular agent, Urbanek. It was dated July 16, 1984, two days after Ken's arrest, and completely corroborated Sorayda Peraino's testimony:

> Re TAYLOR, KENNETH ZACHARY.
> Went to see Kenneth—got info for telegraphic report. He did not wish to sign privacy act or have anyone informed. He said his wife was taking drug pills, they were drinking, got in argument, he beat her.
> Later went to see Theresa [*sic*] at Centro Medico. Theresa was badly beaten, for a time her condition was serious, but she was talking and recovering. She said she didn't know what happened to her.

Then, fresh from a jailhouse visit with Ken, Jean and Zach came to see Venturi. Jean always made him feel uneasy. The reasons were hard to pinpoint. When he met with the Taylors, Zach did almost all the talking. But he could never get over the feeling that Jean was really in charge, that the two of them had first discussed everything very carefully and Zach was simply mouthing what she wanted.

And Venturi still felt that there were deep psychological wounds of a sexual origin in Ken's past that he would never uncover. Just like he would never really know what happened that night in Manalapan. If you held his hand to the fire, Venturi would say that Ken, all jazzed up, probably wanted anal sex and nothing was working for him, not even the phone calls, and it went finally from a rape situation to an assault, "an outright assault."

Zach, fuming, wanted to know why they hadn't had their own toxicologist testifying. Venturi handed him the Niyogi report. He wondered what Ken was telling his parents. Maybe it was fortunate that he had something in writing, after all.

Zach quickly moved to another subject. "What can we do about Acapulco?"

Venturi showed him Urbanek's report. Zach looked as if he'd been kicked in the stomach. Jean, though, remained as impassive as ever.

• • • •

To all intents, it was over. But the dark shadow of Dr. Kenneth Z. Taylor would not go away.

# Part IV

# THE
# CHILD

# Chapter

## EIGHTEEN

It lay there festering even before the trial began.

Who ultimately would have custody of the ultimate victim in all of this, baby Philip?

And right from the start, Ken Taylor drew the lines.

Philip, he informed an investigator from the Monmouth County Probation Department, had been "baptized" Protestant. Jean and Zach, beyond being Philip's grandparents, were his "God parents." The boy had to be "raised in the Protestant faith"—and the Benignos were "devoted Catholics."

Also, Philip must grow up in the "healthy, Christian, moral" environment of Indiana, away from decadent New York.

Anticipating that the age of his parents might be a negative factor, Ken said that his younger brother Tom would gladly look after the child should either Jean or Zach be unable to carry on. Nobody then knew—except, presumably, Ken and his parents—that Tom, thirty, his once bright athletic future over with, still single, still living sporadically at home with Jean and Zach in Marion, picking up a few dollars officiating at sporting events, had drifted into a world of drugs—cocaine, hash and pot. Later, Jean would insist that he had become addicted to cocaine only after he came east to be with her in Manalapan—and had gotten a temporary job as a security guard—during the long months between Ken's arrest and his trial.

And there was Ken's sister. Although it would be news to her—she was at that time living in the South with two sons and a husband now out of the army and recovering from a serious illness—Ken claimed that she was prepared at a moment's notice to return to Marion with her own family to care for Philip.

Zach Taylor also spoke glowingly of the advantages of Philip being "raised in the Midwest rather than in New York City"—in a "good, Christian home," in an ambiance of "old-fashioned values."

So did Jean. Indiana's "low-keyed" life-style, she said, was infinitely superior for rearing a child to "the fast lane of New York," a lane, she suggested, that was largely responsible for the grief which had befallen Ken.

A Taylor family background report from the Grant County Probation Department in Marion was received on April 30, 1985. It described Ken as a "widower." The Taylor home was located in a "rather quiet neighborhood northwest of town." It stated that Zach's salary was approximately thirty-nine thousand dollars, and that outside of a seventeen-thousand-dollar balance on his mortage, he was free of debt.

The report quoted Ernest J. Dalton, Chief Probation Officer for Grant County, as saying "he had known Mr. and Mrs. Taylor and their family for 25 to 30 years and that they have been outstanding citizens of the City of Marion, Indiana. Mr. Dalton stated that the family has contributed greatly to all aspects of community life."

This report, with Dalton's signed approval, concluded that "the child would be most adequately provided for by Mr. and Mrs. Taylor." Ernest Dalton also happened to be a pillar of the First Baptist Church of Marion to which

Jean, especially, gave so much of her time doing volunteer work.

In Marion, word was quietly circulated that the Benignos had Mafia links. It wasn't a hard sell.

Ken further declared his confidence that he would be found innocent of the charge against him. In that event, he would immediately return to Indiana with his parents. If he were sentenced to prison, however, he was not averse to his parents "adopting" Philip pending his release. "They treat him the best," he said.

According to Ken, Jeff and Celeste White had "very poor morals." Jeff not only smoked marijuana on a daily basis, but "sells it." Celeste, he said, was a "scatterbrain." Her sole motivation was "revenge." The Whites already had one infant to care for and "having a second will be too much for them to handle." His great fear, though, was that they "will turn Philip against him and make him believe he is a horrible man, who murdered his mother, when that was not what really happened."

• • •

Jeff White was reported as earning twenty-five thousand dollars as a marine oiler for the Staten Island Ferry Service. The "neat and clean" two-bedroom condominium that he and Celeste occupied was deemed "adequate" for the time being to meet the needs of two small children, although more spacious quarters would eventually be required.

For their part, Jeff and Celeste pointed to the age of the Taylors. While Jean and Zach were "lovely, well-meaning grandparents," they would be nearing the age of seventy when Philip was ten and "with all their good intentions, they will not be able to keep up with him." Jeff and Celeste did not object to the Taylors visiting Philip, but were adamantly against continued contact with Ken. They would allow "Philip to make his own decision when he gets older."

Celeste said that she desperately loved Philip. She wished nothing more than to take her sister's place as his mother. "She has a newborn daughter, Christina, and feels Philip and she will grow as brother and sister."

Although Jeff had no blood ties to Philip, he was reported

as feeling "as close to him as any father could." It was also noted that Jeff's own father abandoned his family when Jeff was four years old, and he knew what a fatherless life could be like. "He agonizes for the child being bounced back and forth and wishes for it to end, one way or another."

• • •

Despite Jean's accusations that Philip had returned "ravished and irritated" after each custody period with the Whites, the Monmouth County Probation Department found him to be in "fine health." It recommended that the child be placed in the custody of the Whites. George Warren, a state-appointed guardian to oversee the child's interim interests, foresaw little likelihood of the Whites and Taylors ever resolving their differences. His position on the issue of permanent custody was "to favor the award of custody to Celeste and Jefferson White."

Still, Judge Julia L. Ashbey, who had ordered the temporary split custody through Ken's trial, reserved final judgment. She wanted additional psychological evaluations.

For these hearings, the Taylors retained Barry Shapiro, the lawyer whom Zach had first contacted on Ken's behalf. As Shapiro would later concede, he became emotionally involved in the case. Although he was a Valley Road neighbor of Ken's, he'd never met him. But during the pretrial months, he had gotten to know Jean and Zach, and in his view, they were "decent, honest, churchgoing people." Shapiro put a reverse spin on a biblical injunction. In this instance, he said, "The sins of the son shouldn't be visited on the parents."

To counter the findings of a psychologist the Whites had hired, Shapiro brought in another one to support the Taylors. Then when neither side could agree on a third, neutral expert, Judge Ashbey herself picked a specialist in child psychology named Michele Rabinowitz, who came with an impressive, single-spaced, three-page résumé of educational and professional accomplishments. And she made the difference.

After extensive testing and interviewing of the Whites

and the Taylors, in and out of the presence of Philip, Dr. Rabinowitz came down on the side of Celeste and Jeff. At the child's current age, she wrote, "bonding" was critical: "Thus it is of utmost importance that the decision concerning custody of Philip be completed immediately so that he be allowed to bond psychologically to one set of parents . . . In a situation such as this, where there are no 'bad guys,' the decision about what is in the best interests of Philip is difficult. However, it is the opinion of this Psychologist that Philip Taylor is best served by being placed in the care of Mr. and Mrs. Jefferson White . . . Philip will need the psychological security of real parents and real commitment. This security may be best identified if Philip were adopted by Mr. and Mrs. White. Whether custody or adoption, Mr. and Mrs. Everett Taylor should be allowed whatever visitation rights they would be given as natural grandparents."

A consent agreement was then worked out between Shapiro and a lawyer retained by the Whites. And on August 27, in an order that really didn't satisfy either side, Judge Ashbey ruled that from September 1 to June 30 each year, custody of the child would be with Jeff and Celeste. From July 1 to August 31, the Taylors would have him, along with an extra week beginning the day after Christmas.

Ken would be permitted one telephone call a week to Philip, the cost to be borne by him. Celeste and Jeff would either take the child, or have the child taken, for a monthly visit to Ken in prison.

The Taylors were also "entitled to liberal visitation, including off-premises visitation, upon reasonable notice."

To ensure compliance, each party was to post a two-thousand-dollar bond. The parties were directed to "confer with each other and discuss all issues concerning the health, education, and welfare" of the child.

"At an appropriate time," they were also to "obtain professional counseling and guidance concerning the manner and wording to explain the situation involving his natural parents."

•  •  •

*How dare she! Mom and Dad had much more experience raising children!*

In the Monmouth County Jail, Ken cursed Ashbey—and Rabinowitz—as he had Chaiet and Farren. Awaiting his sentencing, which had been delayed to October 4, he remained in the medical wing. He could no longer claim a bum ankle, but with two empty cells in the wing, it just seemed simpler to keep him where he was. Now, following Ashbey's order, the time had come to break out.

Inmates in the wing were allowed to roam freely within its confines until the eleven P.M. lock-up. Ken had discovered that the bottom pane was missing in the louvered window of one of the empty cells. Better yet, it was the one cell that had a solid door with a peephole instead of bars. Still, it wouldn't be easy to escape. The window also had a heavy mesh screen with recessed bolts connected to the frame and a steel roll bar over the missing pane.

Ken told the guard he'd been cultivating for an escape attempt that he would need an allen wrench to reach the screen bolts and a pair of hacksaws for the bar. He said his parents were departing the Manalapan house for Marion on Sunday, September 1. They would leave the key under the front doormat, so all the furniture and appliances could be removed that night. Two days later, when Celeste and Jeff drove to Valley Road to pick up Philip's belongings with a key supplied by the court, they found the house ransacked. They called the police, who contacted the Taylors. Zach accused the Whites of the theft.

The following Friday, September 13, the guard brought Ken the wrench and hacksaws. They were hidden in the spine of a novel by Stephen King, *Different Seasons,* that had been taken from the jail library. The next night Ken slipped into the cell, partially closing the door behind him. The other prisoners knew what was going on, but caught up in the excitement, said nothing. Then one of them joined Ken. He needed all the help he could get. The wrench wasn't the right size and excruciating time passed working the bolts loose. The screen crashed suddenly to the floor, but the noise was muffled by sounds from the wing's television set. Then the roll bar kept spinning as the two men tried to saw through it. Finally, Ken wedged pencils in the space at each end of the bar to keep it stationary. But time ran out. They had a quarter of an inch to go when the eleven P.M. lock-up commenced.

The inevitable happened. By morning, one of the inmates had snitched. Ken denied any knowledge of the escape try. The original informant and another prisoner in the wing singled out the guard who was Ken's likely confederate. He, too, denied everything. An effort was made to see who took the novel from the library, but only law books had to be signed out. The guard was forced to resign. That was okay with him, he said. He was planning to move to Florida anyway with his girlfriend. Ken was placed in an isolation cell in the jail's basement.

On October 4, he was brought out for sentencing.

Paul Chaiet told Judge Farren that while the life sentence the defendant faced called for thirty years without parole, he didn't see anything in the statute that prevented the imposition of a minimum of fifty years. "There is," Chaiet said, "a genuine risk that if this defendant is ever released from prison, he could commit further offenses."

Farren agreed that "this was a heinous, savage, brutal destruction of the defendant's wife." Kenneth Taylor had "literally slaughtered his wife with a barbell, wrapped her body in a rug, and drove halfway across the country to visit with his ex-wife for a few days with the decedent still in the trunk of his car."

He said that he'd like nothing more than to grant Chaiet's request. But his reading of the statute didn't permit it. He'd go by the book. It would be thirty years. The earliest the defendant could be released, at age sixty-six, was 2015.

That same afternoon Ken was bused in chains to a state penal receiving center. Three weeks later he was shipped to a maximum security block at New Jersey's main penitentiary, the 150-year-old Trenton State Prison—"Old Dusty," it was called, after its vast recreational yard in which not a blade of grass was visible.

A public defender was appointed to handle his appeal.

• • •

Celeste answered the phone. The operator said, "A collect call for Philip from Doctor Ken Taylor." She felt her stomach turn over. She slammed down the receiver and ran to the bathroom where, gagging, she threw up.

Thirty minutes later, the phone rang again. This time Jeff answered. He listened. Ken's voice cut in over the operator's. "I want to speak to him."

"I'm sorry," Jeff said. "He's asleep," and hung up.

• • •

Suddenly, the composed, cool facade of Jean Taylor cracked.

The letter, dated November 12, was addressed to Judge Ashbey. Ostensibly, it was to complain that Ashbey's orders about accepting phone calls from Ken were being ignored by the Whites. Nor had they brought the infant to see his "Daddy." Further, a Thanksgiving visitation she and Zach requested remained unanswered.

But her letter was truly an explosion of pent-up, disjointed rage. There was, for instance, the matter of Ken's alleged escape attempt:

*A few weeks before Ken left Monmouth County jail an inmate tried to escape by sawing the bars in his cell with a hacksaw blade. Ken heard the inmate's Uncle is a guard at the jail & supposedly got the saw to the inmate. The officer who questioned the inmates was a Mexican detective [Reyes Quinones] who was at Ken's trial & works for the prosecutor's dept. & he knew Ken & we feel the information was used to hold Ken in a holding cell until he was transferred. The inmate who was the one trying to escape was quicky transferred to another jail. Now, Ken has been indicted of trying to escape. This is so unfair . . . Now, they are trying to use this untruth to discontinue the visits which have never started. Circumstances continue to be unfair!*

Then there were the furnishings missing from the Manalapan house:

*The court order was that the Whites were to have Philip's
furniture. Jeff and Celeste & her parents wanted to come
Aug. 31 to Ken's home & take Philip. We were very upset
over the decision, because we know the background of the
White-Benigno family & the life that would be ahead for
Philip. They wanted to come while we were there, but we
couldn't bear them coming & taking Philip's furniture &
him, also. We told them to get the furniture & belongings
after we left . . . Someone or some group removed the
belongings & furniture & did some damage to Ken's home
& we supposedly are responsible. This is really insulting &
only continues to show their characters. We have proof of
being home (in Indiana) the day after the Whites were to
get Philip's furniture & Everett has been at work every day
since. This is just another excuse to use against us. Celeste
& Jeff had a similiar [sic] fake robbery of their own appliances & hid them in the Benigno basement & collected
insurance money, but we cannot prove it. Philip Benigno
& Jeff White burn cars & collect insurance. Our investigator found out the insurance company & the date & claim
but the case was closed & the insurance company didn't
investigate due to costs & etc.*

Memories of "Ken's house" appeared to reinforce her
fury:

*I cleaned & waxed the floors, cleaned windows, polished
cabinets, vacuumed the carpets, cleaned bathrooms &
dusted. Our son, Tom, cut the grass while he was there,
helping to support us, & when he returned home, I couldn't
cut the grass & we payed $180.00 to keep it cut. We had
plumbing work done at $125.00, electrical work for $20.00.
We kept up the mortgage payments, water, sewers, electric, gas, phone, & the expenses for Philip's doctors, medicine for diaper rash, clothes, diapers, formula, & food.
From November 18th until we left, Aug. 31st, we spent*

$12,000 of our money to live in Ken's home & care for
Philip. Now Mr. George Warren is claiming we didn't take
care of the home & property & is considering making us
pay for the loss & damage. I wonder who he thought was
keeping up the mortgage & etc.

We hired North American Movers to ship all of Ken's
clothes, books, bookcase & his stereo (he had it before
marriage), & his golf clubs & Philip's car seat. Jeff White
didn't want us to take the car seat, but since the court
order states we [have to] provide transportation at our
expense, we thought it only fair to take the car seat.

She resurrected the diaper rash issue:

In Jan. after Celeste had her baby, Philip was treated
with diaper rash & it was very bad . . . This happened over
& over & over & I had to take him to Dr. & got prescriptions 3 times & used the treatment recommended by Dr.
(Baking soda baths 3 times per day for about 15 mins., and
when diapered to use the special ointment). Sometimes he
was so raw the warm water would make him cry . . . We
took pictures & I kept records and [it] was verified on several occasions that Philip had diaper rash . . . In Aug.
Celeste asked me, "How do you keep Philip from getting
diaper rash?" Finally, the condition improved. Now, that
she has both babies, I don't know what the condition is. I
am very concerned.

Not only was Celeste so unfit a mother that she had to
be instructed on how to boil an egg, but Teresa was fully
aware of her shortcomings:

Teresa didn't care for her sister, Celeste, & they didn't
get along well at all. Teresa asked my husband & myself
to come & take care of her & Philip when she came home
from the hospital. She just didn't want her sister & mom
taking care of her. We were happy to do whatever we could
& enjoyed them. Ken & Teresa were very happy with their
son & each other. Teresa wanted Philip baptized in our

*church, in Indiana, & we were his God-parents. Teresa really liked it in Indiana & she told us, "If anything happens to one of us, the remaining one should take the child or children to Indiana to live." Dr. Rabinowitz several times in her report referred to Mr. & Mrs. Taylor's low-keyed life style in Indiana. Judge Ashbey, it is a much better place to live & raise a child than in the fast lane of N.Y.*

A sinister conspiracy was afoot against her and her husband:

*When the custody trial was settled, the judgement was unfair. The report of the N.J. Probation officer was incomplete. George Warren's report was very biased. Dr. Rabinowitz's report we couldn't believe! It is our belief that someone or something [influenced] Dr. Rabinowitz . . . The Whites can get away with anything!*

And in a final bitter outburst, Jean Taylor made it abundantly plain how she, as opposed to Celeste and Jeff, would deal with informing Philip about Teresa's death:

*They won't tell him the whole truth, what his Mommy was doing to him, that her body contained at least 3 different drugs, codeine, cocaine, & alcohol. That she was attempting to kill his Daddy . . . was abusing him & would have continued if not caught. What would have become of Philip when Teresa continued sexual abuse of him? When he got old enough to understand what she was doing, what then?*

•  •  •

Jeff and Celeste clung to a portion of Dr. Rabinowitz's report which said that although the Taylors as grandparents should be granted visiting rights, "these visitations should not interfere with the natural and normal bonding process" with the child.

A new, elderly judge, Walter H. Gehricke, had replaced Julia Ashbey in family court. And in October, after an evaluation by a Staten Island psychologist, the Whites petitioned Gehricke to limit the Taylors to "day" visits. The psychologist, Lewis Hill, noting that the Taylors were "resistant to any other figure taking on the mother and/or father label," also recommended "halting all contact with the biological father at least until such time as Philip is ready to face him." Drily, Lewis observed, "An additional complication is presented by the fact that the reason for the father's incarceration is the murder of Philip's biological mother."

In November, Barry Shapiro brought an action before Judge Gehricke which said that the Whites had consistently refused to obey Judge Ashbey's ruling, most specifically in not responding to a request for a Thanksgiving visitation by the Taylors.

Gehricke ordered three day-long visits right after the holiday. Then Celeste learned that on two of the days, Jean and Zach had brought the child to the Trenton State Prison.

On impulse, she'd asked Jean, "You didn't take Philip to see him, did you?"

"Yes," Jean said, as if daring her to do something about it.

The thought of eighteen-month-old Philip in Ken's arms was too much for her to bear. And in December, she and Jeff, after being advised they were on solid legal ground, asked New York State to assume control of Philip's destiny.

This effectively put on hold his upcoming week-after-Christmas stay with the Taylors in Indiana that was part of the original custody arrangement. But before the Taylors were even notified of this, Zach phoned Jeff to say that he and Jean were postponing the visit. They didn't want to interfere with Philip's enjoyment of all the toys they were sure he'd be getting. They'd work out something for later, maybe sometime in January.

Celeste would always remember that. It was so uncharacteristically considerate of them. Kind of scary.

• • •

The New York proceedings dragged on through the end of March. Then, under provisions of the Uniform Child Custody Jurisdiction Act, designed to avoid conflicts between states, the ruling went against Celeste and Jeff. The decision was fairly narrow. Philip had not been living in New York long enough. Besides, his biological father was still a New Jersey "resident."

Nevertheless, it was an outright, unexpected loss, the first one the Whites had suffered. They were crushed. How could they have been let down by their own state?

July and August loomed ahead when Philip would be in Indiana. They could not allow that to happen. Celeste had recurrent nightmares about the interruption to the crucial bonding that all the psychologists talked about. *She* was now Philip's mother. Philip and Christina were growing up marvelously together, just as she hoped. She had read the letter that Jean Taylor wrote to Judge Ashbey. What evil things would the Taylors be saying about Teresa? They would surely see to it that Philip was in constant communication with Ken. For sure, he'd be taken to visit her sister's murderer. Most of all, Celeste was certain that if Philip were taken away for two months, neither she nor Jeff would ever see him again.

Fear of losing Philip consumed them. After the New York decision, they were overwhelmed by apprehension. Every little factor seemed to magnify menacingly against them. White-haired Judge Gehricke, to whom they would now have to return, was even older than the Taylors. Gehricke would view them as kids unable to cope. Physically, the Taylors looked as solid and appealing as figures in a Norman Rockwell painting.

Celeste and Jeff dreaded going back to court. Every time they did, it brought back wrenching memories of Teresa. And what chance would they have? They loved their small condominium apartment, but how could it stack up to the description of the Taylor home in Marion with its three bedrooms, its big yard, its pool? The Taylors were established in their community. Zach Taylor made a lot more money than Jeff. Somehow, Celeste said, they had to get a house of their own with a yard. Somehow, they had to prevent that two-month visitation. She and Jeff flirted with the idea of fleeing to Canada with Philip and Christina. Jeff would find another job. They were young enough to start a new life, and they'd be safe.

But they remained paralyzed. The prospect of appearing before Judge Gehricke was so unnerving. Even though the petition to move everything to New York had been perfectly legal and aboveboard, Gehricke certainly wasn't going to be amused by it.

Then Barry Shapiro forced their hand. On May 29 he filed a contempt of court motion before Gehricke against Jeff and Celeste for failing to obey orders not only issued by Judge Ashbey but by Gehricke himself.

There was a laundry list of complaints. The Whites had failed to post a two-thousand-dollar performance bond ordered by Ashbey; they had failed to effect visitations between Philip and Kenneth Taylor; they had failed to permit telephone calls to Philip from both Taylor and his parents; they had failed to pay court-awarded legal fees to Shapiro after he was forced to go to Gehricke the previous fall to compel the Thanksgiving visits; and now they were trying to evade compliance of the two-month visitation with the Taylors in Indiana.

Shapiro demanded that the visitation be enforced. His motion was answerable on June 16.

After their initial shock, Celeste remembered how Jeff suddenly said to her, "Listen, we've been fools. We're not children, for Christ's sake, we're adults. We can't sit here crying. It's our responsibility for Philip to have a normal, happy life. So it's going to be a long fight. Hey, we're the good guys. And the good guys win! I believe that. Let's stop moaning and groaning."

Frantic, Celeste telephoned the Monmouth County Bar Association. She asked to be referred to a lawyer knowledgeable about custody situations. It was urgent. She was given the names of two attorneys, both men. No, Celeste found herself saying, she didn't want men. She wanted a woman lawyer. Preferably one who was a mother—someone who would understand the agony of what she was going through. She got two more suggestions. Then the woman on the phone said that she shouldn't be saying this, but Celeste ought to try a lawyer named Janice Miller first. "She's real dedicated," the woman said.

Celeste telephoned Miller on June 10. The words came spilling out. She had to see her right away. She was the sister of Teresa Taylor, who had been brutally murdered by her husband. Miller remembered *that*, didn't she?

Janice tried to think. Yes, she did remember. The dentist who bludgeoned his wife to death in Manalapan about a year ago.

Celeste explained about Philip and the court-ordered custody arrangement. Subsequent psychological evaluations showed that the visitation rights accorded the paternal grandparents should be drastically modified. Time was short. A hearing was scheduled in a week.

*In a week?* That made it nearly impossible. Hadn't Mrs. White retained other lawyers in the past? Yes, Celeste said, two of them in fact at different times. But they hadn't been forceful enough. She needed someone who would really fight. Well, Janice Miller had heard that one before.

Then Celeste got more bad news. Besides not having proper preparation time, Miller said that her fee was $125 an hour and she'd require $2,000 "up front."

Oh, God, Celeste thought. There was still eight thousand dollars outstanding from previous court appearances in New Jersey and New York which, with the help of Al and Louise, they were paying off at two hundred dollars a week. And on top of everything else, she and Jeff had just closed on a house, so no social worker could say the condo was too cramped for Philip. The house was nothing grand, but it did have three bedrooms and a tiny yard, only a few blocks from the Benignos. She would simply have to borrow more money from her parents.

"Please, please," Celeste begged. "I don't know where to turn. All I know is that I want a woman representing us."

Janice lived with her lawyer husband, Frank Gaudio, in a rambling house they were still renovating in Monmouth County, one that combined their living and professional quarters, overlooking the Neversink River by the Jersey shore. And that evening during dinner, she recounted Celeste's call.

"What did you decide?" Frank asked.

"I told her that I'd at least see her," she said. "There was just something in her voice I couldn't ignore."

The next afternoon when Celeste arrived, she had the retainer check. She spoke for almost three hours, pouring out her story with the same rapid-fire intensity that she used on the phone, her luminous gray eyes brimming with tears. Janice couldn't help being impressed with her obvious commitment, her anguish and love for Philip.

In a way, she was even more impressed with Jeff. Although Celeste did almost all the talking, his solid honesty, his support for his wife, was unmistakable. When you got down to it, Janice thought, he could have easily said that he didn't need this. It wasn't part of the bargain when he'd married Celeste. Teresa Taylor wasn't his sister. And yet, clearly, he was as committed to Philip as Celeste was.

• • •

There was something more.

Janice did not ask the question that practically everyone else had asked sooner or later. How could Teresa have stayed with such a man? Even if she couldn't recall what happened in Acapulco, wouldn't common sense make her realize what he was like?

Janice didn't ask, because she already had the answer.

Then forty-four, with fine-boned features and short, curly blond hair, she knew the secret shame and humiliation of a battered wife. For nine years she'd been one herself. She came from a New Jersey farm family. She married at sixteen, two months pregnant, without finishing high school. By the time she was twenty-one, she had borne four children. Throughout those nine years, she told no one of the beatings she was receiving at home, hiding out for days at a time so friends and neighbors would not see her black eyes and split lips. Finally, in 1967, after an especially brutal attack that left her with a serious head injury—her husband told the doctor she had fallen down some stairs, and she did not contradict him—she came to a chilling realization. If he touched her one more time, she was certain that she would kill him. So she fled.

And after that, she never gave up. She earned a high school equivalency diploma. During the next fifteen years, while raising two sons and two daughters, she supported her family in assorted jobs—waitress, house cleaner, newspaper distributor. She took typing and shorthand courses and first became interested in the law after being hired as a legal secretary. She graduated from Douglass College, part of Rutgers University. In a stroke of poetic justice, the money to enter Temple University's law school in Philadelphia came from a successful sex discrimination suit that she brought against a law firm where she'd been employed as a paralegal.

At Temple, she met Frank Gaudio, another law student, fifteen years her junior. He also had led an eventful life. The son of a construction laborer from Calabria, in Italy, he arrived in the United States when he was six. He could not speak a word of English when he went to the first grade at a public grammar school in Brooklyn. In high school, he was the class valedictorian. He got involved with Janice in research projects concerning the legal plight of abused women. In their third year of law school, they received a foundation grant to study the status of women in Europe. Despite their age difference, they fell in love.

They had been married for two years when Celeste and Jeff came into their lives. Their practice—primarily civil litigation—was just beginning to show signs of success. Janice devoted every spare moment to counseling at a shelter for battered women. The last thing they needed was a lengthy custody case with clients strapped for money. Janice told Frank that she didn't think it would be that drawn out. But in any event she couldn't walk away. It was, she said, a classic example of how violence in a family ends up affecting everyone.

What appalled her more than anything was the ruling requiring Celeste to accept phone calls from her sister's killer and to bring Philip to see him in prison once a month. It was such a callous disregard of basic human emotions.

And she kept remembering Celeste's terror that if Philip was taken to Indiana for two months, it was the last she'd ever see of him.

• • •

She decided to go on the attack, filing a cross-motion instead of answering Shapiro, pressing for changes in the operative court order. Following a brief appearance with Shapiro before Gehricke on June 18, the matter was adjourned until July 1. Now she had some breathing room. In reviewing the documents Jeff and Celeste supplied, she saw that Dr. Rabinowitz was obviously the key. Rabinowitz was the only objective party, picked by the state in the first place, held in high regard by New Jersey's Division of Youth and Family Services, the only expert who had personally evaluated the Whites, the Taylors and Philip.

Miller was even more convinced when she phoned the psychologist and asked her to testify on behalf of the Whites. "I'm not testifying on behalf of anyone except the child," Michele Rabinowitz said. "He's the only one I'm interested in." On that basis, she'd be available. It was exactly the kind of forthrightness Janice wanted. Judge Gehricke wouldn't miss it. She would lead off with her, and that might be all she'd have to do.

Then the day before the court date, Rabinowitz's secretary called. The psychologist, an avid horsewoman, had been thrown while riding. She was bedridden with damaged knee ligaments and in great pain. It would be impossible for her to appear as scheduled.

On July 1, Janice Miller asked Gehricke for an adjournment pending her recovery. Gehricke refused. There weren't going to be any more adjournments. And suddenly all the concerns about Gehricke bubbled up. He announced that there was no reason why this shouldn't be settled in short order. He was getting sick and tired of the whole business. There didn't have to be further evaluations. It was a simple case. The Whites had not abided by a court order. The child's grandparents had traveled a great distance to be here. If they weren't interested in the child, they would not have come. He himself was a grandfather. Pointedly, he said that he knew what it was like to be separated from his grandchildren. He declared a brief recess, and then they'd get on with it. He had a full calendar.

To buy time, Miller got "lost" in the courthouse. It meant retreating to some corner where you couldn't hear the paging system or couldn't be located. It happened all the time. To fill the courtroom void, there were always other matters for judges to consider, other lawyers waiting to be heard. She wandered back at about twelve-thirty, explaining that because of the Rabinowitz problem, she had to consult with her clients. Without comment, Gehricke recessed for lunch. Well, Janice thought, she'd gotten the morning. If she could stretch things out through July 3, there'd be the regular July 4 holiday break, and with any luck Rabinowitz would be able to hobble in after that.

Celeste, her first witness, said she would welcome visitations between Philip and the Taylors—so long as they weren't overnights. She and Jeff would even take him to Indiana under those circumstances. But then, as Shapiro pounded her in cross-examination, she became rattled and defensive as she tried to explain—he didn't want explanations, Shapiro kept saying, he wanted answers—her failure to comply with earlier court orders, including Gehricke's.

Then suddenly, on the second day, near the end of testimony by Dr. Lewis Hill, the Staten Island psychologist hired by the Whites, Janice thought she discerned a subtle shift in Gehricke's attitude. She introduced portions of Jean Taylor's angry letter to Judge Ashbey in which Jean wrote that the Whites would never tell Philip the truth surrounding Teresa's death and that Ken was innocent. Although Ashbey had placed the letter in the record, it appeared that Gehricke was unfamiliar with it.

And he listened intently when Hill said it showed that Jean, at least, harbored extreme hostility toward the Whites and, further, that she intended to convey destructive information to Philip about his birth mother.

What would the effect of that be?

It would, Hill said, go a long way in wrecking the child's self-image. It could "only hurt the kid."

359

While Shapiro was representing Jean and Zach, Ken had been allowed out of prison to represent himself in court. And now Ken got a long, appraising look from Gehricke when he cross-examined Hill.

Hill was against any visitations in prison, right?

Yes.

Well, his conviction was on appeal. "Isn't it going to be easier for him to be reintroduced to me when I am free to be his father?"

Nonplussed for a moment, Hill said, "It might make that somewhat easier. On the other hand, if you lose, it might be very hard on him."

Jeff White turned out to be a surprisingly effective witness. It was, Janice thought, a result of that same innate honesty she recognized in him when they first met.

He spoke of his feelings for the child and of how, abandoned by his own father when he was four, he knew a special pain.

"What is your relationship with Philip?"

"I consider myself his father," Jeff said. "I love him very much. When we first got custody of Philip, I guess I loved him because I felt sorry for him. But since the time has passed and he's been in my custody, I love him because he's"—he groped for the words—"like I love my daughter. He's my son."

• • •

The next day, July 3, Janice got an unexpected delay bonus. Ken was being brought in each morning from Trenton State Prison, and this time it was nearly eleven before he arrived. Jeff was still on the stand. And the Taylors had yet to testify.

Gehricke sighed. He had a heavy schedule after the holiday period. They'd reconvene on July 29.

Ken rose. He pointed out that his parents were supposed to have custody as of July 1. He assumed that in the interim, Philip would go with Zach and Jean.

Gehricke shot back, "You have not assumed correctly. This hearing is going to be completed and everything is going to be held in abeyance until it is."

Then Judge Gehricke summoned Miller and Shapiro to his chambers. He wanted this settled. What he had in mind was three weeks in Indiana instead of the two months, and another two weeks around Christmas. He made it sound that if the two sides didn't get together, he would go ahead and hand down his own ruling along those lines. Janice, he added, could appeal all she liked.

No way, Celeste said.

And on July 29, Michele Rabinowitz, on crutches, was finally sworn in. Developmentally, she said, children of Philip's age were in a crucial period of adjustment. There was a normal developmental fear called "separation anxiety." It began at around twelve months, peaked at eighteen months, and started to subside at two to two and a half years. Children would suffer psychic trauma if they were separated from mother and father figures during these significant times.

In her reevaluation, she said that the original shared custody ruling "was not in Philip's best interests."

She said an immediate, definitive decision must be made about him, "so that he may be allowed to bond psychologically with one set of parents."

She described Celeste and Jeff as "very positive, loving, and nurturing" parents for Philip. The terms "mother" and "father" for them were "quite appropriate."

She recommended "very limited visitation" with his natural grandparents "over the next few years." At the moment, any overnight visits would be "extremely risky and potentially severely traumatizing."

While grandparental visitation this year could be of "two weeks duration," there should be none that were "overnights." Philip should be picked up for the day and returned home at bedtime. By the age of three, possibly, Philip might be ready for a single overnight visit. He would not be ready for a one or two month stay until he was around ten years old. In any case, Rabinowitz said, "Visits with grandparents of a one or two month duration are highly unusual and interfere with the normal family process."

The court "should consider the strong possibility of psychological trauma that Philip will experience if he is separated from his 'nuclear family' at this most vulnerable time." She said, "This child has suffered enough trauma in his life."

Questioning her, Janice Miller noted that Ken's conviction was on appeal. What about that?

"I believe what's in Philip's best interest is that he have no contact until the appeal is decided."

"And if the appeal is decided where Kenneth Taylor remains in prison for a period of time, would you recommend that Philip see him at that point?"

"Not unless Philip wants to."

• • •

That afternoon, Barry Shapiro, all at once quite friendly, approached Janice in the hallway outside the courtroom. You know, he said, they really ought to settle this. It's what the judge wants.

Miller talked it over with Celeste and Jeff. She was sure Gehricke was leaning their way, but she was equally certain that he would wind up giving the Taylors something. Suppose she offered Shapiro a week's visitation in Indiana? That would at least show Gehricke that they weren't being intransigent.

Okay, Celeste said at last. What could the Taylors do in a week?

To Janice's astonishment, Shapiro did not dismiss the offer out of hand. He said he'd have to talk it over with his clients. Gee, she remembered thinking, Barry must really think he's in bad shape.

In the morning, Shapiro came back with a surprisingly mild counter proposal. How about two weeks?

Now Celeste wasn't so sure.

Look, Janice told her, they weren't going to do any better. Gehricke was already talking about three weeks. If he got irritated, who knew what he might tack on?

On Friday, August 1, everyone returned to the courtroom. At the last second, as Gehricke was about to spell out the agreement, Celeste said she wanted to call Dr. Rabinowitz to find out what she thought about the two weeks.

Wearily, Gehricke said that Celeste could have done that by now, but all right, he'd allow it.

Michele Rabinowitz told Celeste that the only way she would support the settlement was if, during the first week, Celeste spoke by telephone to Philip twice a day and, during the second week, Celeste and Jeff would go to Marion and spend at least an hour a day with him.

When Celeste reported this, Gehricke sighed again and said well, Rabinowitz was the expert. If that's what she wanted, that was what she'd get.

From August 1 until August 16, Gehricke said, the Taylors would have the "infant child" in Indiana.

On Saturday, August 9, Celeste would visit Philip in the Taylor residence for two hours, and for an hour every day after that for the remainder of the second week.

During the week after Christmas, the Taylors would travel to Staten Island for a week's overnight visitation with Philip. Anything after that would be decided "in the best interests of Philip."

In conversation with Philip, the Taylors "will always refer to the Whites as "mother" and "father." The Taylors will be referred to as "grandmother" and "grandfather."

"Under no circumstances," Gehricke said, "will Everett and Jean Taylor allow any contact between Philip Taylor and Kenneth Taylor. There will be no visits to the Trenton State Prison where he is incarcerated. There will be no telephone communication between Kenneth Taylor and Philip Taylor and no letters read to Philip from Kenneth by Everett and Jean Taylor."

Gehricke asked Ken if he had anything to say.

"Not at this time," he replied.

Then, as he was being led out, Celeste saw him wink at his parents. She ran after Janice and clutched her arm. Had Janice seen the wink? What did it mean?

Miller said no, she hadn't. And she didn't know what it meant. All she knew was that, considering everything, they'd gotten the best deal possible.

That same evening, Jean and Zach drove to Staten Island in their Toyota Minicruiser to pick up Philip. He appeared confused and started crying. Celeste, heartsick, tried to console him. He was going off on a wonderful trip with his grandparents.

She gave him his pillow and his fluffy yellow Big Bird from the "Sesame Street" show that he clutched every night in bed. She also gave him a calendar with squares in which she drew pictures of Christina and the Staten Island house, and then in the square for Saturday, August 9, she drew figures of herself and Jeff and labeled them Mommy and Daddy. She pointed to it and told him that was the day she would be seeing him again. She'd be talking to him every day on the phone. And in only a few days, she would be coming out to see him, and she counted out the squares to show him when that day would be.

• • •

Relieved, Janice Miller turned to other cases that had been piling up.

Around eleven P.M. on Wednesday, August 6, she and Frank went to bed. Unaccountably, she couldn't sleep. She tossed and turned for almost two hours. It was no use. She was having a full-blown anxiety attack for no apparent reason. What was wrong with her? She glanced at Frank, peacefully asleep, envying him. Finally, she got up and went downstairs to her office and started doing paperwork. She had rarely worked more feverishly, she would recall, so oblivious to the passage of time that she was actually startled when Frank appeared, ready for breakfast. He had no idea she'd been up all night. They had their usual orange juice and coffee, and then Frank left for the Freehold courthouse. He was trying a big medical malpractice suit, and Janice wished him luck.

Oddly, she still didn't feel the least bit tired.

• • •

In Staten Island, around the same time, Thursday morning, Celeste was dialing the Taylors to discuss her arrival in Marion on Saturday.

Next door, a neighbor, Jack Pierro, was getting ready to go to work. Earlier, he had seen Jeff drive off to the ferry slip. Suddenly, Pierro heard a piercing scream. It was Celeste.

Pierro dashed outside to the front door of the Whites. It was locked. He ran up the narrow walk between their houses and got in the back way. He saw Celeste bent over the kitchen table, her fist hammering on it. She was sobbing.

"Celeste, what's wrong?"

She shrieked through her sobs, "Those sons of bitches. They did it! They did it!"

"What? Did what? Who?"

She looked at Pierro despairingly and then shook her head as if to gather herself together. She went to the wall phone. The receiver was dangling off its hook.

She retrieved it and called Janice Miller. She didn't care what Janice was doing, she told the secretary. She had to speak to her, *now*.

Then Janice was on the line. What was the matter?

The Taylors, Celeste cried. She'd phoned them about travel arrangements. Jean had answered. First, Celeste asked how Philip was doing, and, very sweetly, Jean said there was something Zach wanted to tell her.

And when she heard Zach on the line, she asked again if something was the matter, and he said he wanted to tell her that there was no point in her coming to Marion. They'd just adopted Philip. She'd never see him again.

# Chapter

## NINETEEN

From start to finish, the conspiracy was directed by Ken Taylor. It began to take final form six months after his conviction, around the time Zach postponed Philip's 1985 Christmas visitation in Indiana, a time when, significantly, the Grant County courts in Marion would have shut down for all practical purposes during the holiday season.

Ken had told his parents to find out from Barry Shapiro what action New Jersey might take if Philip was adopted in Marion. They reported that Shapiro said he couldn't see anything New Jersey could do once the child was physically there. They quoted Shapiro as saying, "You can take that boy to Indiana and adopt him. It'll take years before anything is settled. But don't tell anybody I said so."*

---

*While Shapiro would later say that he did not specifically recall such a discussion, he conceded that it was no secret the Taylors wanted Philip. And after all, Jeff and Celeste had displayed more than a little "underhandedness" in trying to move court jurisdiction over the child to New York. In any event, Shapiro said, if a discussion about an adoption in Indiana did occur, it certainly did not embrace anything "illegal."

Next, the right attorney in Marion had to be found. And Jean and Zach did not have to look beyond their own First Baptist Church. Patrick N. Ryan not only was a staunch church member, but enjoyed local renown as a fiercely litigious, anti-establishment practitioner. It didn't matter what the established authority was, courthouse buffs liked to say. You could count on "old Pat" being against it.

Ryan had Ken formally consent to the adoption of Philip by "his parents, Everett and Jean Taylor," and filed it in the Grant County Circuit Court.

On January 17, 1986, while custody proceedings in New York were still going on, Ryan filed a "Petition for Adoption" on behalf of the Taylors. It was artfully crafted.

After identifying them as paternal grandparents of "the said child" and residents of Marion, it stated that "the child's mother is deceased" without any reference to the circumstances of her death. There was no mention of maternal grandparents, or even if they existed.

It said that the "child's father, Kenneth Zachary Taylor," had agreed to the adoption. It did not mention what prompted Ken's consent, or what his current residence was—namely, the Trenton State Prison—or why he happened to be there.

The child, it declared, "has lived with the petitioners from November 12, 1984—the day Ken brought Philip to Marion—until September 1, 1985. It did not say that during this period, there had been in fact split custody with Celeste and Jeff, or that after September 1, the Whites had been awarded dominant custody, or that all during this time—except for the six days after Teresa's murder—Philip had lived in another state.

It further declared that "the child does not have any property," neglecting to list, among other things, the insurance Ken had taken out for Teresa to which Philip was now the beneficiary. Later, Zach Taylor would explain that he didn't consider "insurance" as "property."

Finally, the petition stated that the adoption "will serve the best interests of the child" without noting, to put it mildly, that this was in grave dispute.

The Taylors then authorized Barry Shapiro to file the contempt of court citation against Celeste and Jeff to enforce the original shared custody order—to make sure that Philip got to Marion.

As Shapiro was dickering with Janice over a one or two week visitation, Ken asked his parents if two weeks would give them enough time. They checked with Pat Ryan. Everything was set, they said.

On Friday, August 1, before picking up Philip, Zach telephoned Ryan. They were on their way. Driving in their "motor home," they'd be in Marion Saturday night, Sunday morning at the latest.

Ryan contacted the Grant County Welfare Department to arrange for an appraisal of the Taylors that was required in any adoption petition. These on-premises investigations basically addressed the home environment: how many rooms and beds, its physical condition, the financial resources of the petitioners, and observation of their interaction with the child.

Ryan requested speedy action. The adoption had been hanging fire for nearly seven months and it was time to get going. All the other necessary papers had been filed.

On Tuesday morning, a caseworker arrived at the Taylor residence. She spent about an hour and a half there. A front-page summary of her four-page report confirmed that the child's mother was "deceased."

On Wednesday, once the report was filed, Ryan called Thomas R. Hunt. Hunt was the Grant County circuit judge, who handled adoptions. He had one, Ryan said. Could he come in before court started in the morning? It was all in place. Boy's mother passed away. Father unable to care for him. Wonderful Marion grandparents ready, willing and able to step in. A glowing welfare report on them. It was Indiana—America—at its finest. Almost made you want to weep.

As is customary, Ryan prepared the adoption decree for Hunt's signature. He was careful to touch all bases. It said: "The Court, having heard the evidence and being duly advised in the premises, finds that the natural father has consented to this adoption . . . that the child's mother is deceased; that a custody proceeding is pending in Monmouth County, New Jersey; that petitioners are the paternal grandparents of Philip Andrew Taylor; that they wish to adopt said child as their own; and that such adoption will serve in the best interests of the child.''

Early Thursday, August 7, in the chambers of Judge Hunt, Ryan again cited the incredible love and generosity of the child's grandparents. You just didn't find people like them very often these days.

Hunt glanced at the file Ryan handed him just long enough to ascertain that it included a welfare report. What did catch his eye, though, was the "pending" New Jersey custody proceeding mentioned in the decree that Ryan had prepared. What was that all about?

Oh, Hunt recalled Ryan saying, don't worry about it. Some aunt and uncle of the child were trying "to establish a guardianship in order to gain control over insurance money payable on account of the death of the mother."

The whole proceeding lasted about five minutes, ten at the most. Jean, Zach and Philip were brought in, and Hunt signed the decree. According to Jean, Judge Hunt smiled at them and said, "I'm aware of your situation. I hope this will help."

Ryan lingered in Hunt's chambers. He said that there might be a little flak over the weekend from the New Jersey end because of the insurance business and the guardianship. You could never tell about those money-grubbers back east. If that did occur, he wanted Hunt's assurance that nothing would be decided till Monday and that he would have a chance to respond to any challenges. After all, an adoption always superseded custody. Sure thing, Hunt said. "I'll call you and we'll set a hearing."

Within an hour, when Jean and Zach returned home, Celeste had telephoned and Zach told her not to bother coming to Marion. He then called Barry Shapiro with the good news.

(Shapiro would insist that he was not privy to any of this before it happened. As soon as he heard about it from the

Taylors, he said, he promptly advised Zach to "get another lawyer.")

Meanwhile, at the Trenton State Prison that August as Ken was being kept abreast of these events, he entered into a cabal with five other prisoners to begin plotting an audacious escape.

* * *

Right after she received Celeste's hysterical call on August 7, Janice Miller phoned the Indiana Bar Association for an attorney in Marion. She was given the name of the local association president, Jules Walker. She called Walker. A few minutes later, Walker confirmed that Judge Hunt had signed the adoption decree.

She called Hunt. She identified herself and informed him of Gehricke's custody order. She wanted the adoption decree vacated. According to Miller, Hunt said that he would require a copy of Gehricke's order and also needed a directive signed by Gehricke to serve the Taylors in order to retrieve the child.

Janice then raced to Gehricke's chambers in Freehold. Shaken, the judge listened to her. He put in a call to Hunt. Gehricke told him that he had been "bamboozled." He said, "There was a long, drawn-out affair here and those people have stolen that child in violation of my order."

Hunt said, "I knew nothing of this." The weekend was upon them. If he got the appropriate documents the next day—Friday—Janice quoted Hunt as saying, he would "take care of everything."

(Hunt had a somewhat different memory of these conversations. This "gal attorney" called him, then a "judge." He had no idea if they were who they said they were, or even if what they were claiming was true. He said he said, "If everything you folks are telling me is correct, file a petition to set it aside and I'll give you a hearing.")

Later that afternoon, according to Hunt, Jules Walker, now retained by Janice on behalf of the Whites, "wandered into" his chambers. "Miz Miller" would be in Marion the next day. She better be here by noon, Hunt said. He was due over in Wabash, to sit as a special judge in a divorce case.

After gathering her documents together, Janice met Celeste and Jeff at Newark Airport to fly that evening to Indianapolis. But the Midwest was being trashed by colossal thunderstorms. Their departure was delayed and then canceled. Finally, around ten P.M., they boarded another flight for Chicago. The ride was nightmarish. Celeste was bent over in her seat, moaning, "Why did I let him go?" White-knuckled, Jeff held her as the plane bucked through violent air pockets; it was his first flight ever.

They stayed in a hotel at O'Hare Airport. In the morning, Janice called Walker. They'd be taking the first available flight out—to Fort Wayne, a hundred miles northeast of Marion.

Walker relayed this to Hunt.

"Noon," Hunt said.

Janice and the Whites arrived at Walker's office around one P.M., August 8. The instant she saw him, she realized she'd made a mistake. Everyone in Grant County agreed that Jules Walker, getting on a bit in years, was as sweet a person as you could want, which was why he'd been elected bar association president. There was also widespread acknowledgment that nobody in the county could string a tennis racquet better than Jules. But he was no litigator. His main practice was acting as a trustee in bankruptcy cases. Confrontation was not his middle name.

Walker phoned Hunt and learned that the judge, indeed, had departed for Wabash. Nobody seemed to know when he would be back. Walker said he'd go over to the courthouse. Being on the scene, you could sometimes pick up an interesting tidbit.

Janice waited, fidgeting. Celeste was getting jumpier by the second. Even Jeff was showing signs of unraveling.

When Walker finally returned, he said that an attempt to reach Hunt in Wabash had failed. Hunt's in-laws had a lakeside cottage somewhere. The word now was that the judge had gone fishing for the weekend.

*Fishing?* With all this going on? Every alarm bell in

Janice went off. If the Taylors were capable of this sneak adoption—which, she realized by now, had been carefully planned—what else were they prepared to do? If they found out she and the Whites were in Marion, they could take off.

Well, Walker said, he'd dropped by to see Tom Wright. He was one of two Grant County Superior Court judges, additional major judgeships created by the Indiana legislature when the original circuit court judges, one in each county, like Hunt, were overwhelmed with work. Wright handled all the juvenile cases in the county. Walker said he'd talked over the situation with him, and Wright had suggested they go see Warren Haas, the attorney for the Welfare Department.

• • •

It was then about 3:30 P.M. Warren Haas was getting ready to pack it in. It was his thirty-eighth birthday and to celebrate, he and his wife were going to spend the weekend in Chicago. On the agenda the next day was a ballgame at Wrigley Field to watch his favorite team, the Cubs.

Haas was from Crawfordsville, about fifty miles southwest of Indianapolis. His mild manner concealed an inner toughness. At Indiana University, he had majored in languages, specializing in German. He ended up teaching it at Marion High, when he decided to pursue a law degree. Along with his private practice, he was appointed the Welfare Department's lawyer, and was no-nonsense about it. Sometimes a case would get especially nasty and, because of his German background, he'd be called a "storm trooper." He could not have cared less. Sometimes, too, in one of these cases, he'd think that the party clearly in the right should just take the child and run, but then Warren Haas would remind himself that this was not what he stood for as either a lawyer or a man.

Without warning, Jules Walker, Janice, and the Whites showed up in his office. Walker tried to explain why they were there. Then Janice cut in. Haas was impressed by her. She ticked off the problem—bing, bing, bing. He listened and then examined the papers she had brought with her.

Curious, Haas checked the caseworker's report that had gone to Hunt. It gave the Taylor home high marks for its physical set-up and said Philip appeared to be "a normal, happy child." But it also stated that Ken was serving a thirty-year-prison sentence "for the death of his wife," which had occurred "during some sort of domestic fight with her husband, Kenneth Taylor." According to the Taylors, the report went on, the mother "before her death had been a drug user and consumed combinations of cocaine, alcohol and codeine." Near the end of the single-spaced report, it said: "The child is presently in the custody of another family who lives in New York State. He is here on a two-week visitation with his grandparents, the Taylors. We hope the information in this case will be helpful to the court in deciding this issue."

Granted, Haas thought, the report could have been stronger, but still it was all there. The caseworker, given her mission, had done an excellent job. How could Hunt have signed the decree without a more thorough investigation? Clearly, he hadn't read any of this.

Walker then explained to Haas that before talking to Judge Wright, he'd talked to Hunt, and Hunt had said he might be available on Friday and then again he might not.

"Jules," Haas said, "you can't go around buttonholing judges on something like this. It isn't the way it's done. If you want to attack this, you have to go in and attack it in adoption court before Judge Hunt. If you can't get to him now, you have to decide if you want to wait until Monday."

He told Janice there was one other option. He could file a CHINS—a Child In Need of Services—petition. All he had to do was file it, he didn't have to have a judge's authorization. But it had to be an emergency. What did Janice think about that? She said she couldn't claim that Philip was in physical danger. But what about his emotional well-being? Look, she said, even in the welfare report, the Taylors had accused Teresa of being a druggie and stated that they intended to maintain a close relationship between Philip and Ken. She told Haas what Jean Taylor wrote to Judge Ashbey—that if the child remained with Celeste and Jeff, he would never know the "truth" about his mother. At this stage, she said, she was ready to believe anything. Suppose the Taylors fled with Philip?

Okay, Haas said, he agreed.

To cover himself, he phoned Judge Wright. Had the judge sent the Whites over to him to see if a CHINS petition was in order?

Well, Wright replied cautiously, it was at least to explore that possibility. Haas was more knowledgeable in this area than he was. Personally, he hadn't made a determination.

Haas said he was going to file. There wasn't time to draw up a petition. He'd enter the New Jersey custody order. Under the Uniform Child Custody and Jurisdiction Act, it was as good as one from an Indiana court.

For the first time, Janice Miller began to have some hope. Haas obviously knew what he was doing.

Haas summoned a social worker. They drove to the sheriff's department to round up a deputy. You never knew, Haas said.

The caravan headed for the Taylor home about five miles away, on the northwest edge of Marion in a subdivision called Avondale.

Haas instructed Celeste and Jeff to remain well back. He knocked on the door. Zach answered. Haas identified himself, explained why he was there, and requested entry. Zach refused. If there was a warrant, slip it under the door. Haas said he didn't need a warrant and to open up. Zach said he wouldn't.

The deputy sheriff also identified himself. Zach wouldn't budge. The deputy said he was coming in. Zach said give him a minute. He had to put the dog in the backyard. Then he scurried to the phone and called Pat Ryan.

"Don't let them in," Ryan said.

"Pat, they'll break the door down."

"I'm telling you, Zach, don't let them in. I'll be right over."

The deputy sheriff kept pounding. Finally, Zach gave up. Haas entered, accompanied by the deputy, and took Philip in his arms. Haas had just handed him to the social worker when Ryan roared up. He ran straight at Haas, yelling, "You can't do this. I've cleared all this with Judge Hunt."

Haas stepped between Ryan and the social worker. He did his best to calm Ryan. "Pat, you may be right, but we're not going to argue about it here. The place we're going to do it in is a courtroom."

Zach was yelling at Haas, "You goddamned, no-good Nazi baby snatcher!"

Ryan ducked around Haas and headed for the social worker, but she was already in her car, starting the engine. All Ryan could do was to hammer on the window before she drove away.

Haas told the deputy to radio for backup.

Zach called Janice Miller "a no-good, rotten, little prick." Ryan, fist raised, charged her. She flinched, sure that he was going to hit her. But at the last moment, he didn't. Thank God for the deputy, she thought.

Somewhere behind him, Haas heard Celeste crying, "You sons of bitches." He spied Jean Taylor at the front door. It was eerie, he remembered. In all the furor, she remained standing there absolutely motionless, just watching, "sort of plastic-like."

Suddenly, it was over. Cursing, Ryan and Zach retreated into the house. Haas told the deputy to cancel the backup. Relieved that it hadn't been worse, Haas returned with the deputy to the sheriff's department and filled out a report while Janice, Celeste, Jeff and Jules Walker waited outside.

As it happened, Tom Hunt had not gone fishing. He was in his Marion backyard tending to a family barbecue when Jean Taylor had called him and described the "horrible events" that were, at that moment, taking place at her home. Hunt listened and said, "I can't be talking to you, Mrs. Taylor. Have your attorney call me."

Minutes later, Ryan was snarling, "You gave me your word you wouldn't do anything without a hearing."

Hunt caught up with Haas on the phone at the sheriff's

department. Hunt shouted, "What the hell are you doing? Your goddamned welfare report says these people are perfect to adopt the child, so I act on it, and all at once it's an unfit environment. Get that kid back where you said he belongs."

"Judge," Haas said, "I'm sorry. I've read that report. What you're saying about it is not correct. Everything you needed to know was right there. It's my determination that an emergency exists. If I'm wrong, I'm wrong. But I'm not returning the child. We can discuss this in court Monday morning."

"You can bet on it," Hunt said, slamming down the phone.

That evening there was a new crisis. Haas had arranged for a young Marion couple with two children of their own to care for Philip. He had them come to the welfare center so Jeff and Celeste could be reassured. But in the day's confusion, Celeste had misunderstood. She thought she would get Philip immediately. She was allowed to hold him for a few minutes. When he was taken away, crying and reaching for her, she collapsed to the ground, sobbing. And Jeff, trying to console her, at last lost control. Staring up at Janice, he yelled, "Why aren't you doing something? What is this, Russia?"

Haas brought them to the Marion Sheraton to check in for the night. They had sandwiches before returning to his office where Haas helped Miller and Walker prepare further court submissions.

Past two A.M., Warren Haas finally arrived home. He and his wife left for his birthday weekend in Chicago. He made it for the game at Wrigley Field, but in the middle of the second inning he fell sound asleep.

• • •

Under the illusion that it was only a question of setting the record straight, Janice, Celeste and Jeff boarded a flight to Newark that Saturday. The plan was for the Whites to drive back to Marion. Al Benigno would come with them. Just to be on the safe side, in case of an unexpected delay, Jeff hooked up a small camper he'd bought for vacation outings with Celeste and the children. They'd find a campsite near town while everything was resolved.

By Sunday evening, Judge Hunt had begun to amass the bad news. For one thing, he learned that during the first days of Philip's sojourn in Marion, his mother also had been there—dead, in a car trunk.

Hunt was mad. He was mad at Pat Ryan for duping him. He was especially mad at Warren Haas for making the whole thing public. And he was mad in the abstract. At thirty-nine, a rangy six-footer with a determined stride, he looked forward to being elevated to Indiana's appellate court level. Hunt could just imagine Marion's legal establishment chewing on this one at his expense—at the Marion Cafeteria for morning coffee and at The Nobby Grill, a block from the courthouse, over lunch.

First thing Monday morning, he took out his anger on Judge Wright for interfering in a case that was none of Wright's business. Wright promptly withdrew. Then Hunt stunned everyone by also withdrawing from the case. His excuse was that he had talked to too many people ex parte—outside the confines of the courtroom. The consensus at The Nobby Grill, however, was that Hunt had removed himself to avoid further embarrassment. Celeste and Jeff were distraught. What did this mean?

They were told that it meant the Welfare Department's intervention was voided. Philip would be returned to the Taylors. It also meant that under Indiana's rural legal system, a panel of three judges from other counties would be drawn up. Each side could object to one of the judges. The remaining judge would be assigned the case. And all this would take time.

Everyone's nerves were shot. Raging, Al Benigno said that obviously people had been bought off. Who did *he* have to buy? Even for Haas, that was too much. "Mr. Benigno, you're out of line," he said.

In New Jersey, Janice Miller realized that however likable Jules Walker was, he wasn't what she needed now. She started casting around for another Marion lawyer.

• • •

On Thursday morning, Richard A. Green was having his usual coffee at the Marion Cafeteria. A man who filled a lot of space, he'd been varsity center on the Marion High School basketball team, class of 1960. A graduate of Butler University with a degree in business administration, he went to work in the trust department of a local bank. He decided to study law, got a job in a bank in Indianapolis, and went to law school there five nights a week. He built a thriving practice in Marion with the reputation of being a tough, knowledgeable, all-around attorney. He and his wife, Sandra, also from Marion, loved to fly to New York for theater-going and now and then to work in some sightseeing trips to Europe. Right then, though, the Greens weren't traveling much. He had opened up a second office in the bustling resort town of Syracuse, seventy miles north on Indiana's largest natural lake, Wawasee. He was building a lakeside house, and when it was finished, he was bent on living and practicing full-time there.

That morning, in the Marion Cafeteria, a fellow lawyer tapped Green on the shoulder. "You're going to get a call in about forty-five minutes from a female attorney from New Jersey," he said. "She called me, but it's not my kind of thing. I recommended you. She's got a fact situation that'll knock your fucking dick stiff."

"What is it?"

"Hunt's boo-boo on that adoption."

Of course, he'd heard the gossip. Janice filled him in on the details. Her clients, she said, were still in Marion, at some campsite. They would be calling her. Could she give them Green's number? Yes, he said. If he took the case, he'd need them to sign some papers. She warned him that they didn't have the money for a retainer, but she gave him her personal guarantee that he would be covered. At the time, that did not bother him. It looked like a simple matter to get set aside, an adoption that was clearly fraudulent. After talking to Warren Haas and looking over the documents on file, Green was even more convinced of this.

That afternoon Al Benigno, Celeste and Jeff arrived at Green's office dispirited, bedraggled, paranoid. To top off everything, the shower facilities where they were camping had broken down. "Please, Mr. Green," Celeste said, "I just want my baby back."

As soon as they got a new judge, he told her, he was sure it would be over with. Green didn't underestimate Pat Ryan's wiliness for second. Ryan was a hard-bitten old trial lawyer. He'd try to turn the whole thing into a circus about "issues"—about the best interests of the child, beating the drum about loyalty to Indiana, sympathy for these long-suffering grandparents, and about how adoption superseded custody. One sentence into a discourse on the United States Constitution, Dick Green thought, and Ryan would turn it into a speech about why the Taylors should have the child. Still, this wasn't about issues. The issues had already been decided in New Jersey. This was about the law, and he wasn't going to let Ryan get away from it.

Two weeks later, Green was further heartened when a judge, Bruce Embrey, was selected to preside over the case. Embrey sat on the bench in Peru, in adjoining Miami County, and was first-class. Green drew up a new filing to vacate the adoption. He also prepared a motion for a speedy trial date. Time was of the essence.

In the months ahead, Dick Green often brooded about how hollow those words would sound.

• • •

The block party to raise money—on Cannon Boulevard in Staten Island, where Al and Louise Benigno lived—was the idea of the mother of Celeste's good friend Linda Valente.

Instantly, the reaction of the entire neighborhood was, "What took you so long?" Jeff remembered how people would come up to him and Celeste and say, "You know, we wanted to suggest it, but we didn't want to seem pushy."

By now the events in Marion had made the papers in New Jersey and Staten Island. The *Staten Island Advance* reported, "Murder Victim's Son, 2, Center of Custody Battle." This and other headlines were incorporated in a flyer that the husband of another friend of Celeste's ran off where he worked at Xerox. The flyer said, "FUND

RAISER BLOCK SALE. HELP BRING BABY PHILIP HOME!!" A sign painter down the street prepared banners that said the same thing.

Celeste and other girlfriends distributed the flyer in shopping malls, on car windshields, in front-door mail slots. A friend of a friend supplied a rolling hot dog stand with an umbrella. The House O' Weenies contributed the hot dogs. Another friend provided a pony for kids to ride. Still a third friend, dressed as a clown, would do face paintings. A specialty store gave silk flower arrangements for a raffle. A pizza parlor donated pies to be sold by the slice. A Chinese restaurant sent spring rolls, dumplings and spare ribs. A Jewish delicatessen made up a huge platter of cold cuts. A supermarket provided paper napkins, plates and cups. A novelties store offered ceramic Christmas trees for another raffle.

A big plastic jug was placed in the middle of the block for cash gifts. The son of one of Louise's friends, who played in local clubs, set up a sound system and brought his band. Up and down Cannon Boulevard and on nearby streets, kitchens worked overtime—eggplant parmigiana, baked ziti, meatballs, Italian sausages. Neighbors cleaned out their attics for items to sell—and purchased them back at three or four times their worth. Nuns from St. Charles, where Teresa had gone to parochial school, pitched in.

The block party ran Saturday and Sunday, September 20 and 21. There was a last-second hitch. They had forgotten a permit. The cops came by, but when Jeff explained what was going on, a sergeant said, "Hey, no problem." Then the cops returned to put up street barricades so a car wouldn't inadvertently plow into the crowd.

In all, more than six thousand dollars for legal fees in Indiana was raised. The following night, though, was a downer. When Jeff returned home from his shift on the ferry, he found Celeste in tears. Some friends had been by. She said they had said, "What's wrong with you? Why don't you and Jeff just go out there and grab Philip?"

"Listen," Jeff said. "We can't. If we do that, what's the difference between them and us?"

A couple of days later, she was jubilant. She'd learned she was pregnant again. Now when Philip returned, he'd have another sister—or a brother. It was a good omen, a blessed signal, she said. She was certain of it.

• • •

By the end of September, Ken's plans to break out of the Trenton State Prison were complete. His five confederates were convicts serving lengthy sentences for crimes that included murder, kidnapping and armed robbery. They worked in various areas of the prison's main repairs building. One of them, a lifer in for murder, was in the second floor upholstery and furniture shop. In an empty attic area directly above it, he discovered a window without bars that was level with the top of the prison wall thirty feet away. The problem was that there was a watch tower nearby. "It was very, very bold, very ingenious," a prison official would say about the plan.

They built a makeshift, sectional wood bridge to reach the wall. It was rigged with connecting bolts and steel plates. To take care of the tower guard, a crossbow was fashioned to shoot steel arrows launched with heavy elastic furniture fabric. Other guards within the building would be met with a hail of sixteen-penny nails from a pipe blowgun, built like a bazooka and powered by an air compressor. A half-dozen Molotov cocktails were also made ready. The equipment was assembled piece-by-piece and hidden in the attic. One of the convicts had arranged for an accomplice to be waiting in a van with guns on the other side of the wall. The escape was scheduled for October 4.

But there was a snitch, and this time the snitch was Ken. He later explained to authorities that he simply couldn't be a party to the killings that would inevitably occur. In retrospect, more cynical observers now believe that he was setting himself up for another, more discreet escape in less restrictive surroundings. If that was his intent, it worked. However it happened, word soon leaked that he was the snitch. He was immediately put into protective custody. Then, in a prisoner tradeoff between states to handle situations like this, he was transferred out of New Jersey to the Virginia penal system.

He was received at the main prison, Powhatan, near Richmond, and after about four months was shipped to the Augusta Correctional Center, a new facility in a remote, fog-shrouded valley in the Appalachian chain in western Virginia. He became a model inmate. Because of his educational and professional background, he was assigned to tutor other convicts seeking high school equivalency diplomas. Except for his instructional duties and the morning, afternoon and evening countdowns, he was pretty much on his own.

At once, Ken started looking for a way out.

# Chapter

# TWENTY

After the block party, Celeste kept calling Dick Green in Marion. So did Janice Miller. What was wrong? Why wasn't anything being done? Even Janice started suspecting the worst.

Green was truly embarrassed. Admittedly, just about everyone in Marion who touched the case had fumbled badly. But he tried to explain that the delay wasn't the result of a conspiracy. It was Indiana's judicial system. Judge Embrey, over in Miami County, had been selected to rule on the case, but Embrey had yet to come to Marion to sign in officially. Green was in a quandary. He knew that Embrey was inundated by a heavy trial load. He could pressure him, but he decided not to. Embrey was precisely the kind of judge he desired. There was no point in antagonizing him unnecessarily.

Then in late September Janice had an idea to shortcut the system. She had Celeste file a criminal complaint in Monmouth County Superior Court. Defying Judge Gehricke's custody order was a felony. And it was an extraditable offense. An indictment was returned, an arrest warrant was issued, and the Grant County sheriff's office was notified by teletype that the Taylors were fugitives.

That triggered press attention. Al Benigno was quoted as saying, "It's crazy. If they can get away with this, anybody can kidnap a child and take him to another state and adopt him."

But in Marion, no action was taken. A deputy sheriff named Mark Florence said that while the teletype had been received, "It did not provide enough details about why the Taylors were wanted."

In Freehold, prosecutor Paul Chaiet said a complete set of documents was being dispatched by express mail to Grant County law enforcement officers.

Deputy Florence acknowledged receipt of the documents, but said that an arrest warrant could not be served on the Taylors because no Grant County judge was available to sign the order. All three judges were attending a judicial conference. He referred further inquiries to the Grant County district attorney, Stephen Johnson. But he also was said to be out of town on business.

Pat Ryan sneered that the indictment of the Taylors was a "trumped-up charge." He announced that they would of course fight any extradition if it came down to that. "The issue is moot," he said and provided his own version of the federal child custody jurisdiction act: "It only applies in cases of child abuse or divorce where one spouse kidnaps the child from the spouse with custody. Adoption hearings here in Indiana take precedence and the boy was adopted in August. There is no need for further litigation. The court orders in New Jersey were temporary. Adoption is final."

In light of this, Chaiet, on behalf of Monmouth County, sent a formal extradition request to New Jersey governor Thomas Kean to pass on to Indiana governor Robert D. Orr.

Orr authorized service. Now there was no choice in Marion. Jean and Zach Taylor were brought before the third of the county's judges, Gary O. Thompson. They were released on a five-hundred-dollar bond. Thompson scheduled a hearing for October 20.

"It was just horrible being treated like a common criminal," Jean told rapt members of her Bible-study class. But still, she said, "There was this nice deputy, Mark Florence, he was the manager of the basketball team when my son Tom was on it, and he said he sure hated to be doing this, and Zach said, 'We understand, it's your job," and Mark said, 'Well, I'm not going to fingerprint you and have you mugged. I should, but I'm not.' "

"Praise the Lord," one of her listeners said.

A reporter sought out Dr. Michele Rabinowitz in her New Jersey office for her comments. "The separation from established psychological parents is highly traumatic beyond one or two weeks," she said. "The real victim in this is going to be the child."

• • •

On October 2, though, it appeared that the extradition tactic was superfluous. Judge Embrey finally signed up in Marion. He let it be known that he would get to the case promptly. All the media attention had really helped, Dick Green thought.

Then, suddenly, disaster struck. *The Indianapolis Star,* the state's biggest newspaper, published a major feature story on the case. Judge Hunt was quoted at length. "To tell you the truth," he said, "I was blindsided. I was never completely informed of the New Jersey case. I disqualified myself because I didn't think I could be fair."

Judge Bruce Embrey was also questioned by reporters. Caught off guard, he said that while he could only speak hypothetically, if the facts were as they purported to be, "It's conceivable that [the adoption] could be invalidated."

Green groaned when he read that. Talk about being blindsided. He knew at once what Pat Ryan would do. Ryan wasn't happy having a judge of Embrey's caliber. And Ryan wanted to keep buying as much time as he could. The longer this could be put off, the more he could argue how wrenching it would be to tear Philip from his loving grandparents.

Instantly, Ryan demanded that Embrey disqualify himself because of his prejudicial remarks. Stung, Embrey resisted. But word filtered down from court circles in Indianapolis that, all things considered, it might be wise for him to step down, and he did.

The whole process would begin again. First, there was the presentation of a new slate of three judges from other counties, and then the inevitable wait after one of them was selected.

Now the extradition was crucial.

The hearing was on the docket for late afternoon on October 20 after Judge Thompson finished trial work for the day. Theoretically, once the basics were established—that a crime had been committed and that the wanted persons were, indeed, correctly identified—the process was pretty much automatic. The only exception Green could recall was when a fugitive was able to demonstrate that he could not possibly get a fair trial in whatever jurisdiction was after him. Clearly, that wasn't the situation here.

But Janice, edgy after the Embrey affair, feared that the Taylors might skip Marion before the hearing.

"How far could they get in that camper?" Green argued.

Well, she said, they could leave, and then come back, and there would be another delay and more hassling, more time lost. So Green arranged for private surveillance. Pat Ryan, however, had quite a different strategy.

That day at lunch in The Nobby Grill, most of the conversation was about the upcoming elections, two weeks off. Everyone agreed that Steve Johnson, running for reelection as D.A., was a certain winner. Hardly anyone mentioned the extradition, it seemed so open-and-shut.

Out of idle curiosity more than anything else, Dick Green dropped by to observe the hearing, which would be handled by the D.A.'s office. Ryan would appear for the Taylors. Judge Thompson had already defined the parameters. The issues were authenticity, identity, fugitivity and substance of charges. He was going by the book.

Green stood in the rear of the courtroom. To his amazement, around five P. M., it began to fill up, people streaming in, middle-aged mostly, many of them couples. What was this? Then he spotted the pastor of the First Baptist Church, Darrel Parris. Several people clustered around him, talking and nodding.

Suddenly, the word "flock" crossed Green's mind. It was exactly the right word, he realized. What he was witnessing was a church flock, here with its shepherd. Green no longer was the only one standing. The courtroom was jammed. There was applause when Jean and Zach were ushered in. Judge Thompson hammered his gavel. Green heard someone whisper, "Those poor people. They've been in jail all afternoon." A late arrival pushed past him, saying, "I just got the call. What did I miss?"

There were angry murmurs as an assistant D.A. briefly presented the facts and asked that the extradition warrant be enforced against the Taylors. "That's not right," a voice shouted. "They haven't done anything wrong." Other voices were raised. Again, Thompson gaveled for silence.

Cheers greeted Ryan when he said that the proceeding was a farce. His clients were law-abiding citizens of Marion, Grant County and Indiana. There was nothing illegal here. "These loving grandparents are the only people eligible in the whole country to adopt the child because the father has given his consent."

Someone cried, "Amen!"

Flabbergasted, Dick Green began to wonder if he were at a judicial hearing or a revival meeting.

The warrant, Ryan said, had been issued solely to "satisfy the wounded feelings of some judge in New Jersey."

The assistant D.A. objected on grounds of relevancy. When Thompson sustained the objection, there were angry new shouts.

"The best interests of the child are at stake here," Ryan said, falling back on his favorite theme. "An adoption takes precedence over previous custody orders."

There was another objection. It was sustained. A chorus of boos erupted. Vainly, Thompson pounded his gavel.

There was a hush after Ryan put Jean on the stand. Some women in the audience began to weep as she testified that all she wanted was to care for her little grandson, to see that he was raised in good Christian surroundings.

Then Zach launched into a rambling discourse about all their tribulations back east, how even there, court order after court order had been disregarded, how a behind-the-back attempt was made to move jurisdiction of the case to New York. The mention of New York appeared to inflame everyone. He might as well have said Sodom and Gomorrah, Green thought.

"We love that little boy," Zach said. "He belongs with us here in Marion." Judge Thompson had no choice except to sustain the objection.

"Let the man speak!" somebody yelled.

Thompson tried to redefine the issues, but the hubbub continued. It was getting ugly. Green had a vision of everyone in the courtroom collectively rushing the bench.

That thought also might have occurred to Thompson. Abruptly, he halted the hearing. Both sides would have three days to submit briefs. Jean and Zach would remain under "house arrest." Pointedly, the judge said there would be no official monitoring of their movements. Then Thompson retreated to his chambers.

Slowly, people started to shuffle past Green. Among them, he recognized Ernest J. Dalton, the county's chief probation officer, who had so vigorously endorsed the Taylors as adoptive parents in their original petition. "If you ask me," Dick Green heard Dalton say, "this is man's law interfering with God's law."

• • •

One of the first communiqués to the "Public Letterbox" in the Marion *Chronicle-Tribune* was from Reverend Parris himself. It zeroed right in on electoral retribution:

> If this extradition is allowed to be carried out by our local judicial system, then it seems to me that at the next election we need to make some changes in those who supposedly are to know the difference between the good and bad guys.
>
> One of the trusts we place in the hands of our local

legal system of prosecutors and judges is the trust to look at the people, look at the facts of the charged crime and then strive towards justice. In this case, no justice can be served by extradition.

Let's put the real criminals behind bars, those who hurt and maim. If the persons in charge of our legal system cannot tell the difference in cases like these, then it's time to replace them with those who can.

Another letter echoed Parris's threat:

How can the governor or the Grant County court approve of extradition for an action (adopting a grandson) when Grant County/Indiana judges have already granted adoption papers?

No crime has been committed here by the Taylors who have been law-abiding citizens in our community for over 20 years. It's time for the people of Marion to be heard by insisting that justice be done. Let's not be apathetic citizens! Speak up and be heard!

If our elected officials do not listen, we still have that privilege of removing them from office by casting our vote on election day. Come on, Grant County citizens! Accept your responsibility! You do have a voice in this matter!

Still a third said:

Why should law-abiding citizens such as Mr. and Mrs. Everett Taylor be arrested for legally adopting their grandson?

. . . Mr. and Mrs. Taylor are providing a good Christian home for their grandson. This fact in itself should weigh heavily on the court's decision.

As citizens, we all need to reflect on a judicial system which would permit the arrest of anyone under these circumstances.

The Taylors are not criminals. They are only wanting what they think is best for the child.

The Marion courts should have jurisdiction over this case and do what is best for the child; and at the same time treat the Taylors as law-abiding citizens instead of criminals.

A fourth declared:

... Apparently the maternal grandparents did not or could not seek custody of the child. The paternal grandparents did. Jean Taylor is the closest relative this child has outside of his natural father who, under the circumstances, cannot care for him.

How can any court in our land deny custody of this child to his natural paternal grandparents who want him?

The Taylors need all the legal help and spiritual support they can get from the people of Marion and the State of Indiana.

Among all the letters, there was one dissident note. It said:

I, too, am appalled at the injustice of the Everett and Jean Taylor custody dispute. In fact, I wrote a letter to the letterbox last week saying so, but because my opinion is opposed to that of those who jump on the hometown's favorite bandwagon (including the *Chronicle-Tribune,* evidently), my letter was not published.

I find it easy to believe that the Taylors are good, upstanding people and love their grandson very much, and I would truly hate to see them extradited to New Jersey because I fear they would be treated there the way people on the other side of this dispute are being treated in Grant County.

Imagine if you will what they have gone through. First, their sister and daughter was murdered by the Taylors' son. They obtain legal custody of their slain loved one's child.

After having this little boy for a year as their own child, they are informed that, while he is on a two-week visit with his other grandparents, he has been "legally" adopted by them and to just forget about him.

Yes, I pray for the Taylors. But I also pray for the Benigno-Whites. And in a much larger view, I must pray for Grant County and its judicial system. Had the facts been checked by Judge Thomas Hunt, perhaps this would not be happening now.

But then again, maybe we need something to stand us out from the rest of the state or the nation. We could put up a sign at the city limits: Marion—Illegal Adoption Center of the World.

• • •

Unknown to everyone at the time, except Jean and Zach, Pastor Parris journeyed to Indianapolis to chat with Linley E. Pearson, Indiana's Attorney General. Prior to coming to Marion, Parris had a Baptist ministry in the western part of the state, in Frankfort, and Pearson was a member of that congregation.

What the Taylors were being subjected to was unconscionable, Parris said. They were good people without a blemish on their record. As a matter of fact, if something like this could happen, the extradition law should be changed.

"What do you want me to do?" Parris would quote Pearson as saying.

"Don't extradite them."

"I'll look into it," Pearson said.

Two days later, Steve Johnson took time off from his reelection campaigning for Grant County D.A. and also went to Indianapolis.

On his return he announced big news. Pending a further investigation, Governor Orr was rescinding the extradition warrant he'd signed. Orr was doing this not only on the recommendation of Attorney General Pearson but of Johnson himself—all three of whom happened to be Republicans. "I think just the interest of justice demands and dictates that this be done," Johnson said. He added that he could not go into specifics since the matter was still under review.

In Indianapolis, a spokesman for the governor said, "We wanted to give every opportunity to protect Indiana citizens if they have the right to be protected." He said that the investigation into the facts would be conducted by Deputy Attorney General David Arthur.

Back in Monmouth County, Paul Chaiet urged the assistant counsel to New Jersey governor Kean to press Orr for an early resolution of the investigation.

• • •

Janice Miller and Dick Green had neither the time nor the energy to waste grousing about a fix.

A new special judge, R. Alan Brubaker from Kokomo, was selected to rule on the adoption. But before any hearing could be held to vacate it, a Motion to Intervene had to be entered and granted by Brubaker. At first blush, Jeff and Celeste looked like the aggrieved party in the affair. But, as it now stood, they had no legal standing at all in an Indiana court. They had played no part in the adoption. Their common interest—their connection to Philip—had to be established, and this interest would then justify their intervention in the proceedings. If it were not allowed, they would suffer irreparable harm.

It was basically legalities, briefs followed by oral arguments invoking Indiana case law. Still, it was tricky, given the tenor of local opinion. Pat Ryan could be counted on to throw up every smoke screen he could think of or invent— sympathy for the Taylors, loyalty to Indiana. And success was crucial. Without intervention, the adoption itself could not be contested.

Most crucial of all, it would turn out, was Janice Miller's insistence back in Freehold the previous July, when an agreement on the two-week visitation was reached, that Celeste and Jeff be given sole, permanent custody of Philip. Nothing temporary about it, nothing shared. The visitation to the Taylors, in Judge Gehricke's order, was just that and nothing more.

That was the cornerstone of Dick Green's argument, that

and the fact that the Whites had received no notification of the adoption proceedings, as required by Indiana trial rules and the Uniform Child Custody Jurisdiction Act.

The hearing before Judge Brubaker was held on December 2.

Ryan went all-out.

In a sworn deposition, he declared that New Jersey had no jurisdiction to enter any orders because "Philip had not lived there since his mother died." New Jersey was not his "home state," even under uniform child custody laws.

He picked out state case law and trial stipulations as if they existed in a vacuum. Only the consent of living parents was required for the adoption of a "legitimate child."

Celeste and Jeff had no statutory right to intervene. "The Whites," he insisted, "could neither oppose the adoption or consent to it. If the law does not require a person's consent, he need not be notified."

He invoked Indiana precedent in another adoption where the court said, "If the child has parents living, they alone can interpose objections of the order of adoption in a proper case."

"An adoption," he maintained, "creates new parent-child relationships and terminates any prior, inconsistent custody orders."

He claimed Judge Hunt had recognized in the adoption decree he signed that there was a pending custody proceeding in New Jersey. Hunt had thoroughly reviewed all the pertinent documents—and he had signed the decree without hesitation.

In court, Ryan cried, "Why are we here? There's an Indiana adoption decree that supersedes every other court order there is!"

But in the end he could not escape the finality in Judge Gehricke's order. There was nothing "pending" about it. It had been handed down in accordance with U.S. custody laws which New Jersey *and* Indiana subscribed to virtually word for word.

Judge Brubaker ruled that Jeff and Celeste qualified as "Intervenors." And he scheduled December 18 as the date for an evidentiary hearing to decide whether or not the adoption would be vacated.

• • • •

This, it would seem, was the last go-around.

Jeff and Celeste joined Janice in Marion. There was every likelihood that the adoption would be set aside on the spot, and they could return to Staten Island with Philip.

The strategy Janice and Dick Green devised was designed to keep the hearing focused on the legal issues—that the law had been broken—to keep Ryan from turning it into a best-interest-of-the-child circus, to keep him from retrying what already had been tried.

They would base their case on court documents which couldn't be cross-examined—primarily the New Jersey custody order—and other documents showing, for instance, that although the adoption petition prepared by Ryan claimed Philip had no assets, he had in fact assets totaling more than $110,000.

They intended to call only one witness, Judge Hunt. They wanted to demonstrate that fraud and deception also had played a role in the adoption. In his brief in support of the adoption, Ryan said, "Had Judge Hunt been defrauded, he would have set the adoption aside and chided counsel for same." Ryan further claimed that Hunt had read the entire Welfare Department report before he signed the decree.

However painful it might be for Hunt, Green needed his testimony to refute this assertion. Over the last two months he had mentioned to Hunt that he'd probably be a witness. Okay, sure, no problem, Hunt said. It was such a forgone conclusion that Hunt would testify that Green discarded the idea of a subpoena.

Indeed, on the morning of December 18, Green told Hunt that he would be calling him that afternoon, and Hunt said fine, he'd be around.

The hearing was scheduled for one P.M.

Dick Green got to the courthouse a little early. That was when he got a sinking sensation that this wasn't going to be resolved so fast. He wandered into the waiting area for judges and saw Judge R. Alan Brubaker, just in from Kokomo, beginning to leaf through the pleadings. Clearly, he was looking at them for the first time, and except for Hunt's testimony, they represented Green and Miller's whole case.

Green went out to the courthouse steps to wait for Celeste, Jeff and Janice. Hunt passed by him. He was on his way to lunch. It was a little late for lunch, Green thought, but maybe a trial he was conducting had run over.

"See you later," Green said.

"Yeah," Hunt said.

• • •

Pat Ryan and the Taylors, accompanied by Reverend Parris, entered the courtroom. A handful of church members straggled in. But there was no repetition of the scene at the extradition hearing. It was as if everyone's emotions were exhausted. "Pray for our brother and sister, Jean and Everett," Parris had said the previous Sunday.

Green began submitting papers to Brubaker, asking the court to take "judicial notice" of Gehricke's final custody order which had full legal force in Indiana pursuant to the uniform child custody act, and then introduced a certified copy of Philip's assets.

Ryan had deposed that Philip lived with Jean and Zach from the time of Teresa's death, as if it had all been in Indiana. Green handed Brubaker the first order Judge Ashbey had issued, dated barely two weeks after the murder, which showed that not only had there been temporary joint custody with the Whites, but that it was in New Jersey. He also submitted her second order in August, 1985, that gave Celeste and Jeff custody ten months a year.

Green asked for judicial notice that in his consent to adoption, Ken's residence—the Trenton State Prison—was not included as required by Indiana law. Furthermore, the consent had not been executed before a court, a notary public, or any other authorized person.

No notice of the adoption had been sent to Philip's lawful guardians, Celeste and Jeff, or to the New Jersey court that exercised custodial control, or to Philip's state-appointed financial guardian—all of which Indiana statutes demanded.

Additional documents were offered to show that the adoption was "in direct contravention of the intent and terms of child custody laws in New Jersey and Indiana."

Finally, fraud was alleged.

Green's submissions took about twenty minutes.

The paperwork in front of Judge Brubaker was close to three inches high. He appeared baffled. Wasn't Green going to call any witnesses?

"Yes, Your Honor, Judge Hunt."

The consternation on Brubaker's face was instant. "Are you sure you want to do that?"

"Yes."

Brubaker peered at Green. "You better think about it."

Green realized that Brubaker had not signaled the bailiff to fetch Hunt.

"What's going on?" Janice whispered.

"I don't know," Green said. He asked for a recess. As he and Janice headed for the entry/exit door for attorneys, they crossed Brubaker's path. Green said to him, "What's the problem?"

Brubaker said, "Have you talked to Judge Hunt?"

"Yes, I talked to him this morning."

"Well, you better talk to him again."

Green went to Hunt's chambers. He was not there. With Celeste and Jeff hovering nearby, Green huddled with Janice. Obviously, a message was being sent. Hunt wasn't going to testify the way they expected, or Brubaker wasn't going to expose a fellow judge to any embarrassment. Either way, the implicit threat was that if they insisted on calling Hunt, they were going to regret it.

In court, Green told Brubaker that they would not call Hunt to the stand. Relieved, Brubaker asked who their next witness was.

Green said nobody. He and co-counsel Miller were resting their case. Everything was right there in the documentation in front of him. Brubaker stared at him in apparent disbelief. Pat Ryan seemed equally stunned.

"No more witnesses?" Brubaker said.

"No, Your Honor."

Now Ryan asked for a recess.

Green was exultant. He hadn't given Ryan a single opening to retry the case by cross-examining witnesses. The documentary evidence to invalidate the adoption was overwhelming. All Brubaker had to do was review the material. But then, standing in the hallway outside the courtroom, it was Green's turn to be stunned. A friend of Green's, a member of Marion's legal fraternity, hurried up to him. Hunt had miraculously reappeared in his chambers following his extended lunch. Green's friend had just come from there. "I think you may have a problem," he said.

"What are you talking about?"

Brubaker had stormed in to see Hunt, he said, complaining about Green's tactics. Hunt asked, "What do you mean?" and Brubaker said, "He hasn't introduced any evidence yet, no witnesses, just a bunch of papers."

For the first time Dick Green's confidence in the eventual outcome of the case faltered. He began to fear that either Brubaker was too lazy to go through the documents before him or too dumb to realize that the decision about who had custody of Philip had already been made—in New Jersey.

• • •

Reverend Parris was Ryan's first witness. He began testifying that Teresa had approached him about dedicating her son in the church. Green objected. This didn't have anything to do with anything.

Brubaker called the three attorneys to the bench. Where was this questioning headed? Well, Ryan said, a lot of scurrilous remarks had been directed toward his clients. It was only fitting that the court be informed that no finer folks could be found, that they were merely following the wishes of the child's "deceased" mother and his father. Brubaker, looking uncomfortable, ruled that this was "off the track."

Finally, Ryan gave up on Parris. He called Zach.

Had his grandson lived continuously with him and his wife since his adoption? Had there been any interruptions? Yes, one, Zach said. "That was on, uh, Friday evening, the eighth of August, one day after we adopted the child. We were having dinner about six o'clock, my wife and I and Philip, and I heard a loud knock on the door. I went to the door and there—it—it looked like an army in my front yard. There were two attorneys, uh, Mr. Jules Walker and Mr. Warren Haas. There were two or three, uh, deputy sheriffs. There was a lady from the Welfare Department. There was present, uh, Jeff White and Celeste White and Miz Janice Miller."

Green objected. "Your Honor, he's gotten far enough to indicate that this has nothing to do with the issue before the court."

Ryan said that his clients had been accused of fraud. He just wanted to show that others in this case had used the court to "perpetrate a fraud and this is one of the examples we're going into."

Brubaker suggested that Ryan move on.

"Okay," Ryan said, "now where did Philip stay after the date you learned of—uh—his mother's death? Who did he live with?"

"Philip actually lived with my wife and I from November the twelfth, nineteen eighty-four, until September first, nineteen eighty-five. Part of that time was here in Indiana and rest of the time was in his home in New Jersey."

"What happened after September first?"

Green objected. "Your Honor, this again has nothing to do with the issue. This is not a best-interest hearing."

Brubaker overruled him.

Zach testified, "We were to be allowed to have him in our home in Indiana for seven days on December twenty-sixth . . . Christmas of 'eighty-five."

"Your Honor," Green said, "we're not here to relitigate those things—where the child lived, who he's with and so forth."

Once more, Brubaker overruled him.

"Did you get Philip on December twenty-sixth?"

"We did not."

"Is there a reason for that?"

Now Janice objected. "We are not here to relitigate what

was litigated this past summer. I would respectfully ask the court to sustain this objection, that Mr. Taylor not be allowed to go into every little detail of what occurred. How, in fact, he had problems, my clients had problems, whatever. This is getting off the track of what we're here to decide today."

Maybe so, Brubaker said. But the life of a child was involved. As he put it, "I've got to have some meat to the bare bones."

Zach testified that he and Jean voluntarily postponed the visitation so Philip could enjoy his Christmas toys. Then Ryan moved quickly to the attempt by Celeste and Jeff to "drag" the Taylors into New York.

Brubaker overruled Janice's objection that this was a jurisdictional dispute that had nothing to do with New Jersey and Indiana or the hearing.

Dick Green objected to the use of the word "drag." It, too, was overruled.

Ryan asked, "When did you next get the child?"

"We never actually had him in our possession until August first, nineteen eighty-six . . . That's when we were permitted to bring him back here."

"And then," Ryan continued, "did there come a time— uh, you didn't know whether Judge Hunt would grant an adoption, did you?"

"We didn't know what was going to happen. We certainly hoped that he would."

"And Philip was happy to go with you?"

"Yes."

"Okay, that is all."

"He was happy," Zach repeated.

• • •

It had not gone well, Green thought. Brubaker had let Ryan wander all over the place. He had to get the judge focused back on the New Jersey custody order.

In cross-examination, he said, "Mr. Taylor, you were in court in Monmouth County, New Jersey, before Judge Gehricke, on August first?"

"Yes."

"And you were a party to the agreement which was read into the record by Mr. Shapiro, your attorney, and Mrs. Miller, were you not?"

"I was party to a tentative agreement."

". . . Would you explain to me what's tentative about something that's read into the record and you immediately received benefit or accepted benefit of it?"

"The, uh, tentative part was that it was to be written into document form by Mrs. Miller. That was the tentative part. There was no agreement under oath that day."

"Mr. Shapiro did represent you in that proceeding, did he not?"

"Yes."

"And you heard the agreement read to the judge?"

"I heard it, yes."

"Did the agreement provide that you would take the child on August the first and receive visitation for a sixteen-day period?"

"Yes."

"Did you receive the child?"

"Yes."

". . . So you got benefit out of that hearing?"

"We, we were able to have Philip, yes."

"Did you intend to bring him back on August sixteenth?"

"No." Then Zach, after a moment's hesitation, as if realizing that he'd said the wrong thing, interjected, "I'm sorry. Can I answer that?"

"I wish you would."

"Uh, the agreement that was read in court, the tentative agreement was that Celeste and Jeff were to take him back on August sixteenth. We were not obligated to take Philip back."

"Are you telling me that Mr. and Mrs. White didn't show up on the sixteenth to ask for Philip?"

"Something happened in between."

"What happened?"

"He was adopted on August the seventh."

"You knew when you left New Jersey and New York

that you were going to attempt to finalize this adoption, didn't you?"

"We knew that we were going to try. Yes."

• • •

"Why did you state flatly that he [Philip] doesn't have any property?"

"When I—when I read that in the—is that—is that in the petition?"

"Yes."

"When I read in the petition, uh, what came to my mind as property was, uh, real property in terms of—of—real estate."

• • •

"Mr. Taylor," Green said, "when the Whites filed the New York custody proceedings, you received notice, didn't you?"

"Yes, we did."

"When you filed the Indiana adoption, they didn't receive notice, did they?"

"No."

"That's all we have," Green said.

• • •

In his closing argument, Ryan said, "Mr. Green hasn't brought out anything new. We expected more evidence, more witnesses."

The Uniform Child Custody Jurisdiction Act, he went on, did not apply to adoptions. The "incarceration" of Kenneth Taylor in no way affected the validity of his consent. And Judge Hunt was cognizant of other custody proceedings. Any inadvertent omissions in the adoption petition were fully covered in the Welfare Department report, which Hunt had read.

Dick Green said that all his evidence was contained in the papers in front of Brubaker. He moved to have his pleadings amended to conform to evidence of fraud in the adoption petition.

Flustered, Brubaker denied the motion on fraud. That, of course, would have dragged Judge Hunt back into the proceedings.

He also denied Ryan's motion to throw out the case because of lack of evidence.

Then he ended any thought that he might make an immediate ruling. He would take the case under advisement. He wanted briefs from both sides. Glancing at Green, he gestured toward the stack of documents that had been submitted and said he was not a "history professor."

He wanted the briefs limited to three issues: the notice of adoption as required by Indiana law, the consent required for an adoption, and the validity of the New Jersey custody order.

The briefs were due February 13. After that, Judge Brubaker had sixty days to come to a decision. If he didn't, Green and Miller could move to have him taken off the case. That meant starting the whole process over again, beginning with the selection of another special judge.

Green could only hope that someone—possibly Hunt—would tell Brubaker that documents were as much evidence as witnesses were.

• • •

Crestfallen, Jeff and Celeste, who was now four months pregnant, returned empty-handed to Staten Island. Before Celeste left, Warren Haas did his best to cheer her up. "It isn't over until the fat lady sings," he said.

It was a Christmas of anguish. Philip as a person had disappeared into a legal thicket of motions, briefs and hearings. Celeste was inconsolable. She should have listened to her friends. They should have grabbed Philip.

In Marion, Pat Ryan told the Taylors that he thought they had a "real good shot" at winning. And even if they lost, he'd keep it going through the courts on appeal.

For years.

# Chapter

# TWENTY-ONE

Early in March, 1987, I was writing my novel, ironically called *Father and Son*, when I first heard about the events then taking place in Indiana.

One morning my wife read me portions of a letter she had received from a woman friend in San Francisco. The friend had once worked as a paralegal with Janice Miller. My wife said that she remembered meeting Janice once or twice. The letter described some of the travail that Janice was encountering in a cruel custody case. My impression at the time was that it centered on a dispute between maternal and paternal grandparents. The letter went on to say that Janice was in desperate need of some leverage outside of the legal system, something journalistic, that might help break the logjam. Would I be at all interested?

I said I'd think about it. Then, preoccupied with that day's work on the novel, I promptly forgot about it. In the evening, I met some friends of my own for drinks. One of them happened to bring up a recent segment he'd seen on the television program, "60 Minutes." It was really something, he said. It involved custody fights. If you were in one, and were Norwegian-born, and you could spirit the child to Norway, the Norwegian government, regardless of the merits, would see to it that the child was never returned. I immediately recalled the letter. Norway was one thing. Indiana was quite something else.

I spoke to Janice on the phone. Then, in New York, I had dinner with her and her husband, Frank Gaudio. Janice reviewed everything that had occurred to date, beginning with the call Celeste had made to her in June 1986. Now time was running out. She believed that the chances were odds-on that no decision would be made, and she and the Whites would have to start all over again.

In listening to her, it was obvious to me that she would never be compensated for her time. Why had she put such devotion into the case? It was then that I learned of her own history as a battered wife, and how she continued to involve herself in aiding women who had suffered the way she had. The murder of Teresa Taylor, and its aftermath, she said, was a perfect example of what she was combating.

I told her that it was hard for me to believe, in this day and age in this country, that what, in effect, amounted to a state-sanctioned kidnapping could actually be possible. I said that if I found that she was exaggerating any of this, she would be sorry she ever met me.

Janice had especially singled out the failed extradition of the Taylors as evidence of Indiana's hostile environment.

I drove to New Jersey to see Paul Chaiet in his office in Freehold. Chaiet recalled the prosecution of Ken Taylor, although he did not dwell on the difficulties he had faced in obtaining a murder conviction. As for the extradition, just a couple of weeks before, he had written another letter to John Hayden, the assistant counsel to Governor Kean. Chaiet's letter referred to previous requests for action. He noted that the Taylors had been indicted and that the "Monmouth County Prosecutor's Office has indicated that we will prosecute to the fullest extent of the law." He had not been given "any written explanation as to why this usually routine procedure has dragged on for an inordinate period of time." The letter asked, "Will somebody in an official capacity please get back to me in writing and explain the delay?"

There had been no response. Kean's name was being mentioned then as a possible vice-presidential candidate on the Republican ticket. I asked Chaiet if he thought politics had played a part in this, considering that Indiana's Orr also was a Republican governor.

He said he couldn't comment. I'd have to draw my own conclusions. Afterward, along with documents Janice Miller provided me, I picked up more papers on record in the Monmouth County Courthouse, including Jean Taylor's letter to Judge Ashbey about what Philip would or wouldn't know about Teresa's death.

When I read them, I found little that did not support what Janice had told me. I talked to the Benignos and Jeff and Celeste, and came away convinced of the horrors they'd experienced.

I did not attempt to reach Ken Taylor, still in prison in Virginia. His name as a direct participant in the court fight was not in any of the papers, and I had no inkling at the time of what his true role was in this drama.

Since the clock was ticking—a decision one way or the other, or no decision, was apparently due in mid-April—I approached the editor of the Sunday magazine of *The New York Times,* the only publication I could think of that uniquely met both the demands of time and impact. At first there was some resistance that this sounded like "just another custody fight." I said I thought that it involved a lot more, that in a very real sense it concerned what we as a nation were supposed to be all about. A day later, I got the go-ahead.

I went to Marion.

My first morning there, going around to get a visceral feel of the city, I walked under the great elms bordering the courthouse, including the one from which those two black teenagers had dangled decades before. I discovered that the big talk in town was the expected spring onslaught of the starlings, any day now, settling in the elms—tens of thousands of starlings, perhaps hundreds of thousands, even millions of them. Nobody knew. They'd been arriving for about three years and roosting through October. When I went to Marion's tallest building, the Summit, where so many local lawyers had their offices, the windows on all eight stories that faced the courthouse were strung with trinkets (tiny bells were a favorite) and balloons to ward starlings off the sills. Inflated fake owls had been positioned in the trees. In the past, bird shot had been fired through the branches. Trucks circling the courthouse had blared loud music. Other noises designed to frighten away the starlings had been recorded. Everything short of a howitzer had been tried. But nothing worked. The squealing starlings, along with their deposits, kept coming, and the courthouse square was readying itself for another grim siege.

I met Warren Haas. He confirmed the events of the evening when he had gone to the Taylor residence with Janice, Celeste, Jeff and the deputy sheriff. He made no effort to hide where he stood on the issue. Ever since, he said, when there was the slightest impropriety expressed in a Welfare Department report, he ordered it flagged for a judge's attention. By then, he knew of Judge Brubaker's comment that there had been no evidence, just documents. He shook his head. He couldn't begin to predict how this would wind up. Usually, he said, time was the ultimate victor. People simply wore down and surrendered. It was truly remarkable how Celeste and Jeff had "hung in."

At The Nobby Grill, I heard a rehash of how Judge Hunt had "blown it." There was general amazement that the case was still going on.

Dick Green retraced all the steps he had taken once Janice contacted him. Nothing incensed him more than the declaration by the Taylors that their son Tom was available to care for Philip should something befall them. Green said that he had picked up reliable street talk that Tom was addicted to cocaine. And if he could pin it down, he wouldn't hesitate to introduce it. He dismissed the idea that Tom's blighted athletic career was the cause of his drug habit. He'd been a varsity player himself, he said, and knew many athletes whose careers had been cut short by injuries. That had not prevented them from leading productive lives. In his opinion, Tom's problem was rooted right where he had grown up, at home.

(Three months later, two cops on night patrol in South Marion spotted a suspicious individual, who turned out to be Tom. They chased him to his car and discovered that he had two syringes, one of which had been recently used and contained blood. The arrest report said: "Upon searching the car a spoon, matches and a small plastic bag containing a white crystal substance was found under the driver's seat. The substance was taken to the Marion Police Department . . . and found to be positive cocaine." He was sentenced to probation and ordered to enter a drug rehabilitation program.)

When I saw him, Green still remained confident that things would work out. There had been, however, one disturbing note. He'd recently been in Kokomo. He had planned to invent some reason to drop in on Judge Brubaker. But it was pointless. Brubaker had gone off to a judicial conference in California. Nobody was sure for exactly how long. At least two weeks. Christ, just great, Green thought.

Since the case was still in court, none of the judges who had been involved were available. I attempted to reach the Taylors through their attorney, Pat Ryan. They declined to speak to me. Ryan, however, agreed to an interview.

He behaved as advertised. Over breakfast, he told me that the only issue that counted was the adoption. Every other aspect of the case, including the New Jersey custody order, was "garbage." Although Dr. Michele Rabinowitz originally was appointed by the state, Ryan described the child psychologist as a "hired gun" for the Whites and went on to characterize her as a "real screwball."

In Jean Taylor's letter to Judge Ashbey, she had indicated that she fully subscribed to Ken's version of the murder. I asked him if she were passing this on to her grandson. He couldn't answer that, he said. He had recommended to his clients that they see me, but they were stead-fast in their refusal.

Yes, he said, their son Tom was ready to step in should it prove necessary. As far as he was concerned, Tom seemed "fine." And there also was Ken's sister. Ryan was a little vague about her. The best he could tell me was that she lived down south and was married to "some kind of a military man."

I asked him about the various omissions in the adoption petition he had prepared for the Taylors. He squinted at me. No one, he said, had accused him of "fraud." The implication was clear. I had better not either. As we parted, he said he was confident that Judge Brubaker would hand down a favorable ruling. If not, the fight was far from over.

I saw Steve Johnson, the Grant County district attorney, who had been returned handily to office the previous November. I asked him why he had moved to thwart extradition proceedings against the Taylors.

There was, he said, more there than met the eye. Could he be more specific? Well, he answered, it might well have been that the attorney for the Taylors had led them "down the garden path."

I said that while I was not a lawyer, wasn't this something for the courts in New Jersey to decide? Johnson compressed his lips. He stood up behind his desk. It was nice meeting me, he said. He had to excuse himself. He had to be in court himself.

In New Jersey, I already had contacted John Hayden in Governor Kean's office to find out what he was doing to pursue the extradition. He told me that he'd been in constant touch with the Indiana attorney general's office about it. I asked if there were any written records that would show this. He said he'd have to check his files. I never heard from him.

And in Indiana, I called David Arthur, the deputy attorney general in charge of the investigation to determine whether extradition was warranted. I asked him what was going on. He replied that they were waiting to see what happened on the adoption. I said I didn't see how, legally, one had much to do with the other. "Look," Arthur said, "it's really all very complicated, if you know what I mean."

* * *

My article, titled "The Legacy of a Mother's Murder," was published in the *Times* on Sunday, April 12. The magazine, as usual, was printed ahead of the news sections and advance copies were distributed to selected recipients. I got two copies on Wednesday and gave one to Janice Miller.

Although I did not then know this, Janice telephoned Judge Brubaker's office on Thursday around one-thirty in the afternoon. A woman who answered—with whom Janice had previously spoken—said there wasn't anything to report on the Taylor case. "There's been no final decision." The judge, she said, was occupied in court.

Infuriated, Janice said that she wanted the judge to know that a major article about the case would appear in the Sunday *New York Times*. It reported, she said, accurately enough, the inexcusable judicial machinations that were adversely affecting the fate of a child not yet three years old, that he was being passed around like a basketball in the game the state was so famous for. She read some paragraphs from the article. "The judge may want to take a look at it," she said.

"I'll tell him," the woman said in icy tones.

Janice remembered hanging up, despondent.

Then late Friday afternoon, her husband heard his normally composed wife shrieking in her adjoining office. He rushed in to find out what the matter was.

"We won! We won!" she shouted at him.

After her phone call to Kokomo on Thursday, she had called again on Friday and now she was told that a ruling had finally been made. And then she spoke to Dick Green. The adoption had been vacated. The papers, moments before, had been delivered to the Marion courthouse for filing. After all this time, she thought, it must have been the article.

She called Celeste. "We won!" Janice exclaimed again. "We won!"

Celeste burst into tears, unable to speak. Jeff said, "Is it really over?"

Suddenly sobered, Janice said, "I hope so."

•   •   •

Janice flew to Indiana Sunday evening. Jeff would follow once more details were known. He would come by himself. Celeste, on the verge of giving birth, had been forbidden by her doctor to travel.

The headline across the top of the front page of the Marion *Chronicle-Tribune* said:

> Judge rules Taylors lose
> custody of grandson today

Over an accompanying article, also on the front page, there was another headline:

> 'New York Times Magazine'
> features Taylor custody battle

The lead paragraph said: "An Easterner's view of Marion is being read around the country in a story written about the Midwest-to-East custody fight between a 2-year-old boy's Marion grandparents and his New York City aunt and uncle."

•   •   •

Judge Brubaker's ruling appeared to be hastily written. While it acknowledged the existence of a New Jersey order giving Celeste and Jeff permanent custody of Philip, it was not cited as a decisive factor. He based his decision on the narrowest of grounds. Technically, under Indiana law, the Whites did not have to be notified about the adoption. However, "the spirit of the Indiana adoption statutes would require notice to guardians, courts or agencies having custody or other direct contact with the child."

Well, Janice thought, she'd take it any way she could get it.

Pat Ryan asked for a stay pending an appeal. It wasn't fair to move the child back and forth from one jurisdiction to another.

Ryan put Zach on the stand. It was the same refrain. He

declared that his grandson was happy in Indiana. Indiana was a better place to raise a child than New York, where the houses "were too close together." If Philip remained in Indiana, he would be spared the sordid details of his mother's death. Without mentioning that he had a large pool himself, he added that the Whites had a small above-ground children's pool in their backyard that would be dangerous for a two-year-old who couldn't swim.

In his response, Dick Green asserted that if a stay were granted in the absence of an "emergency"—imminent physical or psychological abuse of the child—a precedent would be set whereby any time a court order was issued, a stay would be granted. So what was the point of an order in the first place?

Brubaker denied the stay. The child would be delivered to the Grant County Department of Public Welfare, and then to his guardians, "on or before noon" on Tuesday, April 14.

Green warned Miller that it still might not be over. He had spotted an Indianapolis attorney named Frank Spencer in the Marion courthouse with Ryan. Spencer specialized in appellate work. He'd bet anything, Green told her, that Ryan would try for a stay in the Indiana Court of Appeals.

• • •

That evening, Monday, April 13, Jeff arrived in Marion.

Throughout the next morning, there were hourly reports from Indianapolis. No motion had been filed. Noon came and went. No Philip.

Green prepared a contempt of court citation. He telephoned Brubaker in Kokomo and got his secretary. The judge was on the bench presiding over a drug trial. Green said he would drive to Kokomo to get Brubaker's signature on the contempt order.

In Green's office, Jeff stared at Janice. Where was Philip? She berated herself for not arranging another surveillance of the Taylors.

He was, in fact, with Jean. Following Pat Ryan's instructions, she was driving around Marion with him, periodically calling in until an application for a stay was granted by the appeals court. At last, around twelve-thirty, she was told that it was. She could go home.

Minutes later, Green heard the news. Tears began rolling down Jeff White's face. He would not be picking up Philip that day after all.

It was the first time that Janice had seen him cry.

• • •

Ryan's maneuverings may have saved Green's life.

In the drug trial in Judge Brubaker's courtroom, the defendant's attorney was a close friend of Green's. Dick would have arrived at the Kokomo court a little before two P.M. when a recess had been called. During the recess, he would surely have stopped to chat with his friend while waiting for Brubaker to receive him. At two o'clock that afternoon, the defendant set off a bomb that killed him and severely wounded his attorney and the local sheriff.

Right then, though, Green knew none of this. He, Janice and Jeff were racing to Indianapolis.

• • •

A new headline in the *Chronicle-Tribune* said:

Emergency order halts transfer of custody

In Indianapolis, they worked through the rest of the day with the lawyer who would represent them in the appeals court, Peter Tamulonis, marshaling their arguments with care, recapitulating the case's tortured legal history, beginning with the New Jersey custody order.

Vicious thunderstorms lashed the city. But at sunset, the rain and lightning had stopped and the sky started to clear. As they headed toward a hotel for a break, Green suddenly said to Janice, "Do you believe in omens?"

"What do you mean?"

"Look, there," Dick said, pointing at a rainbow arching overhead. "See where it comes down on that building?"

"Yes."

"That's where we'll be tomorrow. That's our pot of gold."

The next morning they appeared before a three-judge panel of the appeals court.

On behalf of the Taylors, attorney Frank Spencer argued that Jeff and Celeste had waited too long to intervene in the adoption. The alloted sixty days had elapsed. Further, he said that they were not parties to the adoption to begin with because matters of custody in New Jersey and adoption in Indiana were separate, entirely different forms of physical possession.

"Your position on that point I can only characterize as ridiculous," Judge Paul H. Buchanan, Jr., said.

Peter Tamulonis noted that the delay in the intervention petition had occurred because no judge was available to hear it. And, after citing the ruling for permanent custody that had been awarded the Whites, he said that there was a bottom line to all of this. "The proceedings in Indiana have been shown to be a flagrant attempt to circumvent the orders of the New Jersey court."

Another appeals judge, V. Sue Shields, wondered out loud if fraud wasn't an issue here.

Huffy, Spencer said that the trial court had found no evidence of fraud.

The appeals panel retired for ten minutes.

The emergency stay was denied without comment.

• • •

Dick, Janice and Jeff hurried back to Marion.

Warren Haas and a caseworker went to the Taylor home. There was no repeat of his last visit. Zach and Jean were struggling to maintain their composure. Haas told Jean that he appreciated her feelings. "It probably didn't mean anything to her," he said, "but it did to me." Tom was there, hovering in the background, "like a shadow."

The caseworker took Philip. Haas carried a small suitcase with the boy's clothes. Philip seemed alert, but didn't say anything. It was impossible to know what had been going on in his head all this time.

To avoid the reporters waiting at the welfare office, Haas drove to a friend's house where there were two children around Philip's age. He played tentatively with them. Around five P.M., Jeff and Janice pulled up. Jeff, Haas recalled, was splendid. He swung Philip into his arms and said, "Hi, big guy. You don't remember me, do you?"

But Philip nodded and clung to him.

Then they got into their rented car and drove toward Ohio. "Let's get over the state line before something else happens," Jeff said.

Janice remembered how Philip wasn't saying a word. Jeff had brought along some toys. He took them out and said, "Just show me the one you want."

After an hour or so, Jeff said, "Who's daddy?" and Philip pointed at him.

"I'll tell you what. If you call me daddy, I'll give you a kiss," and Philip spoke at last. "Daddy! Daddy!" he shouted, and Jeff kept kissing him.

They spent the night in an airport motel in Dayton. Philip slept in the same bed with Jeff. In the morning, when Jeff opened Philip's suitcase, he found that none of the clothes fit. They were the same ones he'd gone to Marion with ten months ago.

When they landed at Newark Airport, a number of reporters and television crews were on hand. I also was there. I watched as Jeff placed Philip in front of Celeste. I saw her fall to her knees, despite her swollen belly, and clutch her dead sister's son, sobbing, "My baby, oh, my baby!"

All the local news shows and newspapers in New York and New Jersey covered Philip's return. It was on the wire services and national news broadcasts as well.

Interviewed in Marion, the Taylors said that they were deeply saddened by the loss of their grandson. It was wrong, Zach said, to mix up the killing of Teresa with the adoption. Asked if her son Ken had conveyed any comments about the outcome, Jean replied that he had lost all faith in justice and the law.

At home, Jeff told Celeste that Warren Haas sent his best.

"Oh, my God, I've got to call him," and then on the phone to him in Marion, she said, "Mr. Haas, the fat lady just sang."

• • •

414

That same day, in remote Craigsville, Virginia, Ken Taylor finally found a way to escape from the Augusta Correctional Center.

He'd been alone in the classroom building where he tutored other inmates. Pacing up and down, in a fury after having heard the news from Zach and Jean, he shoved the bar—like a fire-door bar—on the door at the end of a corridor. Ken had always presumed it was locked. To his amazement, it wasn't. He waited, thinking an alarm might go off. It didn't.

He looked outside. A few feet away was a heavy steel-mesh fence twenty feet high, topped with razor wire. In effect, it was a second wall. The cell blocks themselves really formed the first wall. Beyond the fence was forest and in the distance mountains.

To his left, Ken saw that the fence ran right against the administration building. The fence's terminal post rose about two feet over the coils of wire. He was in as good shape as he'd ever been, running every day, working out daily in the weight room. He could shinny up the post, get above the razor wire, leap over it, and come down rolling, like a paratrooper.

Ken confided his discovery to his cellmate, also a tutor. He wasn't interested.

But would he help?

"Sure thing, Doc, whatever you want."

The single-story classroom building had a dropped ceiling. In a small room, where cleaning gear was stored, Ken used a broomstick to pop a couple of the ceiling squares. The cellmate boosted him up so Ken could look around. Ducts for heating and air conditioning snaked around the space. One duct went behind an interior concrete wall hanging from the roof. There were only a couple of inches between the top of the duct and the bottom of the wall, which didn't appear to serve any purpose. Perhaps, Ken thought, it had been part of the original design which for some reason was abandoned. At any rate, he could hide behind it on the duct.

His plan was to remain up there for three nights while

the search for him went on. By then, he figured, the hunt would be concentrated far beyond the immediate area of the prison. He had been told that a mile and a half to the west there was a country store with an outside telephone booth. He'd get to it and call his parents to come for him.

Equipped with candy bars, some cans of soda, and a little cash from poker winnings, he went up through the ceiling after morning classes. He warned his cellmate to be sure to wipe off the sneaker print he left on the wall. He crawled along the duct. When he finished one of the sodas, he would use the can to urinate in.

He heard the commotion below him after the noon count. It sounded as if there were four or five guards in the search party. He saw the beam from a flashlight dancing around. A voice said, "There's nothing up here."

The voices went away. He'd made it. Then that afternoon there were more voices, a lot more. This time Ken knew it was serious. His cellmate must have snitched.

A minute later, the same ceiling squares Ken had come through were popped. A voice said, "Doesn't this look like part of a footprint?"

Again, a flashlight crisscrossed the space. But then he heard another voice, which said, "I'm telling you, he isn't here."

"Keep looking. He's got to be."

He saw the shaft of light picking its way along the top of the duct, just below the concrete wall he was sitting behind. He arched his back to keep from being seen as the light went under him. It came back.

"Wait. I see something. A Coke can. Yeah, he's here, all right."

Ken had forgotten about it—the can for urinating. He called out, "Take it easy. I'm coming down."

He was sentenced to an additional four years.

• • •

Three days after his return to Staten Island, Philip had a new sister, Jacqueline.

On his third birthday, June 11, Celeste said there were still some problems. Not yet toilet-trained, he tensed up instantly at the prospect of going to the bathroom. And he resisted getting into the tub so ferociously that she had to sponge-bathe him.

"It'll all work out," Jeff said. "We're just as calm and collected as any household with a three-year-old, a two-year-old, and a two-month old."

Celeste said she wouldn't mind having another baby.

The problems had disappeared by the time of a party in July to celebrate Jacqueline's christening. The day was sweltering. Some of Jeff's pals jumped into the backyard wading pool to cool off. Philip ran to get his water wings to join them. I watched as they tossed him in the air and to one another.

"More, more!" he kept yelling.

# Chapter

# TWENTY-TWO

In the spring of 1989, I met with Ken Taylor in Virginia's old main prison, the Powhatan Correctional Center, twenty miles west of Richmond.

By then a reversal of his murder conviction—on the grounds of prejudicial pretrial publicity, the "enhanced" photos of Teresa's battered face and head, and the introduction of the Acapulco evidence—had been denied by the New Jersey Court of Appeals. The New Jersey Supreme Court had upheld the verdict, and the U.S. Supreme Court refused to entertain further pleadings.

Jean and Zach had voluntarily returned to New Jersey to face the charges against them. They were sentenced to community service.

In Indiana, their motion to reinstate Judge Hunt's adoption order was turned down by both the state's Court of Appeals and Supreme Court.

In New Jersey, Ken was stripped of all parental rights to Philip, who was then formally adopted by Celeste and Jeff.

The Taylors contested the adoption. In one memorable moment, Jean was asked how she as a mother had dealt with her son Tom's drug habit.

"We do not talk about drugs in our home," she said.

* * *

After his escape attempt in Craigsville, Ken had been transferred to the harsher confines of the Mecklenburg Correctional Center along the North Carolina border. There, it was believed that he had joined a conspiracy with two other inmates to murder a Mecklenburg guard. He was "locked up" for some ten months before being transferred back to Powhatan, where he had been initially received in Virginia.

I had written to him requesting an interview, actually a series of them, for this book.

He replied negatively at first. He had found my article in the *Times* extremely biased. He had, moreover, practically finished a long first draft narrating his side of the story which he hoped to publish. Indeed, toward this end, he had forwarded a great deal of material to a New York literary agent, who was casting about for the right writer to put it in publishable form.

I answered that although I remained anxious to see him, I was going ahead with my own project in any event and wished him well.

Suddenly, he wrote, "I look forward to our visit."

Ken had been at Powhatan for only a few days when I saw him. He was still in segregation in the prison's maximum security wing. While I didn't expect any dramatic revelations from him, I did want a firsthand sense of what he was like—and especially what made him apparently so beguiling to many women.

From my perspective, at least, that was easy to see.

Even though he was manacled hand and foot, in an orange prison jumpsuit, his blond hair now receding and thinning, he was physically imposing. He spoke softly. He had an ingratiating smile. He projected the earnest, almost shy manner of a man buffeted by fate, who nonetheless was bearing up. He came off as, well, charming. If there were any visible signs of tension, it was the way he chain-smoked cigarettes, expertly lighting them despite his handcuffs, accepting a light from me, with profuse thanks, only when he was running low on matches.

Then I saw another side to him, an unexpected toughness that also exerted powerful appeal. Powhatan was not designed for an interview like the one I was conducting. And while the arrangements were being made for us to talk in a glassed-in visitor's cubicle in a cavernous, central corridor just outside the maximum security wing, we spoke in a room in the laundry area inside the wing.

A black convict, about the same size as Ken, also manacled, had spied us through the open door. As we got up to be let out of maximum security, they came face-to-face.

"Who you?" the black convict challenged him, as if no one else were present.

Ken's face instantly hardened. He bent slightly forward, so that they were nose-to-nose no more than six inches apart. "Who *you?*" he said.

For what seemed like an eternity, they glared at one another, eyes their only weapons. Then the black convict looked away.

Afterward, casually, shuffling alongside of me in his leg irons, Ken said, "It's eighty percent black in here. You can't let anybody push you around."

• • •

He immediately told me that he was planning a new appeal. It would be based on incompetent counsel. Jack Venturi, his defense attorney, had really let him down.

I suggested that this might be difficult. Most of the prisons in America would be emptied if inmates could have their way on that.

Yeah, he knew this, but Jack should have gone for temporary insanity. That was the truth, when you thought about it. Worst of all was Jack not getting a toxicologist to speak up for him. It was inconceivable that a "putrid" blood sample could be used to give an accurate reading of how much cocaine Teresa had in her system that night.

I said I had documented evidence that Venturi had approached other toxicologists and, right or wrong, they all reported that their testimony would be the same as the toxicologist for the prosecution. It was just as inconceivable to me, in view of what was at stake, that Venturi hadn't told him that.

He didn't know this, he insisted. After all, he could only tell me what he remembered. It would be a rationale I would hear more than once from him. Afterward, Ken would write me, "Maybe at this late date, Venturi has found prudence to be his best course and has in fact a report or two handy to cover his ass."

His boyhood was idyllic, he said in Powhatan. He could not have been blessed with better, more God-fearing parents. What had happened to him as an adult—"how I fucked up"—was his own fault.

He loved Teresa. And Philip. He loved Marilyn. And Astrid. Listening to him, it was difficult for me to differentiate between them. He smiled disarmingly. What could he say? That was how it was.

He recalled first meeting Marilyn. "She was so sophisticated and so goddamned good-looking and sexy. There was just something about her. She was—I think she was five seven, about a hundred and twenty pounds, solid body, kind of thin—real long legs, long red hair, a knockout. She was a knockout. Plus she picked me up. Sexually, she made the first moves."

Finally, though, in the love he expressed for both women, Teresa edged ahead. "I loved her so deeply. I miss her so much. What happened was a tragedy. I lost my best lover and my best friend." In grand sociopathic tradition, he saw himself as the true victim now. "Why," he asked, "doesn't anybody understand what I've been going through?"

Then his memories of Marilyn grew darker. "I was fed up with her arguing. With her self-righteousness. Her way was the proper, moral way. To do things when she wanted to do them. To have sex when she wanted to have sex, go to a movie when she wanted to go to a movie, go out to dinner when she wanted to have dinner. It's very difficult for me to pinpoint exact things. I can only give you things in general."

He said that the "pain" he felt at not being able to be with his children was enormous. He insisted that the daughter by his first wife was not his. Why then had he not allowed the child to be adopted by her second husband? It seemed such an unnecessarily cruel act. He said that he would still have been forced to contribute support payments. When I said that this simply wasn't so, we reached another dead end. "Look," he said, "I can only tell you what they told me."

Even though his attempt to chloroform Marilyn was not part of his murder trial, he had provided wildly disparate explanations for doing it. Which was right? There was a hesitant, almost helpless smile. "You tell me," he said. "Whether I was trying to scare, rape or kill her remains a mystery to me. I was a zombie that night."

He appeared not to know that Paul Chaiet's investigators had discovered that the phone number of one of the calls the night of the murder—to the Manhattan whorehouse—had also been dialed when Teresa was in the hospital after giving birth to Philip.

Ken flashed another, quicker smile, as if pleased at the chance to be forthright. "Obviously," he said, "I made the call." He told me that he wanted to tell the "girls" that he'd just become a proud father. He would have to think about how Teresa got hold of the number.

Later, when I asked him by letter if he had reached any conclusions about that, he replied that she must have found it in his wallet.

Acapulco, he said, never should have been permitted in his trial. Sorayda Peraino remained an "enigma" to him. *Why* would he have confessed to her? Come on, he said, it didn't make any sense.

After I learned that the U.S. consular agent in Acapulco reported visiting Ken in jail and had received essentially the same confession, I asked him how this could have been so. He said that Chaiet's investigators must have gotten to the agent. My next question—then why hadn't it been part of the prosecution case?—was really pointless. I already knew what his answer would be. He wasn't the prosecutor. Chaiet was. *Ask* him.

Prior to meeting Ken in Powhatan, I had informed him that while I would make my own judgments, I would certainly weigh his side of the story. His sodium amytal interview, he said, proved his innocence—that at the worst, he was only guilty of "involuntary manslaughter."

I reminded him that in that interview, he also said he knew of another instance of a mother sodomizing her son— "a sleazy couple in Ohio."

Could he elaborate?

"Oh," he said, shrugging, "it must have been in some movie I saw."

I later had another query for him about the sodium amytal interview. Why had he lumped together the beating of Teresa in Acapulco, her murder in Manalapan, and the attempt to murder Marilyn in Connecticut as examples of possible psychosexual problems he might have?

Anger colored his reply. "I do not understand the nature of this question," he wrote, "and quite frankly, it seems rude and inappropriate. I am trying to be fair and this does not fit my criteria of being fair."

In Powhatan, I told Ken that after his failed escape from the Craigsville prison, I had heard that a search of his belongings turned up a list of names—which could be construed as a "hit" list—and among the names were Chaiet, Judge Farren and Celeste.

He said that *if* there had been such a list, it was no longer relevant. He had forsaken ideas of vengeance. He knew about New Jersey's death row, its lethal injection chamber. That wasn't for him. He wanted to live. If he ever managed to break out, he'd "head for the hills."

Still, he couldn't disguise his hatred for Celeste and Jeff. Especially Celeste. Jeff was "a nothing." I came away with the impression that it was the thought of Celeste that gnawed so at him, that in the battle over Philip, it was not losing Philip that drove him into such fury, but that

Celeste—this "dimwit," his intellectual inferior—had taken him on and beaten him.

That was what was so insupportable.

• • •

I returned to Marion.

There had been a dramatic change there since my last visit. In the noonday sun, the courthouse looked like an aging courtesan, stripped of her finery. All the great shade elms surrounding it were no more, chain-sawed down in one fell swoop by the county commissioners in a final, desperate effort to drive off the starlings. The next day, too late, an environmentalist from Purdue University arrived to announce it wouldn't work. And he was right. The starlings simply swarmed to trees in nearby residential areas. Hordes of them still perched, despite the balloons and trinkets, on the window sills of the Summit building. Plans to plant new trees and shrubbery were announced. Anyway, the local joke went, there wouldn't be any more lynchings for a while.

• • •

In his chambers, Judge Tom Hunt put all the blame on the Welfare Department. "Attorney Pat Ryan came in," he said, "and indicated that he had this adoption on. He handed me the file and said the welfare report was in it. I read the report. The report was relatively glowing in terms of these people. So I naturally relied on the report, which indicated to me that they felt that it was a good environment in which to place the kid."

He said, "It's impossible for me to conduct an independent investigation on every single case I get. That's why I rely on the Welfare Department in adoptions. They conduct that for the court. So they were well aware of the background in the case, or should have been."

According to Hunt, he did not know that Ken had murdered Teresa, or that he was in prison. "My recollection is that I was told the mother was deceased, the father had signed a consent—I was shown the consent—to have his parents become the adoptive parents . . . Mr. Ryan *did* say there was an aunt and uncle in New Jersey or New York.

They were attempting to obtain guardianship over this child because, in his opinion, the child was going to get some insurance money as a result of the death of his mother. But the kid had been with the grandparents for a length of time . . . So I went ahead and approved the adoption. It was routine."

Hunt remembered the calls afterward from Janice Miller and Judge Gehricke. If everyone had listened to him, Hunt said, none of what then happened would have occurred. He would have held a hearing on Monday morning, and if the facts were as they eventually turned out to be, he would have vacated the adoption immediately.

Instead, he was livid once he discovered that Warren Haas had taken Philip from the Taylors. Hunt said, "I asked him what the situation was, and he said, since I was unavailable, they [the Whites] had come to him. He then went to Judge Wright and got Judge Wright to intervene. I came unglued at that point. Probably shouldn't have, but it made me mad that the Welfare Department—who two days earlier told me these people were absolutely perfect to adopt this child—all of a sudden changed their mind and was saying this was an unfit environment for the child. It made me mad that they had gone and got another judge."

* * * *

Everyone seemed to have a different slant on what was in the welfare report. I asked Haas for it. He'd like to oblige, he said, but he couldn't. The report was under court seal. I managed, however, to obtain a copy.

A few days later I saw Hunt again. In fairness to him, I said, I had to tell him that I had read the report and that it contained everything he said it did not—including Ken's murder conviction, the fact that Jeff and Celeste had sole custody, and that Philip was only on a two-week visitation.

He expressed astonishment. "Is that all in there?" he said. "I don't remember that." He stared at me. "Uh, I will not dispute the fact that there is a possibility that I read it too hastily. That's a possibility. I have a pretty busy court and a number of, an enormous amount of reading to do on a daily basis. I don't consider myself to be without failure. I don't consider myself as never having made a mistake."

Unburdening himself, he went on, "I've been told by the appellate courts in Indiana on occasion that I've made mistakes. And I accept that. I will say that it's possible I didn't read that as carefully as I possibly could."

Did he think Pat Ryan had duped him?

Hunt replied that he'd prefer not to comment.

• • •

At the First Baptist Church of Marion, Reverend Darrel Parris confirmed without hesitation his discussions with Indiana's attorney general—and the local district attorney—about whether Jean and Zach should have been extradited.

He told me that he was upset about allegations that "the child was being mistreated" by the Taylors.

When I asked, "What allegations?" he referred to the weekend Warren Haas and the Welfare Department had taken Philip. He suggested that Celeste and Jeff had spread "lies."

"Someone," he said, "had to come forward and say what good people Jean and Zach were."

His principle in all of this, as far as Ken was concerned, was "love the sinner, hate the sin." Parris was also a flying parson, and during the long court fight over the adoption, he had flown to Virginia—in his Piper Cherokee—to buck up Ken's spirits.

And he said that he'd made it clear how he felt about "the event" of Teresa's death. "Kenny," he said he had said, "what you did was not the right way. What you did was wrong. That was not the right way to settle disputes and arguments," and Ken had acknowledged, in Parris's words, that it had been "inappropriate behavior."

As for Jean and Zach, he said, "My job was to help with the grieving process. This had been a tremendous shock to them. I had to support this mom and dad as they walked through the valley, to help them through that journey."

He told me that he had no doubt that Teresa did not want the child brought up in "the same religion" she had been. When he recommended to her and Ken that they find a church closer to home, she was adamant. She wanted him "dedicated right here, in Marion."

Parris said that he did not believe the Taylors were "treated fairly in New Jersey." Even so, if the Whites had fulfilled obligations set forth in the original court orders, possibly "all of this" could have been avoided. Their "immoral behavior was no better than Kenny's."

But what would have prevented Ken from having the adoption done during the old two-month visitation when the Taylors still had split-custody rights? In all likelihood, under those circumstances, they would have prevailed.

"We'll never know," Parris conceded.

• • •

This time the Taylors agreed to see me.

If, indeed, his parents had made him jump through hoops as a child, Ken was certainly repaying them in kind.

Saddled with legal costs, they were forced to refinance a home mortgage that had almost been paid off. Bankruptcy was a distinct prospect. All thoughts of Zach's retirement, the rounds of golf he had looked forward to, had vanished. And the French company that had taken over the picture-tube plant had instituted extensive employment restructuring. Zach no longer had a desk job as a production engineer. He was back on the assembly line as a supervisor, pounding the concrete on the night shift. "It's hard on a man my age," he said.

Their ranch-style house was modest. There was a formal parlor on the left. Behind it was the kitchen which opened to a dining area that also doubled as a family room with a television set and a sofa. "That's about all we do," Zach said. "Watch TV. Can't afford anything else." Then he tried to look on the bright side. "Jeannie never liked to go out much anyway."

On the right were three adjoining bedrooms. Tom occupied one of them, Jean's mother a second. That was another cross to bear. According to Jean, her mother, with whom she'd feuded for so long, was now senile and bedridden. Her mother, Jean said, would sit up on occasion and shout, "You're not my daughter."

On glass shelves in a corner of the foyer was a sort of shrine given over to memorabilia of Ken, primarily trophies for his athletic accomplishments in grade and high school for football, basketball and baseball. "This one," she said, pointing, "was for peewee football. He was in the fifth grade, which is two years before he could play in regular school. It was in a league sponsored by the Elks."

Other plaques were for softball play in medical school and the Indiana softball association. "Now this one here," Jean said, "was for most valuable player in the sub base softball league. See, Kenny's batting average was seveneighty-seven! He had fifty-two hits and sixteen home runs." She did not mention that it was also the same year he tried to chloroform Marilyn.

They appeared barely able to comprehend what had come crashing down on them, much less the reasons for it.

Zach, ill at ease on the straight-backed parlor sofa, a big, paunchy man in a sports shirt, bald save for a fringe of gray, finally said that it was because of Teresa's cocaine habit. "That's the whole thing in a nutshell," he said.

Jean was baffled by the attitude of Ken's first two wives. She showed me a letter that Emily Latrelle wrote, curtly denying them any further contact with the daughter Ken had disowned.

And she produced a letter from Marilyn written after she and Ken divorced, emphasizing that she'd walked "the last mile" trying to keep faith with her marital vows. I found a sentence in it that also expressed sorrow for the Taylors having raised two failed sons—one in his education, the other in his marriage—due to drugs.

Hadn't that alerted Jean? No, she really didn't pay attention to it. After all, it was before "all this" had happened— the "incident" in Manalapan and "Tommy's arrest."

Looking back, I said, how did they feel about Ken's explanation of what occurred in Acapulco? Zach's face mottled in anger. "It was intruders," he said. "It never should have been allowed."

To my surprise, Jean said after a moment's hesitation that she couldn't say for sure what happened. Kenny had a terrible temper sometimes. Perhaps he did need professional help.

But wasn't his story about Teresa performing fellatio on the baby pretty bizarre?

Not at all, Jean said, gazing at me intently, carefully made up and coiffed, looking years younger than her age, immaculate in a freshly pressed cotton dress, sitting erect, hands folded primly in her lap. As a matter of fact, she'd once seen a television talk show—she couldn't recall what show—in which a pediatrician had said that mothers often "did that" to keep their teething babies from crying.

• • •

While writing his version of Teresa's death, Ken had also taken up fiction. He sent me several efforts for my comment.

One story was about a man, a doctor of all things, convicted of murder. He escapes, flees to Brazil, meets a beautiful woman, they marry, have children and live happily ever after.

A second story, though, was more instructive. In this one, it is a brutally hot New York summer day. He describes a young woman with D-cup breasts, soaked in perspiration, in her apartment. She is thinking of her husband in his air-conditioned office. Why should she put up with this? She goes to a nudist beach, stretches out naked and falls half asleep. She hears a clicking sound. She looks up and sees a man with a camera, who, as luck would have it, has been going out with her best girlfriend. She realizes he's been taking pictures of her. He plops down beside her. She asks where her girlfriend is. He says she's out of town. Why not come by his apartment that night? The implication is clear. If she doesn't, he'll send the photographs to her husband.

She has no choice. Despite the fact that she is being forced into this, Ken lingers over how she perfumes herself and selects her most provocative outfit complete with three-inch spiked heels. Her blackmailer greets her at the door. He leads her to the stereo, tells her to pick any music she wants and to do a striptease. As she dances in front of him,

Ken writes, she feels her growing excitement. Then they have hours of orgiastic sex. Exhausted and gratified, she leaves, already planning her next visit. She can hardly wait.

• • •

In Staten Island, at the Benignos and the Whites, life gradually settled down. All three kids—Philip, Christina and Jacqueline—were thriving. With their expanding family, Celeste and Jeff sold their house and cleared enough for the down payment on a much larger one. Jeff and some of his friends fashioned a basement apartment which was rented to a young couple to help carry the mortgage. And Celeste was hoping to have another child.

• • •

In Powhatan, at the end of 1989, Ken Taylor was suspected of smuggling seven metal blades out of the print shop where he'd been assigned. The blades were found in a cell in the tier above the one he was in. A window bar had been partially cut through. A pair of wire cutters from the shop school was also found in the cell. According to an informant, Ken was the ringleader of the escape attempt—his fourth since his conviction—that involved three inmates. He was again locked up, although there was not enough evidence to try him. Later, however, he would write to me, "It was a damn shame. We were that close."

• • •

And he delivered another ominous message:
"I do not intend to stay in prison."

# AUTHOR'S NOTE

In my preparation of this work, no monetary inducements were offered or editorial promises made to any of the persons portrayed.

Six pseudonyms were used: Patsy Duncan, Kenneth Taylor's high school sweetheart; Emily Latrelle and Marilyn Hope, his first two wives; Astrid, his second daughter; Sal Aurelio, one of Teresa's boyfriends; and Irene DeBlasio, one of her girlfriends. These pseudonyms were employed, solely at my discretion, to protect their privacy.

For additional research, I thank Ed Breen of the Marion *Chronicle-Tribune,* and Lydia Chavez, formerly Cincinnati correspondent for *The New York Times* and now an associate journalism professor at the University of California at Berkeley.

I also want to thank Lorraine Latorroca, who first alerted me, through my wife Suzanne, about the adoption struggle in Indiana.

# ABOUT THE AUTHOR

PETER MAAS was born in New York City and is a graduate of Duke University. He is the author of nine major works of fiction and nonfiction including such bestsellers as *Serpico, King of the Gypsies* and *Manhunt*.